Software Requirement Patterns

Stephen Withall

PUBLISHED BY
Microsoft Press
A Division of Microsoft Corporation
One Microsoft Way
Redmond, Washington 98052-6399

Library of Congress Control Number: 2007926327

Printed and bound in the United States of America.

Second Printing: July 2014

Distributed in Canada by H.B. Fenn and Company Ltd.

A CIP catalogue record for this book is available from the British Library.

Microsoft Press books are available through booksellers and distributors worldwide. For further information about international editions, contact your local Microsoft Corporation office or contact Microsoft Press International directly at fax (425) 936-7329. Visit our Web site at www.microsoft.com/mspress. Send comments to mspinput@microsoft.com.

Microsoft, Microsoft Press, Excel, Internet Explorer, Outlook, and Windows are either registered trademarks or trademarks of Microsoft Corporation in the United States and/or other countries. Other product and company names mentioned herein may be the trademarks of their respective owners.

The example companies, organizations, products, domain names, e-mail addresses, logos, people, places, and events depicted herein are fictitious. No association with any real company, organization, product, domain name, e-mail address, logo, person, place, or event is intended or should be inferred.

This book expresses the author's views and opinions. The information contained in this book is provided without any express, statutory, or implied warranties. Neither the authors, Microsoft Corporation, nor its resellers, or distributors will be held liable for any damages caused or alleged to be caused either directly or indirectly by this book.

Acquisitions Editor: Ben Ryan
Developmental Editor: Devon Musgrave
Project Editor: Maria Gargiulo
Illustrations: Stephen Withall
Editorial Production: ICC Macmillan Inc.

This product is printed digitally on demand.

Contents at a Glance

Part I   **Setting the Scene**

1   Synopsis of "Crash Course in Specifying Requirements" 3
2   Synopsis of "The Contents of a Requirements Specification" 11
3   Requirement Pattern Concepts 19
4   Using and Producing Requirement Patterns 39

Part II   **Requirement Pattern Catalog**

5   Fundamental Requirement Patterns 51
6   Information Requirement Patterns 85
7   Data Entity Requirement Patterns 119
8   User Function Requirement Patterns 155
9   Performance Requirement Patterns 191
10   Flexibility Requirement Patterns 239
11   Access Control Requirement Patterns 281
12   Commercial Requirement Patterns 325

Glossary 341

References 349

Table of Contents

Foreword . . . . *ix*

Preface . . . . *xi*

Part I   Setting the Scene

1   Synopsis of "Crash Course in Specifying Requirements" 3

1.1 What Are Requirements? 4

1.2 Where Do Requirements Fit in the Grand Scheme? 5

1.3 A Few General Principles 6

1.4 A Traditional Requirements Process 7

1.5 Agile Requirements Processes 8

    An Extreme Requirements Process 9

    An Incremental Requirements Process 10

2   Synopsis of "The Contents of a Requirements Specification" 11

2.1 Introduction Section 12

    System Purpose 12

    Document Purpose 12

    Requirement Format 13

    Glossary 14

    References 14

    Document History 15

2.2 Context Section 15

    Scope 15

    Major Assumptions 16

    Major Exclusions 16

    Key Business Entities 16

    Infrastructures 17

What do you think of this book? We want to hear from you!

Microsoft is interested in hearing your feedback so we can continually improve our books and learning resources for you. To participate in a brief online survey, please visit:

www.microsoft.com/learning/booksurvey/

2.3 Functional Area Sections. 17

2.4 Major Nonfunctional Capabilities Section 18

3   Requirement Pattern Concepts. 19

3.1 Introduction to Requirement Patterns 19

3.2 The Anatomy of a Requirement Pattern. 21

Basic Details. 22

Applicability. 23

Discussion. 24

Content. 24

Template(s). 24

Example(s) 26

Extra Requirements. 26

Considerations for Development 28

Considerations for Testing. 29

3.3 Domains. 29

Domains and Infrastructures. 30

3.4 Requirement Pattern Groups 31

3.5 Relationships Between Requirement Patterns 32

Requirement Pattern Classifications. 33

Refinement Requirements 35

Divertive Requirement Patterns 36

Requirement Patterns and Diversity of Approaches 36

Use Cases for Requirement Patterns 37

Business Rules and Requirement Patterns. 38

4   Using and Producing Requirement Patterns 39

4.1 When and How to Use Requirement Patterns. 39

4.2 Tailoring Requirement Patterns 41

4.3 Writing New Requirement Patterns. 42

How to Find Candidate Requirement Patterns. 43

How to Write a Requirement Pattern 45

Part II   Requirement Pattern Catalog

5   Fundamental Requirement Patterns 51

5.1 Inter-System Interface Requirement Pattern 51

5.2 Inter-System Interaction Requirement Pattern 62

5.3 Technology Requirement Pattern. 65

5.4 Comply-with-Standard Requirement Pattern. 71

5.5 Refer-to-Requirements Requirement Pattern. 79

5.6 Documentation Requirement Pattern. 81

6   Information Requirement Patterns **85**

6.1 Data Type Requirement Pattern. 86

6.2 Data Structure Requirement Pattern. 94

6.3 ID Requirement Pattern. 97

6.4 Calculation Formula Requirement Pattern. 102

6.5 Data Longevity Requirement Pattern. 107

6.6 Data Archiving Requirement Pattern. 110

7   Data Entity Requirement Patterns **119**

7.1 Living Entity Requirement Pattern. 129

7.2 Transaction Requirement Pattern. 133

7.3 Configuration Requirement Pattern. 138

7.4 Chronicle Requirement Pattern. 144

7.5 Information Storage Infrastructure 154

Implementation Requirements 154

8   User Function Requirement Patterns. **155**

8.1 Inquiry Requirement Pattern. 156

8.2 Report Requirement Pattern. 161

8.3 Accessibility Requirement Pattern 168

8.4 User Interface Infrastructure 187

8.5 Reporting Infrastructure 189

9   Performance Requirement Patterns. **191**

9.1 Response Time Requirement Pattern. 195

9.2 Throughput Requirement Pattern 204

9.3 Dynamic Capacity Requirement Pattern. 212

9.4 Static Capacity Requirement Pattern. 215

9.5 Availability Requirement Pattern 217

10 Flexibility Requirement Patterns. **239**

10.1 Scalability Requirement Pattern. 241

10.2 Extendability Requirement Pattern 246

10.3 Unparochialness Requirement Pattern 254

10.4 Multiness Requirement Pattern 261

10.5 Multi-Lingual Requirement Pattern. 272

10.6 Installability Requirement Pattern 274

11   Access Control Requirement Patterns 281

11.1 User Registration Requirement Pattern 284

11.2 User Authentication Requirement Pattern 295

11.3 User Authorization Requirement Patterns 305

11.4 Specific Authorization Requirement Pattern 308

11.5 Configurable Authorization Requirement Pattern 313

11.6 Approval Requirement Pattern 318

12   Commercial Requirement Patterns 325

12.1 Multi-Organization Unit Requirement Pattern 325

12.2 Fee/Tax Requirement Pattern. 330

Glossary. 341

References. 349

Index 351

What do you think of this book? We want to hear from you!

Microsoft is interested in hearing your feedback so we can continually improve our books and learning resources for you. To participate in a brief online survey, please visit:

www.microsoft.com/learning/booksurvey/

Foreword

Requirements development is hard! Requirements analysts often are not adequately trained or experienced, so they do the best they can without necessarily knowing how to write high-quality requirements. Analysts struggle with questions such as "Where do I start?," "How do I know when I'm done?," "How detailed should my requirements be?," "Have I missed any requirements?," and "Have I overlooked any critical information in the requirements I've written?" Unfortunately, there's no formulaic approach to the communication-intensive challenge of understanding and specifying requirements.

Stephen Withall's *Software Requirement Patterns* can help any analyst write better requirements. These patterns provide a way to embody comprehensive and structured knowledge about different types of requirements. Requirements development is a journey of exploration, not just a simple collection or transcription process. The patterns Steve presents can help analysts ask the right questions to properly understand and specify requirements of many types in an appropriate level of detail. From the perspective of "know your audience," the patterns include guidance to assist the developers and testers who must take the requirements to the next development stages. People learn from examples, and they work more efficiently with the help of templates rather than blank pages. To this end, Steve's requirement patterns provide both templates and examples.

These requirements patterns are applicable to a wide variety of projects and products. You can apply the concepts in the book to develop new requirement patterns specific to your own industry, application domain, or product line. Too many projects begin specifying requirements from scratch, but the requirement patterns let organizations effectively reuse requirements knowledge captured on previous projects.

This book communicates a wealth of wisdom and insight for writing stellar requirements. Through the patterns, Steve points out the value of using a consistent style when writing requirements, which can enhance every analyst's capabilities. Even if you don't apply the patterns rigorously, the book contains hundreds of practical tips for specifying better requirements. Use the book as a reference: read the relevant patterns, try them, and absorb the ideas and advice Steve presents. Internalizing those patterns that fit your situation will make them a routine aspect of how you explore, analyze, document, and use software requirements.

Requirement patterns just might represent the next generation of software requirements thinking. Stephen Withall's *Software Requirement Patterns* will likely remain the definitive treatise on requirement patterns for years to come.

Karl Wiegers
April 2007

Preface

The Purpose of This Book

There is nothing new under the sun. It has all been done before.

–Sherlock Holmes: A Study in Scarlet,
  Arthur Conan Doyle

The purpose of this book is to help you decide and define what a new software system needs to do and to suggest what extra features to add to make it a *good* system–or even an *excellent* one. It saves you effort and enables you to be more precise, by providing detailed guidance on how to specify individual requirements. Requirement patterns are encapsulated expertise, conveniently prepackaged for reuse. The book contains 37 requirement patterns, each of which describes an approach to tackling a particular type of situation that crops up repeatedly in all kinds of systems, but focusing on commercial business software. Only a fraction of any system is specific to its business area; the bulk occurs over and over again no matter what your system is for. These patterns cover more than half of all requirements in some systems–a lot more if we add the extra requirements the patterns suggest.

If you're wary of the word "requirement" here, don't be; it doesn't mean you have to be embroiled in paperwork. This book is suitable for use by business analysts using a traditional analysis approach and by software architects and engineers who use agile methods. You can use requirement patterns to help you identify and define what a system needs to do even if you don't write formal requirements as a result.

The requirements for a software system specify the problem it needs to solve–its purpose and goals. If they're omitted or done badly–which is, unfortunately, all too frequently the case–a system is unlikely to be a perfect fit, no matter how well it's implemented. A disturbing proportion of computer systems are judged to be inadequate; many are not even delivered; more are late or over budget. Studies consistently show that the single biggest cause is poorly defined requirements: not properly nailing down a system's purpose and what it must do. Even a modest contribution to improving requirements offers the prospect of saving businesses part of a huge sum of wasted investment.

To build good systems more often, improvements are needed all along the chain: Serious efforts have been (and continue to be) made in nearly all of them. But most fundamental of all is what the requirements themselves actually *say* (and, just as importantly, *fail to say*). That's been neglected, but it's what this book concentrates on. If I want to define a requirement of a specific type, what do I need to write? How do I go about it? What extra requirements should I consider writing? What else should I worry about? This book identifies many areas (big and small) for which requirements are frequently inadequate, imprecise, or missed altogether–and suggests what you can do about it. The patterns themselves aim to be down-to-earth and practical–primarily distilled from personal experience–things I wish I'd known all along.

This is primarily *a reference work*, to be pulled out whenever you want help in a particular situation– to explain what a requirement needs to convey, raise questions to ask, point out potential pitfalls, suggest extra requirements, provide example requirements, and generally provide practical advice. You can start using the requirement patterns without having read the book through.

This book contains lots of example requirements—over 400—many of which are suitable for applying unchanged to any system and others that are a useful starting point for a requirement to suit the reader's needs. These examples are the heart of the book. It was from the study of real-life requirements that the requirement patterns in this book were identified. Omissions, ambiguities, and other weaknesses in these real requirements fed much of what the requirement patterns have to say.

This book also provides guidance on how to write other kinds of information that belong in a requirements specification—such as system scope, assumptions, a glossary, document history, and references—and how to structure a requirements specification.

What This Book is Not

This is not a book about the process of specifying requirements or about analysis techniques or requirements management. There are other good books that explain all those things, and this book can be used as a reference alongside them. This book can, however, be used perfectly well by itself; it includes a "crash course in specifying requirements" for readers with no previous experience.

This book doesn't advocate any particular methodology, approach, or specification software tool. It provides relevant advice no matter which way you choose to work. It isn't prescriptive: it doesn't say, "You must do it this way." It steers clear of jargon and avoids introducing its own terminology as far as possible.

You won't agree with everything in this book, and you won't need to act on all the suggestions made by any requirement pattern. But if the time it saves you, when writing requirements or later, is worth more than the purchase price, it has earned its keep. I hope that these patterns prove useful one way or another, by containing enough useful and thought-provoking material to lead you to produce better systems.

Who Will Benefit from Using This Book

The primary audience of this book is **anyone involved in deciding what a new software system needs to do**. This is the business of specifying the requirements for a software system, even if you don't like the word "requirement" or you don't end up writing a full requirements specification. For convenience, we refer to any person who specifies requirements as an **analyst**; they could be a business analyst, a systems analyst, a systems architect, or a software engineer; they could be a business-oriented or technical person. They might have previous experience with specifying requirements, or they might not. They can be divided into those who use traditional analysis processes and those who use more agile methods:

a. **Business analysts**, or anyone fulfilling that role. This book makes no assumptions about how much the reader knows: it's suitable for both junior and experienced business analysts as well as for business executives and software engineers who have never specified requirements before. Requirement patterns can be put into practice quickly.

b. **Software architects and engineers** on any system for which requirements have *not* been written—because the gap must be filled, and it will be one way or another. This book's advice is equally relevant no matter who decides what a system needs to do. Its advice is of just as much value to any organization that does not have dedicated analysts, and particularly those that take an *agile* approach to development. Agile methods place little (if any) emphasis on writing requirements specifications, but still the functionality of the system must be identified—and the requirement patterns in the book can help just as well here as when using a traditional approach. In *extreme programming*, in particular, requirement patterns can help you write user stories, interpret user stories, and formulate "rules" for good practices for developers to follow. Software architects and engineers who are familiar with *design patterns* should be particularly comfortable using *requirement patterns*.

Secondary audiences are:

   c. Anyone asked to **review** a requirements specification, which covers a wide range of technical, managerial, and sales people as well as a new system's user community. This book can help reviewers judge a specification's quality and completeness, and discover omissions.

   d. **Software developers** who must implement requirements. Each requirement pattern contains a "Considerations for Development" section to assist developers.

   e. **Software testers** who must test how well the delivered system satisfies its requirements. Each requirement pattern contains a "Considerations for Testing" section for testers with suggestions on how to test requirements of that type.

   f. **Project managers** who manage a system's requirements, changes to them, and a project to implement them.

Job titles of people who will find this book valuable include business analyst, systems analyst, business systems analyst, software architect, systems architect, software engineer, testing engineer, product manager, project manager, project office manager, and chief technical officer.

Benefits the Reader Will Gain

You, dear reader, will be able to improve your skills and productivity in the following ways from reading this book (and from using it as a reference):

   1. You will be able to define better requirements—with more detail, precision, and clarity, and with less ambiguity.

   2. You will be able to write requirements more quickly and with less effort, by taking advantage of the effort already put into the book (reuse!).

   3. You will recognize extra topics that requirements should specify, further improving their results and making them more complete.

   4. You will be better able to organize a requirements specification and to write general sections (such as the glossary).

As a result you, your colleagues, and the organization you work for will see further benefits:

   5. It is easier to estimate the effort needed to build a specified system.

   6. Development and testing teams will find it easier to understand the requirements.

   7. The resulting system will better reflect the organization's needs, potentially yielding considerable extra return on the investment in it. What price can you put on avoiding a big mistake?

8. Fundamental mistakes, misunderstandings, and omissions will be spotted earlier—with potentially huge savings, given that fixing a defect during the design phase costs roughly ten times more than during requirements, and during development ten times more again.

Skills and Experience Needed by the Reader

This book can be used with no previous experience of specifying requirements. Chapter 1 is a "crash course" containing the bare minimum that a novice reader needs to get started. A good general book on requirements engineering (such as those cited at the beginning of Chapter 1) is a better introduction, and readers who have read them or who are already experienced business analysts are likely to get more from this book. Software engineers using agile methods can use the book in isolation. Anyone responsible for *reviewing* a requirements specification needs no previous knowledge or skills in order to use this book to help them.

This book is accessible to a nontechnical reader. It focuses on writing textual requirements in natural language that can be read by anyone. It is free of arcane diagram formats, deep theory, and jargon. You can read it without knowing UML (Unified Modeling Language) or any other formal technique.

The Structure of This Book

This book is divided into two parts:

- **Part I: Setting the Scene**   These four explanatory chapters open with Chapter 1, "Crash Course In Specifying Requirements," written for someone who is inexperienced at specifying requirements—but everyone should read it, because it states a few principles that are important to the rest of the book. Chapter 2, "The Contents of a Requirements Specification," describes the types of material, in addition to requirements, that belong in a requirements specification. The versions of Chapters 1 and 2 printed in the book are merely synopses of much longer, "full" versions that can be downloaded from the associated Web page (as described in the "Supporting Resources" section that follows). Chapter 3, "Requirement Pattern Concepts," explains what requirement patterns are all about: the basics, what each pattern contains, how they're organized (into domains), and related concepts. Chapter 4, "Using and Producing Requirement Patterns," explains how to use requirement patterns and to write your own.

- **Part II: Requirement Pattern Catalog**   These are sets of patterns for types of requirements that occur repeatedly, to be used as a reference. It opens with a snapshot of the requirement patterns in this book and then has eight chapters (5 through 12) containing the requirement patterns themselves.

Bringing up the rear are a glossary of terms and acronyms used and encountered in the book, plus a list of references.

I advise that you read through Part I to understand what's going on. If Chapters 1 and 2 in the book don't tell you enough, refer to the Web page for the full versions. You don't need to devour Part II systematically: familiarize yourself with the patterns that it contains (unless you're an analyst keen for advancement!), and refer to it whenever you encounter a situation in which one of the patterns will help.

Supporting Resources

You can download the following documents from the book's companion Web page at *http://www.microsoft.com/mspress/companion/9780735623989*:

1. The full version of Chapter 1, "Crash Course in Specifying Requirements."

2. The full version of Chapter 2, "The Contents of a Requirements Specification."

3. "Example Requirements," a complete set of all the examples in the book, plus the requirement templates for all the requirement patterns, to make it easy to copy and paste an individual template or example to use as a starting point when writing a requirement of your own. This document also includes a requirement pattern template, to use if you want to write your own patterns.

4. A "Ready Reference" suitable for printing, containing a diagram of all the requirement patterns plus a list of all the requirement patterns and the "applicability" of each one (to make it easy to figure out which pattern to use when).

The first two are available both as Adobe PDF (Portable Document Format) documents and Microsoft XML Paper Specification (XPS) documents. The last two are available as Microsoft Word documents. To download these documents, you will need about 5 MB of disk space. For system requirements for viewing these files, see the companion Web page.

Acknowledgments

I greatly appreciate the diligent and generous contributions of a number of people, without whose assistance this book would have been much the poorer—or wouldn't even have been completed at all. First, special thanks to Trish Reader for encouragement all the way through, sound business analysis advice, and feedback on various drafts.

I am deeply indebted to all my reviewers, especially those who heroically read and commented cover to cover: to Roxanne Miller, for her deep understanding of what all business analysts will look for in this book, and for keeping me (relatively) honest on analysis techniques; and to Lydia Ash, for her expertise on testing but also countless invaluable suggestions on almost everything. I appreciate the feedback and suggestions of Robert Posener for scrutinizing the text with the all-seeing eye of the consummate project manager; Craig Malone on development methodologies (especially agile matters); Marc Munro for his database expertise on the information and data entity patterns; security guru Eric Fitzgerald on access control; and accessibility experts Annuska Perkins, Norm Hodne, Ramkumar Subramanian, and Laura Ruby. Finally, thanks to Shanno Sanders for perceptive insights on the overall direction of the book. Sometimes I have rashly persisted in disregarding their advice, for which I assume full responsibility—as I do for all errors that remain.

I am grateful to Karl Wiegers for contributing such a generous Foreword, and for the early encouragement that was the nudge I needed to write this book.

I'd like to thank everyone at Microsoft Press, especially acquisitions editor Ben Ryan for his faith in the concept, and editors Devon Musgrave and Maria Gargiulo for their never-failing patience, their good-natured reactions to even the quirkiest of my ideas, and their painstaking copy editing.

Finally, this book could never have been written at all if not for the innumerable people who have contributed to my professional experience over the years. The most valuable have been those at the two extremes of the spectrum: the excellent, from whom I've learned so much about how to specify and develop good systems; and the inept, whose creativity in finding ways to do things wrong is an education in itself. Thanks to you all.

Microsoft Press Support

Every effort has been made to ensure the accuracy of this book. Microsoft Press provides corrections for books through the World Wide Web at the following address:

http://www.microsoft.com/mspress/support/

To connect directly to the Microsoft Press Knowledge Base and enter a query regarding a question or issue that you may have, go to:

http://www.microsoft.com/mspress/support/search.asp

If you have comments, questions, or ideas regarding this book, please send them to Microsoft Press using either of the following methods:

Postal Mail:

Microsoft Press
Attn: Software Requirement Patterns *Editor*
One Microsoft Way
Redmond, WA 98052-6399

E-Mail:

mspinput@microsoft.com

Part I
Setting the Scene

The four chapters in Part I tell you all you need to know to use the requirement patterns in Part II, "Requirement Pattern Catalog." Part I contains two chapters on requirements in general (on the *how* and the *what*, respectively) and two chapters on what requirement patterns themselves are all about.

This is a book about requirement *patterns*, so we don't want it to be bogged down by long explanations of how to specify requirements and what to include in a requirements specification. Yet you need at least a passing understanding of those subjects to make the most of the requirement patterns. How can we reconcile those goals? The answer is to provide longer, full versions of Chapters 1 and 2—just not in the printed book itself. They are available for download from the book's companion Web site, *http://www.microsoft.com/mspress/companion/9780735623989*. The Chapters 1 and 2 that follow are synopses of the full versions and are organized in the same way. They give you the quickest possible overview of these two subjects. If you want to know more about anything in one of the synopsis chapters, please refer to its full version.

Chapter 1, "Crash Course in Specifying Requirements," is a flying introduction to what requirements are all about and how to figure them out, whether you choose to do so in the traditional manner or take an agile approach. In this context, *traditional* means specifying all the requirements before designing and building the system; *agile* means worrying less about specification documents up front, and beginning development as early as possible.

Chapter 2, "The Contents of a Requirements Specification," describes what a requirements specification needs to contain. The full version of Chapter 2 provides a level of guidance about the sections in a requirements specification that is similar to what the patterns provide for individual requirements. This enables you to write a complete, well-balanced, full requirements specification.

Chapter 3, "Requirement Pattern Concepts," describes the role that requirement patterns play, explains what each pattern contains (its anatomy), and introduces a few related concepts.

Chapter 4, "Using and Producing Requirement Patterns," discusses when and how to use requirement patterns, and describes how to produce new requirement patterns by tailoring existing patterns or by writing new ones from scratch.

Chapter 1
Synopsis of "Crash Course in Specifying Requirements"

In this chapter:

1.1 What Are Requirements?. 4
1.2 Where Do Requirements Fit in the Grand Scheme? 5
1.3 A Few General Principles. 6
1.4 A Traditional Requirements Process 7
1.5 Agile Requirements Processes 8

"Would you tell me, please, which way I ought to go from here?"
"That depends a good deal on where you want to get to," said the Cat.
"I don't much care where—" said Alice.
"Then it doesn't matter which way you go," said the Cat.
"—so long as I get somewhere," Alice added as an explanation.
"Oh, you're sure to do that," said the Cat, "if you only walk long enough."

–Alice in Wonderland,
  Lewis Carroll

This chapter tells you the bare minimum that you need to know about requirements to understand the rest of the book. It is a synopsis of a much larger version of the chapter that is available for download from the book's associated Web page at *http://www.microsoft.com/mspress/companion/9780735623989*. (See the Preface for more information.) For convenience, the two are referred to as the **synopsis** and the **full** versions. The synopsis concentrates on defining concepts and terminology that are used throughout the book; it sets the scene. The full version goes into a lot more detail (on *every* topic) and provides justifications and advice—but it is still merely a whirlwind introduction to the subject. Both versions are organized in the same way: opening with some basic definitions and justifications, then describing where requirements fit in the overall process of building a system, and putting forward some principles worth following. Both versions end by describing three overall approaches to requirements, which are: a **traditional** approach, in which requirements are specified in detail before moving on to the development phases; an **extreme** approach, which strives to produce software as rapidly as possible at the expense of formality and documentation, and in which requirements are much less prominent; and a compromise **incremental** approach that specifies some of the requirements up front and some later on. Requirement patterns are equally applicable and equally valuable no matter which approach you take.

A number of good books explain software requirements in general and traditional requirements processes in a lot more detail, present a lot of extra analysis techniques, and cover other requirement-related activities ignored here. Of these, *Software Requirements* by Karl Wiegers (Microsoft Press, 2003), is my favorite. (Others include Robertson & Robertson, 2006; Davis, 1993; and Leffingwell & Widrig, 2000. See "References" at the back of this book for details.) This chapter (even the full version) is no substitute for such a book, and the reader is urged to invest in one (or more) of them.

This chapter assumes that you want to define what a new software system is for and what it must do—though it insists neither that you write a requirements specification nor that you include in your project a dedicated "requirements phase" following which the system will be designed and built. A **system**, as far as this book is concerned, comprises a collection of software components and (optionally) the hardware on which it runs; this book does not regard any of the people who use the system as part of the system itself.

This book makes no assumptions about the manner in which you record requirements. The most straightforward way is to use a word processor. Alternatively, you can use a requirements management tool built especially for the purpose.

1.1 What Are Requirements?

> *At least I have got a grip of the essential facts of the case. I shall enumerate them to you, for nothing clears up a case so much as stating it to another person, and I can hardly expect your cooperation if I do not show you the position from which we start.*
>
> –Sherlock Holmes: Silver Blaze,
>   Arthur Conan Doyle

Let's keep our definition of requirements simple:

The requirements of a system define what *it needs to do–but not how.*

The requirements define the problem that has to be solved: what the system is for and everything it needs in order to achieve that. They do not define the solution. A **requirement** is a single, measurable objective that a system must satisfy. The best way to express each requirement is in plain text. A **requirements specification** for a system is a document stating all its requirements plus any background material needed to make it readable and understandable. It needs to define all the functions and other capabilities that the system must possess.

There's no single "right" level of detail to go into in requirements. Requirements can be specified at various levels of detail. A relatively broad requirement can be broken down into more specific requirements that spell out the implications of the original. It's also possible to write multiple requirements *specifications* at different levels. Some organizations and experts divide requirements into separate levels as a matter of course, often into "high-level" requirements, which capture the business objectives, and "detailed" requirements, which spell out the functions and other capabilities that the system needs in order to achieve the business objectives. This book does not separate all requirements into levels. However, several of its requirement patterns introduce two (or even three) local levels of their own that show how to break down a specific kind of broad goal into clear requirements that are as detailed as developers need. For example, if our system must satisfy a particular standard (the broad goal), we can specify detailed requirements for what the system must do to achieve that goal. (*What*, but not *how*!)

Requirements define most importantly what the system must *do*, the activities it must be able to perform. These are called **functional requirements**. They attract the bulk of the attention, often to the neglect of the other characteristics that the system must possess—called nonfunctional requirements—which cover a wide range of topics from performance to security to standards with which the system must comply.

The *process* of specifying requirements is that of identifying what a system needs to do. It is performed for every system that's ever built, regardless of whether the requirements are spelled out explicitly. A programmer who decides what's needed and simply goes ahead and codes it performs a lightning-fast requirements specification process along the way, even if requirements exist only as fleeting thoughts before being overtaken by more exciting design brainwaves. I argue that it's advantageous to write down all requirement cogitations so that they can be debated and justified in their own right, independent of the design of the solution. A full-blown requirements definition phase isn't the only way to achieve that.

1.2 Where Do Requirements Fit in the Grand Scheme?

I have no data yet. It is a capital mistake to theorize before one has data. Insensibly, one begins to twist facts to suit theories, instead of theories to suit facts.

–Sherlock Holmes: A Scandal in Bohemia,
   Arthur Conan Doyle

Bringing a new system into being involves a number of stages. Exactly how many stages, what each one entails, and who performs them might vary somewhat, according to your organization's culture, who's available, personal taste, and the methodology you're using (and this book leaves that for you to decide). Still, we do need to differentiate the main activities in building a new system. There are endless ways to break them down and represent them. Figure 1-1 shows a simple version that suits our purposes.

Scope

Requirements

Design

Development

Testing

Installation

Figure 1-1   Development life cycle phases

This doesn't assume that you perform the whole of one activity before moving on to the next, so it applies regardless of the methodology that you use. Nor does it mean that you must document every activity: you might just picture a requirement in your mind before designing it, or merely think of a design before coding it. Viewed in this way, methodologies differ mainly in the size of each morsel to which this whole process is applied—from *the whole system* (the traditional approach) at one end of the spectrum to *a convenient unit of coding* (extreme programming) at the other. In a compromise third approach (which we'll call incremental), we specify a chunk of requirements before moving on to design, then perform a chunk of design before starting development; we do more design and specify more requirements as and when they're needed. Both of the last two fit in with an agile outlook. For the key activities, the differences between the approaches look conceptually something like Figure 1-2.

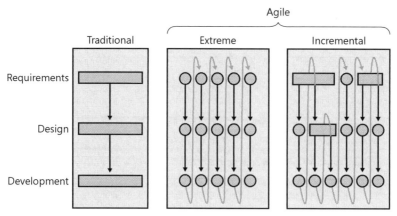

Figure 1-2   Morsel sizes for different development approaches

The second half of this chapter discusses each of these three approaches in turn. Every approach also involves a degree of rework–an iterative element–as errors are discovered in the development, the design, and the requirements.

1.3 A Few General Principles

Like all other arts, the Science of Deduction and Analysis is one which can only be acquired by long and patient study, nor is life long enough to allow any mortal to attain the highest possible perfection in it.

–Sherlock Holmes: A Study in Scarlet,
  Arthur Conan Doyle

This section discusses a few general principles to apply whenever specifying requirements. They will help you deliver good results and can help you decide whether or not to include something. This isn't a systematic set of principles; they're merely a few things that I wish to bring to your attention.

1. **Specify the Problem, Not the Solution.** Saying that requirements define "what, but not how" means that it's not the role of requirements to attempt to specify the solution or any part of it. This is an important distinction, and it is a rule not to be broken.

2. **Specify the System, Not the Project.** Requirements define what a system needs to do: they are a set of *objectives*. A **project** is the mobilizing of a team for a temporary duration to achieve those objectives. Requirements have no place saying how a system's objectives are to be achieved, which means saying nothing about a *project* to implement a solution (including milestone dates, team size, names of team members, costs, budget and methodologies). Also write every requirements specification to be **timeless**, to be equally valid for multiple systems that might be built in different ways at different times: the requirements could be put into a drawer and brought out in a year or two, or we might build a replacement system in a few years time.

3. **Separate the Formal and Informal Parts.** A requirements specification acts like a contract that defines what the builders or suppliers of a system must deliver. But a mass of contractually binding statements are far from enough for a reader to make proper sense of it: it needs background, context, flow, and structure. None of this extra material is contractually binding.

It's invaluable to divide the specification into the binding (**formal**) and nonbinding (**informal**) parts. The requirements themselves constitute the formal part of a requirements specification: the official definition of what the system must do. Everything else is informal.

4. **Avoid repetition.** Express each item of information only once, as far as is practical. Repetition creates extra work and opens opportunities for inconsistencies.

1.4 A Traditional Requirements Process

We choose to specify these things not because they are easy, but because they are hard.

—John F. Kennedy (what he might have said if he'd been a business analyst)

The traditional approach to specifying requirements is to have a distinct requirements phase that delivers a detailed requirements specification before starting to design and build the system. Figure 1-3 sums up the steps in a typical traditional requirements phase. The steps illustrated most prominently are those where the bulk of the work is done. The funny "Gather information" shape signifies that it's not isolated in a single early step, but continues until the final specification is delivered (although with gradually less time devoted to it, signified by the tapering towards the bottom of the shape).

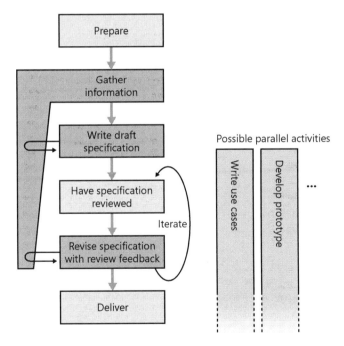

Figure 1-3   Activities in traditional requirements process

The steps shown in Figure 1-3 are:

1. **Prepare.** The analyst must be given an outline of the mission: some kind of statement of the system's objectives, before the requirements process can begin, either by explanation face-to-face or via a short scope document. Also find your feet: familiarize yourself with the environment (and the culture, if you're new to it) and identify all sources of information.

2. **Gather (or "elicit") information.** The main sources of information are people, documents, and existing systems. The key to gathering information well is attention to detail. First, find out as much as you can by reading before talking to people. Familiarize yourself with all relevant systems, too. But people are the best source of information on what your new system must do. The full version of this chapter describes the two prime ways of gathering information from people: individual interviews and collaborative sessions.

3. **Write draft requirements specification.** Start writing the first draft as early in the process as you can, but not until you have a reasonable picture of the major pieces. That, however, should take very little time: just a day or two. Write the "Context" section first. Then identify the functional areas, which form top level sections of the specification. Organize according to what you need to say. Don't be afraid to reorganize as you go along.

4. **Have specification reviewed.** Subject it to serious scrutiny to verify that you've correctly interpreted and represented everything you've been told. There are various ways to review a requirements specification, and these vary in their degrees of formality and thoroughness. The full version of this section discusses two methods for review: the **independent** approach involves distributing the specification to a number of reviewers and asking for their feedback; the **collaborative** approach brings a group of reviewers together at the same time to perform a detailed and systematic *inspection* of the specification.

5. **Revise after review.** Work systematically through all the individual comments that you receive, updating the specification as appropriate. Any comment could hint at other matters that have been omitted or need to be changed; be alert to observations that have wider implications. After creating a new version of the specification that takes into account review feedback, either send it out for review again or decide that you're happy with this version and regard it as finished.

Other activities can be performed in parallel with the main requirements activities. Two common activities are writing use cases and developing a prototype.

1.5 Agile Requirements Processes

> *"You are old, father William," the young man said,*
> *"And your hair has become very white;*
> *And yet you incessantly stand on your head.*
> *Do you think, at your age, it is right?"*
>
> –Alice's Adventures in Wonderland,
>   Lewis Carroll

This section discusses the role of requirements when taking an agile approach to building a system. It is aimed at developers and architects who *aren't* presented with a requirements specification as their starting point. Adopting an agile outlook isn't all-or-nothing; you can take small steps in that direction, or you can adopt it *nearly* wholeheartedly. You can do just some parts of a project agilely. You can take a traditional approach to specifying requirements and then perform design and development in an agile manner. In that case, you can use the traditional requirements process described in the previous section, and then take whatever agile approach you wish to the development.

The agile manifesto (which lives at *www.agilemanifesto.org*) defines an agile outlook as one that values people over processes, software over documentation, collaboration over contracts, and responsiveness over plan. "Software over documentation" is our main guide when deciding how to tackle requirements agilely: we should aim to churn out less documentation. The two approaches that follow concentrate on achieving documentary efficiency while still realizing the value that identifying requirements brings. Let's start with a couple of principles to guide any agile requirements process:

- **Principle 1: Distinguishing problem from solution is valuable.**   One way or another, you must decide what a new system must do. You must also decide how it will do it. This principle merely says it's good practice to recognize the *what* separately from the *how* and to do it first. It gives you something against which you can later gauge the quality of the solution and to compare the merits of two suggested solutions. It gives you a degree of objectivity that's lacking if everything blurs together.

- **Principle 2: If you identify a requirement, record it such that someone else can find it.** This principle does not, however, say where or in what form a requirement should be recorded.

An Extreme Requirements Process

It sounds incongruous to talk about a "requirements process" in the context of extreme programming (XP), because requirements don't appear in concrete form at all in an *extreme* extreme programming approach. Still, no system can be built without someone deciding what it needs to do, so the requirements are there somewhere. And they must come about as a result of some process or another, however fleeting and ethereal it is. That's the kind of requirements process we're talking about here—with a view to catching and bottling its results.

Building a new system using extreme programming begins by asking users to write a full set of "user stories." A **user story** is a short description of something the users want the system to do for them. For user stories to be representative, at least one person from each user area (that is, each "actor") must contribute to them. The end result is user stories for the main user functions of the system. Anyone involved in writing user stories might find the requirement patterns in this book helpful for guidance, for suggestions on topics to cover.

Once a set of user stories has been produced, it is used to plan the order in which they are to be implemented. A user story is assigned to a developer, who then figures out how to implement it (starting by defining a set of tests, which XP calls *acceptance* tests). Each developer must formulate the requirements they are trying to satisfy, even if they are unaware that's what they are doing, and even if the process is over in a split second and never sees the light of day outside their head. The first step in any development task should be to ask: what am I doing? What problem am I trying to solve? Answer those questions before proceeding, and write the answer down as the beginning of the definition of this task's tests. Write it in the form of a requirement (or more than one requirement). Engage a requirement pattern to help you, if there's a relevant one available. A requirement pattern could lead you to recognize the need for extra requirements, some of which might spawn their own development activities.

There are three ways in which requirement patterns can be used in association with extreme programming:

1. To suggest user stories and what to say in them (to make them more precise or more like requirements).

2. To interpret user stories in a more systematic manner, to unearth the actual requirements they allude to, and also to identify extra functionality needed to support a function that implements a user story.

3. To guide the production of a set of "common requirements" to be applied to all systems in your organization, especially rules for good practices to be followed by all developers.

An Incremental Requirements Process

Only perform requirements work as and when it's needed: just in time. That's the premise behind an incremental approach to it. Do a minimum of requirements work up front, so development can begin as early as possible. There are two things to decide here: how detailed the requirements need to be, and when to specify each piece's requirements. At one end of the scale, a full and detailed requirements specification would be written before starting any design and development work; at the other, individual requirements would be defined as part of a development unit. These two are represented by the traditional and the extreme requirements processes already described. An incremental approach is between these two.

Just as agile development involves incremental additions to the software, agile requirements ought to involve incremental additions—that is, gradual expansion of a single set of requirements. Everyone then has the same picture at all times, and we avoid repetition. The requirements specification, like the software, becomes a living being. What's a suitable process for doing this? In keeping with a lean, agile outlook, let's keep it simple:

1. Specify requirements up front sufficient to convince the customer that we understand what they want from the system (making sure we capture the business objectives) and to get the customer's approval to proceed.

2. When developer(s) are ready to begin building a particular area, expand the high-level requirement(s) that apply to that area, and specify detailed requirements for everything the system needs in order to satisfy that high-level requirement.

Chapter 2
Synopsis of "The Contents of a Requirements Specification"

In this chapter:

2.1 Introduction Section 12

2.2 Context Section. 15

2.3 Functional Area Sections 17

2.4 Major Nonfunctional Capabilities Section 18

This chapter discusses what a requirements specification should contain. As with Chapter 1, it is a synopsis of a full version of the chapter that can be downloaded from the book's associated Web page at *http://www.microsoft.com/mspress/companion/9780735623989*. (See the Preface for more information.) The synopsis is a flying overview. The full version goes into considerably more detail and is intended primarily as a reference, to call upon when you want advice on what to put into a particular section and why. Both versions are structured in a similar manner to the kind of requirements specification that this chapter presents.

There's no single right way to organize a requirements specification, but certain topics recur in most systems and deserve their own sections. Figure 2-1 shows a suggested structure for a requirements specification, in the form of a table of contents that identifies thirteen key topics described in this chapter.

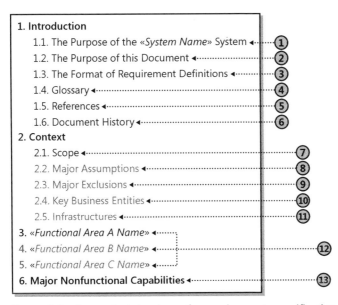

1. Introduction
    1.1. The Purpose of the «*System Name*» System ◄······①
    1.2. The Purpose of this Document ◄······②
    1.3. The Format of Requirement Definitions ◄······③
    1.4. Glossary ◄······④
    1.5. References ◄······⑤
    1.6. Document History ◄······⑥
2. Context
    2.1. Scope ◄······⑦
    2.2. Major Assumptions ◄······⑧
    2.3. Major Exclusions ◄······⑨
    2.4. Key Business Entities ◄······⑩
    2.5. Infrastructures ◄······⑪
3. «*Functional Area A Name*» ◄······
4. «*Functional Area B Name*» ◄······⑫
5. «*Functional Area C Name*» ◄······
6. Major Nonfunctional Capabilities ◄······⑬

Figure 2-1 Suggested structure of a requirements specification, with thirteen kinds of sections

The sections with grayed-out names are optional; include them as appropriate. In practice, all the top-level sections (except those in the "Introduction" and perhaps the "Context" section) will have extra subsections; some are likely to have many. This structure has worked well in practice, is clean and straightforward, and every section is present for a good reason. But no way of organizing a requirements specification is perfect for all occasions, so feel free to adjust it. Treat the thirteen key topics as parts that you can assemble in whatever way suits you: leave out parts that your system doesn't need, and merge parts together if each one is too small to justify its own section.

There are four types of top-level sections, which mirror the four top-level sections that follow in this chapter: "Introduction," "Context," functional areas (which do the hard work of specifying what the system must actually do and where the bulk of the requirements reside), and "Major Nonfunctional Capabilities."

2.1 Introduction Section

This section deals with six topics that belong in the introduction of nearly every requirements specification: system purpose, document purpose, requirement format, glossary, references, and document history.

System Purpose

A requirements specification should open with a description of what the system is for: who wants it, and why? Who will use it? What is the business motivation behind it? These sound like obvious questions, but it's surprising for how many systems they're not asked directly—perhaps because they are *too* obvious. And these questions sound as though they should be easy to answer, but frequently, they're not. Even when they have been answered, there might be much disagreement over the answers—which hints at deeper misunderstandings or disagreements among stakeholders.

Give this section a title that spells out clearly what it's for: "The Purpose of the «*System name*» System" or something very similar. This is to spur you to answer the question of what the system is for and to improve the chances that someone will notice if it hasn't been answered. Titling this section "Scope" or "Overview" leaves its true goal vague, which encourages uninformative waffling, especially when using a fill-in-the-blanks template. I suggest including the name of the system in the title of this section because some specifications make it hard work to unearth the system's name. Also take care to describe the purpose of the *system* itself, not the purpose of a *project* to implement the system.

Document Purpose

Every technical document should state clearly what it's for—the role the *document* plays. The best way to do this is to include in the opening of the document a section called "**The Purpose of this Document**" or something similar, so there's no question what the section is for. You, the author of this section, are its initial audience: use it to force yourself to confront the task at hand, and think about what you're doing. This section makes clear the role a requirements specification plays and more specifically, the role *this* requirements specification plays for *this* system, which might entail further explanation.

You must assume that much of your audience doesn't know what requirements are about or what a requirements specification is for, so you need to explain. Do so briefly and concisely, because if you ramble on, most readers will miss your main points. Beware of people who *think* they already know, but who perhaps don't appreciate the distinction we make between problem and solution. For their benefit, take care to make the explanation clear and strong. Begin by saying something like this:

The purpose of this document is to state the requirements that the «System name» system must satisfy. Its role is to describe the problem to be solved, not the solution: what the system must do, not how.

Other matters to consider addressing in this section are: (a) identify the audience; (b) state disclaimers; (c) say a little about the document's structure; and (d) identify other relevant requirements specifications.

Requirement Format

Much of our audience for requirements either has no idea or doesn't properly understand what a formal requirement is. You must explain, and including a section called "**The Format of Requirement Definitions**" in the introduction of the requirements specification is the best way. It needs to do the following:

- Explain that the material in the specification is split into formal and informal parts.
- Describe the items of information given for each requirement.
- Explain that each requirement defines a single measurable objective.

This book advocates writing the following four items of information for each requirement and presenting them in the form of a word processor table:

Item 1: Requirement ID   This is a unique **identifier** that enables us to refer to each requirement unambiguously. Without an ID, a requirement can't be traced or managed, can be lost, and commands no respect. The first essential quality requirement IDs need is to be **unique**: no two requirements can have the same ID. Whenever we talk about a *unique ID*, we need to clearly understand the *scope* of that uniqueness. Requirement IDs also need to be convenient to use, which means they should be **concise**, **distinctive**, and **sequential**. A lesser consideration is that requirement IDs should be **groupable**, so we can refer to all the requirements in a particular section in a specification. Requirements also *evolve*. The full version of this chapter also discusses strategies for renumbering requirements when you add to them and for handling the removal of requirements. The requirements specification itself needs to explain the requirement ID format that it uses, or it can refer to a separate document that explains it.

Item 2: Definition   This is the description, in free-form text, that formally defines the requirement. The requirement definitions are what our requirements specification exists for; the rest of the document is merely a vehicle for them—albeit with a smooth ride and luxury upholstery, if we do a good job. The **formal** elements in the definition of a requirement are: a formal statement of the requirement plus (optionally) a restatement of the formal requirement in different words, and extra details. The definition can then contain any of the following **informal** things: an example (or more than one); the rationale, motivation, or intent of the requirement; further justification for the requirement's existence; justification for the requirement's *form*; resolution of contradictions (real and apparent); relationships with other requirements (if helpful to the reader); suggestions for implementation; justification of priority; and deletion details (if it's deleted). All of these items are explained in the full version of this chapter. This list might look daunting, but no requirement needs all these.

Item 3: Priority   This states how important the requirement is. Prioritizing requirements provides a sound basis for making sensible decisions about how to build our system (including the order in which to build the parts). Before we can assign a priority to any requirement, we must **define the priorities** we wish to use and explain them to our readers.

Item 4: Summary description   This sums up the requirement as briefly as possible (using two to six words). This improves the readability of the specification and makes it easier to find a particular requirement.

It's possible to squeeze all sorts of other things into a requirement, and for sound reasons, some experts advocate doing so.

The example requirements given throughout the book give only the summary and definition. The requirement ID and priority are omitted because they make no sense in this context.

Glossary

A glossary is often an afterthought that appears by accident or because it makes a document look more weighty or because a document template has a section for it that has to be filled in. This is a mistake, and it explains why so many glossaries are awful. A good glossary in a requirements specification deserves just as much care as any other section. It plays several different roles: establishing the meaning of each relevant term, educating uninformed readers, demolishing misconceptions, and forcing poorly understood domain concepts out into the open. A glossary isn't simply a list of terms. It deserves an introduction, which can include: the scope of the glossary, references to other glossaries, instructions, and disclaimers.

The key to deciding whether to include a candidate term in our glossary is **relevance**. Define just the terms you use or those that are likely to be used throughout the system—and no more.

An entry in a glossary comprises two parts: the **term** itself and its **definition**. When writing a definition, assume nothing. We want our requirements specification to be intelligible by a smart but uninformed audience. **No business or technical term is so obvious that everyone knows it.** The key to writing a good definition is **precision**. The first sentence should constitute the formal definition of the term. If you feel you need to reinforce it to make it clear, follow the main definition with a restatement of the term in another form. After that, add whichever of the following might be useful: an example of usage; references to related term(s); scope (that is, the domain within which the definition applies); part of speech (noun or a verb, if it's not obvious); a note on spelling; and the definition's origin.

Having defined a term in the glossary, do not use that term to mean something else in any document whose scope is covered by the glossary. Our goal is to maintain **consistency** throughout our requirements specification and throughout the system as a whole.

References

Use the "References" section to identify documents and other sources used in the process of writing this document. A list of references is often self-explanatory, but you can introduce it by saying a little about what qualifies a document to be included in the list.

For each reference, provide enough information to identify it unambiguously, which means that you must supply more than just its title. Writers of internal documents within an organization are often slack in including identification details in their documents; they are liable to omit date, version number, the author's name, and sometimes even a title or opening heading.

For each reference give the following details: reference number; title (if it has one); author(s); version number and date of the version to which you referred; and location (where to find it). There are also extra things to say in some circumstances. These items are explained in more detail in the full version of this chapter.

Document History

Use the "Document History" section to record details of each version of the document. A version history is usually self-explanatory, but you can write an introductory sentence or two if you wish. It's normally fine for the document history to reside within the document itself. But if the document is going to be (or might be) distributed outside the organization, consider maintaining the document history elsewhere. A document history is best presented as a table containing four columns: version number; when (typically the version's release date); by whom (the name(s) of whoever made the change); and what changed.

2.2 Context Section

The "Context" section of a specification sets the scene. It provides the first real taste of what the system is all about, and by the end of it, you should have a reasonably good overall picture of the nature of the system—the kinds of things it needs to do and what it doesn't, including where its responsibilities end (that is, what's inside and what's outside its scope). The "Context" section aims to lead the reader—especially the nontechnical reader—into the intricacies of the system as gently as possible. The following are suggested subsections of the "Context" section, each of which is described in it own subsection below: scope, major assumptions, major exclusions, key business entities, and infrastructures.

Scope

The opening section of the requirements specification—"The Purpose of the «*System name*» System"—has already told readers what the system's business aims are, so don't repeat that here. The next step, and the aim of the "Scope" section, is to show how the system fits into the world around it: a local map showing where our territory ends and that of the neighbors starts, if you like. By far the best way to start is pictorially, with a **context diagram**. The full version of this chapter discusses what a context diagram should look like. The main kinds of information to show on a context diagram are

1. **Components** Show all the distinct pieces that must be in place for the system to work properly and how they logically connect to each other.
2. **User roles** Identify the main roles in which people interact with the system (either directly or indirectly). These are the system's actors, though there is no need to explicitly call them "actors" here.
3. **Scope boundary** Clearly separate those parts the system is responsible for from those it is not responsible for, by enclosing everything that's in scope within a closed line.
4. **Intersystem interfaces** Show **all** the interfaces via which the system interacts with other systems or logical components. Label them, so each one can be referred to unambiguously.

Secondary kinds of information you can consider showing are: communication links, major data stores, and grouping of components and people (that belong to the same organization or reside in the same location).

The context diagram should be followed by a brief description of each component, plus explanatory notes. Then describe all the **interfaces** our system has with other systems. Specifications often neglect interfaces, and this is dangerous because designing, implementing, and testing interfaces is hard work and time- consuming—so they need to be properly estimated and budgeted for. Formal requirements must be specified for the interfaces—but the "Context" section is not the best place for them (and they deserve their own section).

Major Assumptions

An **assumption** is an enduring statement that something can safely be treated as fact, as an axiom that can be depended upon (in the context of the system). Proclaim an assumption clearly and explicitly for each thing that you assume to be true (or, alternatively, false) and that would have significant impact on the system if it were not so.

Major assumptions that affect the system as a whole—and possibly the whole *nature* of the system—deserve prominence at the beginning of the requirements specification in their own section titled "**Major Assumptions**" or something similar. Local assumptions are best placed in context where they are relevant, dotted throughout the requirements specification.

Some authors and organizations advocate stating **dependencies** that the system has on external factors in a similar manner to stating assumptions, but doing so separately. External systems on which our system depends are already dealt with by specifying requirements for the interfaces to them. I prefer to regard all other dependencies as assumptions and to present them as such.

Major Exclusions

An **exclusion** is something the system **does not** do ("nongoals"). State an exclusion for any feature which is not planned but which a reader might conceivably expect to be present. The main benefit is in preemptively answering questions that reviewers might otherwise have; the exclusion gives you a place to explain why. It is good practice to write an exclusion for any suggestion that has not been acted upon. An exclusion is not a formal part of the requirements specification. So, more precisely, an exclusion points out something that the system has **no obligation to implement**—not that it **must** not. Anything the system categorically *must not* do should be written as a requirement. As a result, testers can ignore exclusions.

Major exclusions can be placed in their own "**Major Exclusions**" section at the beginning of the requirements specification for visibility, in a similar manner to major assumptions. Lesser exclusions are best placed wherever in the requirements specification they are relevant, again as lesser (local) assumptions are.

Key Business Entities

Use the "Key Business Entities" section to identify the "axis" *business entities* (typically one or two of them) around which the system revolves and to define the salient characteristics of each of these entities. Most commercial systems have only one, two, or three business entities at their core that drive the bulk of the processing: those things the system is built to create and manipulate.

For example, a system for a retail business might have *customer* and *customer order* as the only business entities that deserve the treatment described here.

Each key business concept needs its own subsection and should include the entity's name in its title; "The Life-Cycle of a «*Business Entity Name*»" is a good title format. These entity subsections can either be grouped together within a "Key Business Entities" section or can reside directly within the "Context" top-level section.

The purpose of a section about a type of business entity is to identify its main characteristics, especially what can happen to one in its lifetime. This is where we begin to dig beneath the surface—to go beyond the superficial and the obvious. The best way to express what can happen to an entity is via a **state transition diagram** (sometimes called an *entity life history* diagram, or by UML, a *state diagram*). This shows all the possible **states** an entity can be in and how it can move from one state to another—the **transitions**, for each of which we need at least one function that can perform or cause it.

Infrastructures

The purpose of the "Infrastructures" section of a requirements specification is to point out any "life support mechanisms" that the system depends upon and that are not part of the system itself. Any commercial system exists solely to deliver the functions its owner needs to run their business. But those functions cannot exist in isolation, and we have to deliver lots of extra features simply to provide a well-rounded environment. Implementing some types of requirements relies on underlying software (and possibly hardware, too). For example, any requirement that involves storing data assumes we have a place to store it (typically a database). We call this an *infrastructure*:

Infrastructure: *an underlying set of capabilities needed to support one or more types of requirements.*

Infrastructures are used by the system when it is in production (at *run time*). Nothing that is used during the development or testing of the system is regarded as an infrastructure as far as the requirements are concerned. Likewise, infrastructures are not concerned with nontechnical logistic or operational things: policies, procedures, stationery, training, and such.

The specification of a system can't be regarded as comprehensive unless **proper requirements** are specified for each infrastructure it uses; without them, there are big gaps. But the "Infrastructures" section is not the place for detailed requirements; either include them later in the main specification or write a separate specification for each infrastructure.

2.3 Functional Area Sections

Once we've written all our introductory and contextual material, we're left with the task of specifying the guts of the system. So how should we organize the main body of the specification? It is convenient to divide it into a number of sections to make it more manageable and easier to understand.

Functional areas are the best way of organizing the main body of the specification—which means writing a top-level section for each logical grouping of functions, usually based on the primary interest of each type of user. In short, write a section for each major *actor*.

Name each section for its functional area: "Customer Functions," "Customer Service Functions," "Accounting Functions," and so on. Use the language your customer uses for these areas. It doesn't matter *how many* functional area sections you end up with: there may be one or twelve—both are fine. Create the sections you need, and let everything else take care of itself.

Order these sections according to their importance (from highest to lowest), though what constitutes *important* varies from system to system. It could mean the frequency of use of the functions in each area, the intrinsic relative importance of the actors, or the value, in some other way, to the business. Typically, however, the functional area in which *business originates* is the most important, followed by other areas, according to the length of time it takes new business to flow through to them.

2.4 Major Nonfunctional Capabilities Section

The purpose of this section is to specify in detail the important nonfunctional aspects of the system: those that apply to the system as a whole. It's hard to pin down the contents of this section because it depends very much on the nature of the system, so let's tackle it by suggesting a process by which to write it:

- **Step 1:**   Create an empty "Major Nonfunctional Capabilities" section at the end of the requirements specification when first creating the specification. This serves as a reminder not to forget this area.

- **Step 2:**   Write the main body of the requirements specification. If, along the way, you identify any nonfunctional topic that's too big to fit anywhere else, add it to the "Major Nonfunctional Capabilities" section.

- **Step 3:**   Consider whether there are any extra topics not yet specified. Concentrate on nonfunctional and peripheral aspects. Think especially about flexibility, quality, security, usability and accessibility, standards, and technology constraints.

- **Step 4:**   Move as much as you can of this section's contents to other places in the specification.

- **Step 5:**   Reorganize this section, and give it the most suitable title.

Chapter 3
Requirement Pattern Concepts

In this chapter:

3.1 Introduction to Requirement Patterns 19
3.2 The Anatomy of a Requirement Pattern 21
3.3 Domains 29
3.4 Requirement Pattern Groups 31
3.5 Relationships Between Requirement Patterns 32

3.1 Introduction to Requirement Patterns

In all but trivial systems you'll have requirements that are similar in nature to one another or that crop up in most systems—and probably lots of them. For example, you might have a number of inquiry functions, each with its own requirement. When specifying a business system, a significant proportion of the requirements fall into a relatively small number of types. It's worthwhile to make an effort to specify all the requirements of one type in a consistent manner. To do this, we introduce the notion of a requirement pattern, to allow us to describe how each requirement that uses it should be defined.

Requirement pattern: an approach to specifying a particular type of requirement.

A requirement pattern is applied at the level of an *individual requirement*, to guide the specifying of a single requirement at a time. For example, if you have a requirement for a certain report, you can engage the report requirement pattern to help you specify it. Once you've written the requirement (and any extra requirements it suggests), the pattern's job is done, and you can put it away and move on. But when a software designer or developer comes to decide how to implement the requirement, the pattern is available to give them some hints relevant to their job, if they wish. A tester can similarly use the pattern for ideas on how to test it.

What are the benefits of using requirement patterns? First, they provide guidance: suggesting the information to include, giving advice, warning of common pitfalls, and suggesting other matters you ought to consider. Second, they save time: you don't have to write each requirement from scratch, because the pattern gives you a suitable starting point, a foundation to build on. Third, patterns promote consistency across requirements of the same type. Of these, guidance is of the greatest value. Saving specification time and increasing consistency are nice, but sound guidance that leads to much better requirements can avoid immense trouble and work later on.

The guidance provided by a requirement pattern usually goes deeper than just "say this...." It can give background insight into the problem at hand. It can raise questions you ought to ask yourself. In some cases it can lead you to write a requirement (or several) very different from the one you first envisaged. Answering a big question often raises a number of smaller questions. A requirement pattern is a response to a big question and aims to give both the big answer and the smaller questions.

Some requirement patterns either demand or invite the specification of extra requirements: both **follow-on requirements** that expand on the original requirement, and systemwide **pervasive requirements** to support the pattern itself (for instance, for an underlying feature needed by all requirements of this type). It is therefore useful to be aware of which patterns you have used (perhaps by keeping a simple list), so you can run through them asking yourself whether each one needs its own extra supporting requirements and whether you have defined them. This topic is explained in more detail in the "Extra Requirements" section later in this chapter.

Patterns can vary in their level of detail (their preciseness) and their value. Some types of requirements can be defined in great detail, and instances of them vary little. Others have something worthwhile in common but vary to such an extent that we can't prescribe what they ought to say. These variations are natural. To justify itself, a pattern simply needs to be of value; it doesn't have to do everything a pattern *could possibly* do. On the other hand, just because we encounter a particular type of requirement repeatedly does not mean a pattern for it would automatically have value. If it's hard to encapsulate what the requirements have in common, it's hard to provide guidance on how to specify requirements of this type.

Where do requirement patterns come from? This book defines patterns for a range of common types of requirements, which can be used as they stand. Other patterns may become publicly available in due course. Or you can write your own—see the "Writing New Requirement Patterns" section in Chapter 4, "Using and Producing Requirement Patterns," for guidance. You can also modify existing patterns to suit your own preferences and circumstances.

Pattern Ecosystems

"Each pattern describes a problem which occurs over and over again in our environment." So says Christopher Alexander, the godfather of the technical use of patterns (as quoted by Gamma, Helm, Johnson, and Vlissides, 1995). In a complex environment, there are many niches for patterns to fill, within which different species of patterns can live together harmoniously.

Individual requirements reside low down in the food chain. Designs live high up the food chain, feeding on the requirements (or, in their absence, on whatever unhealthy carrion they can find). In information technology, different species of patterns can coexist at various scales—big or small—and on both sides of the problem/solution divide. They all have their place: it just depends on what you seek guidance about.

Requirement-related patterns have been suggested at the large scale—for *sets* of requirements (by Robertson and Robertson, 2006) and requirements for a *whole system* (by Ferdinandi, 2002). Conceptually, both of these levels are valid.

Martin Fowler's **analysis patterns are** worth mentioning, too. They live on the other side of the fence from requirement patterns, in the design domain next door. Each one serves to guide the solution of a specific application problem. Analysis patterns are one step higher in the food chain than requirement patterns, and design patterns can feed upon them in turn. (Martin Fowler's analysis patterns can be found at *http://www.martinfowler.com* or in his book [1996].) Tony Morgan presents a few handy **business rule patterns** in his *Business Rules and Information Systems* (2002). (A reminder: see "References" at the back of this book for details on the publications mentioned.)

Patterns to apply at the level of individual requirements are especially useful because of the atomic nature of requirements. That is, requirements have a lot more in common with one another than aspects of design do. This is not to say that requirement patterns are in any way better than design patterns—certainly not. It merely means that they are easier to apply because we're always applying requirement patterns to requirement objects that are conveniently self-contained. Also, choosing a requirement pattern delivers a concrete requirement instance to use as our starting point.

Because various species of patterns coexist, this book uses the term "requirement pattern" throughout, rather than just "pattern." For the same reason, it's a good idea to always explicitly qualify the word "pattern" with the sort of pattern you're talking about.

3.2 The Anatomy of a Requirement Pattern

This section describes what a requirement pattern contains, how it is organized, and why. Bear in mind that it talks about *patterns* and how to write them, not the requirements that might result from a pattern. A requirement pattern is considerably more substantial than a requirement. Writing a requirement pattern is correspondingly a lot more involved, too. Indeed, writing a requirement pattern deserves much thought. To be useful as a guide to writing requirements, it needs to take into account all the situations and variations that are likely to be encountered in the type of requirement for which it's written.

A requirement pattern needs to say **when to use** the pattern and **how to write requirements** based on it. It can also give hints on **how to implement** and **how to test** requirements of this type. To convey these sorts of information, each requirement pattern contains the following sections:

1. **Basic details**   The pattern manifestation, owning domain, related patterns (if any), anticipated frequency of use, pattern classifications, and pattern author.

2. **Applicability**   In what situations can the pattern be applied? And when can it not be applied?

3. **Discussion**   How do we write a requirement of this type? What does a requirement of this type need to consider?

4. **Content**   What must a requirement of this type say? What extra things *might* it say? This is the main substance of the pattern.

5. **Template(s)**   A starting point for writing a requirement of this type—or more than one if there are distinct alternative ways.

6. **Example(s)**   One or more representative requirement written using this pattern.

7. **Extra requirements**   What sorts of requirements often follow on from a requirement of this type? And what pervasive systemwide requirements might define something for all requirements of this type?

8. **Considerations for development**   Hints for software designers and engineers on how to implement a requirement of this type.

9. **Considerations for testing**   What do we need to bear in mind when deciding how to test this type of requirement?

Preceding all of this we have the **pattern name**, which appears in the title of the whole pattern. Each requirement pattern needs a unique name so that it can be referred to unambiguously. A pattern name should be meaningful—to clearly capture the nature of the pattern. A pattern's name should also be as concise as possible—preferably a single word, but not more than three. It's also recommended that each pattern name be a noun-phrase. The name of a pattern for functional requirements reflects the function name (for example, "inquiry" for the pattern that guides how to specify an inquiry function).

The number of sections in each pattern has been deliberately kept to a minimum to make them as easy to read and to follow as possible.

Basic Details

The "Basic Details" section of a requirement pattern is simply a convenient vehicle for all those items that can be answered briefly (rather than clogging up our patterns with lots of tiny subsections). In fact, the items lumped together here are a mixed bag. The items indicated by an asterisk (*) are omitted from all the patterns in this book, either because they are obvious from the context (the chapter they're in) or because they're the same in every case.

Pattern manifestation*:	There can be more than one manifestation of a particular requirement pattern, which means different variants or versions. This item tells us which manifestation we have before us, to distinguish it from others. The first manifestation of a pattern is referred to as the "Standard" one. The manifestation can convey one or more of the following things:
	a. The pattern's version number.
	b. The date the pattern was last changed.
	c. The requirements approach (or author).
	d. The customer organization (company name).
	e. The requirements specification language (for example, English).
	(See the "Requirement Patterns and Diversity of Approaches" section later in this chapter and "Tailoring Requirement Patterns" in Chapter 4 for more.)
	"Pattern manifestation" is omitted from all the patterns in this book. All should be regarded as being "Standard."
Belongs to domain*:	Every requirement pattern belongs in a domain, and this states which one.
	Many requirements for which patterns are used need some sort of supporting infrastructure. For example, requirements for reports imply the existence of an underlying reporting infrastructure for producing those reports. Requirements should be defined for the infrastructure itself. (See the next section, "Domains and Infrastructures," for more information.)
	One purpose of identifying whether a particular pattern implies the presence of supporting software is to prompt you to consider whether the requirements for that software have been adequately specified.
	"Belongs to domain" is omitted from all the patterns in this book because it is clear from the chapter in which the pattern resides. This item becomes essential if the domain cannot be determined from its context, such as a single pattern that resides in a stand-alone document.
Related patterns:	This lists any other requirement patterns that apply to related situations. If it would be helpful, this item can also say a little about *how* the patterns relate to each other.

Anticipated frequency:	How many times is this pattern likely to be used in a typical requirements specification? For rarely used patterns, this is best stated as an *absolute number*, or an absolute number for each occurrence of a parent requirement. For more commonly used patterns, expressing it as a *percentage* of the requirements is more useful and easier. Often the frequency is best expressed as a range (of absolute numbers or percentages). This item is also at liberty to point out circumstances in which the frequency might fall outside the normal range.
	For most patterns, this value is indicative only; it might vary considerably from one system to another. Don't lose sleep if your number of requirements falls outside the suggested range.
	The frequencies stated for the requirement patterns in this book derive from a diverse set of real-world requirements specifications. Sometimes the actual numbers encountered have been adjusted to create a broader range, to bear in mind factors not present in the specifications studied.
Pattern classifications:	Each requirement pattern can be classified in multiple ways, and this item lists all that apply to the main type of requirement covered by the pattern. No attempt is made to apply these classifications to any of the *extra requirements* described in the pattern. See the "Requirement Pattern Classifications" section later in this chapter for more information about how to use classifications.
	Classification lists are given in a standard format of "Name: Value", separated by semicolons. For example:
	Functional: Yes; Performance: Yes
	This format is concise, readable, and easy to follow. It allows new classifications to be added without changing the standard structure of requirement patterns.
Pattern author*:	Knowing who wrote a pattern can help you decide whether you want to use it. For patterns written in-house, it tells you who to go to for help.
	For manifestations other than the first, this identifies both the original author and who *tailored* it.
	The pattern author is omitted from all the requirement patterns in this book but should be included in all patterns whose authorship isn't obvious.

Applicability

The "Applicability" section describes the situations in which the requirement pattern can be applied. It should be clear and precise. Conciseness helps too, to let the reader form as quickly as possible a picture of when to use this pattern. It's advisable for the first sentence to capture the essence of the matter, and for the rest to clarify and expand it—just like a requirement, in fact. All such statements in this book begin with, "Use the «*Pattern name*» to...."

Normally, a requirement pattern is applicable in only one clear situation: two different situations usually demand two different patterns. That's not to say that all the requirements that use a pattern will look the same—far from it, because there may be considerable variations between them. Some might have optional extra clauses, and they might vary greatly in their size and complexity. However, they will all share the same underlying nature.

The "Applicability" section can also state situations in which the pattern should not be used, if there's any danger of the pattern being misapplied. If there are no situations of this kind, this statement is omitted. All such statements in this book begin with, "Do not use the «*Pattern name*» to...."

Discussion

The "Discussion" section of a requirement pattern tells you how to write a requirement of this type. It explains everything it can that's likely to help someone who wants to specify a requirement of this type. It generally opens with an overview, to set the scene. It can describe a process to follow, if figuring what to write in such a requirement isn't straightforward. It can raise topics to which to give special thought. It can mention potential pitfalls. The quantity of this discussion material can vary enormously from one requirement pattern to another: from one paragraph to many pages; it all depends on the nature of the requirement and what there can usefully be said about it.

Content

The "Content" section is a detailed list of each item of information that a requirement of this type must convey. Each content item begins with a name by which to refer to the item, followed by an indication of whether it's optional, and then general descriptive material. It is presented like this:

1. **Item 1 name** Item 1 description.
2. **Item 2 name (optional)** Item 2 description.
3. **...**

It's useful for the description to *justify* the item, to explain its purpose if it's not obvious: if the writer of a requirement understands why it's needed, they are more likely to write it (and to write it well). The description can also suggest what to say about the item in the requirement, offer advice, and generally say anything that might help. The order in which the elements of the content are described is implicitly the best order for them to appear in a requirement.

Template(s)

The aim of a requirement template is to allow you to copy it into a requirement description to use as a starting point. A template is a fill-in-the-blanks definition for a requirement that is deemed to be typical of the type.

The "Content" section of a pattern can describe various optional topics a requirement might need to address but that aren't relevant in all requirements. When deciding which of these topics to include in a template, our guide is efficiency: to minimize the effort in using the template. If a topic is likely to be needed in only a small percentage of requirements, it's best left out of the template. But we must bear in mind that it's much easier to delete an unwanted item than to type in an item for which we have no starting point. A useful rule of thumb is to include a starting point for a topic in the template if at least 20 percent of requirements are likely to possess it.

Be warned that templates for documents or parts of documents are dangerous, because they can lull you into avoiding the thinking you really need to do, or they give you the impression that all the thinking has already been done. Another pitfall is that you end up saying what the template writer felt should be said when they had a different situation in mind. Nevertheless, if taken with a suitably large pinch of salt, using a template can save a little time when writing a requirement.

Each template is shown within a table like the one below, which is in a form suitable for direct copying into a requirement:

Summary	Definition
The format of the summary	The format of the definition

Additional explanatory notes can follow the table.

Here's an example of a template, from the inquiry requirement pattern, that demonstrates the main aspects:

Summary	Definition
«Inquiry name» inquiry	There shall be an [*«Inquiry name»*] inquiry that shows *«Information to show»*. Its purpose is *«Business intent»*. For each *«Entity name»*, the inquiry shall show the following: ■ *«Information item 1»* ■ …

Both the summary and the definition can contain **placeholders** for variable information, which are indicated by being enclosed in double-angled brackets and in italics—for example, *«Entity name»* or *«Description»*. Each placeholder must have the same name as that used in the list of content items in the "Content" section (or sufficiently similar that they can be readily matched up). The summary format typically comprises two parts:

1. A fixed word or brief phrase related to the name of the pattern.
2. A brief description to distinguish this requirement from all others of this type.

A template can contain **optional parts**: items of information that are not needed in all cases. This is indicated by surrounding each option part in square brackets: [like this]. This is indicative only; it doesn't mean that everything *not* in square brackets is always essential. Conversely, an optional item might be essential in a particular situation for which you're writing a requirement.

When a requirement can contain a list of items, a sequence number is added to the name of each one (as with '*«Information item 1»*' in the example above), to allow the template to show more than one. An ellipsis (…) indicates that the list continues and might contain as many items as are needed.

A requirement pattern can contain several alternative templates, each tailored to a particular situation. For example, there might be one for a simple case, one containing every possible item, and one or more in between.

Example(s)

Each requirement pattern contains at least one—usually more—example requirement definitions that demonstrate use of the pattern in practice. For instance, a typical requirement that uses the pattern may be very simple, but some might need to say more; in such a case, we might give examples of each.

Each example is shown within a box like the one below, containing information exactly as they would appear in real requirements of which they are representative:

Summary	Definition
Summary for the example	The definition of the example

Anything that follows the box (like this) is explanatory material that is not part of the example requirement itself. There ought to be no need for notes to make clear the meaning of any requirement, because requirements should be self-explanatory, but notes can be used to point out an aspect of a requirement that renders it a useful example.

Example requirements need not be consistent with one another. Each one is present to demonstrate a representative situation. Spanning a range of possibilities often demands requirements from different sorts of system and sometimes requirements that conflict with one another. All examples are intended to be *good* examples; there are no examples of *what not to do*. Examples are also intended to be realistic, which means not simplified when being added to a requirement pattern. Sometimes this involves the inclusion of extra clauses that might make an example look a little long-winded; this is preferable to giving an example that says less than one would want in practice.

Some requirement patterns contain real-world examples that can be copied directly into requirements specifications and then modified as you see fit. For example, the comply-with-standard requirement pattern has examples for a range of frequently used, general-purpose standards. A list of examples, then, can serve as a body of knowledge to be tapped at will and not just as representatives that show you what such requirements might look like.

Extra Requirements

In many situations, one requirement isn't sufficient to say all that must be said: you might (or, in some cases, *always*) need to specify additional requirements to spell out the implications properly. The "Extra Requirements" section in a requirement pattern explains what sorts of extra requirements should be considered and in what circumstances. It provides guidance on what to do beyond simply specifying the main requirement. What other things should you think about? What more needs to be said? If there's nothing further to specify, a requirement pattern's "Extra Requirements" section can be empty.

For example, a requirement that mandates compliance with a particular standard (see the comply-with-standard requirement pattern) is rarely sufficient. Just what does that standard say? Which parts are relevant to our system? What must our system do to satisfy this standard? We need detailed requirements that reflect the answers to these questions. The "Extra Requirements" section of the comply-with-standard pattern is the place that points out what further work needs to be done.

There are two types of extra requirements:

- **Type 1: Follow-on requirements**   These come after the original requirement and define additional things about it. They expand the original requirement. For ease of reading, follow-on requirements should come immediately after the original requirement.

- **Type 2: Pervasive requirements**   These are defined once for the whole system and define things that apply implicitly to all requirements of this type. Usually there is only one pervasive requirement for a particular aspect (for example, "Every page on every report shall show the company logo"), but sometimes there are more, with each applying in clearly defined circumstances (for example, "Every page on every report to an agent shall show the agent's company logo," in addition to the previous example). The use of pervasive requirements of this sort means that each original requirement has fewer topics to cover and can be simpler. They save repetition, and as a result they avoid the chance of inconsistency in their areas.

    Pervasive requirements can also be "catch-alls" that define implicit functions for all instances of this pattern. For example, "All data shall be displayable on some inquiry or another."

An extra requirement could itself be written with the assistance of a requirement pattern. It can have extra requirements of its own.

Figure 3-1 shows how use of a pattern can result in an original requirement plus two sets of extra requirements: follow-on requirements that add details about the original requirement, and pervasive requirements that define common aspects shared by all original requirements of this type.

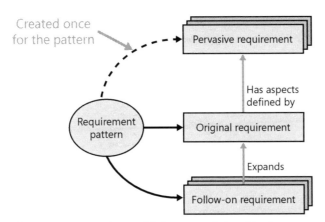

Figure 3-1   Pervasive and follow-on relationships between requirements

You should group related pervasive requirements together, either before all the original requirements to which they relate or after them all. The pervasive requirements for a requirement pattern might look as though they belong in the specification for an infrastructure supporting the domain in which the pattern lives, but actually they should be kept separate. The infrastructure's requirements define what the infrastructure *can* do; the pervasive requirements define what *our system* needs (because another system might use that same infrastructure differently). That's fine, although if both systems use the same instance of software that implements the infrastructure, it can impose extra functional demands on that software. In such cases, you can place the pervasive requirements in a separate "common" requirements specification that both systems refer to.

Take care to alert all readers to the presence of pervasive requirements—especially developers, because pervasive requirements often have profound design and development implications. Imagine how you'd feel upon discovering that some characteristic you demanded for *every* user function was possessed by *none* of them. So,

1. Don't rely on readers reading the whole requirements specification. A developer might read only those parts that look relevant to them, plus the introduction.

2. Don't bury important pervasive requirements where they might be missed (such as at the end of the requirements specification).

3. Make references to relevant pervasive requirements from elsewhere as you see fit.

4. Explain in the requirements specification's introduction the significance of pervasive requirements and the importance of not missing them.

5. Consider putting all the pervasive requirements in one place and pointing all developers unequivocally to it.

6. Consider highlighting each pervasive requirement in some way, such as a clear statement at the end of the requirement's definition. For example, "This is a pervasive requirement" or "This requirement applies across the whole system" or "This requirement applies to all user functions in the system".

An "Extra Requirements" section can contain its own example requirements to demonstrate what each kind of extra requirement might look like. If so, follow-on and pervasive requirements should be kept separate and clearly labeled so that they won't get mixed up. Example pervasive requirements are often suitable for direct copying into a requirements specification. In rare cases, the number of pervasive requirements in a pattern could run to a dozen or more.

In extreme cases, the follow-on requirements resulting from a single original requirement could involve more work than all the other requirements put together. For example, complying with a demanding standard (for, say, safety) might be a massive undertaking and much harder than building a simple system that has the functionality you need.

Considerations for Development

The "Considerations for Development" section is intended to assist a developer who needs to design and implement software to satisfy a requirement of this type. It gives them hints and suggestions and points out things not to forget. The "Considerations for Development" section should be written in the language of developers.

The best way to look at this section is as the sort of guidance a very experienced developer would give to a junior developer. If a grizzled, seen-it-all engineer were asking a wet-behind-the-ears graduate to implement a requirement of this type and giving them advice on how to tackle it, what would they say? The amount to be said varies greatly from one requirement pattern to another. In some cases, the requirement is self-explanatory; in others, there are various pitfalls to point out.

This section can also point out things that a development representative could look out for when *reviewing* requirements. Is a requirement being unreasonable? If it's likely to be impractical to implement, press to have the requirement changed.

Considerations for Testing

A requirement pattern is a useful place to explain how to test requirements of its type. This section is aimed at testers. It is written primarily with user acceptance testing in mind, because that's the sort of testing that can be done most closely against the requirements. But it can be used for other sorts of testing, too.

Since requirements vary considerably in their nature, they vary as much in the ways they need to be tested. Each "Considerations for Testing" section aims to convey three sorts of information:

1. Points to look out for when reviewing a requirement of this type. If a requirement is likely to be difficult to test, suggest how it can be reframed to make testing easier.
2. Overall guidance on how to approach the testing of this type of requirement.
3. Notes on matters to bear in mind and (where possible) tips on how to deal with them.

Universal requirement patterns can discuss testing only in general terms—because a pattern knows nothing about a particular organization's testing practices, the testing tools it uses, the nature of the environment in which the system will run, or the nature of the system.

An organization may well find it worthwhile to tailor—or rewrite—the "Considerations for Testing" sections in its patterns to suit the ways it does testing (taking into account, in particular, whatever tools it uses for testing) and the expertise and culture of those responsible for testing. Indeed, by taking into account the organization's individual situation, it's possible to write sections that are far more than *considerations* for testing; they can become *instructions* on how to test requirements of the requisite type. If you aim to do this, you may find it more useful to leave the "Considerations for Testing" section alone and add (or replace it with) your own "Testing Instructions" section. This could be augmented by additional artifacts to use when testing this type of requirement, such as tailored forms for writing test cases.

3.3 Domains

There is much to be gained by organizing our requirement patterns rather than presenting a monolithic list of them. We do this by assigning every requirement pattern to a **domain**. Each domain has a theme, which all its patterns share, but the nature of the theme can vary greatly from one domain to another. The domains used in this book—each with its own chapter in Part II, "Requirement Pattern Catalog"—are **Fundamental,** for things that any kind of system might need; **Information**, for several aspects of the storage and manipulation of information (data); **Data entity**, on how to treat specific kinds of data; **User function**, for a couple of common types of functions, plus accessibility; **Performance**; **Flexibility**; **Access control**; and **Commercial**, for business-oriented matters. This shouldn't be regarded as a definitive list: new domains might be needed if further requirement patterns are written. For example, if requirement patterns were to be written for a particular industry, they would deserve their own domain (or possibly more than one). The applicability of a domain can range from very broad to very narrow: from nearly all systems, through systems in one industry, to just a couple of systems in a single company.

When you begin specifying a system, you can look through all the requirement pattern domains (in this book, plus any extras you have from elsewhere) and decide which ones are relevant to your system. If it's a noncommercial system, you might decide to drop the Commercial domain. The set of requirement patterns that are available for use in your system depends on the domains you decide are relevant. Regard only the patterns in your chosen domains as available. Conversely, if you want to use some other pattern, it can force you to add a domain you hadn't previously recognized, which can alert you to extra topics you need to address (such as an infrastructure it depends upon). Identifying the available patterns is more useful if you have patterns in specialized domains; the patterns in this book are too general for drawing up a list of relevant domains to make much of a difference.

Each domain needs an introduction to explain its theme. It can then describe features that are common to all its patterns. The size of an introduction could be anywhere from one short paragraph to many pages; it depends solely on how much there is to say. The domain also needs to describe any infrastructure(s) its patterns depend upon (or, more properly, the requirements produced by these patterns), as discussed in the next section.

Domains and Infrastructures

Some types of requirements depend upon infrastructures, as discussed in the "Infrastructures" section of Chapter 2, "The Contents of a Requirements Specification." A requirement pattern gives us the opportunity to identify any infrastructure(s) its type of requirement depends upon, which saves having to figure them out for individual requirements. We can go further and discuss each infrastructure—things to bear in mind when you specify requirements for the infrastructures your system needs. It's not possible to go into detail or specify actual requirements because they will vary considerably according to the demands of each organization and each system. They're called **infrastructure overviews** to make this clear.

Rather than expect that each requirement pattern describes any infrastructure it needs, we pass the burden of explanation up to the domain the pattern belongs to. This is because each infrastructure tends to be needed by more than one pattern in the domain. To avoid repetition, each type of infrastructure is described in only one domain. Each chapter of patterns in this book contains a subsection for each infrastructure in its domain. This book discusses three infrastructures: information storage (in Chapter 7, "Data Entity Requirement Patterns"), user interface, and reporting (both in Chapter 8, "User Interface Requirement Patterns"). The key concepts relate to each other as shown in Figure 3-2.

A requirement pattern is free to use infrastructures in other domains. It's always good practice to avoid mutual dependencies, so if anything in one domain depends on another domain, nothing in the latter domain should depend on the former—that is, if you can avoid it. An infrastructure can also depend upon another infrastructure.

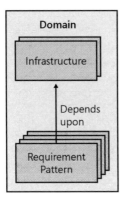

Figure 3-2   Relationships between domains, requirement patterns, and infrastructures

What should such an infrastructure overview say? Its role is to give guidance and advice to someone who's going to specify requirements for an infrastructure of this kind for a particular system, to suggest *topics* for requirements to cover. At a minimum, it should state what a calling system expects from the infrastructure: what it's there for, and its main functions. For problems for which there are obvious alternative solutions, the overview should avoid making judgments.

Each infrastructure overview is divided into the following subsections:

1. **Purpose**   An explanation of why the infrastructure exists, the role it plays.
2. **Invocation requirements**   Suggestions for sorts of requirements that define how a system will interact with the infrastructure—for those functions that the infrastructure must make available to a system—plus any other capabilities systems might want from it (such as access control). The needed functions can be regarded collectively as the *interface* (or *interfaces*) the infrastructure needs to make available to callers.
3. **Implementation requirements**   Some ideas on the other features the infrastructure needs in order to stand on its own feet (for example, inquiry, maintenance and configuration functions). These are brief and merely hint at the likely main areas of functionality to think about when defining the infrastructure itself.

For example, for a reporting infrastructure, our invocation requirements might be very simple: just a function that lets our system request the running of a chosen report. The implementation requirements, on the other hand, would be far more extensive, addressing the complexities of various ways of delivering a report to a user, other ways of requesting reports, designing reports, and so on. (These topics are discussed further in the "Reporting Infrastructure" section in Chapter 8.) To take the analogy of building a house, one of the infrastructures we'd want is an electricity supply. In this case, the invocation requirements would cover how many sockets we want in each room, and the implementation requirements would deal with the parts you can't see, such as the connection to the power grid and adherence to building quality regulations.

3.4 Requirement Pattern Groups

When several requirement patterns have features in common, we can create a **requirement pattern group** and use it as a place to describe all of their common aspects, to save repeating them in each individual pattern. A requirement pattern group is not a requirement pattern: you can't create requirements of this type. But the definition of a group can contain any of the following sections that appear in the definition of a requirement pattern: "Extra Requirements," "Consideration for Development," and "Considerations for Testing." The rule is to include whichever of these sections in which something valuable can be said and to omit the rest. Whenever one of these sections is present in the group, it's worth including a note in the equivalent section in each pattern based on the group as a reminder to refer to it.

The difference between a *domain* and a *requirement pattern group* is that the patterns in a domain share a common **theme**, whereas those in a group have **detailed features** in common. The patterns in a group don't need to belong to the same domain. (For those familiar with Java programming, the relationship between requirement patterns and domains is akin to that between classes and packages: every class belongs to a package just as each pattern belongs to a domain. Also, a requirement pattern can build upon a pattern belonging to a different domain, just as a Java class can extend a class in a different package.)

3.5 Relationships Between Requirement Patterns

When you use a requirement pattern, it generally says everything you need to know to create a requirement of that type. But a pattern might refer to other patterns for several reasons. Two fundamental types of relationship between requirement patterns exist:

1. **Refers to**   A requirement pattern can mention another pattern somewhere in its definition. There are several reasons why a requirement pattern might refer to another:

   a. A requirement defines something that contains (**has**) something else defined by another requirement.

   b. A requirement that's an instance of one pattern **uses** information defined in requirements that are instances of a second pattern. For example, a requirement that defines a data structure might use a value of a kind defined by a data type requirement.

   c. A requirement might suggest the creation of an **extra requirement** of a type for which a pattern is available.

   d. A **divertive** pattern might persuade you to create a requirement using a different pattern. (See the "Divertive Requirement Patterns" section later in this chapter.)

   e. A requirement pattern could refer to another pattern that contains relevant discursive information on a particular topic.

2. **Extends**   A requirement pattern builds upon (or is a specialization of) another pattern. In object-oriented terms, this is an *inheritance* relationship. Instead of extending another pattern, a requirement pattern can build upon (extend) a requirement pattern group. (In object-oriented terms, the group acts like an abstract base class for the pattern.) A requirement pattern is not allowed to extend more than one pattern or group.

We can draw a collection of patterns and infrastructures and the relationships between them in a diagram. Figure 3-3 is an example that shows two domains, with elements of the notation annotated. Inheritance is the most important type of relationship. For simplicity, every other type of relationship is shown as "Refers to," though its role can be indicated by a label on the link. When showing several domains on one diagram, it can become impractical to show all the relationships. In such a case, show all relationships *within* each domain and all *extends* relationships, but omit *refers to* relationships between domains as you see fit. For readers familiar with object-oriented concepts (or UML), this is akin to a class diagram showing relationships between classes.

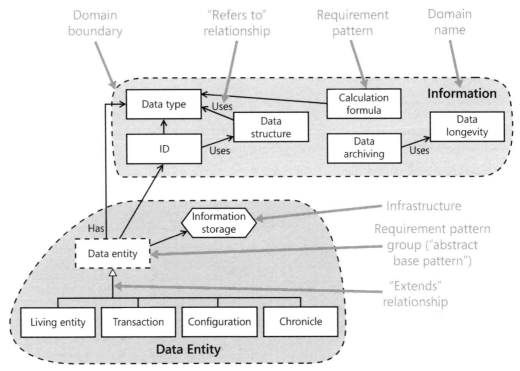

Figure 3-3   Annotated sample requirement pattern diagram

In Figure 3-3, "Data entity" is not a pattern. It's a requirement pattern group: a place for describing the common features of the four patterns that build on it. Any descriptive information that applies to all patterns in a group should be given for the group, rather than repeated for each pattern. Also, by convention, labels for relationships between requirement patterns are placed nearer the subject of the relationship, rather than the object. So, it is a Data entity that *has* an ID (rather than vice versa). The hexagonal shape of "Information storage" denotes it as an *infrastructure*.

See the beginning of Part II of this book for a diagram of this sort for all the requirement patterns in this book. Each of the eight domain chapters contains a diagram of this sort in its introduction, with annotations giving a brief explanation of each pattern, pattern group, and infrastructure.

Requirement Pattern Classifications

Requirements can be classified in various ways (for example, by dividing them into functional and nonfunctional ones). Using requirement patterns has the advantage that if we classify the patterns, we automatically classify the requirements that use those patterns. Classifications tell us a little about the nature of the requirements that result from using each requirement pattern.

Other ways of using these classifications include finding requirements according to their classification and producing statistics. People like statistics (some people, at least, and they tend to be senior executives it's worth our while keeping happy). Statistics on the requirements for a system can be useful in a variety of ways. They can give a rough picture of the scale and complexity of the system. To do this, we need to tag each requirement with whatever values are needed for all the sorts of statistics we want. (Requirements management tools typically do this by letting you define extra requirement "attributes." Then you enter the value of each attribute for each requirement. It's a tedious business.) Using requirement patterns can save some of this effort, because all requirements created using a pattern have attributes in common. They need be defined only once, when the pattern is written. This information is recorded in the "Pattern classifications" section of each pattern.

Once requirements are tagged in this way, it's also possible to search on the classifications to find all the requirements that match your criteria. How you transport this classification information from the patterns to your requirements depends on how you store the requirements. (This is left as an exercise for the reader!) A straightforward way is to copy the requirements into a spreadsheet, add a column identifying the requirement pattern used by each requirement (if any), and add a column for each classification. (Sorting on the pattern name makes it easier to apply classification values many at a time.)

The requirement patterns in this book contain classifications according to a small number of basic classification schemes that are defined below. You can define extra classification schemes of your own and classify patterns according to them. If you do, write proper definitions in a similar manner to those below, and make them available in the same place as the requirement patterns that refer to them.

Classifications can be defined that assist anyone who uses requirements, including developers. As a result, it's not necessary for everyone to understand every classification. For this reason, each classification has its primary audience explicitly stated. If you're not part of this audience, don't worry if you can't follow what it's for or if you're not interested in it.

Requirement pattern classifications need to be properly and precisely defined, or else any statistics based on them can't be regarded as reliable. Each classification needs the following defined for it:

Name:	A self-explanatory, unique name for the classification.
Audience:	An explanation of who is likely to be most interested in this classification: who it's aimed at.
Purpose:	A description of what the classification is intended to be used for.
Allowed values:	A definition of the values that a pattern may have for this classification, and explanations of their meanings. The most common way is to define a list of individual values. Numeric or alphabetic or other kinds of values may be used, provided it's clear to the reader what each value means.
Default value:	This is the value assumed for this classification if it's not present (explicitly stated) in a pattern. This saves cluttering patterns with explicit mentions of classifications that are meaningful for relatively few patterns (that is, the few that have a significant value for it).

There are three requirement pattern classifications used in this book, which we now describe using this format.

"Functional" Classification

Name:	**Functional**
Audience:	Anyone interested in picking out the functionality of the system, or the number of functions.
Purpose:	This indicates whether a requirement of this type defines a function that must be provided by the system.

Allowed values:	**Yes**	Every requirement of this type is a functional requirement.
	Maybe	Some requirements of this type are functional requirements; some are not. If you're writing a pattern, use this value with care. Ask yourself whether your pattern is well-defined; perhaps it ought to be split into two, one for the functional part and one for the nonfunctional.
	No	No requirement of this type is itself a functional requirement.
Default value:	**No**	

"Pervasive" Classification

Name:	**Pervasive**	
Audience:	Software developers	
Purpose:	This indicates whether a requirement of this type is pervasive (that is, applies systemwide). Its intent is to bring to the attention of developers requirements that may apply to them no matter which part of the system they're developing.	
Allowed values:	**Yes**	Every requirement of this type is pervasive.
	Maybe	Some requirements of this type are pervasive; some are not.
	No	No requirement of this type is pervasive.
Default value:	**No**	

"Affects Database" Classification

Name:	**Affects database**	
Audience:	Database administrator (and software developers, too)	
Purpose:	This indicates whether a requirement of this type has an impact on the design of the system's database. Its intent is to highlight those requirements that are of most interest to whoever is responsible for designing the database.	
Allowed values:	**Yes**	Every requirement of this type affects the database.
	Maybe	Some requirements of this type affect the database; some do not.
	No	No requirement of this type itself directly affects the database (though this doesn't necessarily mean a database administrator will have no interest in it).
Default value:	**Maybe**	

Refinement Requirements

It is good practice to keep the size of each requirement's definition within moderate bounds; one that runs to ten paragraphs is way too long. A requirement pattern may identify several pieces of information, although a typical requirement of its type might possess only one or two. From time to time you might have a requirement that possesses more and, as a result, is unreasonably large. In this situation, it makes sense to split the requirement into two or more requirements.

The way to do this is to retain the initial requirement but to cut out parts and make them into additional requirements, which are *refinements* of the main requirement. Each refinement requirement should specify one extra aspect. And each refinement should identify the requirement it builds on. For readability, the main requirement should be immediately followed in the specification by its refinements. This practice makes sense whether or not you're using a requirement pattern—but when you *are*, you can regard the pattern as applying to both the main requirement and the refinements. If a requirement pattern suggests that several pieces of information be present, this is satisfied if all are present in one of the requirements or another. A second reason for splitting a requirement is if different parts of it have different priorities.

Depending on the nature of the system you're specifying, up to a quarter of all requirements could be refinements of other requirements. If you use a very fine level of requirements granularity, you'll increase the number of requirements and with it the percentage of requirements that are refinements.

Divertive Requirement Patterns

Usually when you apply a requirement pattern, the result is a requirement that matches what you asked for. However, a pattern could be sneakier than this: it could try to lead you away from the obvious and towards an alternative, better way of formulating what you want. It explains the difficulties that the obvious way causes (usually for developers), and it provides advice on how to avoid these problems by using requirements that are stated in different terms but that aim to achieve the same underlying aim. A divertive requirement pattern can either explain the alternative itself or it can divert you to a different requirement pattern entirely—or both.

Requirement patterns can be much more valuable than just saying, "If you want to require X, this is what to write…." They can be like having an expert sitting at your shoulder saying, "Hang on! If you specify it like that, you're asking for trouble. Let me explain. Why don't you try this instead?" Several of the performance patterns are divertive, because the most obvious ways to specify performance are often a nightmare to satisfy. (For example, "The system shall be available 24×7" gives developers little idea of what they must do to achieve it.)

Requirement Patterns and Diversity of Approaches

There's no single right or best way of formulating or expressing requirements. **For a given system, there's no single *perfect* set of requirements to define it.** Different requirements approaches might break down a problem in different ways, resulting in requirements that vary in their level of granularity and the way they're expressed. The term "requirements approach" as used in this section simply means a way of going about the specifying of requirements in general or certain types of requirements in particular. Each approach could have its own set of requirement patterns. They might simply be the approach's own distinct manifestations of recognized standard patterns, or they might be patterns specific to the approach.

We can accommodate a diversity of requirements approaches—to let the proponents of each approach create whatever requirement patterns they wish, including their own manifestations of existing patterns. And by recognizing different approaches explicitly, we make the available choices clearer to analysts.

Nevertheless, the greater agreement there is on standard patterns (and the fewer different manifestations of patterns), the better. It's perhaps a testament to the excellence of the choices for design patterns made by Gamma et al. that there's been no apparent call for variants (although lots of extras have appeared), and thus accommodating diverse sets hasn't been necessary. In allowing for multiple requirements approaches, I'm heading off potential criticism of the requirement patterns given here. I can cite it as proof that there's no single "right" set of requirement patterns. If anyone doesn't like them, they can devise their own alternatives without demanding to replace the ones here. There's room for many schools of thought.

To avoid potential confusion, don't mix material for multiple requirements approaches in the same requirement pattern. It is clearer to have multiple manifestations of the pattern and to pick only one to use on your system.

When creating a new pattern (or manifestation of an existing pattern) for a particular requirements approach, state the approach it relates to in the "Manifestation" section of the pattern. Note that when a manifestation is created for a different approach, it takes on a life of its own and might go through a succession of versions independent of the manifestation for the original "standard" approach.

Where two sets of requirement patterns exist that cover the same ground, there are two ways they can be organized:

1. One domain specification can contain both sets of requirement patterns. (A "domain specification" is a document, or part of a document, that contains its requirement patterns and a section about each of its infrastructures. Each of the eight domain chapters that follows is a domain specification.)

2. There can be two manifestations of the domain specification, each containing one set of the requirement patterns.

The second way is easier and less confusing to use (and thus less liable to have an analyst apply the wrong manifestation of a pattern). The second way also allows each manifestation of the infrastructure specification to be tailored to the methodology its patterns use, which is useful if the infrastructure's own requirements use these patterns (which they might).

Use Cases for Requirement Patterns

It is perfectly possible to write use cases for some requirement patterns, those that result in requirements that demand the presence of a well-defined function (or, indeed, more than one function). For example, for the inquiry requirement pattern we could write a use case that shows the steps in a typical inquiry. Use cases for requirement patterns are always *generalizations*, an official UML concept that means they are written to apply in any circumstance that fits, using an "is-a-kind-of" relationship.

One requirement pattern might demand the presence of more than one function for each of the resulting requirement. For example, the configuration requirement pattern implies the presence of create, read (inquire), update, and delete functions (commonly called CRUD) for each item of configuration data. We can write a use case for each of these functions, and four use cases will suffice for all configuration, rather than attempting to write four for each type of configuration (or, more likely, writing use cases for a few but not the rest).

It makes sense to write requirement pattern use cases to suit your particular environment. To attempt to write universally applicable use cases risks them being so high-level as to be of no practical value. For example, a universal "create configuration data" use case has little to say— perhaps just an actor entering the data and the system storing it in a data store. But if we have a browser-based user interface with remote users and a Web server that is outside our system's scope, the use cases will look very different. Also, the use cases' preconditions might insist the actor be logged in and authorized to access this type of configuration data–to satisfy particular security requirements. (All this illustrates how hard it is to write detailed use cases without bringing in elements of the *solution*, even though use cases are meant to reflect only the *problem* to be solved.) No use cases have been written for the requirement patterns in this book.

Business Rules and Requirement Patterns

A **business rule** is a definition of one aspect of how a business operates. For example, a business rule could define how a particular business should act in a given situation (such as when a customer credit card payment is rejected) or a constraint (such as a policy of not selling to anyone under sixteen). A **business rules approach** to building systems recognizes the importance of business rules, with a view to making it easier to understand and change how the business works. In an ideal world, you'd be able to modify your business rules and all affected systems would instantly jump in line. It's a very attractive prospect. There exist **business rules products** to help you do this. They act a bit like a guru who knows your business inside-out and of whom you can ask questions, but there's a lot more to it than that. That's not to say you need a specialized product to adopt a business rules approach. Two places to go for more information are *http://www.brcommunity.com* and *http://www.businessrulesgroup.org*.

Quite a few types of requirements reflect business rules, including several covered by requirement patterns in this book. So why not say which ones they are? The trouble is that there isn't a single agreed-upon set of business rule types. There are many, and it would be arbitrary to pick one. (The same argument applies when you consider mentioning in an individual requirement how it maps to a business rule.) One could create a requirement pattern classification for a selected business rule scheme to indicate how each pattern relates to a business rule. My excuse for not doing so in this book is not wishing to offend any scheme I left out.

It's also worth pointing out that adopting a particular business rule classification scheme might not happen until *after* the requirements have been written. Consider the case where you invite tenders from three prospective suppliers. The first might use one business rules scheme. The second might use a different one. And the third might not think in business rules terms at all.

Nevertheless, if your organization has made a commitment to using a particular business rule scheme, you can write requirements in a way that's friendly to that scheme (and, if you wish, mention the type of business rule that each requirement reflects, where applicable). If you're committed to using a business rule product, you can treat it as an *infrastructure* that your system must interface to. Then, just like for any infrastructure, you can specify requirements for what you need from it, and use those requirements as your basis for choosing the most suitable product.

Chapter 4
Using and Producing Requirement Patterns

In this chapter:

4.1 When and How to Use Requirement Patterns 39
4.2 Tailoring Requirement Patterns 41
4.3 Writing New Requirement Patterns. 42

The previous chapter gave us a tour of the machinery of requirement patterns; now let's bring them to life. The first section in this chapter invites you to sit in the driver's seat and see how patterns can help you reach your destination. In the second section we start to get our hands dirty, to let you tune patterns so that you can get the most out of them *in your environment*. The third section dives into the heavy engineering of building entirely new patterns.

4.1 When and How to Use Requirement Patterns

> *Whatever gets you to the light 'salright, 'salright*
> *Out the blue or out of sight 'salright, 'salright*
>
> *—John Lennon*

This section concentrates more on *when* to use requirement patterns than *how*, because each pattern should be its own guide on how to use it. Familiarize yourself with the patterns available to you, and then exploit them as you see fit.

Requirement patterns are first and foremost to help define what a new system needs to do. They can be used even if you're an agilist who's not writing formal requirements—in which case a requirement pattern can act directly on your thinking rather than through an intermediate step, the requirement. There are two occasions during the specifying of a system in which requirement patterns can be used:

1. **When defining a requirement**, see if a pattern for it exists to guide the specifying of that requirement. The pattern can then provide detailed suggestions on what to say, and how, what else to worry about, and extra topics to consider. Once you've decided to engage a pattern, read through the whole of it (or become familiar with everything it says, so that you don't need to read it all for every requirement of this type). That is, have the pattern in front of you and do what it tells you to.

   Pay close attention to what the "Extra Requirements" section says, because it might have a profound impact on the nature or quality of the system that's needed. Even if you recognize the merit of the extra requirements the pattern suggests, you may not want to be sidetracked by tackling them immediately. That's fine: just make a note that it remains to be done. You also need to take on board each infrastructure on which the patterns you use depends: add it to the "Infrastructures" section of your requirements specification, and then make sure it is itself properly specified.

2. **When considering the completeness of requirements**, scan the set of patterns for topics to cover—to see if you've missed something, or to suggest something to add.

Secondarily, requirement patterns can also be used *after the fact*—that is, after the requirements have been written. The ease of doing this, and the effect, depends on whether patterns were used when specifying the requirements and, if so, how closely they were followed. The main ways of using patterns after the requirements have been written are

3. **When reviewing a requirements specification**, a pattern can help you to check the quality of specific requirements, to identify topics that have not been specified, and to understand the meaning and implications of particular requirements.

4. **When estimating** the scale of a system and the effort needed to build it, based on its requirements, you can use patterns to get a better feel for the implementation complexity.

   If you have records from which you can tell how long particular features took to implement in previous projects, you can calculate the effort needed to implement an average requirement of a particular type—that is, metrics you can attach to each pattern, which would allow quick estimation of the effort for all requirements for which patterns were used. Effort figures are not available for the patterns in this book, and even if they were, they would need recalibrating to suit each organization's environment.

5. **When implementing a requirement**, a pattern can give you a deeper understanding of its intent. The "Considerations for Development" section of the pattern is aimed squarely at the designers and developers of the software. It contains hints on how to approach implementation and suggests things to bear in mind.

6. **When testing a requirement**, the "Considerations for Testing" section, which is written specifically for software testers, serves to suggest approaches to testing this kind of requirement.

If we look at a requirement, how can we tell if a pattern was used when it was written? In one sense we don't need to: after a pattern has been applied, the requirement stands on its own feet. But it's useful to know, because it lets readers know that the pattern is there to assist after the fact (points 3–6 above). There are three ways to indicate use of a pattern. First, the requirement summary can reveal it, if the summary matches a form for a particular pattern. Second, you could add a little note at the end of the requirement definition, something like "(This requirement uses the «*Pattern name*» pattern.)" Third, if you're using a requirements management tool, you could store the name of the pattern as an attribute behind the scenes.

Using requirement patterns has several benefits:

■ **Requirements are easier to read**—because a lot more thought can be put into producing a pattern than you can afford to spend on any single requirement.

■ **Requirements are easier to compare with others of the same type**—because they are similarly structured.

■ **You can tell if something is missing**—because comparison of the requirement against the pattern indicates if something in the pattern is missing in the requirement.

■ **Requirements are easier to write**—because you have a checklist of topics to think about. This is of greatest help to inexperienced analysts.

■ **Readers can be referred to the written pattern for more information**—about why the requirement is formulated as it is and for explanations of what each part of the requirement means.

- **You can refer to a list of patterns when writing your requirements specification**—to check whether there are any types of requirements you should specify but that you've forgotten about.

The benefits of requirement patterns greatly outweigh the reasons for not using them—but be aware that there are a few potential drawbacks. There's a simple mantra that lets you sidestep them all: don't be lazy. Beware of the following:

- **You might be lulled into not thinking enough**—because if you apply a pattern mechanically, especially if you copy in text from a template and fill in the blanks, you might not put your mind fully into gear.

- **You might misapply a pattern**—if you use it in inappropriate circumstances. To guard against this, make sure you properly understand each pattern you use (especially the situations in which it's suitable), and make sure that any requirement you apply a pattern to fits the circumstances.

- **Lots of requirements might be worded similarly**—your readers will get bored more quickly and might have less faith in what you are saying, both because they fear a lot has been copied in and may not have been properly tailored in all cases, and because you have obviously not written everything from scratch. Introduce a bit of variety into your requirements, to make reading them a little more interesting and to let your readers know you put some thought into them—and that they're not a big copy-and-paste exercise.

You won't find a pattern for every requirement. A high proportion of requirements (perhaps a majority) don't have a neat pattern that can be applied to them. Our intent in using patterns is to reduce the amount of work and do a better job wherever we can, not to apply them to everything. The proportion of requirements covered by the patterns described in this book varies considerably from system to system and could be anywhere from 15 to 65 percent. (A self-contained business system would be at the high end of that range. The less a system fits that stereotype, the lower the percentage of the requirements for which these patterns apply.) These figures come from study of real-world requirements specifications. We could write more and more patterns to cover more types of requirements, but we'd quickly reach the point where diminishing returns render it not worthwhile. A substantial system will always have many requirements that will need to be written from scratch.

For certain types of requirements, it's tempting to group them together in their own section in the requirements specification (for instance, a section for all of a system's reports). This has some advantages, such as reducing the chances of duplication (for example, specifying the same report twice in different sections), but on the whole it's preferable to keep all requirements for each *functional area* together. A functional area often has a constituency of users, and it's easier for these users to read the specification if every function they need is described in *their* section. If necessary, one section can refer to a requirement for a function that is defined in another section.

4.2 Tailoring Requirement Patterns

The phrasing of individual requirements is to a large extent a matter of personal preference—their author's own writing style—which we don't want to suppress unduly because it can help to enliven otherwise turgid technical documents. Phrasing also needs to suit the organization's culture, such as the appropriate degree of formality in speech. And, as always, speaking the customer's language is of overriding importance in a requirements specification. For all these reasons, the language used in the **templates** in requirement patterns should accord with the language used in the rest of any requirements specification that use those patterns. Sudden changes in style will strike readers as odd and make them feel uncomfortable. At worst it can be obvious that some of the specification's language comes from outside the organization, which can damage the author's credibility.

In a non-English-speaking country, a software designer who speaks English can perfectly well use a *design pattern* expressed in English. In the same environment, however, a *requirement pattern* wholly in English is acceptable only if requirements specifications are being written in English. If this isn't the case, at least the templates in the requirement patterns should be translated into the local language.

You can also refine requirement patterns based on *your* experience with them in *your* organization. Some insightful organizations take a little time to reflect on how well a just-finished project ran, to find ways of doing better in future. (This is usually called a postmortem, but I prefer to call it a "postnatal," because it's more hopeful to imply it happens after the birth of the system, rather than its death.) If any problems arose as a result of badly written requirements, you could refine any patterns that were used by adding advice to guard against that problem. If no pattern was associated with a troublesome requirement, you could consider writing one, even if it's just as a vehicle for a small piece of advice. If a pattern itself was a cause of trouble, correct it so that it won't be again.

For these reasons there's a greater need to tailor requirement patterns than design patterns. So be prepared to (and don't be scared to) do this tailoring. The fundamentals of the pattern remain the same; tailoring merely tweaks the bits that appear in requirements created using the pattern. Sometimes only the requirement definition templates need to be changed (because they're the only part that ends up in actual requirements), but then modify the examples too to reflect the changes to the templates. Also check the rest of the pattern for consistency with the modified templates, and adjust it as necessary.

Each time we tailor a requirement pattern we create a new **manifestation** of it. In this context we can take the term "manifestation" to mean one instance of a pattern tailored to suit a particular environment and approach. (We can't use the term "version" because each manifestation could have its own history and thus go through several versions.) In some organizations, this means that multiple manifestations of requirement patterns might be needed. If so, make sure the right ones are used for each project. Add an explanation to each one indicating which manifestation it is and when it should be used. In practice, this should be a straightforward matter if done from the moment a second manifestation of any pattern is created.

4.3 Writing New Requirement Patterns

This section deals with writing one or more new requirement patterns from scratch, on fresh ground for which no patterns exist already. It doesn't cover modifying an existing pattern or creating a new manifestation or version of one. The process is divided into two stages: **finding** a pattern or patterns to write, and then **writing** a new pattern. Writing a new pattern also includes analysis and review steps, which makes the process similar in many ways to that for specifying requirements themselves.

Don't tackle new patterns lightly or just because you like the idea. Do it only if each new pattern delivers enough value to make it worthwhile. That will be a subjective judgment, based on how much time will be saved in specifying requirements of this type—how many requirements will there be, and how much time will be saved on each one?—and also how much can be gained by writing better requirements.

On the other hand, don't be put off because it sounds daunting. If, in your environment, certain types of requirements crop up repeatedly and would benefit from being specified in a consistent manner, or simply are sometimes specified badly, then go ahead and write a requirement pattern for them. It's not that hard!

How to Find Candidate Requirement Patterns

Are patterns invented or are they already out there, lurking in the undergrowth waiting to be discovered? The tenet that a pattern "describes a problem that occurs over and over again in our environment" suggests we're surrounded by a menagerie of wild patterns that have yet to be captured. Yet they inhabit an artificial world of our making, a world we can strive to improve, so we're at liberty to adjust or create patterns accordingly. Capturing patterns is first a matter of hunting for them among the world of requirements already written. If we don't find what we want, we can engage in a little genetic engineering to create patterns for fashioning our brave new world.

As with any kind of hunt, there are two ways to find our quarry: the *systematic*—methodically scouring an area and flushing out most of its inhabitants—and the *opportunistic*—catching whatever we stumble upon. That's not to suggest the systematic approach is always preferable. Use them as follows:

- **Systematic**   Our aim here is to build a list of candidate requirement patterns. You might do this if you're contemplating creating a set of industry-specific and/or company-specific patterns. Gather all existing requirements specifications that you want to use as your hunting ground, and proceed through them looking for requirements in your area of interest.

    Study each such requirement and try to classify it: what type is it? If an existing pattern can be applied to it, note that fact and move on. If an existing pattern doesn't quite fit, study the requirement to see if a new, more specialized pattern could be devised for it. Otherwise, can you envisage a pattern being of assistance in specifying this requirement? If so, suggest a name for this pattern and add it to the list of candidates. Don't be fussy at this stage; requirements don't always conveniently fit the patterns. Nor are there hard and fast rules for identifying patterns. When you've gone through all the available specifications, review the list of candidate patterns. You might spot some duplication or overlap. Resolve these inconsistencies.

    (The patterns in this book arose in this way. I loaded sets of requirements into a spreadsheet and added a column for the name of a candidate pattern of which each requirement is an instance, where relevant. This yielded a list of patterns, which was gradually refined and improved. The spreadsheet also provided statistics on the prevalence of requirements for each pattern.)

- **Opportunistic**   When specifying a requirement, you may realize there will be others of the same type. If you find it tricky to write this type of requirement, a pattern might be worthwhile to help other people when they come to write similar requirements—and to promote consistency. For example, in a banking system, this might happen for a requirement that defines the characteristics of a type of bank account. When you identify a pattern in this way, beware of taking too blinkered a view of it. Before writing it, try to think beyond the requirement at hand. What variations might there be? Don't rush into creating a pattern that's too narrow.

If you anticipate writing more than one or two requirement patterns, it's better to do a systematic study first, rather than writing each one in isolation. This lets you see how the patterns relate to each other, and you can write them so that they fit together coherently.

Ask yourself if analysts or developers will easily understand a pattern's purpose. If it's too abstract or hard to explain in a short sentence, or if it's hard to name clearly in a way that users will understand, there might be something wrong and requirements written using the pattern might themselves be hard to understand. Consider whether the pattern can be split into two or more patterns whose purpose is clearer. You might find multiple variants of a candidate pattern, each of which fits a particular situation much more closely than one broader pattern. Several well-targeted patterns are better than one pattern that tries to cater for several situations. The tighter the fit of a pattern, the more your pattern can guide an analyst who uses it and a developer who implements the resulting requirements. On the other hand, don't divide patterns up to the point where any particular pattern has little to say: a pattern deserves to exist only if it delivers sufficient value.

Don't go overboard. Don't try to find a pattern for every requirement: they don't all deserve one. Some requirements will only ever be one-offs, whose like will never be seen again. A pattern is only worthwhile if the effort of writing it is more than offset by the benefits accrued by using it. This happens only if it is used more than a handful of times. Because a pattern is a net benefit only if the effort saved in using a pattern is greater than the effort involved in writing it, in general concentrate on the patterns that will be used most frequently.

Our patterns don't have to mirror the requirements we encounter. Keep your eyes open for superior ways of expressing requirements. One goal of requirement patterns is to specify better requirements in the future. That doesn't only mean finding easier ways to write requirements just like those written in the past—it could also mean formulating requirements in a new way.

Decide which domain each requirement pattern belongs in. Feel free to add new patterns to an existing domain, including the domains in this book, but don't do so just for convenience. If a pattern doesn't rightly belong in any existing domain, create a new one for it. If you plan to write several new patterns, assign them all to domains at the same time. Doing so might help you decide the scope of each new domain, especially since your patterns are likely to be related (and thus might belong to the same one or two domains).

Creating a New Domain

If you've identified a new domain, first make sure it has a clear **theme**, one to which you can give a clear and concise name and whose role you can explain in a sentence or two. You need a document in which to describe the domain, its patterns, and any infrastructures it has. This normally means creating a new document specifically for it. But if your domain is just for one or two patterns you don't expect to be useful in other systems, you could include a section for the domain at the end of this system's requirements specification.

There are a few other things to think about:

1. Look at the patterns you've put in the domain and ask yourself if there are any **gaps**. Can you think of any other patterns that belong here?

2. Avoid mutual dependencies between domains as far as possible. Ways to do this include splitting a domain in two, merging two domains, or moving a pattern to a different domain.

3. Is any supporting **infrastructure** needed to implement the patterns in this domain? If so, write an overview of the infrastructure, to a similar level of detail to the infrastructure overviews in this book. If you're in the middle of specifying the requirements for a system, you probably need to add an instance of this infrastructure to it—and specify requirements for it, too.

How to Write a Requirement Pattern

This section assumes you want to write a requirement pattern for a known purpose. The best place to start is with example requirements: gather as many as you can find. Then write the rest of the pattern in order from beginning to end. There's a significant iterative element, too: revisit and refine any previously written material as appropriate. It's also far from a mechanical process; you need to devote serious thought to every stage. Here's a suggested step-by-step process for writing a requirement pattern, which reflects the way the bulk of the patterns in this book were written:

- **Step 1: Is there enough value in it?**   Before going to the trouble of writing a pattern, ask yourself whether it's likely to repay the effort. Do a quick cost-benefit analysis, based on three key factors. First, how many times will the pattern be used? Second, how much value will the pattern provide each time it's used? Third, how long will it take to write the pattern? Thus a pattern that yields little benefit each time is worthwhile if it's used a lot, and a rarely used pattern is worthwhile if it has a big payoff each time it's used. The benefits can be both in time saved when writing requirements and in improved quality, which can result in a better system and avoiding mistakes. Judging the net value is educated guesswork, but if it doesn't look promising, proceed no further.

- **Step 2: Create a skeleton pattern.**   Include all the requisite headings and the items in the "Basic Details" section. The easiest way is to copy in the contents of the requirement pattern template document. (See the "Supporting Resources" section of the Preface for details of where to obtain it.) Then fill in the "Basic Details" section.

- **Step 3: Write the "Applicability" section of the pattern.**   Describe what the pattern is for, taking care to be as precise as you can. Capture the essence of the pattern in the first sentence, and say more if necessary. If you find this difficult, it might be a sign that its purpose isn't as clear in your mind as you thought. Sort this out before going further.

  Also, in a separate paragraph, describe what this pattern is **not** for—to reduce the chances of it being used in inappropriate situations. If you can't think of any such situation, that's fine: just leave out this paragraph.

- **Step 4: Gather example requirements.**   And build a list of all that you find—as many as possible, from the widest possible range of sources. Scan through old requirements specifications looking for requirements that fit the bill—that is, that are *potentially* instances of this pattern—and copy them into the pattern as candidate examples. Don't be fussy at this stage: don't limit yourself to requirements that conform to your notion of how this kind of requirement should be specified. Cast your net wide.

You might be unable to find any suitable existing requirements—for instance, when you have a new kind of requirement that you expect to recur in a forthcoming specification. In this case, write a few representative requirements (at least one!) and use them as your candidate examples. Before you can advise on how to write requirements of a particular type, you must be comfortable writing them yourself, be aware of possible variations, and understand what information they should contain.

Also gather possible extra requirements as you go along—that is, any requirement you encounter that is related to this topic. Create a separate list of these requirements in the "Extra Requirements" section of the pattern. This list is likely to be expanded in Step 9.

■ **Step 5: Examine the example requirements.**   Determine what they have in common and how they vary. Identify the kinds of information they contain. Bear in mind that few real requirements are perfect: they tend to be incomplete, imprecise, hard to understand, or otherwise flawed. (If they weren't, there would be little to be gained by writing a pattern for them. Our goal is to help do better in the future.) Pay particular attention to requirements that are out of the ordinary or that tackle this topic in an unusual way. They might give you a fresh insight and lead you to realize there's another way to look at this kind of requirement than the one you had in mind.

This is a good point at which to sit back and take stock. Don't simply look for ways to explain how to write the kinds of requirement you encounter—look for **better** ways. Would it be more useful to restate the requirement in another form?

■ **Step 6: Describe the items of information a requirement may contain.**   Distill the content of the examples into a set of distinct constituent snippets. Give each item a concise descriptive name (suitable for using in the requirement template—or, at least, one that recognizably maps to the equivalent placeholder in the template), state its purpose, and suggest what a requirement should say about it. If it's optional, say so—and, ideally, say when to include it and when it can be omitted.

■ **Step 7: Write the requirement template(s).**   Start with the best (most representative and exhaustive) example requirement you can find. Devise a requirement summary format that's descriptive, concise, and distinctive, which is sometimes a tough balancing act. Then, in the description, replace each specific item of information by a descriptive placeholder in double-angled brackets (such as «*Data type name*»). Enclose in square brackets ([...]) each optional item and any explanatory text related to it.

You might need more than one template, but if they are radically different from one another, it might indicate that you should be writing more than one pattern. Don't act hastily: reflect on what you've uncovered. Do the two templates really represent separate topics? Could you divide the content and extra requirements in two as well? Would two patterns deserve a base requirement pattern group for any material that applies to them both? Would each of the spun-off pieces have enough to say to justify its existence? Don't split a pattern in two just because it's the logical thing to do, if it will result in feeble offspring about which there's little to say.

(One case in this book of splitting a pattern in two occurred when I was writing a capacity requirement pattern. I ran into trouble because I realized that there are two fundamentally different kinds of capacity, so I created separate patterns for *dynamic* capacity and *static* capacity. A similar split resulted in the specific authorization and configurable authorization requirement patterns. This second case deserved a requirement pattern group for common material, but the first case didn't.)

■ **Step 8: Write the rest of the "Discussion" and "Content" sections.**   Ask yourself what the writer of a requirement of this type ought to worry about, which aspects they should consider, and which considerations they're liable to miss. What sorts of mistakes could an analyst make when specifying a requirement of this type (ideally based on your experience of mistakes made in the past)? Reflect on the different circumstances in which a requirement of this type might arise, taking into account different types of system, size of project, and skill and experience level of the analyst and developers. If you were sitting next to a novice analyst as they embarked on writing a requirement of this type, what would you tell them—what advice would you give them? Think about the complications that can occur in practice. If these can be serious, consider alternative ways of specifying such requirements. Turn it into a "divertive" pattern if it'll help.

Think about what a *developer* needs to do to implement a requirement of this type, and how a *tester* would test it. These things can have a major bearing on how you formulate the pattern. For instance, the performance requirement patterns in this book tend to eschew obvious quantitative targets and prefer requirements that give more helpful guidance to developers.

■ **Step 9: Build a list of examples of potential extra requirements.**   Or extend it, if you've already created a list as a byproduct of Step 4. Scan the requirements specifications again. Concentrate on the requirements that follow examples of this pattern. Add to the list any requirement that is in some way related to this pattern. But look elsewhere in the specification, too; *pervasive* requirements can live anywhere.

■ **Step 10: Identify candidate topics for extra requirements.**   What extra requirements are commonly needed—both follow-on and pervasive? Examine the list of potential extra require-ments (from Step 9), and group similar requirements together. Then ask yourself what else could be said on the subject: are there any other aspects that have been missed?

If a particular kind of extra requirement is sufficiently important (that is, it occurs reasonably often, and there's a decent amount to say about it), consider writing a separate pattern for it. (The inter-system interaction requirement pattern in this book came about in this way.)

■ **Step 11: Write the "Extra Requirements" section.**   This constitutes the bulk of the work in some patterns. First write a list of the topics for which extra requirements might be written, giving an explanation of each one. If what you have to say about a topic is too much to fit in the list, write a separate subsection for it (below the list). Include as many examples as you can—of both follow-on and pervasive requirements (if relevant). Aim to give at least one example of each possible type of extra requirement. Write example pervasive requirements in such a way that they can be pasted directly into a requirements specification. The report requirement pattern, for instance, has lots of pervasive extra requirements (for report headings, end-of-report line, date run, and such like) that are eminently suitable for reuse.

Emphasize anything in the "Extra Requirements" section that involves significant effort or has other important implications. Consider describing further actions the analyst might be well advised to take, such as publicizing as soon as possible the discovery of large unexpected demands on the system. If the "Examples" section is large and the "Extra

Requirements" section is important, you could add a reminder at the end of the "Discussion" section not to overlook the "Extra Requirements" section.

■ **Step 12: Write the "Considerations for Development" section.**   Discuss this with one or more senior developers. Ask them what advice they'd give to an inexperienced developer who needs to satisfy a requirement of this kind. What would they say to prompt a good solution? What implementation pitfalls are there?

■ **Step 13: Write the "Considerations for Testing" section.**   Ask one or more senior testers what they'd tell an inexperienced tester. How would they go about testing that a system satisfies a requirement of this kind? What difficulties have they previously encountered when testing requirements of this kind? Testers are a good source of wisdom on causes of ambiguity and on what sorts of information are often omitted. Also, what advice do *you* have to offer?

■ **Step 14: Was it worth it?**   A reader can get out only what the author puts in. If the pattern you write doesn't say enough of value, stop, file it away, and waste no more of your and other people's time on it. It's worth recording its existence, though, so that anyone with a real interest can find it. It would be a shame if someone else embarked on writing a pattern on this topic and duplicated your effort without realizing it.

(During the writing of this book several patterns fell by the wayside at various stages of development. Nearly all were dropped soon after being identified as candidate patterns and requirements were tagged as examples. They fell for several reasons, but mostly because they were too obscure or too broad in scope to be able to generalize their content. Those few that were dropped later did so mainly because there turned out to be insufficient material of value to say.)

■ **Step 15: Have the pattern reviewed.**   Ask analysts to check clarity and usability. Ask software designers and engineers (and perhaps database designers, too) to check practicability and to contribute to the implementation considerations. Ask testers to check (and enrich) the testing considerations. Take review feedback seriously. Be prepared to change the whole direction of a pattern if someone finds it confusing—or even to scrap it altogether. A badly formulated pattern could have unfortunate effects in every system in which it is used.

Writing a requirement pattern is not as daunting as the length of this list would have you believe. Treat this more as a guide to things to think about. You don't have to adhere to it doggedly.

Part II
Requirement Pattern Catalog

Part II presents a total of 37 requirement patterns for topics that recur repeatedly across all kinds of commercial systems. They are divided into eight domains, as shown here. For readability, this diagram shows only the most significant relationships between patterns in different domains (rather than *all* of them).

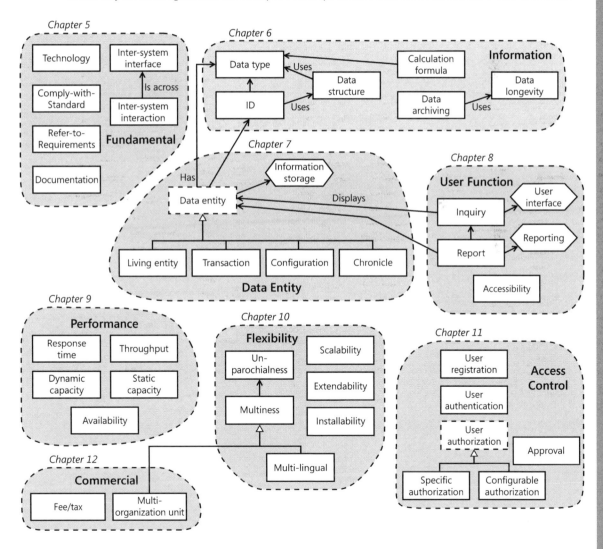

Each of the following eight chapters deals with one of these domains and contains its requirement patterns. The domains are shown in a top-to-bottom ordering so that those domains common to the most types of systems tend to come first, with the rarer or more exotic ones last.

When you're writing a requirements specification, it's useful to have a summary list of all the requirement patterns that might be used for the kind of system you're specifying, to make it easy to find the one you want. Not all patterns are applicable to all kinds of systems, so it can be worthwhile to draw up a list containing only those relevant to *your* system.

Chapter 5
Fundamental Requirement Patterns

In this chapter:

5.1 Inter-System Interface Requirement Pattern 51

5.2 Inter-System Interaction Requirement Pattern 62

5.3 Technology Requirement Pattern 65

5.4 Comply-with-Standard Requirement Pattern 71

5.5 Refer-to-Requirements Requirement Pattern 79

5.6 Documentation Requirement Pattern. 81

Fundamental requirement patterns are for various things that might be needed in any kind of system, as summed up in Figure 5-1.

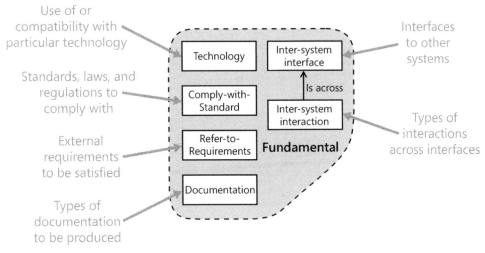

Figure 5-1   Requirement patterns in the fundamental domain

5.1 Inter-System Interface Requirement Pattern

Basic Details

Related patterns:	Inter-system interaction, throughput, availability, extendability, comply-with-standard, documentation, technology
Anticipated frequency:	Four or fewer requirements in a small-to-medium system; possibly a dozen or more requirements in a complex system
Pattern classifications:	None

Applicability

Use the inter-system interface requirement pattern to specify basic details for an interface between the system being specified and any external system or component with which it needs to interact.

Do not use the inter-system interface requirement pattern for *user interfaces* (though you can treat interactions to *user devices* and user interface *infrastructures* as inter-system interfaces if they behave in a similar way to an external system). Also, do not use this pattern for *internal interactions* between different parts of the system, unless an external system might participate in those interactions at some time in the future (that is, if it might become an external interface).

Discussion

Getting one system to cooperate with another can be a time-consuming and unpredictable undertaking. Developers might have little idea how hard it will be to implement a particular interface until they get their hands dirty. If we're using an interface defined by someone else, it might not do exactly what we want or might not work as we expected; if we're designing the interface ourselves, we're dependent on the owners of the other system to implement it properly. As a result, it's important that we treat inter-system interfaces with respect and that we don't underestimate their complexity: give them plenty of visibility, pin them down as early as possible, and allocate them sufficient resources. Often these don't happen, in many cases because the requirements specification glossed over the interfaces—or even failed to recognize some altogether. As a result, a system's interfaces might be weak links.

This requirement pattern cares neither about the nature of the interface nor whether the external system is local or remote. It uses the general term "interaction" to describe an activity across the interface (which usually means an *exchange* of information).

Every requirements specification should contain a system context diagram, and it should be near the beginning. (See the "Scope" section in Chapter 2, "The Contents of a Requirements Specification.") This is where interfaces make their first appearance, so take the opportunity to give them star billing. On the context diagram, show all external systems (and other components) with which our system needs to interact, and label every connection to them explicitly with an interface ID. Figure 5-2 shows a sample context diagram with features related to interfaces indicated.

There are several points to observe. First, each interface is identified by its unique interface ID (using the convention described in the "Content" section later in this pattern). Next, each interface ID is either inside or outside the boundary line of the system's scope. Every interface must eventually be either *wholly inside* or *wholly outside*. If ownership of the interface has yet to be determined, the interface can be shown straddling the scope boundary; highlight this unresolved issue with a large question mark. Finally, when there are multiple similar systems to which to interface (such as the multiple credit card clearing houses in Figure 5-2), each must be treated separately, because they are all different. The connection to each is a separate interface. Don't lump an indeterminate number together. See the "Interface Adapters" section that follows for a discussion on how to handle interfacing to multiple systems for the same purpose. If we need to be able to handle *multiple instances* of a particular type of interface, then there are various extra factors to consider—such as deciding which to use and when. These factors are discussed in the extendability requirement pattern in Chapter 10, "Flexibility Requirement Patterns."

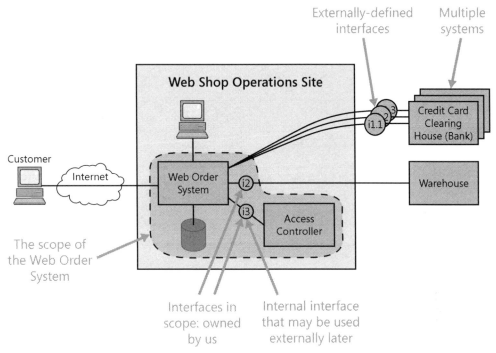

Figure 5-2   Sample system context diagram

Interface Adapters

We're building a beautiful new system. We want to keep at arm's length anything messy that would spoil its pristine elegance—such as having an indeterminate number of interfaces of some kind (like the credit card clearing houses in Figure 5-2). We can avoid our core system dealing with lots of external interfaces for the same purpose by interposing a single interface of our own choosing and plugging in a piece of software, called an *adapter*, to do whatever's necessary to convert this into what a particular external interface expects. This is shown conceptually in the following diagram:

The core system deals only with a single interface for this purpose (I_A), and the adapter deals with the external component's interface (I_E). We can build as many different adapters as we need to. This is especially beneficial when building a product because third parties (including our customers) can build their own extra adapters, and we don't have to modify the core system every time. We can, on a case-by-case basis, place each individual adapter either inside or outside the scope of our system.

If there's a widely-accepted standard for a particular interface, we could adopt and use that interface—yet we might still encounter external systems that don't use it. In this situation, we could build adapters for the one-off cases but would need no adapter for the standard interface. Before adopting an externally-specified interface definition and asking third parties to use it, first check whether you're allowed to; it might be proprietary and confidential or carry licensing restrictions.

Adapters are ordinarily a design matter, but it becomes very beneficial to introduce them in the requirements whenever we want the freedom to place interfaces of a particular type in scope and leave some out of scope. See the extendability requirement pattern in Chapter 10 for discussion of additional factors.

Between two systems, there might be more than one interface (for example, a custom messaging protocol for transactions and email for sending monthly reports). Treat each different communication medium as a separate interface, because they'll have to be built and tested separately and will function independently.

Interfaces that are wholly within the system's scope (and don't involve any component outside that scope) normally don't need to be dealt with in requirements. One exception is if development is to be split between multiple teams (especially if one team is not in-house or if the teams are physically remote from each other). Requirements can only deal with this if it's known at requirements time and if the system is clearly segregated—in effect, if we're specifying a "federation" of systems. Another exception is when we envisage part of our system being spun off in the future and used by other systems (as for the Access Controller in Figure 5-2).

If interfacing to a third-party system, it is reasonable to define requirements that its supplier must satisfy: documentation, performance, availability of a test system, test accounts and so on—everything *we* need to be able to build and test our end of the interface. Bear in mind that third parties might have very different standards and abilities from those of your organization; they might be capable of meeting far higher professional standards than you need—and might charge you accordingly if you use them. At the other end of the scale, they might have poorer practices and skills than your own developers.

The Ups and Downs of Interface Ownership

Sometimes we'll use an existing interface; sometimes we must define an interface ourselves; occasionally we can choose whether to take responsibility or leave it to whoever owns the system at the other end. How do we choose? There are arguments both ways. It's useful to understand them even if the decision is forced on you.

The great benefit of defining an interface yourself is control: you can make sure it does what you want, how you want, and you know it's not going to change unless you want it to. You can do it your way. The downside is that you have to do all the hard work of defining it—as well as explaining it to everyone else who will implement it, which means documenting it and possibly supplying them with your interface software.

> Using an interface defined by someone else means living with what they provide: it might be awkward to use, badly documented, involve technology that you don't use or with which your developers aren't familiar. A widely-used interface might be overly complex for your needs–perhaps designed by committee. The interface might change, presenting you with ongoing upgrade work– possibly to tight time deadlines outside your control. The interface's owner might be unresponsive to changes that you need–if they're prepared to make changes for you at all–and then charge you for the privilege. On balance, doing the work yourself is often a price worth paying to avoid these risks–but sometimes it's too expensive a price.
>
> Overall, the most successful outcome is likely to be achieved if the interface is owned by whoever has the greatest vested interest in its success.

Content

An inter-system interface requirement contains the following:

1. **Interface name**   Give each interface a concise meaningful name–something convenient for people to use in discussion.

2. **Interface ID**   Give each interface an identifier that is unique within the scope of this system so it can be easily and unambiguously referred to. One convention that works well is using "i" (lowercase to distinguish it from the numeral 1) followed by a sequential number. Where multiple interfaces serve the same purpose, use a two-part number, where the first identifies the purpose and the second distinguishes the interfaces (such as i1.1, i1.2, ...).

3. **The system at each end**   It's possible for the same interface to appear more than once on the system context diagram. But show the same interface ID only if two interfaces serve the same purpose. In this case, explain the roles the two systems play in the interface, or cite each pair of systems explicitly.

   Also identify which of the two systems can *initiate* an interaction; both might be able to.

4. **Interface purpose(s)**   Describe each distinct purpose–all of them.

5. **Interface owner**   Which organization is responsible for the definition of the interface? It could be designed cooperatively, but one organization should be the ultimate arbiter (to avoid misunderstandings and to settle arguments definitively). See the previous section titled "The Ups and Downs of Interface Ownership" for the relative merits of owning or not owning the interface's definition.

6. **Standard defining the interface (if any)**   Also state its *version* explicitly. Refer to the comply-with-standard requirement pattern later in this chapter for guidance on what else to say about the standard: the location of the standard, in particular.

7. **Technology to be used for the interface (if relevant)**   If particular technology *must* be used for the interface, describe it. Otherwise omit this item: don't make technology choices. See the technology requirement pattern later in this chapter for further details on what to say.

A single requirement like this usually isn't sufficient to fully specify the interface (although it might refer to a standard that does). Its main role is to give the interface "official recognition," so it's treated with the respect it deserves.

Template(s)

Summary	Definition
«Interface name» interface (*«Interface ID»*)	There shall be a clearly defined interface (called *«Interface ID»*) between *«Component 1»* and *«Component 2»*. Purposes: 1. *«Interface purpose 1»*. 2. … Interactions across this interface can be initiated by *«Initiating components»*. This interface's definition is the responsibility of and owned by *«Interface owner organization»*. [This interface shall comply with version *«Standard version»* of the *«Standard name»*, whose definition can be found at *«Standard location»*.] [*«Technology statement»*.]

Example(s)

Summary	Definition
Payment clearing interface (i4)	There shall be a clearly defined interface (called i4) between the system and payment clearing houses. It is invoked by the system only. Its purpose is to allow a customer to pay for an order. Ownership of this interface is within the scope of the system.
Alarm monitor interface (i5)	There shall be a clearly defined interface (called i5) between the system and an external alarm monitor. It is invoked by the system only. Ownership of this interface is within the scope of the system. Its purpose is to notify appropriate personnel of any event that is relevant to them (which usually means only serious problems).
Accounting system interface (i6)	There shall be a clearly defined interface (called i6) to an external accounting system. It is invoked by the system only. Ownership of this interface is within the scope of the system. Its purpose is to pass accounting entries (or information from which accounting entries can be generated) resulting from all activities in the system that have financial consequences.
Certification authority interface (i7)	There shall be a clearly defined interface (called i7) between the system and a certification authority (CA). It is invoked by the system only. Its purpose is to verify a digital certificate presented by a customer. It shall be possible to support multiple CAs (for example, eSign, Baltimore). Each CA shall prescribe its own interface (though at least some are expected to use the PKCS #10 standard—see *http://www.rsasecurity.com/rsalabs/pkcs/pkcs-10* for details).

Extra Requirements

An inter-system interface requirement might be followed by several extra requirements, although sometimes none are needed. Run through the following list of topics to see which you need to address:

1. **Individual types of interaction**   The main interface requirement states the purpose(s) of the interface, but you might wish to say more about the main types of interactions. There might also be secondary interactions that deserve a mention; apply the inter-system interaction requirement pattern for each one.

2. **Throughput**   How much traffic must the interface be able to handle? Follow the throughput requirement pattern.

3. **Scalability**   How well must the interface cope with increases in throughput? Follow the scalability requirement pattern.

4. **Extendability**   Do you need to be able to slot in extra interfaces of this type? This has been referred to several times in this requirement pattern. If you do, write suitable requirements as described in the extendability requirement pattern.

   Also, do you need to be able to switch the interface on and off? And what configuration parameters does it need? The extendability requirement pattern tackles these questions, too.

5. **Resilience and availability**   Do we need to detect missing or duplicated traffic? How well and how quickly must the interface recover from a failure? During what hours does it need to be running?

6. **Traffic verification and recording**   Must we be able to tell exactly what was sent and received? To *prove* we sent or received something? Or that the other system acknowledged receipt of something?

7. **Upgrading**   What happens when the interface changes? Must we be able to support old and new versions simultaneously?

8. **Security**   An interface is a door into (and out of) our system. To what lengths must we go to verify access and to stop intruders? Are we worried about strangers getting their hands on the information that is passing along the interface?

9. **Documentation and third-party interface development**   If you're defining the interface, how are you going to tell the developers of the system(s) at the other end what they need to do? How will they test their part?

The first four topics are covered in their own requirement patterns; each of the last five is discussed in its own subsection that follows. This list looks daunting, but it isn't as tough as it appears. The requirements for a typical interface need worry about few of these topics; most can be left to the development team to sort out.

The extra requirements are most readable if they immediately follow the main requirement for the interface to which they relate. But it can be beneficial to group all the main inter-system interface requirements together and then have the extra requirements later on (perhaps even in a later section of the requirements specification). This has the advantage of giving a clear overview of all the interfaces in one go without getting bogged down in the details.

Resilience and Availability Requirements

Most interfaces involve some sort of communications mechanism, which occasionally have traffic hiccups. **Resilience** in an interface means being able to identify anomalies and deal with them: to spot when messages are missed and ask for them to be re-sent and to spot duplicate copies of messages. Some message protocols and other types of interfaces take care of these things for us, but if you want to play it safe, you can write a requirement demanding this kind of resilience, which acts as an instruction to the developers to take care of it. The requirement needn't worry about how it's achieved. If the developer knows that the underlying messaging protocol handles resilience already, there's nothing more they need to do.

Here's an example interface resilience requirement:

Summary	Definition
Warehouse interface fixes omissions	The interface between the system and the warehouse (i2) shall detect missing messages and arrange for them to be re-sent and shall detect and ignore duplicates of messages already received.

Requirements for the availability of an interface—both its normal availability window and downtime targets—can be written in the same way as for the availability of a system as a whole. Follow the availability requirement pattern but limit your focus to the interface only. Clearly identify the interface to which each resulting requirement relates.

Traffic Verification and Recording Requirements

This is a mixed bag of features that collectively act as a sort of passport control for the interface. They come into play once messages have safely completed their journey (or before they set out). Consider whether you need to do any of the following:

1. **Verify the identity of the sender**   This could mean the identity of the other system, the organization to which it belongs, an individual (such as the author of an email)—or all these things.

2. **Record messages (logging)**   Think about incoming and outgoing traffic separately: do we need to know what we *sent*? Do we need to know what we *received*? Do we need to record all types of traffic, or just some? The volumes might be large if we record everything, making it awkward to store and harder to find an individual message—even if only marginally so, in this high-capacity age. Refer to the chronicle requirement pattern in Chapter 7, "Data Entity Requirement Patterns," for information on what to say.

3. **Record acknowledgment of receipt**   This is a special case of recording a message for the special purpose of being able to prove that the other party received the information we sent them. It can be used, for example, along with other steps, to prove that both they and we possessed particular information (or a document or another resource) at a particular time.

The motivation for such steps is sometimes legal: to provide proof that another party requested, saw, possessed, or did something. This being so, you need to understand the level of proof needed in your country (or in all the countries in which your system will operate). You might be in for some nasty surprises. You might, for example, need to record messages on a write-once read-many (WORM) medium, to prove that it hasn't subsequently been tampered with.

Here is an example requirement for each of the three topics discussed:

Summary	Definition
Verify identity of affiliate	Whenever an affiliate establishes a remote connect to the system, their identity shall be verified. A secure mechanism shall be used for this verification such that interception of communications traffic between the affiliate and the system does not disclose any information that could help a third party impersonate the affiliate.
Record all emails	Every email sent by and every email received by the system shall be stored persistently.
Record all acknowledgments received	The system shall record every acknowledgment received from the warehouse system for dispatch requests sent to it. Each acknowledgment shall be regarded as proof that the warehouse system has accepted responsibility for fulfilling that dispatch request.

Upgrade Requirements

An interface can be tough enough merely to get going in the first place, so why on earth would you want to change it? Well, the functionality might need to change, or a new version of an interface standard might come along. There are two strategies for switching over to a new version of an interface:

Strategy 1: Change the software at both ends of the interface at the same time.   This is the easiest option to implement, but it demands careful coordination of the upgrading of the systems at both ends. It's often impractical even if only two systems are involved, and it becomes steadily more impractical as the number of systems grows.

Strategy 2: Have each participating system accommodate both the old and new versions.   This is necessary until every system has stopped using the old version, and then it can be dropped. If it takes a long time to switch all systems (or, indeed, if some *never* switch), then more than two versions must be supported at once. The complications don't end there: to be smart, each system needs to be able to tell which version(s) are supported by each other system it talks to. This involves storing this information and/or including an interaction that allows a system to ask another system what it supports. Life is easier if interactions of this sort are present in the first version of the interface.

These sound like design questions, but they must be addressed in the requirements because they affect external systems. If an interface development guide is written, it should say which strategy is to be used—although it is conceivable for one version to use a different strategy than the previous version used.

For an interface not owned by us, the requirements should say the extent to which we are committed to keeping our system compatible with future versions of the interface. If nothing is said, readers can reasonably assume the system merely has to work with the stated version (or whichever is the current version when the system is built). Refer to the comply-with-standard requirement later in this chapter for further discussion on this subject.

Here are example requirements for strategies and situations discussed in the preceding section:

Summary	Definition
Warehouse interface simultaneous upgrade	Any change to the interface between the system and the warehouse system shall be installed simultaneously by both systems.
	The intent of this requirement is to simplify the interface and its implementation by eliminating the need to support more than one version of it at a time.
Multiple versions of affiliate interface	The system shall support multiple versions of the affiliate interface concurrently. All versions of the interface released within three years shall be supported.
	The intent of this requirement is to avoid forcing all affiliates to upgrade whenever a new version is released, and to have to do so at the same time.
Credit reference interface upgrade	Whenever the credit reference agency releases a new version of the interface to its credit reference service, the system shall be amended to use the new version. Amendments of this nature shall be installed within three months of the new version being released.

Security Requirements

Whenever the subject of security arises, it's likely to be complex and tricky. This little section has no pretensions to being systematic or comprehensive; it merely raises a few issues for you to consider. Let's divide the problem into two parts: the *communication medium* used by the interface and the *traffic* that travels along it.

The communication medium used by the interface needs to be protected to prevent intruders from using it to gain general access to our system (hacking in). Requirements can easily address this in solution-independent terms. (No mention of firewalls or virtual private networks or such here!) Unfortunately, it's difficult to decide or express *how much* protection we need: it can't be quantified. Here's an example requirement of this kind:

Summary	Definition
Warehouse interface intrusion protection	The communications medium used by the warehouse interface (i2) shall be protected to prevent an intruder from using it to gain unauthorized access to the system.

As for the *traffic*, there are various kinds of attacks we could be subjected to, but they boil down to the active and the passive. In an active attack, an attacker modifies the traffic: creates bogus messages, modifies genuine messages, or prevents the transmission of traffic. A passive attacker simply listens to our traffic to get hold of sensitive information. You need to write a requirement to protect against each type of attack you're worried about. Again, specify what you aim to achieve: avoid specifying in terms of solutions—though you can *mention* an approach if it's obvious. (Common approaches include encryption to prevent the reading of information, hash codes to detect tampering, and digital signatures to verify who sent messages.) Here are a couple of example requirements:

Summary	Definition
Warehouse interface bogus traffic detection	It shall be possible to detect bogus traffic on the warehouse interface (i2). Bogus traffic is any message that was not generated by one of the components legitimately participating in the interface, or any message generated erroneously by a legitimate component.
Warehouse interface traffic not readable	It shall not be possible for an intruder who can listen to the traffic across the warehouse interface (i2) to read its content. (It is anticipated that this be achieved by encrypting all messages.)

In sensitive applications, an eavesdropper can glean useful snippets merely by knowing that there is traffic or knowing its quantity—but this is unlikely to be a concern in commercial environments. If it is, engage a security expert to work out your security requirements.

Documentation and Third-Party Interface Development Requirements

If we own the interface, the developers of the system(s) at the other end will need to know what to do, and it's our responsibility to inform them. This means we need to write some kind of "Interface Developer's Guide" for this interface—even if it's rudimentary. How thorough a job we need to do depends on who they are and how many of them there are: if we're building a product, and lots of customers will be implementing this interface, we'll need a slick and comprehensive guide; we don't want our developers spending all their time explaining it over the phone or in emails. Here's an example requirement for an interface developer's guide:

Summary	Definition
Warehouse interface development guide	A development guide shall be written containing sufficient information to allow a competent software engineer with suitable skills to develop software that implements the warehouse interface (i2).

This sort of requirement is very similar to requirements to allow third-party development of drivers, as described in the extendability requirement pattern. See also the documentation requirement pattern, discussed later in this chapter, for further details on what to say.

The external developers also need to be able to *test* their interface software. This probably means making a test system available for them to use and running it for as long as necessary. If we're writing software to help test the interface, perhaps we can make that available to them—which involves packaging it up neatly. Last, the developer's guide needs to explain all these testing issues. Write requirements covering everything that you decide is needed, and point out suggestions that were rejected.

Considerations for Development

When designing an inter-system interface, start by running through the topics in the list at the start of the "Extra Requirements" section of this pattern. Some of these topics might be covered in requirements, but most probably aren't. A well-rounded interface design and implementation take these matters into account and can cope without panic when changes are made in the future.

Consider writing software to simulate the interface (and the system at the other end). The value of this depends on the importance of the interface (does your company's future depend on it?), its complexity, and the availability of a test system by the other system's owners. Testing error conditions can be difficult and tedious; some are impractical to cause at all. Sometimes it's useful to have the test software simulate certain types of errors. (One system I worked on let us specify, in the messages themselves, the type of error to simulate during testing. This was very powerful. But we had to take *great* care that all trace of this feature was removed—compiled out—before the software went into production. I'm not promoting this approach.)

Considerations for Testing

The organization who builds a system must test every component, within the system's scope, that participates in the interface. Treat each participating component separately. Identify, from three sources, all the kinds of interaction that can occur across an interface:

1. Explicit interaction requirements (as per the inter-system interaction requirement pattern that follows).

2. Implicit interactions, which help to satisfy goals stated indirectly. For example, resilience, traffic verification and security requirements (and possibly others) might involve additional kinds of interactions.

3. Interactions not discernable from the requirements at all.

See the inter-system interaction requirement pattern that follows for more about how to test each kind of interaction.

Most commonly, one end of an interface is outside the scope of the system being implemented. Check that a test "other end" system is available. Things become tricky and risky if not. This is often an important issue—especially when dealing with big, powerful organizations such as financial institutions (to test, say, credit card transactions) and government bodies. Sometimes, it even becomes necessary to build a working simulation of another system, which can involve considerable extra time and effort.

See the previous "Considerations for Development" section. Encourage the development team to build software to test the interface, and then make use of it. But don't rely on test software of this sort for all testing, in case it's incomplete or doesn't simulate the interface faithfully.

5.2 Inter-System Interaction Requirement Pattern

Basic Details

Related patterns:	Inter-system interface
Anticipated frequency:	Between zero and five requirements per inter-system interface
Pattern classifications:	None

Applicability

Use the inter-system interaction requirement pattern to specify a particular type of interaction across an inter-system interface.

Discussion

A typical interface involves a range of different types of interactions. A credit card payment service might exist primarily to enable retailers to debit a cardholder, but its interface will do various other things, such as reverse a transaction and check a card's credit limit. These are business-related functions, but the interface might also possess a number of more technical and supporting interactions: initiating a connection (and shutting it down); requesting resend of a previous message; notifying status; and so on. An **interaction type**, for the purposes of this requirement pattern, means the exchange of a particular type of information—which could involve messages in both directions. For example, a request and corresponding response count as an interaction.

Whether we want our requirements to address specific types of interactions depends very much on who owns the interface. There are four distinct situations in which we might find ourselves, and they have a direct bearing on our reasons for wanting to specify individual types of interactions, which in turn affect how much we should say:

■ **Situation 1: We own the interface.**   It's our responsibility to make the interface complete, so use the requirements to prevent something from being forgotten. You don't have to scratch your head trying to think of all the secondary interactions the interface needs; certain capabilities can be stated in very general terms.

■ **Situation 2: We don't own the interface but can influence its design.**   Use the requirements to identify and describe features we'd like to see in the interface. Treat the interface owners as the primary audience for these requirements, so aim to make a strong case for the inclusion of each one.

Beware that each of these requirements is outside our control, so until the interface owner accepts it, we don't know that the interface will satisfy it.

■ **Situation 3: We don't own the interface and cannot influence its design, but know what it looks like.**   Rather than force all readers of the requirements specification to refer to the interface specification to understand what it involves, it can be useful to sum up the individual interactions in requirements. Our requirements can capture the essence of the interface—to make effort estimation easier, for example. The earlier we get a feel for the difficulty of implementing this interface, the better.

Alternatively, you can write an informal summary of the interface rather than formal requirements. (You still must include it within the requirements specification, though.) This gives you the opportunity to include subjective judgments (such as on the quality of its documentation, its overall complexity, and so on). You could ask a developer to study the interface and write a summary.

■ **Situation 4: We don't own the interface, cannot influence its design, and don't know what it looks like.**   This is a risky situation to be in, but it happens. We're obliged to commit to building an interface without knowing what it involves—how extensive or tricky it will be. Flag this as an area of concern, and do all you can to obtain the necessary information as quickly as possible. We won't be able to write interaction type requirements until we know what the interface looks like.

Content

An inter-system interaction requirement needs to contain the following:

1. **Interaction type name**   This allows us to refer to it.

2. **Interface name and ID**   The interface over which the interaction occurs must be clear; the requirement's context (for example, following the interface's main requirement) is not enough. When referring to an interface, mention its interface ID to prevent misunderstanding.

3. **Interaction purpose**   Describe what this interaction is for. Make clear who initiates it.

4. **The information to pass**   This needn't be comprehensive. (Indeed, sometimes there's no need to say anything at all.) Concentrate on the important information. If the interaction involves flows of information in both directions, you can spell out what each one contains—but if the requirement grows too large (perhaps over half a page), split each flow into a separate requirement.

Template(s)

Summary	Definition
«Interaction summary»	The *«Interface name»* interface (*«Interface ID»*) shall *«Interaction purpose description»* [that passes at least the following information: *«Information to pass»*].

Example(s)

Here are a couple of example inter-system interaction type requirements for interfaces we own:

Summary	Definition
Raise alarm with alarm monitor	The alarm monitor interface (i6) shall allow the system to raise an alarm (that is, to pass an alarm message and cause all appropriate people to be notified). A raise alarm request shall include at least the following information: ■ Message ID ■ Message text ■ Time of occurrence ■ Alarm raised by (person or process name) The alarm monitor shall respond with an acknowledgment (or an error response indicating that it has been unable to raise the alarm).
Warehouse interface status	The interface between the system and the warehouse (i2) shall provide the ability to verify the operational status of both the interface and the warehouse system itself.

Extra Requirements

None

Considerations for Development

Refer to the inter-system interface requirement pattern earlier in this chapter.

Considerations for Testing

Refer to the inter-system interface requirement pattern for the big picture of testing an interface as a whole.

An inter-system interaction *requirement* specifies only what the interaction must achieve, its goal. The implementation might turn out to be more complex. For example, a requirement might imply there will be one request and one response, whereas in practice, it takes two of each. Therefore, testing an interaction *requirement* must be concerned with only whether the *goal* is achieved, not the intricacies of the implementation. Additional testing should be done to verify that the physical interactions work properly. Data flow diagrams can be useful in devising tests for the physical interactions but will be less so for the logical interactions.

Formulate both valid cases and invalid (erroneous) cases. In the first case, identify *valid but unexpected* cases. Does the interface deal properly with valid interactions that won't happen every day but can come along at any time? It's never possible to test every eventuality, but try to cover as representative a spread of situations as possible.

5.3 Technology Requirement Pattern

Basic Details

Related patterns:	Comply-with-standard, inter-system interface, accessibility
Anticipated frequency:	Usually no more than six requirements
Pattern classifications:	Pervasive: Maybe

Applicability

Use the technology requirement pattern to specify technology that must (or *must not*) be used to build or run the system, or with which the system must be capable of interacting or otherwise compatible.

Do not use the technology requirement pattern to make technology *choices*.

Discussion

Technology is any externally-produced hardware or software that is used in building, installing, and running a system. That's what it means here, at any rate. Requirements must not *make decisions* about which technology to use; they must describe whatever is known about the technology landscape into which the system must fit—to constrain in some way the technology that can be used in the system. We can conveniently divide that landscape into the following three areas:

- **Area 1: To *use* in production**   Hardware, operating system, database, Web server, firewall, uninterruptible power supply, and any other paraphernalia needed to provide life support for our application software.

- **Area 2: To *interact with* in production**   Such as a Web browser. This includes *indirect* interaction, such as exporting files or data that are to be read by some other application (and vice versa, importing files).

   All inter-system interfaces should be specified according to the inter-system interface requirement pattern. Each inter-system interface requirement must state the technology to be used for the interface, insofar as it is mandated.

Sometimes you need to make a judgment call about whether to regard something as *technology* or as *a standard*; some things can be regarded as both. For example, if our system needs to produce HTML pages to be displayed in a Web browser, are we complying with the HTML standard, or are we interacting (indirectly) with a browser? The best way to decide is to look at the underlying purpose: why are we doing this? If the purpose is to allow use of a Web browser, no one will care whether we use HTML (nor what version of HTML) providing the browser is able to present our output satisfactorily. In this case, specify the technology rather than the standard.

- **Area 3: To use in development**   Such as a programming language. Documenting, testing, and installing are regarded as falling within this area too. Common motivations for development technology requirements are

    a. For the *skills* needed to build the new system to match those that the organization already has.

    b. To be compatible with *existing software* (so we can reuse as much as possible).

    c. To fit in with existing *development practices*.

    d. To allow use of *development tools* already purchased and familiar.

Specifying development technology is most important when outsourcing development, especially if maintenance and ongoing development will be done *in-house*: constrain the external developers so the system suits our existing environment and skills. When developing in-house, we can usually rely on the development team to pick technology that is compatible with other systems and their skills, but not always. A developer might have their pet programming language or might just want the chance to learn a popular new skill—and you might have good reasons for keeping them to tried and true old ways. Carelessly introducing a hotchpotch of technologies contributes—invisibly, and probably significantly—to incompatibilities between systems—and thus inflexibility as well as extra development cost.

All requirements for technology to be used in development must have the highest priority; it's not practical to change these things after development starts.

It's not necessary to specify all this stuff—or, indeed, any of it. Just specify whatever is a given. The less we specify, the more freedom the development team has to pick whatever technology best fits the constraints placed upon it plus the goals of the system.

Where do technology requirements come from? We can expect demands for the technology that must be used (or not used) and interacted with in production to become apparent during the requirements process: someone's likely to mention them. On the other hand, we're likely to discover development environment matters only if we go looking for them—by talking to the development team. But that doesn't mean we should mechanically record such information: only specify it in requirements if there is a good reason to.

Content

A technology requirement should contain:

1. **Description of technology**   What technology are we talking about? This can be as specific or as general as appropriate. It doesn't have to name specific products. It can embody a formula for determining one product or more, in a similar fashion for working the version(s) of technology that must be supported, in point 3(c) below (though formulae of this kind can become intricate).

2. **Usage of the technology**   What role must this technology play in our system? At a minimum, convey which of the preceding three areas it relates to (use in production, interact with, use in development). Usage can be *negative* as well as positive: "the system **must not** use such-and-such technology."

3. **Version(s) of the technology (if relevant)**   Mentioning versions in a requirements specification is always problematic, because we don't want to tie the system just to specific versions that are liable to become out of date; neither do we want to make an open-ended commitment to each and every new version that might come along in the future. We also don't want to be unnecessarily specific or restrictive. There are three possible approaches:

   a. **Don't mention versions at all**. Sometimes there's no point in making a fuss. If everyone's likely to understand what's needed and what is customarily involved when a new version of this particular technology is released, or if there won't be a problem whenever a new version comes along, there's little to be gained by talking about versions.

   b. **Mandate one or more specific versions**. This is likely to be fine in the short term, but it conflicts with the goal of a timeless specification. What happens when a new version is released? Taken literally, the requirement says that any new version needn't be supported. But if that's what we mean, say so explicitly—because the average reader won't see it that way. If we expect the system to work with future versions, it's better to express the versions in a formula—which is approach (c).

   c. **Devise a formula**, based around *the most recently released version*, that is expressed in terms that don't mention that version explicitly and that identifies one or more versions that must be supported. For example, we could describe the most recent version and the two previous versions, or all versions that have been, at any time in the past two years, the most recent version. Do your best to minimize the number of versions that must be supported at once. For example, you could add a caveat to rule out any version that was soon superseded (and thus not widely used).

   Bear in mind that accommodating a new version might involve significant extra development effort. This, in turn, means there might be a delay between when that new version is released and when our system begins supporting it. If so, it's worth having the technology requirement grant the system some leeway, in case anyone expects instantaneous conformance.

   Always give at least a little thought to the matter of versions, even if you end up deciding not to mention them in the requirement itself.

4. **Motivation**   Why are we mandating this technology? The reasons for some technology requirements can be far from obvious; in fact, they are all liable to appear arbitrary if not justified in some way. People can have strong opinions on particular technologies (even stronger when they're negative opinions), so stating good reasons why one technology is essential can prevent a potentially vehement argument before it raises its head.

If the system must work with a range of technologies (for example, a couple of popular Web browsers), write a separate requirement for each one. This makes it harder for any one of them to be neglected (that is, it's easier to trace that each technology is supported), and it allows each one to be assigned its own priority.

Template(s)

Summary	Definition
«Technology summary»	*«Technology description»* shall be used for *«Technology usage»*. [*«Technology version statement»*.]
	«Motivation statement».
«Technology summary»	The system shall use *«Technology description»* for *«Technology usage»*. [*«Technology version statement»*.]
	«Motivation statement».

Use one of these templates as a starting point only. As the examples that follow demonstrate, the most suitable phraseology varies considerably depending on what an individual requirement says.

Example(s)

The following examples should not be regarded as advocating (or deprecating) any of the technologies they mention. This is not a coherent set of requirements that apply to one system: a few contradict one another. The second example demonstrates how expressing technology and versions in terms of a "formula" can be tortuous to specify precisely.

Summary	Definition
User access via Web browser	All user functions shall be accessible via a Web browser.
Popular Web browsers	The user interface shall be Web-based, and all functions shall operate fully with all popular Web browser/operating system family combinations (up to a maximum of eight such combinations) as nominated by a designated person (who is expected to be the marketing manager).
	All versions of any such Web browser that have been the latest version at any time in the past two years shall be supported, except for any version that was superseded within a month of its release.
	The list of popular browser/operating system family combinations can be modified periodically, but not more than four times per year. When a browser/operating system family is added to the list, support for it shall be provided within two months of that time.
Internet Explorer Web browser	The user interface shall be Web-based and all functions shall operate fully with the Microsoft Internet Explorer Web browser. All versions that have been the latest version at any time in the past two years shall be supported, except for any version that was superseded within a month of its release.
Widely used database	The system shall store its data in a widely used, well respected relational database product.
Oracle database	The system shall use the Oracle database.
	For each installation, data shall reside in the same Oracle instance used by the company's other systems. A noteworthy consequence of this clause is that the system does not need to concern itself with database transactions spanning multiple databases.

Summary	Definition
Programmed in widely used high level language	Software shall be written in a widely used, high-level programming language. A scripting language is not acceptable.
	The company has a preference for software written in C#.
Java programming language	The primary programming language for the server-side software shall be Java. The "primary programming language" is that in which the main application software is written. This requirement does not preclude the use of other programming languages in special situations (such as database stored procedures), but it does demand that other languages not be used for the development of any part of the core software.
	All tasks and processes that must be run regularly or frequently in order to keep the system operating shall be regarded as part of the main application software.
Widely used operating system	The server components of the system shall run on a widely used operating system that has proven dependability and scalability.
Windows operating system	The software shall be written to run on hardware running a version of the Microsoft Windows operating system.
No development facilities in production	There shall be no means to write software on the production system and no programming tools (including compilers, editors, linkers, and debuggers).
	The motivation for this requirement is to prevent unscrutinized, untested software from being run in a live environment.
No PERL scripts in production	No PERL scripts shall be used on a production machine (further to the previous requirement).
All scripts in PERL	All scripts shall be written in the PERL language.
Apache Web server	The system shall interact with the current corporate approved version of the Apache Web server.
Documentation in Word	All documentation that is written as proper documents (as opposed to Web pages) shall be written using Microsoft Word.

Observe that these examples are *not* divided into the three areas discussed (use in production, interact with, and use in development), yet mixing them up does not confuse the role of each requirement.

Extra Requirements

Some **nonfunctional requirements** that we wish to impose on our system also need to apply to technology that we use. In this case, write extra requirements for the purpose. One example is accessibility: our system can't be regarded as satisfying its accessibility requirements if some of its functions are implemented using a third-party product that doesn't satisfy them. (See the accessibility requirement pattern in Chapter 8, "User Interface Requirement Patterns.") Write extra nonfunctional requirements for each of the technologies used. That's usually preferable to attempting to broaden the original nonfunctional requirements so they also apply to the technology used. The latter is certainly easier to specify, but it isn't helpful to developers because the work involved in building a feature into our own software is of a different nature than that of choosing a compliant product. It's equally unhelpful to testers for similar reasons.

Considerations for Development

Technology is too varied to be able to make suggestions here on how to tackle particular types. But it is possible to say a little about how to react to the two main kinds of technology requirement, because they are very different as far as development is concerned:

1. Technology the system **uses** (or must not use). This kind of requirement influences (often in profound ways) the *process* of building the system, including who will build it. For example, once you mandate the programming language, you need a development team competent in that language. But a technology use requirement typically has less effect upon the *design* of the system. For example, a given design could be implemented in many different programming languages.

    When reviewing this kind of requirement, development representatives should check that adequate technology that satisfies the requirement can be found. Also check that the prospective development team has suitable skills to use this technology.

2. Technology with which the system must be **compatible**. This kind of requirement directly affects the software that needs to be built. It might mean that at least one developer must be (or must become) an expert in this particular technology. For example, if our system must interact with a particular credit card clearing service, someone will have to get to know it in detail and develop software for it.

    When reviewing this kind of requirement, developers should scrutinize it and contemplate its implications. Try to get an early feel for how difficult it will be to implement.

Considerations for Testing

As with development, the two main kinds of technology requirements place very different demands on testing:

1. Technology the system **uses** (or must not use). This is generally straightforward to test: for each technology requirement, find out what technology was used in that area, and verify that it's in accordance with the requirement.

2. Technology with which the system must be **compatible**. There are no shortcuts here: it must be tested in detail—occasionally in excruciating detail. For example, if the system must be accessible via a particular Web browser, then every type of page delivered by the system must work.

For both kinds of requirement, pay special attention to any requirement that insists that the system work with **multiple** different technologies (and/or multiple versions of each one), especially if the number of permutations looks impractically large. Be alarmed if two or more technology requirements have impact on each other, yielding vastly more permutations. This situation is likely to be hard to test—because you have to acquire, configure, and run all the technologies to test them. Then tests must be repeated for each one. It's tolerable for client technologies with which the system must interact (such as several Web browsers and browser versions). But it's a major headache when it relates to the system's own environment, such as testing that server applications run on several different operating systems or types of hardware.

5.4 Comply-with-Standard Requirement Pattern

Basic Details

Related patterns:	Accessibility
Anticipated frequency:	Rarely more than 12 requirements
Pattern classifications:	Pervasive: Maybe

Applicability

Use the comply-with-standard pattern to specify that the system must comply with a particular standard.

Discussion

A **standard**, for the purpose of this pattern, is any document or collection of documents that makes demands on how things in its sphere are to be done. It includes laws (tax, privacy, access by people with disabilities), government regulations, industry-specific regulations and codes of conduct, company standards, quality standards (such as ISO 9001), information standards (such as currency and country codes), and technical standards of diverse kinds (for example, file formats, communication protocols, and user interface conventions).

Comply-with-standard requirements tend to be very straightforward: you must comply with whatever-it-is. But more often than not, it isn't good enough to leave it at that, and you should write extra requirements that expound the implications. See the "Extra Requirements" section later in this pattern for more. (Note that this pattern has been named "*comply-with-standard*" for clarity: calling it the "*standard*" requirement pattern would invite misreading its purpose.)

Let's divide standards into a few categories for the purpose of saying a little about how to approach them:

1. **Industry-specific legislation, regulations, and codes of practice**   Complying with these sorts of standard often involves a lot of work, which is justified because they usually have a major bearing on the central purpose of the system. But you might still be in for a nasty surprise when you find out just how extensive and tough they are, especially if you're new to the industry in question.

2. **Legislation that applies to all companies within the jurisdiction to which it applies**   (Such as sales tax and financial regulations.) Usually, it's not necessary to study the laws themselves: turn to an expert in that area, such as the company accountant, lawyer, finance department, or auditors, to ask them what's needed. Often it's not necessary even to mention the laws that underlie the need to support taxes and such.

3. **Company standards**   These are usually concerned with software quality and consistency, though they might mandate certain support functions (such as system monitoring). The line between company standards and company-mandated use of common software or common requirements can be blurred. If you have any control over these things, it's best for company standards to stick to nonfunctional matters, and to have common requirements specifications for the rest.

4. **Technical standards**   (Such as file formats and communication protocols.) Normally, you don't need to go into detail here: if you find that building your system involves developing your own implementation of a general technical standard (when that is not central to the purpose of your system), it might be a sign that something's wrong. For example, if someone asks for the system to support a peculiar file format for which no off-the-shelf software is available, you should seriously question whether it's justified.

Complying with Multiple Versions of a Standard

If complying with a standard is bad enough, dealing with multiple versions adds all sorts of complexities. It might not just mean complying with multiple versions at the same time; it might encompass changing the version(s) over time—in particular, complying with the *latest* version on an ongoing basis. This is very easy to state in an innocuous-sounding requirement, but in it likely lurks a can of worms. Consider the requirement "The system shall read all versions of PDF files, including the latest." What are developers and testers to make of that? Do we retest every time a new version is released? And what do we do if something suddenly doesn't work? These sorts of questions must be answered one way or another, so everyone knows where they stand.

Factors to consider:

1. Does the standard affect the functionality of the system? If not (for example, a standard that deals with *quality*), moving to a different version of the standard probably involves no work beyond its new demands. (That is, *switching* versions is not itself a problem.)

2. Does a new version of the standard supersede an old version, or must the system support multiple versions of the standard at the same time?

3. Does the standard affect any of the system's external interfaces? If so, switching to a new version must be coordinated with whoever is at the other end of the interface. You have two choices:

   a. Support old and new versions at the same time. This means the developers must build more sophisticated software.

   b. Install a new version of the system at exactly the same time as the external system(s) switch to the new version of the standard. This is akin to a juggler taking over from another juggler while the balls are in the air: it takes precise timing and even a small mistake can create a big mess.

4. Does switching to a new version (or even from one standard to another) have to happen on a specified date? For example, this is likely to happen if a new tax regime is being introduced (or when a country introduces a new currency—such as adopting the Euro). Changes like this imply the same two choices described for the previous factor— but with the extra risk of leaving you no control over when it happens.

5. Do we actually have *multiple different standards* for the same thing, rather than multiple versions of the same standard? For example, if the system has to deal with the tax regulations of different states, more than just the tax rates could vary (and if we're taking about different *countries*, they certainly will). Situations like this can have a big

bearing on the system's design (and might invite use of the *extendability* pattern to make it easier to introduce extra instances of a like standard), so they need to be identified early and spelled out in detail. But they can be difficult to spot. At the very least, if you think this is not a problem for a particular standard, state that as an assumption in the requirements specification so that readers can check it.

6. Does the advocate of the standard expect to verify your compliance with it? If so, what compliance demands are there, and how tough are they? (They can be so onerous as to influence the whole development approach and warrant the building of many extra system functions.) If compliance is going to be hard, make everyone aware of the implications early.

Spell out the answers to all these questions in extra requirements.

It's impossible to enumerate all situations here. This rather alarming list of factors illustrates how tricky it can be to deal with multiple versions of standards—which leads to these tips:

Tip 1:   Don't commit to more than you need to. Find as many simplifications as you can: make the requirements less onerous(as far as possible). If it suffices for your system to comply with one identified version of a standard, require that only.

Tip 2:   Don't gloss over the complications involved in handling multiple versions of standards. Any complexity you ignore in the requirements won't go away and will only be harder to deal with later on.

Content

A requirement that mandates a standard should specify:

1. **The name of the standard**   State the name clearly, such that it cannot be confused with any other standard. To achieve this, you might need to prefix it with the name of the organization who produced the standard (which means the jurisdiction in the case of laws and government regulations).

2. **The purpose of the standard**   If the name of the standard does not convey its purpose, include a summary of what the standard is for. Usually you can do this apparently in passing (for example, "ISO3166, the international standard for country and region codes, ..."). You can't expect your readers to know what an arcane code for a standard means, especially one that is numbered, and it's rude to force readers to go find out for themselves.

3. **The version of the standard with which to comply**   If the system must comply with more than one version, or must comply with the *latest* version on an ongoing basis, see the preceding "Complying with Multiple Versions of a Standard" section for the extra factors you must consider. When specifying compliance with a law or government regulation, state the year it was enacted if it has no "version." If the system will only ever need to support one particular version of the standard and never any other version, say so explicitly—to avoid anyone having to worry about the awkward multiple version questions.

4. **Parts of the standard with which to comply (if relevant)**   If the system need only comply with some parts of the standard, identify them—but be brief. If there are more than a handful of items to identify, do so using extra requirements. If you need lots of extra requirements, consider splitting them off into a separate requirements specification. Also identify any parts for which you have or might be able to obtain a *temporary dispensation* from compliance.

5. **Location**   State where a copy of the standard can be found. Cite all sources likely to be available to members of the project team: the URL (Uniform Resource Locator) of a publicly available online source, hard copies (where they are stored, or who possesses them), the location of a soft copy on disk, and so on. It is advisable not to follow the location by a period ("."), to avoid the risk of it being interpreted as part of the location.

If a suitable standard exists for a particular aspect of a system, it is generally a good idea at least to seriously consider using it before devising something in-house for the same purpose. If you're not sure whether a standard exists, go and look. There are plenty out there. (This is not quite the same as the famous saying, "The nice thing about standards is that there are so many of them to choose from.") A few good starting points are

- *http://www.iso.org*: ISO, the International Organization for Standardization, produces a wide range of standards related to quality (the ISO 9000 series), company organization, and management, as well as industry-specific and domain-specific standards.

- *http://www.w3c.org*: The World Wide Web Consortium is responsible for a wide range of standards that define key aspects of the Web and adjacent subjects, including many XML-related standards.

- *http://www.ietf.org*: The Internet Engineering Task Force (IETF) manages the RFC (Request For Comment) standards which cover a broad range of software-related subjects, including many pertaining to the Web.

- *http://www.ieee.org*: The Institute of Electrical and Electronics Engineers (IEEE) produces a very large number of technical standards, including many areas of computer technology, telecommunications and quality.

- *http://www.omg.org*: The Object Management Group produces standards for software analysis and design (including the UML–Unified Modeling Language–standard), security, business modeling, security, and for a few specialized areas.

- *http://www.oasis-open.org*: The Organization for the Advancement of Structured Information Standards (OASIS) has a range of standards related to XML and connected areas, including for business processes and security.

Template(s)

Summary	Definition
Comply with «*Standard name*» standard	The system shall comply with [parts «*Standard parts list*» of] the «*Standard description*» standard [in order to «*Standard purpose*»]. «*Standard version statement*».
	Source: «*Standard location*».

Example(s)

All the examples that follow relate to real standards (except for a couple for a fictitious company). They are divided into the four types already discussed: industry-specific, applicable to all companies, company-specific, and technical. Examples relating to accessibility legislation can be found in the accessibility requirement pattern. The first examples are industry-specific:

Summary	Definition
HIPAA privacy	The system shall protect the privacy of all protected health information in compliance with the privacy rule of the U.S. Health Insurance Portability and Accountability Act (HIPAA), 1996.
	Protected health information is any information about an individual that concerns their health, the provision of health care to them, or payment for health care.
	Source: *http://www.hhs.gov/ocr/hipaa*
HIPAA security	The system shall comply with the security provisions of the U.S. Health Insurance Portability and Accountability Act (HIPAA), 1996 with respect to the secure storage, use of and access to protected health information (as per the previous requirement).
	Source: *http://www.hhs.gov/ocr/hipaa*

These examples demand compliance with various laws:

Summary	Definition
SOX	The system shall comply with the U.S. Sarbanes-Oxley Act, 2002 (commonly referred to as SOX) to the extent of faithfully recording, protecting from improper modification, monitoring, and providing accountability for all activities within the system that have financial consequences.
	The intent of this requirement is to be confident that the financial information embodied in the system accurately reflects the business transacted by it, and to provide means by which auditors can verify the correctness of this information.
	Source: *http://frwebgate.access.gpo.gov/cgi-bin /getdoc.cgi?dbname=107_cong_bills&docid=f:h3763enr.tst.pdf*
U.K. Data Protection Act	The system shall protect personal information in accordance with the U.K. Data Protection Act, 1998.
	Source: *http://www.opsi.gov.uk/acts/acts1998/19980029.htm*
Australian Privacy Act 1988	All usage of information about customers and their activities, and exchange of this information between organizations, shall be in accordance with the provisions of the Australian Federal Privacy Act, 1988.
	Source: *http://www.austlii.edu.au/au/legis/cth/consol_act/ pa1988108*

Here are a couple of example requirements for company-specific standards:

Summary	Definition
Company coding standards	All software shall be written in compliance with the company's coding standards for the programming language in which it is written.
	Whenever a new programming language is introduced, a suitable coding standard shall be adopted for it.
Company Web style guidelines	All Web pages produced by the system or written in association with it shall comply with the company's Web style guidelines.

Here are example requirements for a few technical standards:

Summary	Definition
ISO 639	Spoken languages shall be identified internally in the system by codes defined in ISO 639, the international standard for natural languages.
	(Note that this requirement does not cover the *display* of language choices to users—for which it is preferable to use the *names* of the languages.)
	Source: *http://www.loc.gov/standards/iso639-2/langhome.html*
ISO 3166	Countries and geographic regions (subdivisions) shall be identified internally in the system by codes defined in ISO 3166, the international standard for such codes.
	(Note that this requirement does not cover the *display* of countries and their subdivisions to users. It is strongly advised that only their names be shown unless there is a good reason to do otherwise.)
	Source: *http://www.iso.org/iso/en/prods-services/iso3166ma/ 02iso-3166-code-lists/list-en1.html*
ISO 4217	The currency of all monetary amounts shall be identified internally in the system by codes defined in ISO 4217, the international standard for currency codes.
	(Note that this requirement does not cover the *display* of currencies to users. It is strongly advised that only currency names and symbols be visible to them unless there is a good reason to display the ISO code.)
	Source: *http://www.xe.com/iso4217.htm*
X.509	Digital certificates used for user authentication shall comply with X.509, the ITU-T's standard for public key and attribute certificate frameworks.
	(Note that this requirement does not mandate the use of digital certificates, merely that *if* they are used, they must be X.509-compliant.)
	Source: *http://www.itu.int/ITU-T/asn1/database/itu-t/x/x509/1997/*

Summary	Definition
PKCS #10	Interactions between the system and Certification Authorities shall comply with PKCS #10 (RSA Laboratories' standard for the syntax for certification requests sent to a Certification Authority).
	It is recognized that PKCS #10 defines message syntax in an abstract manner (ASN.1), so compliance with it is not in itself sufficient for a given calling system to be able to talk to a given Certification Authority.
	Source: *http://www.rsasecurity.com/rsalabs/pkcs/pkcs-10*

Extra Requirements

The natural reaction to reading a typical comply-with-standard requirement is bemusement: what's it mean? What are developers and testers supposed to do with it? If it's clear, the original requirement will suffice. If not, someone has to figure out the implications for the system by going through the standard in detail—and for consistency and efficiency, it makes sense to do this only once, rather than having several people independently making their own, uncoordinated interpretations. That person should be the analyst, and extra requirements should be their medium. It still makes sense for representatives of the development and/or testing teams to verify the analyst's interpretation against the standard itself, but the importance of that depends on the nature of the standard. Also, a small project might not have the resources to perform a lot of double-checking.

There are three levels of detail at which compliance with a standard can be specified by using requirements:

- **A single requirement**   (As per this requirement pattern.) This suffices only if this requirement says all that needs to be said. For example a requirement that says "The 'Save as HTML' function shall produce output that complies with the HTML 4.0 standard, which resides at ..." is sufficient. There's no need for the requirements to delve into the HTML 4.0 standard: it's clear to developers what HTML constructs are allowed, and testers can rigorously verify whether output complies.

- **A set of requirements in the system's requirements specification**   If only a handful of requirements are needed to specify in detail how to comply with the standard, then include them directly. In this situation, you can omit the comply-with-standard requirement itself—though it's advisable to preface these requirements with an explanation of what they're for.

- **A separate requirements specification**   If the standard's requirements are so numerous that they would cause the main specification to grow significantly, or they'd dominate it, create a separate requirements specification for them. Make this separate specification as general as possible: aim to specify what any system must do to comply with the standard—with a view to reuse. This isn't always possible, though, because you might write the requirements to suit the particulars of your system. So make clear whether the separate specification is suitable for reuse or not, and, if so, in what circumstances. (In an ideal world, standards would be written to be usable as requirements specifications in the first place—but I've never seen one that is.)

If you write a separate requirements specification for the standard, the original comply-with-standard requirement must identify the separate specification (its name, version, and where it can be found), and state explicitly that all its requirements must be satisfied. The comply-with-standard requirement then takes on the role of a *refer-to-requirements* requirement, and you should use that pattern instead.

Usually, you need to specify requirements for everything that the system must do to comply with the standard—just as if the standard were replaced by a customer who insists on everything in the standard. There are a couple of situations where it's not necessary to go into such detail: first, if you are outsourcing development to an external organization that can be expected to properly determine the implications of the standard for themselves; and second, if you intend to purchase a product. But beware of suppliers that comply with the letter of the standard but not its spirit. If you're worried about this, add requirements covering areas of potential concern.

Standard-related requirements needn't all have the same priority. For example, when a new standard is introduced, it might introduce its provisions gradually over time. (Some imposers of standards are reasonable!) Or a compliance auditor (say, for a government regulator) might grant dispensation from some demands for a given time (just like a health inspector granting a restaurant time to clean its dirty kitchen).

Some requirements that have been requested already might contribute to compliance with a standard. Add a note to this effect to each such requirement. Every requirement that contributes to compliance with a standard should say so explicitly, unless it is obvious from its context (such as being in a section of the requirements specification devoted to that standard).

If you're supplying your requirements specification to a third party (outside your organization), they must have access to all the standards you expect them to comply with. This means you must make internal organization standards available to them, and supply industry standards if the third party is unable to obtain them because they don't belong to the requisite industry body (or to save them the expense of buying them). Wherever possible, distribute copies of standards to third parties along with the requirements specification itself: it saves everyone the time of asking for and supplying them later, and it brings to light any supply problems before you suffer any embarrassment. Also bear in mind that standards can be relatively expensive, and those available only in hard copy can take significant time to order and receive. This can cause considerable difficulties if you're asking for responses (bids) from third parties, especially if you impose a closing date (for example, for a tender). This reinforces the fact that it's always helpful to your readers to spell out in detail the implications of a standard, so they don't have to pore over it themselves. It's a much better use of time for one person to figure out the implications than for multiple readers each to do it for themselves, particularly since they know less about the author's intent. It also minimizes differences in interpretation.

Many standards appear to be intentionally mean and bloody-minded. But if we consider they're nearly all written by people who aren't directly accountable for any unreasonablenesses, ambiguities, contradictions, and omissions in them, and who don't have to pay for or carry out the work necessary to comply with them—well, perhaps we should be grateful that standards aren't worse than they are.

Considerations for Development

Developers are strongly advised to consider the factors discussed in the "Complying with Multiple Versions of a Standard" section.

Be especially careful when a standard defines an interface (for example, for a communications protocol) or some other aspect of system interoperability (for example, when one system must read files produced by another system). It's very easy for two systems built to the same standard not to be able to talk to each other: it only takes very small differences in interpretation of the standard. If possible, coordinate development as closely as possible with the other organization(s) implementing the same standard.

Considerations for Testing

Standards vary considerably, so testing depends on the nature of the standard. The key to thorough and sensible testing against a standard is to get to know it firsthand.

If requirements have been specified for all the detailed implications of the standard, the parent requirement for the standard itself need not be tested.

5.5 Refer-to-Requirements Requirement Pattern

Basic Details

Related patterns:	None
Anticipated frequency:	Up to six requirements, but usually fewer
Pattern classifications:	Pervasive: Maybe

Applicability

Use the refer-to-requirements requirement pattern to specify that some or all requirements in an external requirements specification must be satisfied as if those requirements were present in the current specification.

Discussion

A detailed requirements specification for a serious commercial system is a significant document that takes considerable effort to write and, equally importantly, to read and review. Moving certain parts into separate specifications makes it easier to deal with. Spinning off the less visible or more technical parts gives the main specification a clearer focus on the matters closer to the heart of the business, but at the risk of masking from key stakeholders the overall scale and complexity of the system. Improved clarity and manageability is one good reason for referring to external specifications. Another is that those specifications can be referred to by other systems, thus saving effort (via reuse) and increasing consistency between systems. A third reason is that a specification on a specific subject tends to be written more diligently than when it's an afterthought in another specification.

Make sure that the referenced specification is accessible to the whole audience of the current system's specification. If that's not possible, either create a version of the referenced specification that everyone *can* access, or copy the individual requirements into the main specification. Developers *must* be able to read all requirements that they are expected to satisfy.

Content

A requirement that refers to external requirements needs to contain:

- **Name of the referenced specification**   Use the name the specification calls itself, with extra clarification if it might be confused with some other similar specification.

- **Version of the referenced specification**   This is essential. Without it, confusion might result if there's more than one version—or if a new version is produced later. Don't commit to a moving target: we're saying the requirements in *this version* suit us, and satisfying them is enough. In due course, it might well be beneficial to switch to a later version of the referenced specification—indeed, we might be obligated to— but do that consciously. It might involve software changes, which mustn't slip in by the back door: deal with them the same as you'd deal with any requirement changes.

  Including the *date* of this version of the referenced specification is helpful, too.

- **The requirements that apply**   Must our system adhere to the whole of the referenced specification or just some of it? If all its requirements must be satisfied, say so. If not, clearly identify which parts must be satisfied— which is best done by referring to the IDs of the requirements that apply. If you need to refer to several sets of requirements, write a separate requirement for each set. If it's more convenient, you can identify those parts of the referenced specification that **don't apply**—that is, that all requirements must be satisfied except for those identified.

  If only one or two requirements are referenced, you could copy them into the main specification directly; the convenience to the readers probably outweighs the drawback of duplication.

- **Location of the referenced specification**   Where does the specification live? State where it can be found.

- **Information about priority**   Give serious consideration to the priority of the referenced requirements; don't gloss over this subject. The referenced specification might define the priority levels that it uses in a different way than our current specification does. If not, we're lucky—and we can adopt their priorities directly. Otherwise, we need to state the priorities explicitly, either by assigning one priority to them all, saying which requirements have which priorities, or defining a translation between the priority schemes used by the two specifications.

  If this information can be expressed concisely, put it in the requirement's "priority" column; otherwise, explain it in the requirement definition and say, "various" or something suitable in the "priority" column. If a normal priority level is placed in the "priority" column, then that priority applies to **all** the referenced requirements—though it helps to state this explicitly in the requirement definition.

Template(s)

Summary	Definition
«Domain description» requirements apply	The system shall satisfy *«Requirements that apply»* specified in *«Specification version»* of the *«Specification name»*, which resides at *«Specification location»*.
	«Priority statement».

Example(s)

Summary	Definition
All common requirements apply	The system shall satisfy all the requirements defined in version 2.0 of the Common Requirements Specification, which resides at x:\Specs\Common\CommonReqtsV2.0.doc.
	All referenced requirements have priority 1.

Summary	Definition
Basic security requirements apply	The system shall satisfy all the basic security features requirements (SR1.1-SR1.11) specified in version 1.3 of the Security Requirements Specification, which resides at x:\Specs \Security\SecurityReqtsV1.3.doc.
Access control requirements apply	The system shall satisfy all the access control requirements (SR2.1–SR2.9) specified in version 1.3 of the Security Requirements Specification, which resides at x:\Specs\Security \AccessControlReqtsV1.3.doc.

Extra Requirements

None.

Considerations for Development

Treat each applicable requirement in the external specification as if it were present in the current specification.

Considerations for Testing

The suggestion in the "Considerations for Development" section applies to testing, too.

5.6 Documentation Requirement Pattern

Basic Details

Related patterns:	None
Anticipated frequency:	Up to 10 requirements
Pattern classifications:	Pervasive: Maybe

Applicability

Use the documentation requirement pattern to specify that a particular type of documentation needs to be produced.

Discussion

Documentation can be regarded as anything that is written about a system, no matter what form it takes—not just traditional documents. Online help, presentations (in Microsoft PowerPoint, for example) and comments and other annotations in program source code all count as documentation. Some people might dispute whether anything in source code should count as documentation, but the output from utilities like Javadoc—which generates a coherent set of HTML pages about a body of Java software—must certainly count as documentation, and it seems artificial to include some types of annotations of source code but not others.

For the purpose of this requirement pattern, it's also possible to extend the definition of documentation beyond what's written, to include instructional videos, interactive tutorials, and informative material in other media. In an increasingly multimedia age it seems inappropriate to place artificial limits on what counts as documentation in the broad sense.

Content

A requirement for documentation should contain those parts of the following that are appropriate:

1. The **name** and/or **type** of the documentation. What's this sort of document called?

2. A **description** of what the documentation is to contain. Go into whatever level of detail is necessary such that any documentation that complies is likely to satisfy you.

3. The **format** or **medium** to use, which can be as precise as necessary (such as a Word 2007 document or HTML 4.0 pages) but preferably left as open as possible (for example, "a document" or "online").

4. The name of a **standard** to which this type of documentation must conform, if any (for example, use of company document templates), along with a description of where this standard can be found. This typically applies when a company has internal standards for particular kinds of documentation. Also explain the extent to which adherence to the standard is mandated (if relevant).

5. The **language** the documentation is to be written in, if this is not obvious. In some cases, it might be necessary to state the dialect to use, too (for example, for English, whether it should be British, American, Australian, or some other kind). For a multilingual system, some documentation might need to be provided in *multiple* languages, in which case those languages must be explicitly identified.

Template(s)

Summary	Definition
«Document type name»	There shall be a «*Document type name*» that contains «*Document description*». [It shall be in the form of «*Document format or medium*».] [It shall comply with the «*Document standard name*».] [It shall be written in the «*Language name*» language.]

Example(s)

Here are representative requirements for several common (and one or two uncommon) types of documentation. The mention of a type of documentation here is not a suggestion that it should be produced for every system.

Summary	Definition
Online help	There shall be online help for every online function in the system. Online help for functions available to customers shall be aimed at them; online help for other functions shall be aimed at internal users.
	For each function, the online help shall describe how to use that function, such that an uninformed user of average intelligence shall be able to use it as intended.
User guide	There shall be a user guide for all functions available to internal users.
	The online help could form the basis for satisfying this requirement if it can be consolidated into an attractive printable form.

Summary	Definition
Operating instructions	There shall be operating instructions that explain to an operator (system administrator) how to run the system. It shall cover at least startup, shutdown, and the monitoring of the system's health.
Procedures manual	There shall be written operational procedures for all business processes that involve use of the system.
Security procedures manual	There shall be written security procedures for the system. It shall, at a minimum, include instructions and advice on the choosing, changing, and protection of user passwords.
Error message explanations	There shall be a set of explanations of error messages. It shall contain an explanation of the meaning of each error message that satisfies any of the following criteria: a. An intelligent but inexperienced user could not deduce the full meaning. b. The error indicates a severe problem. c. There is more to explain about the error. Where appropriate, each explanation shall also describe how to correct or otherwise respond to the message, and (if possible) identify the system component in which the error originated.
Installation instructions	There shall be installation instructions covering each step necessary to install the system.
Upgrade instructions	There shall be instructions for each version of the system to describe each step necessary to upgrade from a previous version of the system.
System design	The design of the system shall be documented.
Javadocs or equivalent	Every Java source file shall contain meaningful Javadoc annotations for every class, interface, method, and public variable. Every source file written in a programming language for which a utility equivalent to Javadoc is freely available shall contain equivalent annotations.
Commenting of source code	All source code shall be commented to a professional standard, sufficient to permit maintenance by a developer other than its author.

Extra Requirements

A documentation requirement is usually self-contained. There are the following rare cases when extra requirements might be needed:

1. If special software must be written to support the documentation, specify requirements for that software.

2. If the system's software must be written in such a way as to facilitate a special kind of documentation, specify requirements for what the software must do. An example might be special software hooks to drive an interactive tutorial. Unless you find a dedicated product to help you do it, this kind of thing is very exotic and to be undertaken only if you really

know what you're doing. Writing a requirement that says "There shall be an interactive tutorial" is not adequate by itself; you need to provide a better idea of how extensive and how fancy it needs to be—for which extra requirements are necessary.

3. If you are *outsourcing* the development of your system, you might want to insist on being able to tailor its documentation. This is especially true for online help, user guide, and other instructional material—although you might as well insist on it for everything except material within source code. Here's an example:

Summary	Definition
Documentation tailorable by «*Our company name*»	It shall be possible for «*Our company name*» to modify any piece of documentation written for the system, except that residing inside program source code.

Considerations for Development

The development team's biggest interest in complying with documentation requirements is in producing whatever is expected of them. When reviewing documentation requirements, check that those demands aren't unreasonable.

It is, of course, good practice to comment source code when writing it. It's also very helpful to the whole development team to make good use of tools that generate source code–based documentation (such as Javadoc) and to generate it for the whole system regularly as a matter of course (say, whenever a build of all the software is performed).

Considerations for Testing

For the purposes of testing, we can divide documentation into four types, each of which needs to be tested in a different way:

1. **Traditional**   This means the sort you can print out and read anywhere. Test by reading it and checking its accuracy and completeness. Non-interactive instructional material using other media (principally video and/or audio) can be regarded as falling into this category, in the sense that testing it involves scrutinizing it from start to finish.

2. **Online**   Test help pages by calling up the help page associated with each function and checking it for helpfulness and for compatibility with the function to which it relates. If there is a requirement that says every online function must have help, you need to invoke every function to check compliance.

3. **Within source code**   It's better to give developers responsibility for source code quality, including commenting, through peer reviews (though in some organizations testers also participate in code reviews). But if testers are asked to check that a requirement in this area is satisfied, it's not necessary to expect them to verify the quality of comments and other annotations in source code. If they exist and appear to be coherent, that's good enough evidence that developers are taking the trouble to properly document their source code.

4. **Interactive**   Any form of documentation that permits the user to interact with it (such as tutorials) means you have to devise a set of paths through it to exercise all options at each decision point. This can be a major undertaking.

Also test that all documentation complies with any accessibility requirements. See the accessibility requirement pattern in Chapter 8.

Chapter 6
Information Requirement Patterns

In this chapter:

6.1 Data Type Requirement Pattern. 86

6.2 Data Structure Requirement Pattern. 94

6.3 ID Requirement Pattern. 97

6.4 Calculation Formula Requirement Pattern. 102

6.5 Data Longevity Requirement Pattern. 107

6.6 Data Archiving Requirement Pattern. 110

Information is the lifeblood of commercial systems: IT is *Information* Technology, after all. It used to be called Data Processing (DP), but information has more prestige than mere data; this book treats the two as synonymous. Both names reflect the central nature of the information—entering, storing, displaying, reporting, and so on—in the vast majority of systems, especially those that play a part in running a business. So requirements that specify data and how it's handled play a crucial role in defining a system, and patterns for them can help get them right.

Most of the requirement patterns in the information domain are for describing various aspects of the information the system needs. They relate to each other as shown in Figure 6-1.

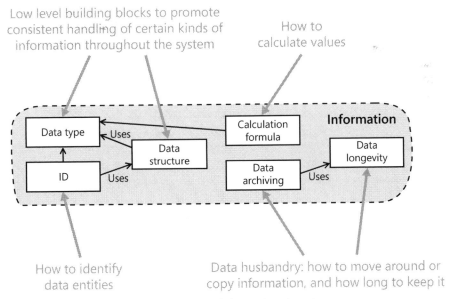

Figure 6-1   Requirement patterns in the information domain

6.1 Data Type Requirement Pattern

Basic Details

Related patterns:	Unparochialness
Anticipated frequency:	Usually fewer than 10 requirements, but more if you wish to specify how common data types (such as dates) are to be displayed
Pattern classifications:	Pervasive: Maybe; Affects database: Yes

Applicability

Use the data type requirement pattern to define how a particular atomic item of information (a single field) for a particular business purpose is to be represented and/or displayed. Also use the data type requirement pattern to specify how a *standard data type* is always to be displayed (for example, *all* dates).

Discussion

Define a logical data type for each unit of information that serves a clear logical role in the system, such as product type code or company ID. Don't bother doing this for items of information that are so clear and simple that they need no further explanation, such as a count of transactions or plain text.

Writing requirements for logical data types isn't essential, but it's good practice. It promotes consistency across the system, saves repetition, and prevents developers arbitrarily making their own decisions on something that's very visible to users. A data type requirement's primary responsibility is to describe in detail the *form* of the information the data type must convey (for example, six alphabetic characters, or a date). It can also state how all occurrences of this type of data are to be *displayed* to the user. Sometimes describing the form is easy, and the bulk of the requirement deals with display.

Any data type defined in a requirement is a *logical* data type, so also define it in terms of what the customer needs: its business purpose, the role it plays. Even if two data types have the same form (say, a three-character code), if they serve different business purposes, they're still logically distinct and must be treated as such. Don't mention technical data types (as used in databases or programming languages): maintain independence from the technology, unless forced to by circumstances. In any case, a logical data type can be represented in multiple ways depending on the technology (for example, one way in the database and another in each programming language).

The table that follows lists the form of various common data types, in the self-evident terms best suited to nontechnical readers (and it's reasonable to assume you'll always have some of these), along with suggestions on what else to say about them (and what not to say), plus other things to consider. If you want to state precisely what a particular common data type means in the context of the current system, write a requirement for it. You can also use a requirement to describe extra characteristics a common data type needs in your system; a few possibilities follow.

Form	Suggestions and Extra Considerations
Characters	"Characters" on its own implies that a value can contain anything the user can type in using a keyboard. If you want to restrict this somewhat, you can instead refer to "**alphabetic characters**" or "**alphanumeric characters**." (Don't call them *strings* or *varchars* or other jargon.)
	Whenever a data type allows alphabetic characters, consider *case*: must it all be uppercase, all lowercase, or either? If either, is it case-sensitive (so "a" and "A" are treated as different) or case-insensitive ("a" and "A" are treated as the same)? When entering such values into a screen, you can usually prevent unacceptable case values from being entered. But this isn't possible for all sources of data (such as messages sent by another system, or data read in from flat files). If your system has any of these, consider what should be done if a letter arrives with the wrong case. Should it be automatically converted to the correct case, or should it be rejected?
	Extra characteristics to consider include which languages' character sets must be allowed: letters with accents, multibyte characters (for languages such as Chinese)? Allow special symbols to be entered? Bear in mind that some users are likely to have keyboards that contain different characters to yours (especially if they come along from anywhere in the world across the Web). It may be worth defining two "characters" data types: one narrow and one broad.
Number	"Number" on its own implies a whole number made up of the digits 0 through 9 (an *integer*—but don't call it that; also avoid programming terms such as *float* and *double*). If it's not a whole number, state how many decimal places you want to allow. (In commercial systems, numeric values that genuinely might have an arbitrary number of decimal places occur relatively rarely.)
	Some numbers are allowed to take *negative* values, and some aren't. Often it's clear from the context whether negatives are allowed, but it's usually a good idea to state explicitly in each place where a number is used whether it's **signed** or **unsigned**.
	A **percentage** is simply a type of number. So are numbers to bases other than ten (**hexadecimal**, **binary**), but it's unusual to find them mentioned in the requirements of commercial systems.
	Any value that has a type of *unit* associated with it is not a type of number. In particular, a **monetary amount** isn't a type of number, because every amount is denominated in a particular currency. But you can treat a number-with-unit as a plain number if you're *sure*—cross-your-heart-and-hope-to-die sure—that the unit will always, *always*, **always** have the same value in your system (for example, one currency).

Form	Suggestions and Extra Considerations
List of values	If you list all the possible values a data type can have, you don't need to say how they're held (or stored). Nor should you, because that's a design decision. In any list of this kind, just give *logical* values. Find a word or two that sum up the meaning of that value, and then add a brief description of it. Don't invent either coded values for the system to use (that's a design matter) or the text values to show to the user (which you shouldn't tie the system to at this early stage and which will vary in a multilingual system anyway).
	When giving a list of allowed values in a requirement, include every value you know: **never end it with "etc.,"** which is a cop-out that's likely to bite you later.
Yes or no	This is the simplest of all data types, but it's a little awkward because it's preferable not to inflict the word *boolean* on non-technical readers and there's no clear alternative. Still, it can be helpful to list the possible values in the user's terms (yes or no, true or false, male or female, member or not, on our mailing list or not), because that's how it needs to be presented to users. Also consider whether there are more than two alternative values (such as *maybe* or *don't know* or *unspecified*), which means it's a list of values rather than a boolean.
Date	This indicates the value holds an actual calendar date (such as 19th March 2012). If you want to be able to support special values (such as **"today"** or **"tomorrow"**), describe what you need (for example, whether they're solely for the convenience of users entering dates, and then manipulated and stored in the form of an actual date).
Date and time	Use this for an instant in time (such as 4:13 a.m. on 19th March 2012). If you need values to record the time as well as the date, say so. If you just say "Date," it won't include the time. **"Timestamp"** is a good word to use to indicate the current date and time at which an event happened—but add this term to your glossary first.
	See the "Endless Fun with Dates and Times" sidebar later in this pattern for more things to consider.

This table might give the impression that some of these forms are awkward to express, but when you write requirement text it's easy enough to phrase the surrounding words to make the whole description flow nicely. A few other data types that are often handled untidily are discussed in the unparochialness requirement pattern in Chapter 10, "Flexibility Requirement Patterns."

Most data types have a simple form. But a few are **compound**—that is, they comprise more than one part. Spell out compound data types in detail, especially the intricacies of how users are expected to type them in. Are separator characters needed to divide the different parts (such as dashes in a telephone number)? Conventions for separators can vary from one country to another (as discussed in the unparochialness requirement pattern). Entering a compound value in a single field can be quicker than having a field for each part (especially for power users), but using separate fields makes it easier to provide lists of allowed values and to report errors.

Check Digits

People can make mistakes when they type in values, especially numbers. One way to catch the majority of such mistakes (roughly 90 percent) is to tag on the end an extra one or two digits calculated from the number itself. These are called check digits, and if the check digit(s) entered by the user disagree with the calculation, ask the user to try again. The downside of check digits is that the user has more digits to enter (and perhaps to remember). Check digits are often used for things like customer numbers and account numbers, and if you need to introduce numbers like these, you could consider whether adding check digits would be worthwhile. But don't go overboard: use them sparingly.

For data types that include check digits (or wherever one part of the data is calculated from another), explain how the check digits are calculated. Either cite a document that describes the algorithm (you could put it in an informal part of the requirements specification and then refer to it, or put it in a separate requirement to save overloading the requirement), or describe the algorithm in the requirement itself. This pattern's examples include one for a number with check digits, which specifies its algorithm explicitly.

Consider whether your data type definition is *parochial* (that is, restricted in scope or outlook somehow). Is it tied geographically? Does it limit your system to use within only one country or state, or within one company or industry? If so, is that acceptable? Even if it is acceptable, might removing such a limitation open extra possibilities? Spell out any such limitations so that readers are aware of the possible implications. Many companies have built such a nice system for themselves that they've decided to sell it—only to find that it's a lot harder than they ever imagined, one reason being little company-specific data types that pervade the whole system. Making provision for wider use of this kind is straightforward when a system is first built, but difficult and expensive to change later, usually prohibitively so. (See the unparochialness requirement pattern for more on this subject.)

For some common data types you can find a standard that defines a suitable format (occasionally more than one acceptable format) and sometimes lists of allowed values, such as the ISO standards for currencies, countries, and languages. The comply-with-standard requirement pattern (in Chapter 5, "Fundamental Requirement Patterns") has example requirements for a few such standards. When mandating the use of a standard to define a data type, we end up with a requirement that combines the data type and comply-with-standard requirement patterns.

Endless Fun with Dates and Times

What could be more straightforward than asking a customer for their date of birth or than recording when a transaction occurred? Dealing with dates and times sounds deceptively easy and as a result various pitfalls are often ignored and fallen into later—the most notorious case being the Y2K problem, which was a failure of requirements as much as anything else. Lest we forget! Following are a few traps to avoid by specifying suitable preventive requirements. (Some of these have representative requirements in the "Extra Requirements" subsection later in this section, and some have further complications discussed in the unparochialness requirement pattern.)

1. **Time zones**   Dates and times can be held using more complex structures that contain their own time zone. This gets around any confusion but causes extra processing—introducing the need to keep converting between different time zones when displaying them and with it new opportunities for errors. Time zone issues are more important for distributed systems, especially for Web-based ones that can be accessed from anywhere in the world.

2. **Daylight saving time**   Storing any timestamp (even if it's just the date part) according to a time zone that is subject to daylight saving time is asking for trouble. Any event that occurs in the hour before the clocks go forward (assuming they go forward by an hour) might look like they happened *after* events that occurred later. Avoid this sort of unpleasantness by always, always, *always* storing timestamps according to an unchanging time zone. The standard time zone for such purposes is UTC (Universal Time Co-ordinated), effectively what used to be called Greenwich Mean Time, and what pilots call Zulu.

   The first "Extra Requirement" that follows covers this topic. But beware that even spelling out the reasons in detail (as that requirement does) may not be enough to get the message through to some nontechnical readers, who can still be worried about having times inflicted upon them according to a strange time zone, despite your reassuring them at every opportunity.

3. **Date display formats**   These vary around the world (dd/mm versus mm/dd, and so on) and need to be borne in mind if you have users in more than one place. People are usually reasonably tolerant when using a foreign system—but real problems could be caused if 3/12 is read as 3rd December when it's actually 12th March. If this is possible, add a note somewhere explaining the format used for dates. This is a matter of unparochialness.

4. **External timestamps**   Beware of timestamps that are allocated outside your system (by another system, or an unknown Web user's PC): don't trust them. If you want them, supplement them by timestamps generated by your own system. (Actually, this isn't strictly a data type matter, but this is a good place to mention it.)

5. **Full year**   Oh, and don't forget to store the *full year* for all dates. We don't want our descendents to endure a Y2100 problem. When you're storing dates in a database using its date-related data types, you should have nothing to worry about. But you might find dates stored in other places (for example, if you store copies of messages or formatted flat files, or if developers embed them in file or directory names).

Content

A data type requirement should contain

1. **Data type name**   Give this data type a unique name that reflects its business role. Make it self-explanatory yet succinct, because it's likely to be referred to frequently.

2. **Purpose**   What's this data type used for? What role does it play, in business terms? Write a separate data type requirement for each purpose, even if two or more share the same form.

3. **Form**   The sort of values the data type needs to convey. Common forms are listed above. This is used to help decide the best way to manipulate (in program code) and store (in a database) values of this type—though they are design decisions to be left for later.

4. **Display format**   For both output and input. If values of this kind need to be displayed in a particular way, describe what it is. This typically means including separators to make it easier to read (dashes in credit card numbers and phone numbers and such like). For some data types, the commonly accepted format varies from one place to another. If you want the system to accommodate such variations, explain what it needs to do. (See the unparochialness requirement pattern for more.)

   You can also describe any other aspects of input that are relevant. A common one is presenting the user with a list of values from which to choose. If the number of options is large, ask yourself if there's a better way. For example, Web sites that ask for your address often confront you with a list of all the countries in the world—which I find unfriendly. Then the valid options might depend on another value already entered. If I've already said which country I'm from, don't present me with states for another country. Use the data type requirement to indicate how smartly you want the system to handle it—but bear in mind that the user interface technology might make it difficult (plain HTML, for example).

5. **Constraints**   Limits on values—for example, they must be positive, or within a given range, or the value's *length* must be within a given range. Avoid mentioning field lengths if possible, but if you do, try to stick to *minimum lengths* that must be accommodated (such as "email addresses at least 60 characters long must be allowed"—so a system that allows more is acceptable). If your system might be used in multiple countries, be prepared to support longer values, especially for those that hold natural language text.

   Constraints can specify other restrictions on allowed values, including the detailed form of any value. For example, we might want to insist that an email address has the correct form (in accordance with RFC 2822, the standard that defines it). For complex forms like that for email addresses, it's better to refer to the relevant standard than to attempt to enumerate constraints in the data type requirement—because a requirement doesn't have room to replicate the intricacies in a standard. Merely insisting that an email address contains one "@" isn't good enough, and trying to be more precise starts you on the path of duplicating the standard.

   Constraints must be only those that apply to *all* occurrences of this data type: state constraints that apply in particular circumstances separately. For example, not allowing a savings account's balance to be negative is very different from saying that no monetary amount anywhere can be negative.

6. **Special handling**   Some data types need rules for particular ways in which they must always be treated. If so, describe what they are. For instance, a password must never be displayed and must be stored in an indecipherable form (hashed or encrypted), and a new value must be entered twice before it's accepted. A credit card number must be displayed with its last four digits hidden. Describing these kinds of special handling as part of the data type requirement saves repetition and demands that they apply systemwide.

Template(s)

Summary	Definition
«*Data type name*» data type	«*Data type name*»s, which are used for «*Data type purpose*», shall be of the form «*Data type form*». [«*Display format statement*».] [«*Constraints statement*».]
	[«*Special handling statement*».]

Example(s)

Summary	Definition
Email address length	The system shall allow email addresses at least 60 characters long.
Telephone number form	Employee telephone numbers shall be of the form: AA-LLLL-NNNN xEEEE where AA is the area code, LLLL is the locality, NNNN is the individual number, and EEEE is the extension.
Card number format	The card number of a customer membership card shall be a number of up to 16 digits, the last of which is a check digit. For a card number of the form $N_1N_2N_3N_4N_5N_6N_7N_8N_9N_{10}N_{11}N_{12}N_{13}N_{14}N_{15}C$, the check digit C shall be calculated as follows: $ODD = N_1 + N_3 + N_5 + N_7 + N_9 + N_{11} + N_{13} + N_{15}$ $EVEN = N_2 + N_4 + N_6 + N_8 + N_{10} + N_{12} + N_{14}$ $CHECK = (ODD * EVEN) + ODD + EVEN + 7$ $C = CHECK$ modulo 10 (that is, the last digit of CHECK)

Extra Requirements

Few data type requirements have a need for follow-on requirements. One situation is when you need to say something about the *context* of the data, when a data item's value alone doesn't tell you what it means. For example, for a date and time you need to know its time zone to know which moment in time it refers to. In a case like this, a follow-on requirement can nail down a context to apply systemwide—as the following example does. Note that the second paragraph is unusually detailed. This was a riposte to a nontechnical customer who wanted to insist on *not* using UTC and had difficulty understanding the trouble that could lead to.

Summary	Definition
Timestamps in UTC	All timestamps recorded by the system shall be in UTC (Universal Time Co-ordinated) **when in some form of permanent storage**. A "timestamp" is a record of the current time, as attached to transactions for the purpose of fixing when they occurred. The purpose of this is to avoid problems when switching to and from daylight saving time. (Without it, a transaction occurring just after the clocks went back will appear to have occurred before a transaction just before they went back—and, short of shutting the system down for an hour, nothing can be done to prevent any subsequent unpleasantness.) **It is worth repeating that this requirement applies only to the form in which times are *stored* (in a database and other stores). It does not apply to the display of times to users; for that, see the following requirement.**

Summary	Definition
	This requirement does not care what is the designated local time zone of the machine(s) and/or database product on which the system is run. It is simply saying that when timestamps finally hit the database, they must be according to UTC. The system is responsible for doing whatever it takes to achieve this. (In practice, it is anticipated to be a straightforward task.)

Here are a couple of other examples that define other systemwide aspects of date/time handling:

Summary	Definition
Show user times as per their time zone	Whenever a time (or date-and-time) value is shown to a user, it shall be according to the user's designated time zone.
	This requirement does not apply to
	■ Times obtained from an external source (for example, a data feed) from which the time zone cannot be discerned.
	■ Times for events that clearly occurred (or will occur) at a remote place, for which its local time zone may be used (for example, when inquiring on times of concerts in a selected city).
	In circumstances where there is no known user, the system local time zone shall be used instead of the user's time zone. (For example, this might occur when the system automatically runs reports.)
	A user's "designated time zone" is the one they have specified as a personal preference or, in the absence of that, the system's local time zone.
Time zone of time obvious	Whenever a time is displayed, its time zone shall be obvious.
	This can be achieved either by displaying the time zone as part of the time, by displaying the time zone prominently elsewhere, or by using an implied time zone (provided it is obvious). A case where an implied time zone is obvious is when displaying the times of a user's previous actions: it should be clear they're according to the user's own time zone.
	It is acceptable to display commonly used acronyms for the time zones. (Note, however, that ambiguities might exist because there is no international standard for these acronyms, not even in ISO 8601, the standard for date/time formats. As a result, these acronyms should not be used when *inputting* times.)

Observe the extent to which these requirements go into detail. This is primarily to make the need for the requirement clear to nontechnical readers, who might otherwise not appreciate the difficulties likely to result otherwise. The second reason is to limit the applicability of these requirements, because there are circumstances where they aren't appropriate. Requirements relating to the context of any data type commonly deserve to be specified in such detail.

Any data type requirement that defines the structure of a data type is in effect already a pervasive requirement, so it needs no pervasive requirements of its own. But if you're writing a requirement that defines how a particular data type is to be *displayed* in certain circumstances, consider whether it's worthwhile to add a pervasive requirement for the structure of the underlying data type itself (if no such requirement already exists).

Considerations for Development

Database designers need to consider how to store this data type in a database: what database data type is most suitable for it? A nonsimple data type may be best stored as two (or more) columns in a database table. For example, a monetary amount that comprises the value plus the currency might warrant two columns, though any entity that has multiple monetary amounts might get by with a single currency column shared by them all. The database designer should liaise with the application developers on such matters, because what best suits the database might be awkward for the application software.

Application developers need to consider how to represent this data type in software: will a built-in data type (such as an integer or string) suffice, or is a special (object-oriented) class needed? If a special class is needed, does such a class exist already, or must one be developed?

Considerations for Testing

Verifying that a system properly handles individual items of data is one of the staples of testing, and one of the most fertile test areas. Any good book on testing (for example, Ash [2003]) will cover this topic in detail. Testing needs to cover the entry, interpretation (parsing), storage, manipulation, and display of all occurrences of each data type for which requirements have been specified. Occurrences can be found in requirements for, among other things, data entities, inquiries, reports, and other user functions. Further occurrences can also crop up in the delivered system, in areas that weren't specified in detail.

Testing that a data type can be entered correctly (and that invalid values are rejected) is likely to constitute the largest number of test cases. Draw up a list of values to enter. This list should include boundary conditions (values at, near, and beyond the limits of what's acceptable) and values that might be treated by the system as special (an empty value, zero, all spaces, for example). Also test values with various kinds of formatting—for example, thousand separators and decimal point in numeric amounts, or dashes and brackets in telephone numbers.

In addition to testing what users of the system see, testers can also study everywhere that data is stored (especially databases) to verify that defined data types are held in a correct way— for example, that dates are stored with the full year, and numbers are held to the right number of decimal places.

6.2 Data Structure Requirement Pattern

Basic Details

Related patterns:	Data type
Anticipated frequency:	Fewer than 10 requirements
Pattern classifications:	Pervasive: Maybe; Affects database: Yes

Applicability

Use the data structure requirement pattern to define a compound data item (one that comprises multiple individual pieces of information) that occurs in more than one place or that contains too much to define neatly in one requirement. A requirement for a data structure is used to avoid repetition (and the consequent risk of inconsistency), both in the requirements specification and to encourage the same in the implementation.

Discussion

A data structure, as far as requirements are concerned, is a logical definition of a collection of pieces of information. It does nothing useful on its own. It defines no storage or functions. It's merely a building block that other requirements can refer to, to save them having to define this structure for themselves.

Ordinarily a data structure requirement isn't the place to specify which items of information are mandatory, which are purely optional, or more complex rules (such as "either A or B must be present"). That's because the data structure might be used in multiple places, each of which needs to apply different rules.

Content

A data structure requirement needs to contain

1. **Name**, to sum up what the data structure represents.
2. **A list of items of information**, each of which is a textual description for one of the following:
   a. **A previously defined data type**—that is, one that has already been defined using a requirement (for which the data type requirement pattern can be used).
   b. **A description of a data type**, that defines the data type itself. See the data type requirement pattern for details of what to say here. If it runs to more than two or three lines, consider splitting it off as a separate requirement.
   c. **Another data structure**, either by referring to a requirement that defines it or by defining it in situ.
   d. **A list of items**, all of the same type, each of which is one of the previous types of item.
   The sequence in which items appear in the list is not significant. For example, there is no suggestion that this is the sequence in which they would appear in a data entry screen. You might find it worthwhile stating this explicitly in the requirement. Order the items for readability, with the most prominent items first and related items grouped together.

Don't attempt to decompose data structures into smaller pieces: that's part of the design process. If you find you need to pull part of a data structure out into its own requirement to avoid having to define it more than once, or to stop a requirement getting too big, that's fine—but only do so for those reasons.

Template(s)

Summary	Definition
«*Data structure name*»	«*Data type description*» shall comprise the following items of information:
	■ «*Data item 1 description*».
	■ ...

Example(s)

Summary	Definition
Personal name details	The name details for a person shall comprise the following items of information: ■ Given name ■ Middle name(s) ■ Family name ■ Initials ■ Title
Personal contact details	The contact details for a person shall comprise the following items of information: ■ Personal name details (as defined in the previous requirement) ■ Address ■ Work telephone number ■ Home telephone number ■ Mobile telephone number ■ Fax number ■ Pager number (used for employees only) ■ Email address

Extra Requirements

None.

Considerations for Development

In an object-oriented programming language, a requirement for a data structure suggests the presence of an equivalent class.

Database designers can consider whether the structure deserves its own database table. Database designers also need to be aware that this requirement pattern permits *lists of items* to be present in a data structure—because it's a convenient way to describe them. Such structures must be normalized during the design of the database.

Considerations for Testing

A data structure cannot be tested directly, only via other requirements that refer to it. Check that all requirements that refer to a data structure are consistent with it. The system as implemented might also have additional functions not explicitly mentioned in the requirements that use a data structure. Test these functions against the data structure requirement, too.

Look for places in the system that should use the data structure but don't. For instance, are there any functions that ask for entry of values pertaining to a particular data structure but don't show all the values?

6.3 ID Requirement Pattern

Basic Details

Related patterns:	Data type, data structure
Anticipated frequency:	Between one and six requirements
Pattern classifications:	Affects database: Yes

Applicability

Use the ID pattern to define a scheme for assigning unique identifiers for some type of entity or to indicate that a data item (or combination of data items) can be used as a unique identifier.

Discussion

We give IDs to things to unambiguously identify them so that we can go directly to whatever an ID refers to. IDs also let us prevent duplicates (such as two customers with the same ID). IDs look simple, but they have a few subtle complexities. It's not good enough to say "customers shall be identified by a six-digit number"; more needs to be said.

An ID can either be added solely for the purpose of identification (such as a customer number, which tells us nothing useful about a customer per se) or it can be a piece of information that's present anyway that's suitable for identification (such as a customer's email address). Write an ID requirement for each type of ID you actually need—not for values that *could* be used as IDs but which you have no reason to.

The form of an ID can be either a **simple data type** (such as a number or name) or it can comprise **multiple parts** (for example, an order ID made up of customer number plus a sequential order number for that customer). Multipart IDs are sometimes needed to uniquely identify an entity, or they may be simply be more convenient (easier to understand, allocate or manage). Multiple ID parts can be used to extend the scope of uniqueness. For example, if we tack on our company's Web site address, we can create IDs that are unique worldwide (as email addresses are). Conversely, part of a multipart ID is unique within a smaller scope. For example, if we allocate order IDs as customer number plus a sequential number, each sequential number is unique within the scope of a single customer—and will suffice, if we confine ourselves to that scope. Audiences for IDs needn't always be aware of every part of an ID. For example, when showing order numbers to a customer, we needn't show the customer number part.

The predominant data types used for IDs (or parts of IDs) are characters (strings) and numbers. Dates and times of day come in a distant third. If you're fortunate enough to be free to choose the most suitable form for a particular type of ID, how do you decide? The key factors to weigh up are

Factor 1: Uniqueness   Containing enough information to pick out the single entity it refers to.

Factor 2: Meaningfulness   Making inherent sense to a person (for example, names), if they're going to be visible to people (and they usually are).

Factor 3: Conciseness   Needing as few characters or digits as possible.

Factor 4: Memorability   Being easy for a person to remember. Meaningfulness and conciseness contribute here.

Factor 5: Simplicity   Inflicting as few distinct parts on people as possible. This isn't the same thing as avoiding multipart IDs—as the discussion on that subject demonstrated (in the big paragraph preceding). No, it means needing to *make visible* as few parts as possible.

Factor 6: Who allocates   A person or a machine? It's easier for a person to devise a name and easier for a machine to allocate a number.

Factor 7: Connection to other IDs   Basing an ID on another ID that's already known. This is convenient when the base ID is known to the user. For example, banks don't inflict on their customers huge transaction numbers that are unique within their system. Rather, they allocate sequential numbers for each customer that are unique within the bank when tacked on to the customer ID.

Factor 8: Flexibility   Being able to handle IDs of unknown type or several different types. This might occur if we must accommodate IDs supplied by an external system or by several different external systems.

Some of these factors go hand-in-hand; others conflict with one another. In particular, the uniqueness factor tends to conflict with the others.

Content

An ID requirement should contain the following:

1. **Owner entity name**   To what are we allocating IDs of this kind? Examples might be *customer* and *employee*. In rare situations, we may want more than one type of entity to share the same ID scheme. For example, we could have transaction IDs that are used for both customer orders and defective item returns. Do this if there's a genuine business need, but avoid it otherwise.

2. **ID name**   If the owner entity has more than one ID, to clearly distinguish one from another.

3. **ID form**   Restrict an ID requirement to what's actually needed; don't make decisions about the form of IDs if you don't have to. Say what you need to achieve, and no more. One reason is that allocating IDs can have performance impact, especially if all IDs must be allocated by a single allocator (which would represent a bottleneck). Give developers the freedom to allocate IDs in the most efficient way if you can.

   For IDs that contain characters, state whether they're case-sensitive. Is "MAC" the same as "Mac"? IDs that *aren't* case-sensitive are usually better—to avoid confusion.

4. **Scope of uniqueness**   What are the bounds of the context within which an ID of this kind is unique? It's important that you give some thought to this and not make the scope of uniqueness too small, because it might make life awkward later in the life of the system. For example, if you install multiple instances of your system that all allocate sequential customer numbers and later you want to merge them all into a single database, you'll need something in addition to the customer numbers to distinguish the customers. You could include this something (perhaps a company ID or office ID) in the scope of uniqueness from the outset.

   If the scope of uniqueness isn't stated in a requirement, assume that the ID is to be unique for entities of this type within the scope of the system but not beyond it. Take note of that "of this type" qualifier, because it means we can have the same ID for different things—which is usually no problem, because they're unlikely to collide. For example, we could use "JPY" as the ID of currency details about the Japanese Yen and also as the ID of an employee with these initials. If you want to have only one entity with the ID "JPY," you must define the scope of uniqueness such that it spans every type of entity affected.

5. **How allocated**   IDs don't appear magically out of thin air, so where do you want them to come from? There are three main ways IDs can be allocated, each with its own advantages and drawbacks:

   a. **Automatically by the system.** For this way, you could describe how the system is to allocate IDs, or you could leave that as a design question. The most common approach is sequential numbers—in which case you should consider the first value (start at one?), whether it should be reset (and, if so, when), how big it must be to avoid the risk of it overflowing, and what should happen if it does overflow (it mightn't bear thinking about!).

   b. **User choice.** Let the user type in the value they'd like to use as the ID. The system must cater for them entering a value that's already used as an ID. When this happens in the case of a *user ID*, it's common practice to ask them to choose a password at the same time and to say there's a problem with either the user ID or password, so as not to alert the user if they stumble upon someone else's user ID. (It doesn't fool an alert user, though.)

   c. **From an external source, such as another system.** A value a user possesses and is asked to type in counts as from an external source (for example, a credit card number), but there is the extra risk of them entering it incorrectly. So validate it thoroughly before using it as an ID.

   There are variations that look like combinations of these ways, but they usually boil down to one of the three. For example, the system could generate a *suggested* ID and then let the user modify it, thereby boiling down to user choice. Or the system might create an ID based on the user's choice—if it's already used, say—thereby boiling down to one of the first two, depending on whether we give the user the chance to modify the ID the system created.

   Just for good measure, there are a couple of obscure ID allocation factors to keep an eye open for. First, *hidden significance*: might an ID's value reveal something you'd rather it didn't? For example, if a customer is allocated customer number 0000012, you're revealing you've done little business and the customer might trust you less. Second, *continuity*: if an old system allocates IDs in a particular way, doing it differently in a new system might have unexpected consequences, even if it functions perfectly. For example, veteran employees in some companies take pride in having a low employee number; a new system that allocates employee numbers in a different way could be resented. Your ID requirement might respond by demanding that each ID allocated must be higher than all previous IDs.

6. **Display format**   As per the data type requirement pattern. This is usually only warranted for complex ID forms, but you could use it to state, say, that numbers are to be shown with leading zeroes removed (or present, up to a specified number of digits, if you're so inclined). If an ID has multiple parts, how should it be displayed to people, to make each of the parts clear? For example, we could add separators like dashes and dots. Also consider describing how a multipart ID is to be typed in on a screen: should it be divided into multiple input fields?

7. **Sort order**   If it's different from the obvious, or if you want to prevent the development team being silly. This applies especially with multipart IDs. For example, you may want "61-001" to come before "123-001," which is likely to happen only if sorting treats the ID as two separate numbers. Avoid sort orders that aren't intuitive or that involve interpreting the meaning of any part (such as extracting the date meaning from a form like, say, "21AUG12").

When sorting on textual values, consider whether you need to worry about the sort order of characters used in languages other than yours. For example, if it's important that "é" and "ë" are sorted as if they are next to "e" (or the same as "e"), say so.

8. **Reuse conditions, if necessary**   When an entity expires, you may want to be able to reuse its ID. For example, if an employee identified by their email address "chris@ourco.com" departs, a new employee called Chris might want this email address. Avoid reusing IDs if possible, because it opens the door to ambiguity (and consequently mistakes): the new Chris might carry the can for the mistakes of the old one. But if the system must permit reuse, say so, and impose conditions to minimize the chances of the wrong entity being identified. If no reuse conditions are stated, it's reasonable to assume that IDs of this type won't be reused.

Template(s)

Summary	Definition
«*Owner entity name*» [«*ID name*»] ID	Each «*Owner entity name*» shall have a unique ID that is in the form of «*ID form*» allocated by «*How allocated*». [«*Display format*».] [Each «*ID name*» shall be unique «*Scope of uniqueness*».] [«*Sort order statement*».] [«*Reuse conditions statement*».]

Example(s)

Summary	Definition
Customer number, with check digit	Each customer shall be uniquely identified by a customer ID that is in the form of a number allocated sequentially plus a check digit calculated over that sequential number using the «*algorithm name*» algorithm (as explained at «*algorithm location*»).
Order ID	Each order shall be uniquely identified by an order ID that is in the form of the number of the customer that placed it plus an order number allocated sequentially for that customer, starting at one for the customer's first order. Order IDs shall be displayed in the form "«*Customer number*»-«*Order number*»" (for example, "10762-1").
Employee ID	Each employee shall have an employee ID that is a five-digit number allocated externally (and entered manually when an employee's details are first entered). Each employee ID shall be unique within the scope of the system; even if an employee departs, their employee ID shall not be reused for another employee.
Loan approval decision rule ID	Each loan approval decision rule shall have an ID by which it can be referred. Rule IDs shall be allocated in such a manner as to not become invalid or incorrect when another rule is added or removed. For example, a rule's sequence in a list of rules cannot be used because that will change if an extra rule is inserted before it.

Extra Requirements

An ID requirement is usually self-contained. But extra requirements might be needed for the following couple of topics:

1. Rules to be followed for every "**invisible**" ID scheme that developers choose to add. An "invisible" ID is one that is used internally by the system in order to function but that is not normally visible to users. For example, if we wanted to give customers the option of changing their customer ID, we might assign them a second, invisible customer ID that never changes. We can't demand anything for a particular ID scheme that's not itself mentioned in requirements, but we can write requirements to apply to all invisible IDs (or more widely to all IDs).

2. Continuity of IDs from a system we're replacing. If our system is taking over from a previous system, we'll have to import all its old data—including all its old IDs. Once our system goes live, it needs to take over from where the old system left off (or, at least, it must start allocating new IDs sensibly, without breaking anything). What must we do to achieve this? What pitfalls do we want to avoid? This can be a significant issue if we're replacing multiple old systems that used different ID schemes.

Here's an example pervasive requirement of the first kind, that cover *all* IDs (not just invisible IDs):

Summary	Definition
All IDs viewable	Every ID that can be used to identify an entity shall be viewable by some means, regardless of whether that ID is intended to be seen by normal users.
	The purpose of this requirement is to assist developers, testers, and auditors in examining the workings of the system.

Considerations for Development

It's possible to add extra ID schemes beyond those specified in requirements, and it's sometimes necessary. In particular, it can be useful to add "invisible" IDs that users need never see. If you use these "invisible" IDs for most processing, less reliance is placed on "visible" IDs, which makes it easier to change them. Conversely, if it **is** possible to change an ID, you're likely to need unchanging "invisible" IDs to hold everything together.

Martin Fowler's *Analysis Patterns* (1996) has an identification scheme analysis pattern.

Considerations for Testing

Test the overflow of sequentially allocated numbers. That is, contrive to reach the highest possible ID and then see what happens when you attempt to go past it.

Is it possible for unusual or special values to be used as IDs, such as zero or all spaces? If so, are they properly handled? If not, what happens if you *try* to these values as IDs?

If an ID allocated to an expired entity can later be reallocated to a different entity, scrutinize this situation closely. Do the two entities ever get mixed up? Make sure information about one isn't presented as if it belonged to the other.

6.4 Calculation Formula Requirement Pattern

Basic Details

Related patterns:	Data type
Anticipated frequency:	Between zero and a dozen requirements, depending on the nature of the system
Pattern classifications:	Pervasive: Maybe

Applicability

Use the calculation formula requirement pattern to specify how to calculate a particular kind of value, or how to determine a value via a process of logical steps.

Do not use the calculation formula requirement pattern directly for unduly complex formulae or logic. A mathematical treatise doesn't lend itself to squeezing into a set of requirements. In such cases, write a requirement that refers to an authoritative source that defines the calculations; don't attempt to duplicate such a source. Nevertheless, the calculation formula requirement pattern may still be useful in suggesting points to mention in the requirement.

Discussion

Getting calculations correct is vital, especially when they affect the revenue of a business. The way a calculation is to be performed deserves to spelled out clearly so that everyone can see and scrutinize it. It's made more important because computers don't let us observe the act of calculating and formulae embedded in software cannot be observed by nondevelopers. It's surprising, then, that critical calculations are often not mentioned anywhere in a system's documentation, leaving the business to trust that unguided developers do the right thing. That's not good enough—and it's the requirements' responsibility to see it doesn't happen.

Write a requirement for every significant calculation the system must perform. Don't be afraid to spell out even the most obvious formula—first, because no formula is so obvious that every reader can be sure to know it, and second, because it might turn out to be not so obvious after all when you sit down to specify it properly.

Formulae for calculations need to be stated precisely, or else they risk being misinterpreted and implemented incorrectly. A calculation that's *close* and *looks about right* to the naked eye is still wrong. Expose as much as possible how the system works, and what it's doing. Let users understand, and they'll be more likely to spot when something's not working properly and they'll have more faith in the system (because it becomes less of an inscrutable monster).

For convenience, this requirement pattern uses the term "calculation" to mean a formula that yields a single result value from a number of variables and "determination" to mean a list of instructional steps to follow to yield a result value. A determination step can itself contain a calculation formula.

First get your facts straight. Don't just write what you think is common sense off the top of your head, because it may be more complicated than that. Do your homework: find a reliable source that explains your formula, if you can. It might contain an unexpected twist or two. For instance, if you think calculating simple interest for a bank account is . . . well . . . simple, you need to think again, because there are subtly different alternatives (which are spelled out in the example requirements later in this section). It's not until you discover something unexpected that you even appreciate the obvious formula might be inadequate.

Be alert to possible geographic variations (for example, again, how interest is calculated), or variations from one industry to another, or from one company to another. Don't be parochial. If you intend to support only one environment (or some other subset of all possibilities), say so explicitly. Allow variations to be accommodated via configuration where possible.

Content

A calculation formula requirement should contain these items:

1. **Value description**   What is it that this formula is used to calculate?

2. **The formula itself, in the form "«*Value name*» = ..."**   Choose the name of the value carefully, because the formula constitutes a definition of this name. Make the name clear and unique within the scope of the system. Split it into more than one formula if it makes it easier to explain.

3. **Explanations of all the variables used**   For each variable state all the following that are relevant:

    a. **Variable name**. Capitalize the first letter to make it easier to distinguish in the formula. Use names consistently, especially when a value is the result of another calculation.

    b. **Origin**. Where does the variable come from? It might be the result of another calculation formula.

    c. **Data type** (if relevant). If a logical data type has already been defined for this value, refer to it. Otherwise, describe what kind of value it is (a whole number, a percentage, and so on) if it's not clear.

    d. **Allowed values or range**, if relevant. For example, if the variable is a percentage, perhaps it must be in the range 0–100%.

    e. **Number of decimal places**, if relevant.

4. **Calculation refinements**   If the result must be calculated to a particular level of precision or rounded in a particular way, say so. It's usually reasonable to assume that calculations will be performed accurately, but software finds innumerable ways to trip the unwary–so if you're worried that $2 + 2 = 4.000012$, explicitly insist on perfect accuracy.

5. **Applicability limitations**   If this formula is suitable only in certain circumstances, say what they are (for example, for use in the United States only) so that if the system is used outside these bounds, it's clear there might be problems.

6. **Reference**   Few calculation formulae used in systems are novel. Whenever possible, cite an external reference (or more than one) that explains the formula. This is important when there is a standard, law, or government or industry regulation that defines precisely must be done, especially for monetary calculations. Deviating from a prescribed way to calculate something might have unpleasant consequences.

7. **An example**   If you think it makes things clearer. Or more than one.

Split a formula into more than one requirement if a single requirement would be large and unwieldy or if a subcalculation is used in more than one formula. Note that if you're using subcalculations, the variables listed in the original requirement might not be all you need, because a subcalculation might use additional variables. For example, the interest calculation formula that follows has a "number of days" variable, but the requirement specifying it uses "start date" and "end date" (among other variables).

Pay attention to the visual formatting of the formula and variables, to make them clear and easy to read. Don't try to impress your readers by making formulae look more complex than they need to be; impress them by making the complex easy to understand.

A requirement that determines a value using a sequence of logical steps is similar to a calculation requirement in its content, but it has a *list of steps* instead of the formula and explanations of variables. Each step is an instruction on what to do, which may itself be a formula.

Template(s)

Summary	Definition
«*Value name*» calculation	«*Value description*» shall be calculated as follows: «*Value name*» = «*Formula*» where «**Variable 1 name**» is «*Variable 1 description*»; «**Variable 2 name**» is «*Variable 2 description*»; ... [«*Calculation refinements*».] [«*Applicability limitations*».] [«*Reference*».] [For example, «*Example*».]
«*Value name*» determination	«*Value description* » shall be determined as follows: 1. «*Step 1 description*». 2. «*Step 2 description*». 3. ... [«*Applicability limitations*».] [«*Reference*».] [For example, «*Example*».]

Example(s)

Summary	Definition
New deposit principal calculation	The new principal of a deposit is calculated as the old principal plus the interest accrued since interest was last paid.
Simple interest calculation	Simple interest for a period of not more than one year shall be calculated as follows: Interest = Principal * Interest rate * Period in days / Days in year * 100 where **Principal** is the monetary amount upon which interest is earned; **Interest rate** is the percentage rate applicable; **Period in days** is the number of days' worth of interest, calculated as per the next requirement; **Days in year** is the number of days in the year for which the calculation is being performed, calculated as per the next requirement but one.

Summary	Definition
Interest days determination	The number of days in a period for interest calculation shall be determined as follows:
	1. Determine the calculation's **month basis** ("30," "30 European" or "actual") as per the next requirement but two.
	2. If the month basis is "actual," calculate and use the **actual number of days** between the period's start and end dates.
	3. Let D_1, M_1 and Y_1 be the day, month and year of the start date, and D_2, M_2 and Y_2 be those of the end date.
	4. If D_1 is 31, change it to 30.
	5. If the month basis is "30 European" and D_2 is 31, change the month basis to 30.
	6. If the month basis is not "30 European" and D_2 is 31 and D_1 is 30, change D_2 to 30.
	7. Calculate the number of days as:
	$$\text{Days} = (Y_2 - Y_1) * \text{Days in year} + (M_2 - M_1) * 30 + D_2 + D_1$$
	where **Days in year** is determined as per the following requirement.
	This requirement was written with reference to *http://www.investmentz.co.in/Debtz/Glossary.htm*.
Interest days in year determination	The number of days in the year for which an interest calculation is to be made shall be determined as follows:
	1. Determine the calculation's **year basis** ("360," "365," or "actual") as per the following requirement.
	2. If the year basis is "360" or "365," use that year basis as the number of days.
	3. If the year basis is "actual" and the time period between the interest calculation start and end dates contains 29th February, use 366 days; otherwise use 365 days.
Year basis determination	The year basis to use for an interest calculation ("360," "365," or "actual") shall be determined as follows:
	1. Use the year basis specified for the combination of **banking product type** and **currency**, if present.
	2. Use the year basis specified for the currency alone, if present.
	3. As a last resort use "360."
Month basis determination	The month basis to use for an interest calculation ("30," "30 European," or "actual") shall be determined as follows:
	1. Use the month basis specified for the combination of **banking product type** and **currency**, if present.
	2. Use the month basis specified for the **currency** alone, if present.
	3. As a last resort use "30."

The complexity of these interest calculation requirements—despite the formula in the first one being so straightforward—demonstrates how complexities can lurk just beneath the surface. (That's my excuse for including such long-winded examples.)

Extra Requirements

A calculation formula requirement is usually self-contained. There are, however, two kinds of extra requirements you can add if you want to do an unusually good job:

1. **A calculation test utility**   A function that allows a formula to be tested in isolation—without crediting a customer with interest or charging them a fee—is useful for developers and testers. Include this utility in the production system, to let users play with it and so that the actual formula being used can be tested in production.

   If a variable in a formula is calculated by another formula, insist on the ability to enter all variables explicitly. That is, enter the values that come from the original business situation, not intermediate values (though it's helpful to display what any intermediate values are). For example, for an interest calculation utility, allow the start and end dates of a time period to be entered—even though the main formula uses a number of days—but display the intermediate calculated number of days, too.

2. **Justify each calculation**   The idea here is that each time a calculation formula is used, it creates a record of what it did (principally the values of the variables), so that it can be reviewed later. So few systems attempt this that it must be regarded as exotic—though it strikes me as odd that it's acceptable for such a critical aspect of systems to remain opaque and impenetrable. (Household bills, such as an electricity bill that shows "Amount charged = Unit price x Number of units," are a rare example, though even they tend to bother only when it's easy.) Perhaps tougher financial regulation of companies (such as SOX in the U.S.) might create the incentive to do this.

Considerations for Development

Develop only one implementation of each formula. Don't duplicate the code, no matter how simple the formula is. The only exception is when you need implementations in more than one programming language. For any calculation test utility you build, have it use the standard implementation of any formula it uses.

Considerations for Testing

Identify all the places where a particular calculation formula is used, and then test that in each place it is performed as promised. If you can tell that every place uses the same implementation of the formula (asking the developers is one way to find out), you need test the nitty-gritty only in one place. A calculation test utility (as just described in the "Extra Requirements" section) can be that one place; it's a convenient way to test that the formula works properly in detail. An even more convenient way is to use another utility that performs calculations using prepared test data and automatically verifies the outcomes against expected results.

Test that subcalculations (if any) or the steps in an algorithm are performed in the correct sequence.

Pick a representative set of values for each parameter in a calculation, including these: values on the limits of what's allowed (the biggest and smallest), negatives, values with different numbers of decimal places, zero. Pick another set of values that shouldn't be allowed, because they are too small or too big or for some other reason.

For each calculation you perform, work out the result you expect *before* the test. Otherwise you might be influenced unconsciously by the result you already have, and you might judge a slight flaw in the calculation as the way it should be done.

For each type of calculation, put yourself in a user's shoes. Does the system provide sufficient information for a user to be able to verify a calculation? Is all the information conveniently available in inquiries and reports? If not, is that acceptable? How would an auditor react if they are unable to prove the system is behaving as it should?

6.5 Data Longevity Requirement Pattern

Basic Details

Related patterns:	Data archiving, comply-with-standard
Anticipated frequency:	Rarely more than two or three requirements; in many systems, none at all
Pattern classifications:	Affects database: Yes

Applicability

Use the data longevity requirement pattern to specify for how long a certain type of information must be retained or for how long it must be available with a given degree of ease.

Discussion

Data longevity requirements are often needed to satisfy legal obligations, accounting rules, or other regulatory demands. For example, a company is normally obliged to keep financial records for a certain number of years. There are two ways of approaching data longevity requirements: either do what the customer tells you, or take a systematic look at the whole system. Doing what you're told is easy, and writing a longevity requirement is straightforward enough and usually arises from a clear need. Looking at the whole system isn't hard either but involves a bit more thought.

Data longevity has three distinct variants. The first covers how long data must **remain online**, the second how long it is to be **stored somewhere**, the third how long it is to be **stored offline**. In this context, *online* means stored in the main system (typically in its database) and directly accessible by it, and *offline* means stored somewhere else, such as on a backup tape. Although these three variants look almost identical, the first and third are very different in implementation and the second is a mixture of the other two. Use the third option only if you have a clear need for it; otherwise use the second option.

Requirements that determine when data can be deleted are rare, which is rather odd when you think about it. The result is that the timing of data disappearing is driven by technology (how much space is available, and what the database lets you do—for example, by enforcing referential integrity) and by developers' choices. Technical rather than business considerations reign, which is not ideal. A few other requirement patterns make their own suggestions, as piecemeal contributions in their own areas. Here are a couple of default rules for which requirements could be written:

1. Retain all transactions online for a stated length of time (90 days?) after each transaction's latest date.

2. All data must be retained offline for an *indefinite* period. Never throw anything away. (Why would you? Well, except if you've got something to hide, and we'll naively assume you haven't.)

Online longevity steadily shrinks in importance as disk capacity steadily grows and becomes cheaper. For some systems this is balanced by exploding ambition, most prevalently by launching on the Web to sell to the world. Online longevity requirements retain usefulness as an expression of for how long data is wanted, even as it loses its practical importance with the ability to retain data for far longer. Retaining all data online indefinitely is an option worthy of serious consideration. (It happens by default in many places because no one's thought of going to the trouble of deleting unwanted data.)

Content

A requirement that defines data longevity should specify

1. **The data it relates to**   This may be a narrow type of data or a broad category. Either way, make it clear what the requirement applies to.

2. **The manner of storage**   How must the data be stored, or how conveniently must it be available, until it is eligible to be removed? Normally, this should be expressed only in general terms, such as "online."

3. **The length of time to retain the data**   After how long does it become acceptable to remove (or lose) the data? "Indefinitely" is a valid option.

4. **The duration start trigger**   When does the clock start? What is the length of time measured from? It's usually from a date associated with the item itself, such as the date it was deleted. For a transaction, it might be the date it occurred.

5. **The action at deadline**   For online longevity, be clear about what is to happen when an item of data reaches its time limit. This affects the implementation approach to take. The common options are as follows:

    a. **It can be retained for longer ad nauseam**. That is, the requirement merely specifies a minimum, and it's perfectly acceptable to keep it for longer—or much longer, or forever.

    b. **It can be retained for a moderate extra period**—perhaps the end of the day in question or the end of the month.

    c. **Once it reaches its time limit, it must become invisible** to at least some users (for example, customers). It can be physically removed later.

    d. **It must be promptly removed** at the deadline.

    When deciding, aim to avoid users perceiving the system's behavior as arbitrary. If old transactions are sometimes gone in a day but other times stay around for a week, users are liable to become confused and lose a little faith in the system. Users are more contented if they understand what's happening.

    If data is to be copied elsewhere before removing it, use the data archiving requirement pattern to specify the copying activity.

6. **Purpose**   Why do we want to keep this information for this length of time? Data longevity is sometimes mandated by law, industry practice, or company policy. If so, cite that source and identify where it can be found (its location) in the manner described in the comply-with-standard requirement pattern.

Template(s)

Summary	Definition
Store «*Data description*» «*Storage form*» for «*Duration*»	«*Data description*» shall be stored «*Manner of storage*» for «*Retention duration*» from «*Duration start trigger*». [When data is eligible for removal, «*Action at deadline*».]
	«*Storage purpose*».

Example(s)

Summary	Definition
Store orders for 90 days online	Customer orders shall be retained online for 90 days from the date the order was shipped.
	Orders shall not be visible to customers after this date, but they may continue to be stored online.
	The purpose of this is so the details of an order are easily available in the event of a problem with delivery.
Store transactions for 12 months	All transactions shall be retained for at least 12 months.
Seven years' financial data	Financial data shall be retained for at least seven years (for legal reasons).
	For the purpose of this requirement, financial data is any information that pertains to the payment of money from one organization or person to another, or an obligation to pay money, including all information needed to calculate or otherwise justify such an amount of money.
	(Storing tape or other offline backups of the relevant data is deemed to satisfy this requirement.)

Extra Requirements

None.

Considerations for Development

A data longevity requirement simply states for how long a particular class of data must be retained. Developers are at liberty to archive it (as per the data archiving requirement pattern), even if no data archiving requirement has been written.

Considerations for Testing

Because data longevity periods tend to be long (often years), you won't be able to wait for test data to grow that old. Two ways round this are

1. Keep changing the system's clock so that you can simulate time passing very quickly. This is liable to annoy anyone else who's using the system or the machine(s) it's running on, so this kind of testing might need a dedicated system to itself.

2. Devise a way to created back-dated data. This means the data is somewhat artificial, so check carefully that the tests adequate mirror real "old" data. You also need to take care that whatever means are used to create back-dated data are not available in the production system.

Test whether it's possible to delete an item of data prior to the date until which the system is obliged to retain it.

Create data items that are eligible to be deleted on a range of dates, including all likely boundary conditions: the first and last days of several months, the first and last days of several years, the February 29th on a leap year, weekend days, public holidays, days on which the system wasn't running. Then check whether each item of data is deleted when it should have been.

6.6 Data Archiving Requirement Pattern

Basic Details

Related patterns:	Data longevity
Anticipated frequency:	Zero to three requirements, rarely more
Pattern classifications:	Affects database: Yes

Applicability

Use the data archiving requirement pattern to specify the moving or copying of data from one place of permanent storage to another.

Do not use the data archiving requirement pattern to specify the regular *backing up* of a database. It's reasonable to assume that whatever database product is being used supports the regular backing up of its data (and restoring it in the event of trouble). If you want requirements to this effect, specify them for the information storage (that is, database) infrastructure. (See the "Information Storage Infrastructure" section in Chapter 7, "Data Entity Requirement Patterns.")

Discussion

Archiving is one of those Information Technology terms that's uncomfortably vague, with tattered boundaries. Many people have different interpretations of it. Here's a definition of its meaning in this book:

Archiving: The moving or copying of a body of data from one medium of permanent storage to another. A "body of data" archived can be any subset of the available data. The backing up of a whole database is expressly excluded: it is not archiving.

This is, like many definitions, rather stark and cold. It's expressed in narrow functional terms—not technical, exactly, but neither does it hint at what business purposes archiving might serve. So for what might we want to use it? Archiving is commonly used for the following purposes (and possibly more than one simultaneously):

1. **Historic**, to create an offline record of data that's due to be deleted because it's no longer needed in the online system.

2. **Performance**, by minimizing the quantity of data to be searched and processed and by allowing data to be duplicated somewhere else so that heavy work on one copy doesn't affect the performance of another.

3. **Noninterference**, to create a copy of data that can be worked on and mucked around with without affecting the original data.

4. **Security**, because it's impossible to improperly access information that's no longer present.

More obscure uses for archiving include

5. **Proof of existence**, so that we can prove that certain data was present at the time an archive copy was made.

6. **Expiry of permission**, if the data belongs to someone else and our authority to continue using it has ended. This might occur if the data is associated with a third-party product or belongs to a company on whose behalf we have been doing processing but no longer.

Sometimes the benefits of using data archiving don't reveal themselves until the system's being designed, which is fine. So it's not always necessary for the requirements to specify data archiving, even if the system ends up using it. Write a data archiving requirement if you have a specific need. It's worth pointing out that this requirement pattern delves into technical matters more than we like to in requirements, but it's important to understand the implications of what we specify because they can profoundly affect the nature of the whole system. This is especially true of the "Extra Requirements" section, which deals with some of those implications.

A straightforward commercial system could have a database that will happily store all the data it ever accumulates in its lifetime and whose data conveniently stays in the same place all the time. Such a system might have no need for data archiving. Also, disk space is so plentiful and machines so powerful that the need to delete unwanted data has all but disappeared in many organizations, to the extent that the thought of doing so is alien to many developers. The cost of building software to purge data becomes harder to justify (but, surely, it's still the right thing to do!).

Data Archiving Model

Data archiving requirements are good at elucidating the details of all the kinds of archiving a system needs, but they can be made clearer by painting an overall picture of what's going on: what data goes from where to where? A relatively simple diagram like this one does the job:

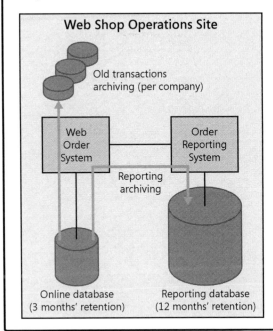

It can help us decide what archiving is needed and help us spot omissions. As such it deserves to be treated with respect, which is more likely if we give it a fancy name: a **data archiving model**. In most systems, data is usually in the right place at the right time, but only data administrators know the whys and wherefores of the copying and movement of data. That's not good enough—everyone, especially testers and auditors, should be able to tell what's going on.

Use whatever format best suits what you have to say. This diagram uses a cylinder for all permanent storage, so it doesn't influence the choice of storage media—but it uses cylinder size to suggest relative quantities of data. Supplement the diagram with textual explanations if it'll make it clearer.

Avoid mentioning specific technology in a data archiving requirement, as far as possible. If you can, leave it up to the development team to pick the most suitable storage media and products. But place whatever realistic demands you wish upon the *characteristics* of the storage medium, such as the ease of reading it or use of nonproprietary formats. Ordinarily data is archived to machine-readable media, but it needn't be. Purely human-readable media is sometimes acceptable, and there are circumstances where it is preferable. Reports printed on paper are harder to tamper with undetectably than most digital media (unless you go to the trouble of using digital signatures and the like), and they can be read with no technology at all. Filing away piles of paper may seem old-fashioned, but it has its merits. Then there are intermediate technologies such as microfiche, which require low-tech readers but surely have more chance than a digital medium of being readable fifty years hence. (I can't help but reflect that our digital era will leave to posterity fewer enduring artifacts than the books and scrolls and tablets of earlier ages.)

Data archiving is often neglected, both in specifications and in systems themselves, partly because it's not prominently visible and partly because most archiving is unimportant when a system is new. It takes time for data to grow old. It's usually quite legitimate (and not detrimental) to give archiving-related requirements a relatively low priority and not to worry about them in initial versions of a system. The building of systems is dominated by short-term priorities: everyone wants to get their hands on a new system and start using at quickly as possible. Data archiving is all about the long term, which is why it's put on the back burner and why functions for manipulating very old data are all but unheard of in normal systems.

Content

A data archiving requirement should contain the following:

1. **Data description**   What information is to be moved or copied? State as clearly as possible the criteria for selecting the data. It may be narrow (one type—from a single database table, say) or broad (many types); it may involve a small quantity of data (possibly none at all, sometimes) or lots. The nature and quantity of data to archive can have a major bearing on the implementation (and type of storage media), but the requirement need not concern itself with that.

2. **Move or copy?**   Is the original data to be left where it is, or is to be removed? The word "move" implies that the original data is deleted, but you might want to say so explicitly, to forestall misunderstandings.

3. **Origin**   Where does the data being moved or copied originally reside? It is most commonly a database.

4. **Destination**   Where is the data to be moved or copied to? It might be an offline medium or another database. Keep an open mind about the storage medium, as far as possible.

In most cases, archiving involves one origin and one destination, but it can be more complex. Data in one place could be split up and saved separately, especially if it is segregated (as described in the multiness requirement pattern in Chapter 10)—for example, to create an archive tape for each company in a multicompany system.

Conversely, data from several places could be loaded into a single destination—for example, if we have a consolidated reporting database into which is placed data archived from several other systems. A situation like this involves various other complications, so properly analyze it and specify additional requirements as appropriate.

5. **Frequency**   How often should the archiving be done? This might also encompass at what time of day, though try to express this in terms of *intention* rather than a specific time of day (for example, on the first day of each month, in the wee small hours when system activity is at its lowest). Frequencies can vary enormously—from once a year to every few seconds— which has a huge bearing on the nature of the implementation. If the archiving is manually initiated, the frequency is indicative only—to assist the devising of operational procedures.

6. **Initiator**   What starts the archiving process? Should it run automatically, or only when a person requests it? Or doesn't it matter (as far as the requirement is concerned)?

7. **Purpose**   Why is this data being archived? It might be because it is no longer needed online, to improve performance, or for any of the other reasons listed above.

One further item might be needed in rare circumstances, but avoid it if possible:

8. **Archive format**   Say as little as you need to, and be as nonspecific as you can. Stating the archive format might be necessary if you're producing archives to be read by another system or to satisfy some external standard. It's possible to offer multiple archiving formats (perhaps pluggably, as per the extendability requirement pattern, also in Chapter 10).

Template(s)

Summary	Definition
«Data summary» archiving	*«Data description»* shall be [moved]/[copied] from *«Data origin»* to *«Data destination»* *«Frequency»*. *«Initiator description»*.
	[The purpose of this is to *«Archiving purpose»*.]

Example(s)

Summary	Definition
Customer order archiving	Customer orders and all details pertaining to each order shall be eligible to be moved to an offline storage medium a configurable number of days (expected to be of the order of 90 days) after the whole order has been fulfilled, and actually moved the next time the order archiving process is run thereafter. The resulting offline storage media shall be retained indefinitely.
	This requirement makes no judgment about how the order archiving process is to be initiated; it may be manual or automatic.
	The purpose of this is to reduce the quantity of transactional data in the online system (to assist performance) and to reduce the adverse impact of unauthorized access to the online data.

Summary	Definition
Reporting database archiving	All changes in the data in the Web order system (including new data) shall be archived to the order reporting system. This archiving shall be performed sufficiently frequently that any update to the Web order database shall reach the order reporting database within 60 minutes.
	The purpose of this is to keep the contents of the order reporting database reasonably up-to-date.
Whole company archiving	It shall be possible to create an offline archive of all data belonging to a nominated company.
	The purpose of this is to allow a company to obtain a copy of its data, particularly if it wants to end its participation in the services run by the system.
Customer statement archiving	For every printed statement sent to a customer, another printed copy shall be produced for archiving purposes. A statement for archiving shall be produced within one lapsed month from the printing of the original statement, and it must contain the same information as the original.
	All statements printed at one time shall be sorted by customer number. If more than one statement is printed for one customer, they shall be in statement number sequence.
	This is for legal reasons: to be able to defend the content of any statement disputed by a customer.

Extra Requirements

A data archiving requirement might deserve extra requirements for some of the following things:

1. **Keep track of archives.** Cabinets full of offline media aren't much use if you can't tell what each one contains. How do you know what data you have stored offline in archives? What data is stored where? How do you find what you want? Being able to answer these questions demands "indexes" of the archives' contents, which can either be stored on the archive media themselves or in the main system. The latter makes it easier to locate what you want. The level of detail needed in the "indexes" depends on how easily you want to be able to find specific items of data. They could, for example, go so far as to record which archives contain data for which customers. Some archives are simple enough in their content to be managed manually (or by using a spreadsheet).

2. **View archived data.** Archived data is of no use unless you can access it. How are we going to look at what's in our archives? This is described further in the "Viewing Archived Data" subsection later in this section.

3. **Reload archived data.** One way to view archived data is to load it back into the original system and use the normal functions it has for viewing—or doing other things with—data of this kind. See the "Reloading Archived Data" subsection for more.

4. **Allow rearchiving.** If you're serious about keeping your archived data in a usable form, you should be able to transfer an offline copy to another offline medium. Most media degrade over time. And most eventually become obsolete, so you need to copy data stored on it before

you dump the last device capable of reading it (such as your last big reel tape reader or your last eight-inch diskette drive).

5. **Deal with unreliable archiving.**   An archive process can be unreliable if the destination is remote from the origin (that is, dependent on unreliable communications) or if the destination media has inadequate capacity (or it asks you to load an extra medium, and you don't have one). When moving data, it should not be removed from the source until it has definitely been stored at the destination—and it's reasonable for any data archiving requirement to assume this implicitly. A "move" could separate the copy and the remove stages, with the remove being conditioned on acknowledgment that the copy succeeded (or for there to be a delay to give time to take another copy if the first failed). Acceptance of the copy might demand more than merely that it was produced successfully; it could also include successful delivery to its recipient. It could also involve creating more than one copy.

6. **Allow access control.**   Once data is placed on an offline medium, the system's own access control mechanisms cease to protect it. (Also recognize that anyone capable of creating offline media might be able thereby to gain access to data they otherwise couldn't.) Data can be protected by encrypting it, but this raises its own headaches of tools for accessing it, management of encryption keys, and so on, which is too much for this requirement pattern to cope with. You must work this out for yourself.

7. **Prevent *copies* of data being modified.**   If we're archiving data *into* a database, we may want to prevent the software that uses it there (which might be the main system's software) from modifying it, if we want it to be purely a faithful copy of the original data. In that case, write requirements to this effect.

8. **Take over an old system's archives.**   If we're replacing an old system, are we taking responsibility for the data archives it produced during its life? Does that mean the new system must be able to access these archives? If so, write requirements specifying what we want. One option is to write a utility to convert the old archives into a format used by the new system (a kind of rearchiving, as described above). This achieves the goal without necessarily involving the main new system.

These features are remarkably rare in commercial systems. The reasons aren't hard to find: they're unsexy, infrequently used, obscure, hard to implement, and unimportant while the system is young—in short, too much work for too little return. Then, because systems tend not to have them, no one expects them. Nevertheless, a system that has gaps in its functionality as a result can't be regarded well-rounded and complete. And perhaps their omission contributes in a tiny way to dissatisfaction with a system and with systems in general.

Viewing Archived Data   There are several possible approaches to take to viewing archived data:

1. **Reload the data into the main system**, which will already have a wide range of familiar functions for viewing it. This is the subject of the next subsection, "Restoring Archived Data."

2. **Store the data in an easily viewable format** so that commonly available software can view it (a Web browser, or a plain text editor). There can be a trade-off here between convenient viewing by a person and convenient reading by a machine. Decide which is more important. For example, we could archive data as HTML pages to be easily viewable (but more problematical for a machine to extract the raw data), or we could use a more formal structure that suits a machine but is harder for a person to read.

There is scope for more creative answers to this dilemma, but to express one in requirements without it sounding like a solution (without mentioning specific technology, say), you must be nippy on your feet. A good basis for an answer is to store the data in a properly structured format and to write a definition of a way to transform it into a human-readable form. (For example, XML could be the structured format and an XSLT style sheet the definition—to facilitate converting it to HTML.) It's good practice to store any auxiliary definitions on the archive medium, too, so that it becomes self-sufficient.

3. **Write special software to view the archive**. This might sound over the top, but you might encounter circumstances where it's appropriate—for example, if the archive must be viewable by an external party to whom you can't or don't want to provide the main system's software. Also consider the platform(s) on which this software is to run: make it as widely usable as possible. Again, for self-sufficiency, place the software on the archive medium itself if there's room for it.

Functions for viewing archived data can usually be treated as low priority: to be built after the mad scramble to get the main system working is over. After all, they're of no use until our data begins to age, unless our system has taken responsibility for old data belonging to an earlier system it replaces. The danger here is that these functions will be forgotten about and never built: more pressing demands on resources will keep coming along. (Strictly speaking, you could forget about archive access functions altogether until you need them—if the chances of actually using them are low. This might be a valid attitude if archives are there only as a last resort—for instance, in case your company is sued.)

Information outlives the system that stores it. What happens to requirements for viewing archives once the system shuffles off its mortal coil? Should they not continue in effect? This is an interesting philosophical issue. When specifying a system, there is a tendency to see it as being born into a pristine new world and being able to live for ever. This ignores its responsibility to take ownership of any system(s) it replaces or to make it easier to hand over information to any system that comes afterwards. The latter may seem an awfully long way off, but a system is properly specified only once and that might be the only opportunity to think about it.

Reloading Archived Data   Accessing archived data by loading it back into the original system sounds like the obvious thing to do, but it's fraught with practical problems, so don't ask for it unless you know what you're doing (and you're aware how much trouble you might be causing). In short, reloading old data can confuse a system. It will probably want to archive it off again (delete it!) at the first opportunity, and it might interfere with other functions (such as statistics). One way around some of these difficulties is to load the data into a separate database, distinct from the main database, which might or might not be looked after by the main system.

Another cause of trouble for reloading archives is changes in the structure of the database during the system's life. For instance, data to be reloaded might be missing values for columns that have been added subsequently. The software for reloading must be able to cope with these inconsistencies, which, unless you're careful, might mean having to enhance it whenever the structure of the database is changed. If you want your archives to be reloadable even if the database is modified, say so in the requirements—though it may involve significant ongoing effort to achieve it. This is perhaps another argument against reloading archives back into the original system as a means to view it.

Here are a couple of requirements related to restoring archived data:

Summary	Definition
Restore offline transactions	It shall be possible to restore selected transactions from offline storage to online storage in a convenient manner. "In a convenient manner" means that the number of offline media (for example, tapes) that must be loaded must be small. For example, having to load a daily tape for each day of the two-year life of a customer in order to restore that customer's history is **not** considered convenient.
	Criteria for selecting the transactional data to restore must include:
	■ For a given customer ID, and date range (with all activity back to the customer's registration being a special option).
	■ For a given company ID, and date/time range.
No inquiries load from offline storage	No inquiry shall directly request the loading of data from any offline storage medium.
	The purpose of this requirement is to prevent casual use of any inquiry from asking for the manual intervention that loading an offline medium is likely to involve.

Considerations for Development

The "Extra Requirements" section touches upon many technical considerations, more so than is normal in a requirement pattern.

Consider the format in which to store offline data. Keep it as open and accessible as possible, not tied to any particular storage product, in case you (or whoever accesses it) don't have that product at the time (perhaps because it's no longer available by then). Consider flat files in some generic format, such as XML, perhaps with an XSLT style sheet included, to make the data self-displaying by suitable software.

Considerations for Testing

The testing of archiving can vary considerably, depending on the nature and format of the destination and the frequency of archiving. You might need to simulate a relatively long time period before the system is due to archive any data at all. (See the data longevity requirement pattern earlier in this chapter for a couple of suggested ways.)

It's impractical to test retrieval of old data following upgrades to the system that affect the structure of data until such an upgrade occurs. Then you can have some fun! Get hold of some data stored offline, and attempt to reload it. If you don't have access to data from a live system, you need some forethought. Create some offline data during earlier testing, and store long-term the test archives you create for each version of the system.

If you're allowed to reload data from an archive into the main system, do so. Test whether the system deletes the reloaded data at the first opportunity. This can be irritating if whoever reloaded the data hasn't had the chance to look at it. If it's unclear (unspecified) how the system should behave in this situation, decide whether you think what it actually does seems sensible.

Chapter 7
Data Entity Requirement Patterns

In this chapter:

7.1 Living Entity Requirement Pattern. 129
7.2 Transaction Requirement Pattern. 133
7.3 Configuration Requirement Pattern 138
7.4 Chronicle Requirement Pattern 144
7.5 Information Storage Infrastructure 154

Builders of systems tend to take a cavalier and ad hoc attitude to information: we lack rules for when data can be deleted; we're relaxed about losing data; we permit data to be modified without retaining a record of what it was before; we don't know who did what; we can't tell how amounts were calculated. It's hardly surprising that so many systems handle data in a sloppy and messy manner. This chapter aims to impose some order and consistency, by introducing a scheme for dividing all data entities into fixed categories that share many important characteristics. It then presents a requirement patterns for the most important categories of data entity, namely **living entity**, **transaction**, **configuration**, and **chronicle**, and suggests demands to make on all entities in each category. These categories are shown in Figure 7-1.

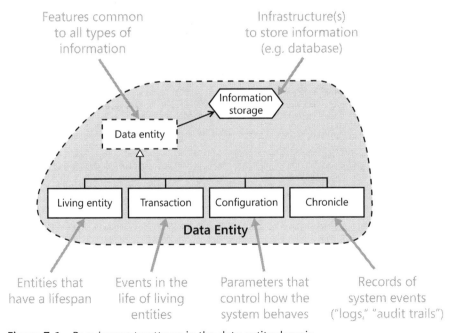

Figure 7-1   Requirement patterns in the data entity domain

To satisfy information-related requirements, a system needs a supporting infrastructure for **information storage**, to store information persistently (most commonly in a database); sometimes it needs more than one. The requirement patterns in this chapter are organized and written with a view to using a database as the main storage mechanism, which is true for almost all business systems. These patterns do, however, work perfectly well for data stored in flat files and more specialized repositories (for example, electronic directories for finding addresses, such as those adhering to LDAP, the Lightweight Directory Access Protocol). A database provides all the operations we need to store and retrieve our data. But these operations are at too low a level to relate meaningfully to requirements. We need a stepping-stone to help bridge the gap. This chapter divides a typical business system's data into *seven key categories*—according to the ways in which that data should be handled. We can then define, for each category, rules that apply to all data in that category (via pervasive extra requirements), to save having to worry about such matters for each individual type of data. In a typical business system, we find the following categories of data:

Name	Summary	In requirements?
Living entity	**An entity that has a lifespan**. It is created, might be modified a few times, and is eventually terminated. Examples are a shop customer and a bank account.	Yes
	Any entity that is for configuration purposes is categorized as configuration rather than as a living entity. (See the configuration category that follows.)	
Transaction	**An event in the life of a living entity**. In a commercial system, most transactions have a financial impact of one kind or another. Examples are a purchase from a shop, a bank account withdrawal, and a magazine subscription renewal.	Yes
Configuration	**Parameters that control how the system behaves**. Examples are sales tax rates and bank account types. It's reasonable to assume that anything not explicitly required to be configurable won't be, in which case, every change in behavior means a change to software.	Yes
	Any item of configuration of which there can be more than one (such as account types, or currencies) has a lifespan just like a living entity. The easiest way to distinguish between configuration and living entities is to imagine the organization has yet to open for business for the first time: anything that can be set up at that time is configuration (for example, account types and products); anything that can't is a living entity (for example, customers and their accounts).	

Name	Summary	In requirements?
Chronicle	**A record of some event that happened.** Examples are: an error, a record that some system process ran, a change to a living entity, and approval by a manager of a large withdrawal from bank account. Records of this sort are often called "audit trails" or "logs," but we avoid the first term because many people associate it just with financial transactions, and the second because it conjures up specific solutions (such as using a single log as a dumping ground for everything, and storage in flat files).	**Yes**
Derived	**Data computed from the other kinds of data.** Examples are daily order totals and total balances for each account type. Derived data can be identified by asking the question, "If I lost it, would I be able to regenerate it from the other data available?" In theory, you can regenerate all derived data from the data it is based on, though in practice, it demands a sound database design (so there's some risk).	Usually not
Administrative	**Data used to keep the system running smoothly.** Examples are the time that month-end processing was last performed and counters such as the last-used customer number. Administrative data is either global or associated with a living entity (such as a customer's last order number). Data of this sort results from design decisions, so it doesn't appear in requirements.	Usually not
Historic	**Old, inactive data that no longer affects current business,** but needs to be retained for legal or future investigative reasons. The *structure* of historic data is dictated by the original data, which is why requirements are not needed to define it.	Usually not

Each type of information is placed in one (and only one) of these categories, each of which has been chosen to recognize the special characteristics the information has. We can then define requirements to enforce rules for the sound handling of each category. Potential requirements are discussed in the requirement patterns in this chapter. Don't worry if one or two of the category names look rather abstract: you needn't expose readers of requirements specifications to them.

In the preceding table, the **In requirements** column indicates whether requirements are needed for that category of data. Not all data in a database is visible or of direct use to users; some is intermediate "massaged" data, is there to improve performance, or helps in other ways to keep the system running smoothly. Structures for this sort of data are created during the design of the database and don't appear at the requirements stage. Only data of direct interest to users is reflected in requirements (indicated by a **Yes** in the table), and only those categories of data have had requirement patterns written for them. Data entities for which **Usually not** is shown don't result directly from requirements, but there could be a requirement or two that refers obliquely to or implies the presence of such data. Also "Usually not" is preferred to "No" because it would be rash to say that there will *never* be requirements for these categories of data.

Each entity, regardless of its category, needs a name. Make it concise, unique, and descriptive— describing the kind of thing it stores. A useful convention is to express each one in the singular (so "customer," not "customer**s**"). Avoid vague collective terms, such as "inventory," that don't tell you what that entity contains.

Extra Requirements

Requirements for specific sorts of information define both the data needed to operate the business and any associated functionality. But there are several areas, common to all types of information, for which extra requirements are sometimes appropriate or for which it is worthwhile to specify supporting functionality once rather than each time. Some areas to consider are:

1. **Information integrity, including database back-ups and restore/recovery**   It can be dangerous to assume that all your information will magically always be there for you, intact, pristine, and available. Some judicious extra requirements can proclaim a few things that we should be able to rely on—partly for insurance and partly to remind the developers of pitfalls to avoid.

2. **Multi-part information entry**   Any function that involves entry of information in multiple parts (that is, split over multiple screens) needs to be able to handle failure partway through. The simplest way is to record nothing (or act as if nothing has been recorded) until everything has been entered—but expect users to find this frustrating, because they then have to rekey the first information if the user exits partway through. However, if information is stored after each screen is entered, the system should provide a way for the user to pick up where they left off—which can be complicated and cumbersome to implement (so it costs more).

3. **Co-ordination of multiple data stores**   If your system interacts with another system, and both store data, trouble could result when one of them fails: their data could be inconsistent. This is a technical matter, but point it out so it won't be forgotten, and think through possible problems (which might be significant) and how to deal with them—such as special corrective software, for which we'd need requirements.

4. **Timed and co-ordinated changes**   Sometimes, changes to information in a system need to be made at a precise moment in time (such as a change in a tax rate at midnight on a specific date, mandated in legislation). Sometimes a collection of changes needs to be made at the same time (such as a revamping of a shop's pricing and discounting). Special provision must be made if you want these sorts of changes to be made while the system is available to users, with minimal risk of human error.

5. **Approval of actions**   A user of a computer system usually goes ahead and does what they want, but a business sometimes wants some actions approved by a second person before those actions take effect. See the approval requirement pattern in Chapter 11, "Access Control Requirement Patterns."

    Areas 4 and 5 have aspects in common, especially if your system ends up having a general mechanism for storing changes before applying them (which is discussed in the "Considerations for Development" section of the approval requirement pattern).

6. **Inquiries**   When you're specifying a particular type of information (or a function for entering it) is a good time to ask yourself who will want to look at this information and why. For each function for entering information, there should be at least one function to view it–at the very least to let the user see whether what they entered was actually recorded, in the event of a system failure.

The subsections that follow deal with each of these areas in turn–except Areas 5 and 6, which are covered in the approval requirement pattern in Chapter 11 and the inquiry requirement pattern in Chapter 8, "User Interface Requirement Patterns." Areas 1 and 6 are likely to be relevant in all commercial systems; ask yourself whether the other areas apply to your system.

Information Integrity, Including Database Back-Ups and Restore/Recovery   First of all, what do we mean by "information integrity"? It can be summed up by the **ACID** properties possessed by any reliable database, which are: **atomic**–any change is made either completely or not at all; **consistent**–whichever way you look at the data, you get the same picture; **isolated**–no change is affected by any other change that's in progress but not yet completed; and **durable**–any completed change stays there. **Backing up** the information can be regarded as providing durability even when a storage disk is lost. **Restoring** is the act of copying from a back-up when the main data is lost, and then **recovery** is the act of bringing the restored data up to date using an **update log** of changes made since the back-up was taken.

Strictly speaking, if we want information integrity at all, we should define requirements for it. But if we're storing our data in a proper database, it's reasonable to assume that it will take good care of our data and guarantee its integrity. (If you're not happy with that, then by all means specify requirements you expect your database product to satisfy.) This isn't true for other places where information is stored: flat files provide no protection against data loss, for example. Developers like using flat files for such things as configuration parameters and imported/exported data, and they often forget about the integrity of this data–so it's a good idea to add a requirement to demand the integrity of **all** data, and emphasize that this includes flat files. Such a requirement can also demand (implicitly or explicitly) that any online directory (such as LDAP) or similar product that you use must store its data in a proper database.

You could draw up a list of all the types of information in your system (taking a broad interpretation of "information" for this purpose), including:

1. Web pages, including page templates (such as JSP or ASP pages), style sheets, and help pages.

2. Images, sounds, and other multimedia resources.

3. All flat files referenced by the system, especially configuration files. Don't forget files that belong to third party products (since they are indirectly part of your system). Including files used by the operating system is perhaps going too far.

4. Emails and any other types of electronic messages sent and received, including attachments.

5. Document templates (such as for letters generated using a mail merge facility).

6. Data recorded by sensors.

Then go through the list asking what would happen if you lost the disk on which those files live. Bear in mind that even if you have back-up copies of these files, you will lose all changes made since the last back-up copy. If some of the possibilities scare you, take steps to protect against them–for which you need to define some requirements. The more of this information you can store in a database, the better.

Here are some suggested pervasive requirements for this area. The first one is uncompromising, and is impractical for some systems and over-the-top for others. The second one is a gentler alternative—but its laxness still means that a disk failure could leave an unpleasant mess (though you will at least know how big a mess). It's possible to specify a compromise in between these two.

Summary	Definition
All information in database	All information updated by any mainstream function in the system shall be stored in a core database.
	The intent of this requirement is to ban the use of flat files to store information needed for the smooth running of the system. But it by no means limits its scope to flat files. It also mandates that any data in, say, an LDAP directory must use a database as its data store (or that its data be stored in a database *as well*).
	For any information stored both in a core database *and* in some other place, the database shall be regarded as the primary store.
	For the purposes of this requirement:
	■ A **mainstream function in the system** is any function needed to satisfy any business requirement (including those used by a user and automated functions). Low-level configuration activities that *must* store data outside core databases for technical reasons (such as configuration files used by the operating system or third party products) are excluded.
	■ A **core database** is one that is backed up regularly, for which transaction logs are stored on separate disks, and for which recovery procedures are in place.
	The prime motivation for this requirement is to avoid data loss when a disk is lost. Data stored in a core database is recoverable in such a situation; data stored in flat files is not.
	A secondary motivation is security: databases offer several degrees of protection (access control, protection against tampering, and logging of changes).
Record changes to information outside database	Whenever a change is made to information that is stored outside a database, the fact of the change shall be recorded in a database.
	The intent of this requirement is that in the event of the loss of a disk, we will at least know which files have been changed.
Recover secondary copies of information	For all data that exists in the database and also in a secondary form outside the database, the database recovery process shall cause the recovery of the secondary form.
	For example, if certain information is stored both in a database table and in an LDAP directory, then database recovery must bring the LDAP copy into line with the database table (after recovery of the latter), including removing entries no longer present in the database table.

Multi-Part Information Entry   Have you ever bought anything from a Web site that involved a longer succession of Web pages than you expected, and just when you thought you'd entered everything, they hit you with yet another page? Then you quit because one little piece of information isn't at hand, and when you returned later, you had to start from the beginning again? Or you couldn't tell whether your order was in there somewhere, and if so, what state it was in? Systems abound that give an unpleasant experience through lack of consideration for their users—for example, by not accommodating users who deviate from the expected path. The main reason is neglect that can be avoided by specifying suitable requirements. (One could argue that use cases that emphasize the primary path can be partly to blame. Also, having to write a second use case to cover the completion of a half-finished process is somewhat tedious, and hard to in an easy-to-follow way without repetition.)

Things that can be done to improve multi-part information entry include:

1. Allow the user to recommence entering information later on, from the point they had reached previously.

2. If the system assigns a transaction number (for example, an order number), tell the user what it is as soon as it's allocated. This lets them know that the system has registered at least some of the information that they've taken the trouble to enter. (You could go further and inform them of incomplete transactions—say, the next time they log in, or via email.)

3. Inform the user where they are in the process: first, the status of the transaction (for example, has an order been placed yet?), and second, how many more screens are yet to come. If this isn't possible (because the number of steps depends on what values the user enters), then at a minimum, tell them there's at least one more screen to come. A help page that explains the steps in the transaction (perhaps as some kind of flow chart) is also useful.

4. Let the user go back to the previous screen. This might sound obvious, but unless you state it as a requirement, the system has no obligation to provide it.

If you want the system to do any of these things, write requirements for them. Here are a few sample extra requirements that apply to *all* multi-stage data entry functions:

Summary	Definition
User can return to complete multi-stage data entry	If a user exits any multi-stage data entry function before completion, they shall be able to return later and complete it without having to reenter details that were received by the system.
	The system may impose a time limit, such that if the user does not return within a reasonable time, the data can be deleted. This requirement does not specify a precise time limit, but it shall be at least 48 hours.
Go back to previous multi-stage step	The second and subsequent pages in any multi-stage data entry function shall provide a way for the user to go back to the previous page.
	If accessing the system via a Web browser, then using the browser's "Back" button shall be a valid way of returning to the previous page.
Multi-stage data entry completion clear	The system shall make it clear to the user when any multi-stage data entry has been completed and accepted.

You could write a version of any or all of these requirements to cover a specific function instead of all of them.

Co-ordination of Multiple Data Stores   This means co-ordinating your system with one or more other systems, when each system stores data for itself. Imagine you're specifying a system for a Web-based retail site (a Web shop). You subcontract some products to a supplier, by passing a suborder to them. What happens if either your system or the supplier's system fails while in the middle of processing an order? Systems can be built to deal with situations like this—but if all the possible failures aren't recognized and handled, you could be in trouble when one that you don't accommodate occurs.

Requirements shouldn't worry about *how* to co-ordinate the updating of data in multiple systems. But they *should* identify what each system involved must be able to do to play its part, especially in the area of resilience. This is particularly important for each system to which we're interfacing, for various reasons. First, any external system is outside our control. Second, it might already exist. Third, it might require modification, even if it otherwise has all the functionality we need of it—it might already handle a "here is an order" message, but not "did you get this order?" or "delete this order" messages. Fourth, it might not be modified quickly enough. Fifth, it might be expensive to modify. Sixth, it might not be within our power to have it modified at all. In short, the implications could be significant, and they need to be brought to light as early as possible.

For each type of action that involves two or more systems, nominate one system—usually the first one in which data storage occurs—as being *in charge*. This system is responsible for three things in addition to its own processing:

1.   Keep track that other systems have fulfilled their responsibilities. This involves recording each step in the processing, including when requests are sent to other systems and when acknowledgements are received.

2.   Detect when another system hasn't done its job.

3.   Complete the processing once the system that failed is back. This can be initiated either manually or automatically.

If the system we're specifying is the one in charge, specify requirements to cover these three things to our satisfaction. If our system *isn't* in charge, write requirements to cover what the system in charge expects of us. (But don't be surprised if it expects nothing, because systems poorly built in this respect are abundant.) Usually, one system is in charge for all types of actions, but it is possible for one system to be in charge for some actions and another system to be in charge for others.

Let's reiterate that the steps described in the previous paragraph must be performed for *each type of action* that involves two or more systems—although in practice, the number of types of action is usually very small—perhaps only one. While completing incomplete actions must be done in action-specific ways, the initiation of them can be grouped together. So, when we know that an external system that failed is now back, we could have a single function that initiates completion of all types of incomplete actions involving that system.

One way to provide integrity for transactions that span multiple databases—and one that avoids having to figure out all this messy co-ordination for ourselves—is to use a transaction processing monitor product (usually called a TP Monitor), but this can be impractical for technical, performance, cost, or business reasons.

A couple of further subjects you might want to consider are:

1. Would it be beneficial for the system to modify the way it behaves once it has detected that a particular external system is not responding? For example, we could stop accepting orders for that supplier's products, or we could send subsidiary orders to an alternative supplier instead.

2. What if a failed external system never comes back? This is an extreme situation, but it is worthwhile devising a fallback plan in case a company you deal with disappears.

Here are a couple of sample extra requirements for a Web shop customer order transaction:

Summary	Definition
Customer order recovery from failure	The system shall be able to recover cleanly from failure during the processing of an order received from a customer, whether the failure occurs in the system itself or in a supplier's system with which an order is placed. This shall include a user function to initiate upon request the completion of incomplete orders involving a selected supplier.
Incomplete order inquiry	There shall be an inquiry that shows a summary of orders received from customers for which processing is incomplete. For each supplier to which at least one subsidiary order has been sent without acknowledgment, this inquiry shall show the following information: ■ Supplier name ■ Number of unacknowledged orders ■ Total monetary value of unacknowledged orders ■ Date and time of last acknowledged order ■ Date and time of first acknowledged order ■ Date and time of last unacknowledged order This inquiry does not show a list of individual orders because such a list might be too large to view.

Timed and Co-ordinated Changes   A **timed change** is a change to information that needs to occur at a precise, predetermined moment in time. For example, switching to or from summer time might need to happen at precisely 2 a.m. on a designated Sunday morning. And moving the Ruthenian Dinar across to the Euro might need to be done at midnight on a published date.

Co-ordinated changes are a collection of related changes to information that all need to be applied at exactly the same time. When a retailer changes its pricing schedule—raising some prices, lower others, modifying discount rates, introducing a range of special offers—it won't want them to be done in dribs and drabs; it'll want them all to happen at once.

Timed changes and co-ordinated changes have much in common with each other (including the possibility that a set of co-ordinated changes could happen at a specified time), which is why they're dealt with together in this section. Both also have much in common with the approval of actions (the subject of the approval requirement pattern)—first, because all involve the need to store the details of actions before acting on them, and second, because we might want to *approve* timed or co-ordinated changes before accepting them.

Innumerable systems have managed to get away without proper provision for timed and co-ordinated changes. After all, making changes manually at the right time, and a set of individual changes one after the other offers only a tiny window during which the system doesn't behave exactly as it should. The hope is that no one will notice. In the main, that's true—and if something should go askew, it might not be tracked to its actual cause. Also, if your system doesn't need 24-hour-a-day availability, you can make these changes when nothing else is happening. But if you need to make such changes while users are active, and you don't want to risk something like this going wrong, take the trouble to see that these changes are made *properly*. While there is a tendency for more systems to be available at all times, the mentality of system builders has lagged behind: nearly all seem unaware of all the implications—and the extra functionality that such systems need.

A further reason for allowing timed changes and co-ordinated changes to be entered beforehand is so they can be reviewed and checked, and any mistakes can be corrected—that is, to reduce human error. (This is also a reason for having them approved, too.) In any case, changes made in the wee small hours by whoever's working that shift, based on scribbled notes left by someone else, sound more at risk of human error than most.

Even if you manually make a timed change at the right time, you're still likely to need to know what the previous value was and when it was changed. For example, if a sales tax rate is changed at midnight on a certain date, we still should be able to calculate sales tax amounts on orders placed before this date. Again, systems have managed to survive without being able to do this—by performing calculations immediately—but it's untidy: it's hard to justify (say, for audit purposes) what the system did, and if any mistake was made, it's difficult to rectify. (You'll probably have to go, cap in hand, to the developers whose omission led to the problem in the first place.)

Timed and co-ordinated changes most commonly apply to changes in *configuration*, but they can happen to other types of information. Indeed, they could conceivably apply to any type of *function*. But worry about that eventuality only if and when you encounter it.

Timed and co-ordinated changes are another area in which lurk all sorts of easily forgotten things, including:

1. Don't allow *backdated* timed changes. If you were to enter a time in the past, in all likelihood the change wouldn't be made at all—but you can't be sure what the software would do.

2. What do you want to happen if a user is in the middle of entering a timed change (particularly a half-finished set of co-ordinated changes) when its time is reached? For instance, a user is halfway through entering some price changes to be applied at midnight when the silicon clock strikes twelve. Should we do nothing, or should we apply the changes that have been entered? Is Cinderella better off wearing just one glass slipper, or neither?

3. What happens to a timed change that needs approval but hasn't been approved by the time it's due? Should we warn someone when this situation looms?

4. Provide at least one inquiry that lists pending changes. Let users see both timed changes and unapproved changes (regardless of whether they are timed); they can be shown in a single inquiry or separately in two. Decide which sorts of changes each user can see.

5. Allow timed changes to be modified and removed before they have been applied. This includes the ability to modify the *time* at which a change is to be made.

6. Prevent entry of two separate changes to the same thing at the same time. When a user's entering a timed change, it would also be helpful to warn them of any other pending change to the same thing.

Once you've discovered one thing for which approval, a timed change, or a co-ordinated change is needed, your eyes are open to spotting more. As soon as you have more than one of these things (or if you see prospects for introducing more in the future), it can become worthwhile to introduce a general mechanism for storing actions that aren't ready to happen. Such a mechanism can be used as the basis for approvals, timed changes, and co-ordinated changes, as well as combinations of them. This involves creating a place where you can store any kind of pending action you wish and a range of functions for updating and viewing it—for which you need to specify requirements. But ask for a general mechanism of this kind only if it's worthwhile, because it's a big and complicated undertaking.

Here are a few requirements for timed and co-ordinated changes:

Summary	Definition
Sales tax rate change timed	When making a change to a sales tax rate, it shall be possible to nominate a date and time at which the change is to take effect.
	Every proposed change to a sales tax rate must be approved by a member of the finance department.
Pricing changes co-ordinated	It shall be possible to enter a set of pricing changes and to have none applied until all have been entered.
Pricing changes timed	It shall be possible to have a set of pricing changes automatically applied at a predetermined date and time.

7.1 Living Entity Requirement Pattern

Basic Details

Related patterns:	Data type, data structure, configuration
Anticipated frequency:	Up to 5% of requirements
Pattern classifications:	Affects database: Yes

Applicability

Use the living entity requirement pattern to define a type of entity for which information is stored and which has a lifespan (that is, is created, can be modified any number of times, and eventually terminated).

Do not use the living entity requirement pattern for any entity that is part of the system's configuration; use the configuration requirement pattern instead.

Discussion

A requirement for a living entity is primarily to define the information that needs to be stored for it (field by field), as well as related details such as how each entity can be uniquely identified (using IDs or other keys). Secondarily, a requirement for a living entity can also cover functions for editing (adding, modifying, and removing) and viewing an entity; these can be achieved either explicitly, or implicitly by the use of pervasive requirements that mandate such functions for all living entities. However, if there's anything particular to be said about any one of these functions, write a separate requirement for that function.

Content

A requirement for a living entity must define at least:

1. **Entity name**   Make it clear, unique, and concise.

2. **An explanation of the entity**   This is to make it clear what it is, what it's for, (and, if appropriate, also what it's not for).

3. **The information the entity contains**   Present this in the form of a data structure. Usually the requirement itself defines the data structure, but it can alternatively refer to another requirement that defines it. In both cases, the data structure is as described in the data structure requirement pattern. These map roughly to the columns of a database table.

   The definition of each item of information can also contain relevant details about the entry, validation, display of its value (including whether it is to be displayed at all), and/or such things as whether it can be amended after the entity has been added. Such information can be included in a requirement defining the data type in question if it applies to all occurrences of it (as per the data type requirement pattern in Chapter 6, "Information Requirement Patterns").

4. **The way(s) in which an entity is uniquely identified**   State its ID (or IDs) plus any other ways of uniquely identifying it. (These later turn into indexes of a database table.)

5. **Parent entity details**   (If any.) An entity of one type can sometimes only be created if some other entity already exists. A banking system might insist that a bank account can only be created if the customer it belongs to already exists. Describe the relationship with the parent or parents (because there could be more than one, and they could be different types of entity), including whether it is essential or optional.

Template(s)

Summary	Definition
«Entity name»	The system shall store the following information about a *«Entity name»*: ■ *«Data item 1 description»*. ■ ... A *«Entity name»* is *«Entity explanation»*. Each *«Entity name»* is uniquely identified by *«Entity identifier(s)»*. [*«Parent entity details»*.]

Example(s)

Summary	Definition
Basic customer details	The system shall store the following information about a customer: ■ **Customer ID** (as defined in requirement XR99.1). ■ **Password**. ■ **Personal contact details** (as defined in requirement XR99.2). ■ **Credit card details** (as defined in requirement XR99.3). ■ **Date of birth**. ■ **Registration date**. ■ **Status** (active, blocked, or terminated). This is never displayed to the customer. Each customer is uniquely identified by its customer ID.

Extra Requirements

See also the "Extra Requirements" section in the introduction to this chapter.

There are several kinds of *pervasive* requirements that can be written to apply to all living entities, to avoid having to specify them repeatedly for each type of entity. These are:

1. **Editing functions**   We need to be able to add, modify, and remove an entity. Each function to modify an entity needs to identify which information can be modified (or, if it's more convenient, which cannot). If your system allows people to modify information about themselves, distinguish what *they* are allowed to change from what *other users* are allowed to change. For example, a Web shop customer might be able to change their personal details and preferences; an employee of the shop might be unable to change these things. Refer to the user authorization requirement patterns in Chapter 11 for how to specify in more detail who is allowed to do what.

2. **Inquiry functions**   Specify one to list all the living entities of a certain type (or, if there are too many to list, some sort of selection or search mechanism), and one to display the details of a selected entity.

3. **Change history**   This is typically a record of every modification to an entity (including adding and removing). It could either record every changed value (so as to have a complete picture of every change) or merely the fact that *something* changed. Knowing every changed value is attractive—but it's also a lot more development effort (and raises other matters—such as restricting access to sensitive information in change histories), so ask for it only for those entities for which it's justified. If in doubt, leave it out.

4. **Common data**   These are items of information to be present in every type of living entity. They are typically used for information such as *who last changed* an entity and *when*.

   If an adequate change history is maintained for each entity, common data identifying who made changes and when is not strictly necessary, because it can be derived from the change history.

5. **Logical remove only**   When we ask for a living entity to be removed, we don't want all trace of it to disappear (because that might cause difficulties); we merely want it to behave as if it's no longer active. All respectable databases will prevent something from being removed if it is being referred to (that's called *referential integrity*), but we don't want it to be removed even if nothing refers to it.

Here are sample pervasive requirements for some of these things:

Summary	Definition
Living entity last changed date and time	Every living entity shall store within it the date-and-time it was last changed.
	This value shall be updated automatically each time the entity is modified, and it shall not be possible for it to be modified in any other way (such as by a user changing it explicitly).
Living entity last changed user ID	Every living entity shall store within it the user ID of the user who last changed it.
	This value shall be updated automatically each time the entity is modified, and it shall not be possible for it to be modified in any other way (such as by a user changing it explicitly).

Summary	Definition
Living entity added date and time	Every living entity shall store within it the date and time it was added.
	This value shall be set automatically when the entity is added and never modified thereafter.
Living entity added user ID	Every living entity shall store within it the user ID of the user who added it. This value shall be left empty for any entity that was added as a result of customer action (such as a customer entity resulting for the customer self-registering).
	This value shall be set automatically when the entity is added and never modified thereafter.
Living entity change history	Every change to a living entity shall be recorded so as to build up a complete record of what values were changed, when, and by whom.
Remove means logical remove	Any living entity that is removed shall be logically removed only.
	The intent of this requirement is to allow details about any entity that has been removed to still be available when viewing historical data. For example, a report of user actions should still be able to show the names of employees who have departed.

Follow-on requirements (for a specific living entity) can also be written for any of the first three kinds of pervasive requirement, regardless of whether a pervasive requirement has been written on the same subject. A requirement can override any of the pervasive requirements by stating which of them does not apply to a particular living entity or class of living entities. Similarly, for any of these standard functions, a requirement can be written to describe features needed by a particular type of living entity (or class of living entities). This requirement would then override the standard function as specified in the pervasive requirement. If you do this, check that it's clear that only one function of each type is needed for each type of entity: you wouldn't want developers to build one to satisfy the pervasive requirement and another for the specific requirement.

User Preferences

A user preference is an item of information that is set by a user to indicate one aspect of how they wish the system to behave. User preferences should be encouraged, because they improve users' experience of our system by discouraging a one-size-fits-all outlook. A requirement for a living entity that represents a class of users (for example, customers) can be followed by requirements that define user preferences (one requirement for each preference).

A requirement for a user preference should contain:

1. **Name**   A unique, descriptive, and concise name for the preference.

2. **User class(es)**   To which users does this preference apply?

3. **Allowed values, or data type**   Let a user avoid making a choice if they don't want to: let them choose "unspecified," "not applicable," or "I don't care," or for potentially impertinent information, "I don't wish to tell you."

4. **Default value**   If the user doesn't set the value explicitly, what value will it have? If you've defined a non-choice value (such as "unspecified"), make that the default.

Don't ask a user to express a preference that's not used (for example, because the piece of software that would use it hasn't been written yet). If someone realizes that something they took the trouble to key in is ignored, they have a right to feel a little cheated.

It can also be worth writing one or more further requirement to ask for the ability to easily add extra preferences—at least to the extent that we don't have to modify the database structure each time—and perhaps a function for adding a user preference.

Here are three requirements that define preferences:

Summary	Definition
Customer mailing list preference	A customer shall be able to indicate whether they wish to join the product mailing list, which periodically sends out emails about new products.
User time zone	A user shall be able to specify the time zone in which they reside.
Preferred notification method(s)	A user shall be able to specify by which means they wish to be notified of events pertaining to them. They shall be able to specify different notification method(s) for each event severity level. For each severity level, they shall be able to nominate one or more of the available notification methods.
	This requirement does not concern itself with *which* events each user is notified of.

Considerations for Development

Even if no pervasive requirements have been specified for the topics discussed in the previous "Extra Requirements" section, you might regard some of them worth acting upon—simply as good practice.

Considerations for Testing

Check that add, modify, remove, and inquire functions exist for every living entity. There might be more than one function for each of these four things. A suitable range of tests needs to be prepared for each of these functions.

7.2 Transaction Requirement Pattern

Basic Details

Related patterns:	Data type, data structure
Anticipated frequency:	Usually fewer than 10 requirements; more if one or more fundamental transaction type has subtypes that have their own requirements
Pattern classifications:	Affects database: Yes

Applicability

Use the transaction requirement pattern to define a type of event in the life of a living entity, and/or a function for entering such a transaction.

Discussion

Transactions are the lifeblood of any commercial system: they're usually where the money comes from. So handling them well is critical to a system's success. A system might have only a small number of types of transaction, and it might take surprisingly few requirements to specify them; even so, it's important to get these few right. Examples of transactions: a purchase from a Web retail site, renewing a magazine subscription, making a successful bid at an auction.

A **transaction** is a representation of something that happens at a point in time. For most kinds of transactions, this is clear and straightforward. A bank customer requests a cash withdrawal, which is deemed to take place the moment the cash is handed over. **The transaction's details are fixed at the moment it is deemed to happen.** This is an important rule: systems that break it are asking for trouble sooner or later. After the bank customer has walked off with their cash, the bank can't play around with the amount withdrawn or pretend it was paid from someone else's account: changing any of the transaction's details would be incorrect. If a genuine mistake was made (such as the wrong customer's account being debited), the only way to fix it is by means of one or more further transactions. Who'd trust a bank that did otherwise? (The purpose of the first pervasive requirement in the "Extra Requirements" section is to enforce this rule.)

A simple after-the-fact record that some event occurred (for example, an entry in a log or in a change history of a living entity) is **not** a transaction for the purposes of this requirement pattern; it is categorized as *chronicle* information (as defined in the introduction to this chapter).

Complex Transactions

Transactions can be complex. First, the *time* at which a transaction happens might not be clear-cut, and second, a transaction can comprise *subtransactions*.

A customer places an order with a Web shop. When exactly does *this* transaction happen? The obvious answer is as soon as the customer placed it—but that's not necessarily the right answer or the best answer. The shop takes a while to verify availability of the products. Can the customer change the order before it does? They'd find it very convenient! The shop discovers a couple of products are unavailable and is forced to remove them from the order; the rest of the order is confirmed. Does the order happen now? The shop dispatches those products that are ready for shipping and sends the rest later. What effect does this have?

In fact, a complex transaction (like this Web shop purchase) involves subtransactions (of more than one type), each of which happens at a particular moment, after which it can't be changed. It's well worth building a solid understanding of the different types of subtransaction involved in a complex transaction. A key matter is deciding when each subtransaction is deemed to happen, because this has a major bearing on who can do what, up till when. Paying attention to when each subtransaction happens can unearth subtleties you might otherwise miss. In the case of our Web shop, we might find ways to give the customer greater flexibility to change an order. Conversely, we might discover situations where it's not obvious to the user what state the transaction is in. How many times have you made a purchase from a Web site and not known the order status, how much it's going to cost you (especially mailing charges), and whether you can change your order? These are flaws in their system.

Sometimes it's useful for information to devolve (that is, to pass or appear to pass) from a transaction to its subtransactions—and to permit changes to that information in any subtransaction until that subtransaction happens. For example, consider the delivery address in a Web shop order. When our system creates one suborder for the part to be delivered now and another for the part that can't, the original delivery address can devolve on to the two suborders. We can then let the customer change the delivery address of the second suborder—because that subtransaction hasn't happened yet. But notice that the original order never changes after it is placed. Devolving information like this can add to the attractiveness of the system, as directly perceived by the users—in this case, the customers. So it's not simply a design issue; it affects requirements. Conversely, if the devolving of information is ignored, situations such as this might never come to light—until customers moan about the *inflexibility* of your system.

If a complex transaction becomes *too* complex, simplify it—artificially if necessary. Options include applying an extra restriction on when it or a subtransaction can be changed, or omitting or limiting some function. For example, our Web shop might decide not to allow a customer to change anything about an order after submitting it. A transaction becomes too complex when you don't properly understand it, you can't model it to your satisfaction, or you're unsure whether it could result in an unpleasant combination of circumstances (such as an order being changed after commitments have been made). Whenever you simplify a complex transaction, state it clearly in the requirement and explain the reason for it. You don't want a developer to remove the simplification (just because they're smart enough to), because it might still lead to the unpleasant combination of circumstances or be hard to test thoroughly enough.

Viewed one way, a complex transaction can itself appear to have events during its life—which makes it look a bit like a living entity. The easiest way to distinguish the two is that a transaction comes to the end of life naturally (such as when an order is fulfilled), whereas a living entity stays alive until explicitly terminated (for example, when a customer closes their account).

Now for another subtlety to worry about! If a transaction doesn't happen immediately, and its processing uses one or more configuration values, consider what to do if one of those values changes *after* the transaction was entered but *before* it happened. For example, if our Web shop's mailing charges change after receiving an order but before shipping it, should we levy the old charge (which is what we told the customer) or the new one (which is what it'll actually cost us—if we're merely passing this on)? Neither way is ideal. We could do better if the mailing charge changes were entered in advance, but even then we probably won't know beforehand whether shipping will occur before or after the change. A simple solution usually suffices once a situation like this has been spotted, but it's still worth recognizing it in the requirement. A picky, intricate answer is rarely necessary and is a sign that your solution is too complicated—which means potentially fragile and unsatisfactory software.

Content

A requirement for a transaction needs to define at least the following:

1. **Transaction name**   State what it's called.
2. **An explanation of the transaction**   Describe what it is and what it's for.

3. **The information the transaction contains**   Give this in the form of a data structure. This can include details about how particular values are entered, validated, and displayed. (See this part of the living entity requirement pattern, earlier in this chapter, for a little further explanation.)

4. **How a transaction is uniquely identified**   This enables us to distinguish two transactions whose details might otherwise be identical (or at least hard to tell apart). Computer systems are sufficiently fast that to differentiate on the basis of *time*, you need to get down to very small gradations of time–certainly much less than a second, and possibly finer than the accuracy of the machine's clock). The safest way is to allocate a transaction ID to each transaction–even if people rarely need to refer to them.

5. **Owner living entity details**   This identifies the entity on whose behalf the transaction is being performed: the customer making a purchase, the bank account from which cash is being debited. (Assume every type of transaction belongs to a living entity, because you're unlikely to encounter one that doesn't.) A type of transaction could conceivably have more than one owner–but they're rare.

6. **When the transaction is deemed to happen**   State this in terms of steps in the life of the transaction. It could be when the transaction's *entered*, when it's *accepted* (in a sense meaningful to the system–such as when a shop has checked that it has in stock all the products in an order), or when it's *approved* (say, manually by a person). This is the moment from which no changes are allowed. If the "happen time" isn't stated in the requirement, the transaction can be assumed to happen immediately when it is entered. Even if a transaction has separate steps for acceptance, approval, or other actions, its entry time could still be regarded as the time it happened.

7. **Transaction longevity**   (Optional.) How long should transactions of this sort hang around? That is, after how long does it become eligible for deletion? This effectively incorporates the intent of a longevity requirement (as per the data longevity requirement pattern in Chapter 6), which is good practice to consider for each type of transaction, even if you decide not to state it in the requirement explicitly.

Template(s)

Summary	Definition
«*Transaction name*»	There shall be a function to create a «*Transaction name*» transaction for a «*Owner living entity name*». Each «*Transaction name*» shall contain the following information: ■ «*Data item 1 description*». ■ … A «*Transaction name*» is «*Transaction explanation*». Each «*Transaction name*» is uniquely identified by «*Transaction identifier(s)*». A «*Transaction name*» is deemed to have happened «*Transaction happen time description*». [«*Transaction longevity statement*».]

Example(s)

Summary	Definition
Account adjustment	It shall be possible to post an adjustment (debit or credit) to the account of a selected customer. An adjustment shall contain the following information:
	■ **Customer ID**
	■ **Adjustment amount**
	■ **Adjustment reason**—free-form text intended to explain why the adjustment was raised
	A unique ID shall automatically be allocated to each account adjustment.
	It is expected that authority to use this will be restricted to very few employees.

Extra Requirements

See also the "Extra Requirements" in the introduction to this chapter.

If you're going to specify performance requirements for anything in your system, it's most likely to be for the processing of transactions—because they're usually the highest volume, most visible, most financially significant part of a commercial system. It's illuminating to try calculating daily or monthly volumes for each type of transaction—even if only in a cursory manner, and even if it only serves to point out that you have little idea how busy your system's likely to be. Refer to all the requirement patterns in Chapter 9, "Performance Requirement Patterns," for types of performance for which you could consider specifying requirements.

Here's a pervasive requirement to enforce the rule stated previously:

Summary	Definition
Do not modify transactions	No database row that acts as a transaction with actual or potential financial consequences shall ever be modified after the transaction was originally recorded such that its financial effect is or might be altered. In particular, errors in financial transactions shall never be rectified by modifying the transactions themselves. Instead, additional transactions shall be the only way to make the necessary adjustments.
	For the purposes of this requirement, a financial transaction is any row in any database table that causes some financial value (such as a customer's account balance) to change.
	The motivation for this requirement is to force a clear history of financial-related activity to be maintained. This is impossible if values in transactions are overwritten, because it results in both an inability to see what happened and quite possibly in errors that are hard to make sense of and to rectify.

Considerations for Development

Always adhere to the rule of never modifying any transaction after the fact. And take care processing transactions, because they're important.

Considerations for Testing

Testing that transactions are handled well is perhaps the most important testing of all, because the functions to process transactions tend to be the most heavily used and are highly visible. So testers should prepare a large number of test cases that cover all eventualities. Identify all the relevant permutations that a complex transaction can have, including states, transitions between states, and error conditions. Then build test cases for them all.

Pay special attention to the statement in a transaction requirement about *when* a transaction is deemed to happen. Test that a transaction cannot be changed after this point. When testing a complex transaction, ask yourself at each stage whether it's clear where you stand: is it obvious whether the transaction has been accepted? Can you tell what you're allowed to change? Are the financial implications spelled out? For example, is it clear to a customer how much they must pay? And are the actual computed consequences what you expected?

7.3 Configuration Requirement Pattern

Basic Details

Related patterns:	Data type, data structure, living entity
Anticipated frequency:	Up to 10 percent of requirements
Pattern classifications:	None

Applicability

Use the configuration requirement pattern to define parameter values that control how the system behaves.

Discussion

Configuration values are either **systemwide** or they are associated with **configuration entities** that behave very much like living entities—but the emphasis is on the *values* rather than the entities, and configuration requirements tend to reflect this. A **systemwide** configuration value is one for which there is only one instance: the same value is used everywhere in the system; other configuration values have multiple instances, each one used in a different circumstance. A bank might set a different cash withdrawal limit for each currency; in this case the currency is the configuration entity, and each instance of a currency has its own withdrawal limit configuration value.

A configuration value can exist at one of several degrees of flexibility, which run as follows (from least to most flexible):

1. **Hard-coded** Values defined in the software itself are to be avoided. It's bad practice. Every configuration value must be modifiable so it can be set without involving developers. Do this even if you can't envisage it ever changing. Even if you're building a system just for your own company's use, the company might want to sell it if it's really nice; this has happened to systems in the past—only to run into severe trouble and embarrassment when hard-coded company-specific values come to light.

A hard-coded value can occasionally slip in without anyone (even the developer) realizing. Pay special attention to calculation formulae. For example, bank interest calculations vary from one currency to another. (See the calculation formula requirement pattern in Chapter 6 for the gory details.) You need to be on your toes, especially if you're new to the industry you're working in.

2. **Systemwide**   For each systemwide value you identify, ask yourself whether it's genuinely a single value. Sometimes shortsightedness leads to parameters being made systemwide when they should actually vary—by country, by language, by currency, by customer type, by account type, by company, in some other way, or in a combination of more than one thing.

3. **In a configuration entity**

4. **In several configuration entities**   (And perhaps systemwide, too.) This includes successive defaulting if the value isn't explicitly present at a particular level.

Don't Mess with a Running Production Line

Any change to a factory production line can upset its smooth flow—even bring it to a halt and smash things. A commercial computer system is like a production line, and its smooth processing of transactions and other everyday activities can be disrupted by a change made while it's running—a change to its configuration, that is—even if it's a sensible, necessary change. A configuration change function can, in extremis, behave like a self-destruct button—and, given the opportunity, someone will eventually press it.

So we need to consider the effect of the very *act of changing* a configuration value. In general, the more fundamental a value is, the more traumatic is the effect when it's changed. (In addition, the less frequently a value is changed, the less attention tends to be paid to the software that makes the change.) Imagine the effect if you suddenly changed the designated local currency, local time zone, tax rates, or the length of time before transactions are archived. Developers would probably consider these to be unreasonable things to attempt—but where does it say so? Unless the matter's properly addressed (starting with the requirements), users have no reason to suspect that normal use of some system function could cause trouble.

One answer is to examine each configuration value and decide *when* it's likely to be safe to change it. This can only be a guess at the time the requirements are written—so be conservative, and err on the side of being restrictive, because we don't want to raise expectations that are hard for developers to realize. Assign to each configuration value one of the following times at which it can be changed:

1. **At any time**

2. **Only while normal processing is halted**

3. **Only before the system goes live**   Some configuration values are so sensitive that they should be set once and never changed again during the life of the system. (An example might be the designated local currency.)

You might want to add other options relevant to your system. It must be clear which time category each configuration value belongs to. To avoid having to state it explicitly for every value, assume that (a) **all systemwide values can be changed only while normal processing is halted**; and (b) **all nonsystemwide values can be changed at any time**.

Some changes might have to be accompanied by the running of special conversion processing or by taking other extra steps—which might become apparent only during development.

Configuration editing functions must prevent any value being modified at the wrong time. To achieve this, we must be able to tell when the system is in each of these states: whether normal processing is underway or not, and whether the system has gone live or not. We then need one or more functions to switch the system between these different states. (Such functions can be useful for other purposes, too—such as shutting out users when the system experiences a problem.) We need extra requirements for these things; see the examples in the "Extra Requirements" section later in this pattern.

A couple of other recurring subjects have special considerations when applied to configuration:

1. **Access control**   Examine the access control needs for each configuration value. Don't simply assume that one important person will look after all the configuration, because it's risky to put control over everything into one person's hands. Give proper thought to organizing your configuration values, so that values with a related purpose are grouped together; it's not necessarily the same as the physical organization of the data. Separate the editing of sensitive, rarely-changed values from others, so they're harder to change by mistake. This is best worked out after all the configuration requirements have been determined, for obvious reasons. Grouping values according to *when* they can be changed is a good starting point. (See the user authorization requirement patterns in Chapter 11 for more.)

2. **Integrity**   Configuration, like all data, is best stored in a database. Recall the discussion about data integrity in the introduction to this chapter (Area 1). Storing configuration values in a flat file might be convenient for developers (especially if new types of values keep being added), but it's dangerous. Consider first what happens if you lose the disk that the file's stored on: what changes were made since it was last backed up? And second, when do changes take effect? If a configuration file is read into memory when the system starts up, will a change be read into memory straight away? If not, how do we cause it to? The whole situation is messy, and the best answer is to avoid the risk altogether: mandate that all configuration data is to be stored in a database. If developers really want the flexibility that they use flat files for, they can choose to store a whole configuration "file" as a blob in a database—but that doesn't by itself solve all these complications.

Content

There are two ways of structuring a configuration requirement:

A.   Define a **configuration value**, and then describe the level (or levels) at which it lives.

This way is preferable purely because it focuses its attention onto a single aspect of configuration, which makes it hard to escape describing it properly. It also saves duplication if you want to configure a value at multiple levels. One drawback of this way is that it doesn't let you see together all the configurable values defined for a particular entity, which also means developers and database designers have to pull all the values together for themselves.

B.   Define a **configuration entity**, the whole of which forms part of the configuration.

This way is more convenient if you have several items of information to specify at the same level, but it discourages saying much about each one.

A requirement for a **configuration value** needs to contain:

1.   **Name and purpose**   It's important to make clear the intended use of each configuration value, especially where there are multiple values with similar meanings. If developers inadvertently use the wrong value, the resulting errors could be subtle and hard to detect; much damage could be done before it's sorted out.

2.   **Representative value**   For a systemwide value, this is either the *expected* value (if this is known) or a *sensible* suggested value. It gives readers an idea of what we have in mind. It can sometimes stimulate useful discussion: someone remarking that it's not a realistic value might be a sign we've misunderstood something. These representative values can also be used when initially setting up the developed system, both for testing and for live use.

3.   **Data type**   Either specify this in-line as described in the data type requirement pattern in Chapter 6, or refer to a separate requirement that defines a data type.

4.   **Level(s)**   This is either "systemwide" or the name of the configuration entity to which the value belongs (per currency, per account type, and so on). A value may exist at more than one level; if so, explain how precedence (and perhaps defaulting, too) is to be handled. For example, if an approval limit is set for a person, use that; otherwise if a limit is set for a role, use that; as a last resort, use a systemwide default limit.

5.   **When the value can be changed**   See the preceding section "Don't Mess with a Running Production Line." Note the rules for what value to assume if the requirement doesn't say explicitly.

A requirement for a **configuration entity** contains:

1.   **Entity name**

2.   **The purpose of the entity**   What is it, and what is it for?

3.   **The entity's contents**   Write it in the form of a data structure. *When* each value can be changed can be stated explicitly as necessary. An example can be given for each value.

4.   **How an entity is uniquely identified**   State its ID (or IDs).

5.   **When the entity can be changed**   This applies to all the entity's values, except those for which it is explicitly overridden. If omitted, a default is assumed, as described in the preceding section "Don't Mess with a Running Production Line."

Every value in a configurable entity is regarded as a configurable value (we don't count its ID and supporting information such as last-changed-date as "values" in this sense), and configurable values live only in configurable entities. So none of the values in any living entity (say, a customer) constitutes part of the system's configuration.

Template(s)

The first template here is for specifying a single configuration value; the second is for a whole configuration entity.

Summary	Definition
«*Configuration value name*»	It shall be possible to specify «*Configuration value name*» for the purpose of «*Value purpose*». This is a «*Data type description*» value (for example, «*Representative value*») and is «*Configuration level(s) description*». [This value can be changed only «*Change time description*».]
«*Configuration entity name*»	The system shall store the following information about a «*Configuration entity name*» for the purpose of «*Entity purpose*»: ■ «*Configuration value 1 description*». ■ … Each «*Configuration entity name*» is uniquely identified by «*Entity identifier*». [Such an entity can be changed only «*Change time description*».]

Example(s)

Summary	Definition
Local currency	It shall be possible to designate which is the systemwide local currency. This value cannot be changed after the system goes live.
Cash withdrawal limit	It shall be possible to specify the cash withdrawal limit, which is a monetary amount expressed in local currency that determines the maximum value of a cash withdrawal transaction that a user can perform. This value can be set for: (1) an employee; (2) an employee role; (3) a department; and (4) a systemwide default, such that if not specified at one of these levels, the one at the following level shall be used. It is optional at all levels except systemwide. It can be changed at any time at any level.
Currency details	It shall be possible to specify the following details for a currency: ■ **Currency code**, as per ISO 4217 (e.g. "USD"). Three characters long. ■ **Descriptive name** (e.g. "U.S. Dollar"). ■ **Symbol** (e.g. "$," "A$"). Up to three characters are allowed. ■ **Number of decimal places** (e.g. 2). A number between 0 and 3. * ■ **Interest calculation days in year** (e.g. 360). Allowed values are 360, 365, and *actual*. * ■ **Interest calculation days in month** (e.g. 30). Allowed values are 30 and *actual*. * * Values identified by an asterisk cannot be modified after the system goes live (though they can be entered for a new currency when it's being added). Each currency shall be identified by its ISO 4217 code. The descriptive name shall also be unique (to prevent confusion).

Extra Requirements

See also the "Extra Requirements" in the introduction to this chapter.

Here is a pervasive requirement to enforce a "no hard-coding" rule:

Summary	Definition
No hard-coding of parameters	No parameter used to control the way in which the system behaves shall be hard-coded in the software; systemwide variables shall be used instead. A parameter for the purposes of this requirement is a value for which it is possible to conceive realistic circumstances in which a different value could be substituted.

Here are a few basic requirements to facilitate preventing configuration values from being edited at the wrong time:

Summary	Definition
User access state	It shall be possible to specify what access by users is currently permitted. The allowed states are: ■ **Normal access** ■ **Login not allowed** Users already logged in can continue as normal, but no one else can log in. ■ **No access allowed** Users are not allowed to do anything. Access by system administrators for the purpose of operating the system are unaffected by these states.
System processing state	It shall be possible to specify whether system processing is currently permitted or not. For the purposes of this and following requirements, **system processing** is processing carried out by the system itself as part of its usual operation.
Overall processing state	The overall processing state of the system is determined from the user access state and the system processing state. For the purpose of changing configuration, normal processing is deemed to be halted when no user access is allowed and no system processes are currently running.
System activity inquiry	There shall be an inquiry that shows current activity in the system. It shall show: ■ The number of users currently logged in. ■ The number of logged-in users for which the system is currently performing processing. ■ The number of system processes currently running.
System gone live state	It shall be possible to specify whether the system has gone live or not.

These requirements do not pretend to be adequate for proper system management.

Considerations for Development

Consider the effect of changing each configuration value while the system is running. If this might cause problems, take steps to prevent damaging changes from being made. Also publicize the potential danger, so everyone who ought to know does know and so that it is properly documented.

Introduce extra configuration values if you need to; it's perfectly natural for extra ways to control the system to arise during development. Don't hard-code values. Again, publicize any new value and have it properly documented.

Considerations for Testing

The testing of the basics of configuration—adding, modifying, removing, and viewing values—is essentially the same as for living entities. But once that's been done, test the effect of changes of configuration upon the functions that use it. As has been noted previously, changing certain configuration values can have profound effects—possibly very negative effects. Many of these sensitive things are systemwide variables, so take a look through all the systemwide variables for ones that look dangerous to modify.

Bear in mind that extra configuration values, over and above those specified in the requirements, might have been introduced during design and development.

7.4 Chronicle Requirement Pattern

Basic Details

Related patterns:	Transaction
Anticipated frequency:	Between one and twenty requirements
Pattern classifications:	None

Applicability

Use the chronicle requirement pattern to specify that a certain type or range of types of event (occurrence) in the life of the system must be recorded.

Do not use the chronicle requirement pattern to record anything that has a financial role of any kind; use the transaction requirement pattern for them.

Discussion

One dictionary defines a chronicle as "**a record or register of events in chronological order.**" As a verb, it means "**to record in or as if in a chronicle.**" These match perfectly this requirement pattern's uses of the word: a chronicle is a place where events are permanently stored. You can avoid using the word "chronicle" in requirements, though, so you don't have to explain it to your readers. The aim of chronicling is to build up a picture of anything that happens in the day-to-day life of the system and might be of future interest: like built-in closed-circuit television cameras. Its primary use is to assist investigation when something goes wrong—whether it be a software problem, employee fraud, attack by hackers, or hardware or other kind of failure. Chronicles can also yield a wide range of statistics, based on the volumes of different types of events.

This requirement pattern uses the terms **event** and **occurrence** interchangeably to mean anything that occurs within the system while it's running and which the system is aware of and is able to act upon. We can chronicle any event (occurrence)—which means pretty much whatever we choose to; it's not restricted to events that *trigger* some kind of system action. Events can include database updates, errors detected by the system, user actions, milestones in system processes (such as starting up and shutting down), and passing preset thresholds (such as when free disk space goes below a certain level). We also use the verbs to **record** and to **store** when talking about what we do with an event; it means the permanent storage of information about the event, which is to remain unmodified and unmodifiable (a faithful snapshot of the event).

Anything that's recorded in a transaction (in the sense used by the transaction requirement pattern) needn't be recorded in a chronicle as well. Conversely, a chronicle requirement merely states that an event must be recorded, not how—so it's quite acceptable to record it in the form of a transaction (provided it is never subsequently modified).

The key features of a chronicle are that it must be:

1. **Chronological**   It records event in the order in which they happened.
2. **Faithful**   It records exactly what happened. Record the details correctly, and don't let them be tampered with afterwards.
3. **Complete**   It records *all* events of any type being chronicled, because to record some but not others would be misleading. Also, don't allow events to be deleted.
4. **Reliable**   It is not susceptible to system failure. Among other things, this prevents a wrong-doer from covering their tracks by causing the system to crash.

This requirement pattern makes no judgment about how many distinct chronicles a system has: it might put everything in one, or it might use different chronicles for different things (or separate them for other reasons, such as per company in a multi-company system); that's an implementation matter. Chronicle requirements should do likewise. Nor do we stipulate in what form chronicles are to be stored (such database tables or flat files), though the "Extra Requirements" section suggests demands that may render some forms unacceptable. That's one reason why we don't use the terms "log" or "logging" here, because it might lead your readers (especially developers) to make inappropriate assumptions—both about what does and doesn't belong in a log and about the implied use of a logging product (which might in fact not satisfy our requirements). Use the words "log" and "logging" in requirements if you choose, but bear in mind that this could influence the implementation by implying a particular kind of solution. For similar reasons, we don't talk about "audit trails," because readers might interpret that in different ways.

It's useful to recognize the difference between occurrences that are related to a living entity and those that aren't, because of their relative volumes. (We'll have a lot more of the former.) Think about how many occurrences of each type are likely to occur.

It's possible (and often convenient) to incorporate the need to record each *use of a function* in the requirement for that function, but strictly speaking, they are separate requirements (as demonstrated by the fact that verifying the resulting records is a separate testing step). Writing a separate requirement also prompts you to give proper thought to what information should be recorded. You can also write a chronicle requirement that applies to a set of functions. (This, too, sounds like lumping separate requirements together, but they are all of the same nature. It's better to add several apples together than an apple and an orange.) Make a conscious decision at the start of the requirements specification process about which approach you wish to take. Being consistent throughout has the benefit of reducing the chances of some kinds of chronicle entries being neglected.

Individual chronicle requirements concern what events are recorded and what information is recorded about each one. (Functions that enable us to make use of this information are covered in the "Extra Requirements" section later in this pattern.)

Content

A chronicle requirement should contain:

1. **The type(s) of occurrence to record**   A chronicle requirement can specify the recording of a *specific type* of event or the recording of a *range of types* of events—in ways that can be defined quite broadly. It's attractive to be specific, but in doing so, we risk both missing certain things and also causing an explosion in the number of requirements. The best answer is to specify *classes* of events (defining their scope in terms of criteria that let someone test whether something fits or not), and if necessary, write another chronicle requirement for each specific type of event that we definitely want recorded.

    A system cannot record things that it cannot perceive, so don't ask it to. Recording all break-ins and unauthorized access, for example, is impossible: a system can only record those it *detects*.

2. **The information to record about each occurrence**   Every occurrence pertaining to a user action must include the ID of the user. Every one reflecting a change in data should enable both *before* and *after* values to be determined (which doesn't necessarily mean storing both in the change itself, so long as both can be obtained from somewhere—such as obtaining the *before* value from the previous change). Every one pertaining to an organization must identify that organization. Every one pertaining to a server machine must identify that machine.

3. **Severity**   (Optionally.) If the occurrence indicates a problem, the severity tells how serious it is. Either identify a severity value defined in a separate severity scheme requirement (as explained in the "Extra Requirements" section later in this pattern), or describe it in general terms (to allow it to be mapped to a formal severity level when they are defined later). If you say nothing about severity, it means you're happy for it to be decided later, either by the development team or by whoever configures the system before it goes into production. If the occurrence is clearly not an error, don't mention its severity.

    In some cases, it's appropriate for the severity to depend not just on the type of event but also on one or more other values. For example, the severity of a low disk space event might become more serious as the free space dwindles.

Template(s)

Summary	Definition
Record «*Occurrence type(s) summary*»	Every «*Occurrence type(s) description*» shall automatically be recorded. For each, the following shall be recorded: <ul><li>Date and time</li><li>«*Occurrence detail 1*»</li><li>«*Occurrence detail 2*»</li><li>…</li></ul> [Each such event shall be treated as having a severity of «*Severity description*».]

Example(s)

A relatively extensive list of example requirements is given here to identify a number of types of events that a typical commercial system might want to chronicle and to demonstrate a few variations in approach. As a result, there is a degree of overlap and consequently repetition in these requirements.

Summary	Definition
Store all order events	Every event that occurs during the life of an order shall be stored permanently. For each such event, at least the following information shall be recorded: ■ Type of event ■ Details of change (which will vary from one type of event to another) ■ Date and time of change ■ User ID of person who made the change (if relevant) ■ User ID of person who approved the change (if relevant) Note that there is no implication that all events are stored in the same way or in the same place.
Record significant user actions	Every user action of business significance shall be recorded. The caveat "of business significance" is included to filter out trivial actions such as navigating the system's user interface. Nevertheless, even actions of small business significance still fall within the scope of this requirement. This requirement shall be read as including all the following types of actions: ■ Use of any function described in this specification. ■ Anything that causes a database change. ■ An employee viewing or changing any sensitive data, including a customer's or an employee's details. ■ A user logging in or logging out, including each unsuccessful attempt to log in. ■ A system operator starting up or shutting down parts of the system, or changing system operational parameters (whether permanently or temporarily). (Some actions fall into more than one of these categories.) The information recorded for any such action shall include at least the following (when, who, what): ■ Date and time. ■ The identity of the user who performed the action (user ID and company ID). Identifying the company is particularly important if action affecting one company is taken by an employee of another (for example the system operating company's action affecting a Web shop company). ■ Details of the action. Note that this requirement does not suggest that all actions are stored in the same way or in the same place. If a particular type of transaction is stored in its own database table, that would suffice, provided it recorded the details listed. Note also that nothing is said about which details of the action are to be recorded—and we do not demand that **all** details be recorded. This is left for resolution on a case-by-case basis.

Summary	Definition
Record significant system events	Every significant system event shall be recorded. By "significant system event," we mean things that affect the system's availability and important actions started on the initiative of the system itself—plus any other things that are worthy of showing on the system events report. These include (but are not limited to):
	■ Startup and shutdown of system components (such as server machines)
	■ Failure of any system component or interface
	■ The passing of any defined system threshold, including measures of performance and available resources (for example, to report reduction of available disk space to less than a critical level)
	This requirement excludes events that, by their very nature, are incapable of being recorded by the system (such as failure of the system itself).
	The information recorded for any event shall include at least the following (when, who, what):
	■ Date and time
	■ The identity of the system component in which the event occurred
	■ Details of the event
Record access to sensitive data	Each successful access by a user to an item of data deemed sensitive shall be recorded. "Sensitive data" is not defined.
	The information to be recorded shall include the date and time of access, the ID of the user, and details of what data was requested.
	(Note that *unsuccessful* accesses are covered by the next requirement and are not to be recorded again under the auspices of this requirement—to avoid recording the same event twice.)
Record unsuccessful data access	Each unsuccessful attempt by a user to access an item of data shall be recorded.
	This type of event shall be treated as having a low severity.
Record failed user actions	Each failed attempt by a user to perform an action shall be recorded. (This requirement excludes unsuccessful attempts to access data, which is covered by the previous requirement.)
	This type of event shall be treated as having a low severity.
Record errors	All error conditions detected by the system shall be recorded. Validation errors and other minor conditions pertaining to a single user, that can occur through normal use of the system and which are reported directly to the user, are expressly excluded from this requirement.
	It shall be possible to assign a severity level to each type of error.

Summary	Definition
Record security violations	All security violations that the system detects shall be recorded.
	Every security violation shall be regarded as serious, but some kinds could be more serious than others.
Record incorrect password entry	Each entry of an invalid password (or any other secret information used to authenticate a user) shall be recorded.
	This requirement applies to every function that asks a user to enter their password or other secret information.
Record configuration changes	Each change to configuration parameters shall be recorded. For each change, the following shall be recorded:
	■ The before image. (The after image is not explicitly recorded for the change, because it is held in either the current value or the before image of the next change.)
	■ The ID of the user making the change.
	■ The date and time of the change.
Record software changes	Each change to the software loaded on production server machines shall be recorded. This covers both server software and software which is available to be downloaded to client machines. The information recorded shall include what was installed and what version.
Record number of active users	The system shall periodically record the number of active users. The frequency at which this is to happen shall be a configuration parameter.
Record report run request	Each request to run a report shall be recorded. At least the following shall be recorded:
	■ User ID of the requester.
	■ Date and time of the request.
	■ Report name.
	■ Report selection criteria. (That is, the parameters that control the report and determine what information it shows.)
	This requirement serves two purposes: first, to make it possible to see which users requested what information, and second, for report usage analysis—to facilitate study of which reports are used most frequently and which are used rarely or never.
Record report design changes	The addition of a new report definition and any change to an existing report definition shall be recorded.

Extra Requirements

There are various types of extra requirements that can be specified for chronicling. They are all easier to apply across the board to all chronicling in the system (or selected parts of it), rather than following on from an individual chronicle requirement. These types of extra requirements are:

1. **Access control**   Who's allowed to see what in chronicles? This topic appears at the top of this list because the others need to take it into account—and access control requirements can have a significant bearing on what kinds of solutions are acceptable.

2. **Common chronicle features**   What characteristics do we want our chronicles to demonstrate? The most important are the key features described in the "Discussion" section earlier in this pattern: to be chronological, faithful, complete, and reliable.

3. **Chronicle view functions**   There's no point in creating chronicles if there's no way to see what's in them. See the "Chronicle View Functions" section that follows.

4. **Severity levels**   For chronicles to work properly, the severity levels used in all events must be consistent: it's unacceptable for minor events to look as though they're severe. We can write requirements to define severity levels and others to assign levels to different types of events.

5. **Purging chronicles**   For how long should chronicle data be kept? It's possible to retain different types of events for different lengths of time—particularly if they are stored in different chronicles—but this makes it harder to interpret what happened during those periods of time affected. To make sense of them, we certainly need to keep track of the date from which each type of event is present, so it's possible to tell whether omission of data could be due to it having been removed (which is covered in the third example requirement in the "Common Chronicle Features" section that follows).

6. **Archiving chronicles**   If chronicles are archived and loaded into another database for study (let's say a "reporting system" database), care must be taken if actions on the secondary database are chronicled—because these events could pollute the chronicles. The answer is to have two distinct sets of chronicles that are strictly kept apart. If you're doing anything along these lines, carefully think through what might transpire, and specify suitable requirements to prevent trouble.

7. **Triggering other actions**   It's useful to be able to notify people when a severe event occurs. The best way to do this is to build it into the chronicle mechanism itself, so it works for any type of event. This could be extended to allow other kinds of actions to be triggered by events. Work out what you want, and write requirements for it.

8. **Turning chronicling on and off**   Recording events in chronicles can affect the system's performance, especially when recording a high volume of events. It can be useful to turn the chronicling of certain types of events on and off. Allow this only for non-error events. Being able to switch off low-volume events serves no purpose.

   Switching chronicling on and switching it off are themselves events that must be recorded, because they affect what we can expect to see in chronicles. Without doing so, we could never tell whether the absence of an event was due to an event not occurring or because chronicling was off at the time. (This point is dealt with by the third example requirement in the "Common Chronicle Features" section that follows.)

The first four of these topics are covered in more detail in the following subsections.

Chronicle Access Control   If we control which information each user can access, the same restrictions should apply when that information finds its way into chronicles. After all, we're wasting our time if a user can bypass access control restrictions by examining events recorded in chronicles. (This is in addition to control over who can access the chronicle view functions themselves.) Strangely, this loophole is common in systems, though rarely recognized as such (often because systems administrators keep chronicles to themselves, and chronicles commonly lack detailed information). Here's a requirement for plugging the gap:

Summary	Definition
Access control for records of events	Any information recorded about an event shall be subject to access control rules at least as strong as those that apply to the original information. This requirement applies regardless of the form in which event information is stored (including flat files and "logs"). For example, if a user is not allowed to access a particular customer's details, they shall not be able to view details of an event that records changes to that customer's details (though it is acceptable for them to be made aware of the *presence* of the event).

The explicit reference to "logs" is just so there can be no misunderstandings on this point. This requirement might look innocuous, but it's likely to have a major impact on the implementation of chronicling: it makes it appreciably more complex and rules out many off-the-shelf products. So don't ask for "proper" access control of this sort unless you really need it–because it won't endear you to whoever has to implement it.

Common Chronicle Features   We can only expect chronicles to be chronological, faithful, complete, and reliable if we ask for these things in requirements, as these examples do:

Summary	Definition
Event date and time	Every event recorded shall store the date and time at which it occurred. The event date and time shall always be determined by the system itself; any date and time originating externally is to be considered unreliable for this purpose.
Event records unmodifiable	No user (including a system administrator) shall be able to modify in any way, or to delete, any record of an event.
Event record sequence number	Every event recorded shall be assigned a sequential number that shall be one greater than the previous event recorded in the same place. The purpose of this requirement is to be able to detect whether an event has been deleted.
Record actions affecting event recording	Any action that affects which events are recorded (or which are still present—that is, not yet archived) shall itself be recorded. This requirement covers, but is not limited to, the following actions: 1. Switching the recording of any types of event on or off 2. Removing (archiving) any recorded events (due to their longevity) The purpose of this requirement is to make it possible to tell both which types of events are liable to be present at any point in time and also for how far back in time events are present.
Record events in database	Any record of an event shall be stored in a database. If the event itself records a database change, the record shall be in the same database and performed in the same database transaction. The purpose of this requirement is to provide protection against the failure of a disk drive.

Chronicle View Functions   Chronicles that store a wide variety of events are a rich resource that can tell you much about what the system—and consequently the business—has been doing. Functions for viewing chronicles can be divided into the *detailed*—which show individual events (and can be used for investigative purposes)—and the *statistical*, which summarize them into totals (for various purposes—including management, marketing, and system load analysis).

The number of chronicles a system has, and what events are recorded in which one, is an implementation matter that doesn't concern the requirements. Consequently, requirements for chronicle view functions cannot distinguish separate chronicles; they must limit themselves to the types of events that are to be shown. However, it is possible for chronicle view functions to include chronological-based information—especially transactions—from elsewhere in the database to give a more complete picture of what was going at the time. The case for doing this is strong if it's a close call whether to regard something as a transaction or a chronicle event.

Summary	Definition
Recorded event inquiry	There shall be an inquiry that lists recorded events that match given selection criteria. The selection criteria shall include (but need not be limited to):
	■ Start and end date/time range
	■ Customer ID
	■ Whether to include customer-related events (yes or no)
	■ User ID (to select actions performed by this user)
	■ Company ID
	■ Machine ID
	■ Event type
	■ Severity level (to show all events with this or higher severity)
	The user shall be able to supply or omit whichever criteria they wish.
	Any item of information to which the user does not have access shall not be displayed.
	The user shall be warned if particular types of events requested are unavailable for some or all of the time period being shown (due to their having been archived).

Severity Levels   Should a requirements specification define event severity levels? Defining a complete set constrains the implementation, but defining none makes it hard to describe the severity of a type of event in the requirements. A middle course is best: define a few fundamental severity levels, but allow the implementation to have more. The bare minimum severity levels are "normal" and "severe." **Normal** is for something that can be expected to happen during the normal running of the system, which is not an error. **Severe** is for a problem that warrants attention by a person. But you should include at least one level in between these two. Choose different names for the levels if you wish. When devising severity levels, consider differentiating between errors that affect just a single entity (such as one customer) and those that affect the system as a whole—and have separate severity levels for the two types. (The example requirement that follows *doesn't* do this.) Write a requirement that identifies the severity levels you want. Every definition of a severity level must include a readable description of its meaning.

Take care when assigning the severity level of a type of event. Don't let severe events be neglected, but don't "cry wolf," either. The volume of severe events must be kept small, or their impact will be lost.

Chronicle requirements can specify the severity of particular types of events, but their severities can be defined in other ways—in particular, by making them configurable. This adds a degree of flexibility, but changing severity levels once the system is in production is potentially dangerous and can lead to confusion.

Summary	Definition
Event severity levels	The system shall support at least the following event severity levels (or their equivalents): ■ **Normal**—nothing is wrong. ■ **Warning**—worth bringing to someone's attention, but no action is required. ■ **Moderate**—corrective action is needed, but it's not urgent. ■ **Severe**—immediate action is needed. ■ **Catastrophic**—the system should be shut down immediately.
Event type severity	Each type of event that can be recorded shall have a **severity** defined for it.

Considerations for Development

Performance is a major consideration. It's straightforward enough to develop chronicle capabilities but much harder without having an appreciable impact on the processing time of the occurrence being recorded. If possible, use chronicle software already written for this purpose—provided you can find such software that satisfies all the requirements laid down.

Estimate the likely volume of each class of events. Base it on the sizing model, if there is one (and perhaps extend the model). Consider keeping high-volume and low-volume chronicles separate from each other.

Record all occurrences using a timestamp generated by the system itself— because if it came from elsewhere, we shouldn't trust it.

Considerations for Testing

Having as many as possible of a system's activities recorded is of great assistance during testing, because these records provide invaluable information about what happened in the system. So, when reviewing requirements, testers should press for as many types of events as possible to be recorded.

You should cause all the types of events for which chronicle requirements are specified. This can be difficult, especially for obscure error conditions. Insisting that every conceivable condition must be tested is rather picky in typical commercial systems; if you insist upon it, one option is to ask developers to modify the software to allow it to simulate them.

Separate broad-scope chronicle requirements (those that ask for a range of occurrences to be chronicled—according to specified criteria) from specific chronicle requirements; it's clear what to test for the latter. But the former are open-ended; to test such a requirement properly, identify within the delivered system all the functions and occurrences that satisfy the criteria, and then test each one in turn. Both the identifying and the testing could be very onerous.

7.5 Information Storage Infrastructure

Purpose

An information storage infrastructure lets us store information persistently—that is, it's still there when we switch the machine off—and retrieve it later. Information infrastructures vary significantly in their characteristics, and for this reason, a system might use more than one of them, and sometimes more than one of the same type (such as a heavyweight server database plus a lightweight database on client PCs).

The most prevalent kind of storage mechanism for commercial systems is a database. Other kinds are a file system for reading and writing flat files (though there's usually—but not always—little point in saying anything about this as an infrastructure, because it's built in to every operating system and programming language, so it's there anyway); a *transaction monitor* (if we need to co-ordinate changes made to more than one database); and a *document management system* (if our system accesses the contents of "documents"). You can also regard information *retrieval* mechanisms as information infrastructures that make use of information stored elsewhere; these include a directory service (such as one adhering to LDAP) and a search engine (to provide powerful means of finding things). This is a very diverse range of types of products, and we can expect requirements for them to vary accordingly.

Invocation Requirements

What will a calling system expect to be able to ask this information infrastructure to do for it? What kinds of requests will it make? If we're asking for a database, a system will invoke it using standard database operations (of which the most important are the so-called CRUD ones: *create*, *read*, *update* and *delete*). It's reasonable to assume that any database product will supply these operations, so there's little to be gained by spelling them out. Similarly, we can expect any file system to let us read and write the raw content of any flat file and to read the file system to see what files are present.

We might want the ability to easily replace one product with another. In this case, it might be helpful to go into a bit more detail about how we talk to it—perhaps by mentioning a standard (such as SQL or ODBC, for a database), which will, in theory, let us use any product that adheres to that standard.

Implementation Requirements

One way to look at implementation requirements is to see them as specifying the criteria by which to choose the most suitable information storage (or retrieval) product.

Some behind-the-scenes capabilities that we might want an information storage infrastructure to have are the ability to create back-ups of data and to recover data in the event of a failure (such as losing a disk drive). We might also want to ask for all changes to be atomic (all or nothing), to maintain data in a consistent state, and for each change to be isolated from other changes being made at the same time. (These are three of the ACID properties: *atomic*, *consistent*, *isolated*, and *durable*—the last of which is implicit in an information storage infrastructure.) Other considerations that might be important include capacity (especially if you need to be able to store huge quantities of data) and security features (such as being able to encrypt data, and access control).

Requirements for any kind of storage infrastructure other than databases must take into account its special characteristics.

Chapter 8
User Function Requirement Patterns

In this chapter:
8.1 Inquiry Requirement Pattern 156
8.2 Report Requirement Pattern. 161
8.3 Accessibility Requirement Pattern 168
8.4 User Interface Infrastructure. 187
8.5 Reporting Infrastructure 189

User functions are so diverse that it's hard to identify categories that have enough in common to make it worthwhile to write requirement patterns for them. Patterns for two types of functions, the **inquiry** and **report** patterns, are presented here—plus a third on **accessibility**, which covers steps for making a system accessible by people with disabilities while at the same time improving usability for everyone. These three patterns are shown in Figure 8-1. More specialized user interface functions are described in many of the other requirement patterns in this book.

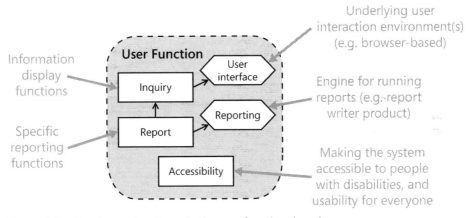

Figure 8-1   Requirement patterns in the user function domain

To work, our user interface functions need a **user interface infrastructure** (for example, a browser-based one that produces and delivers HTML pages to users). If our system has reports, it also needs a **reporting infrastructure**, which is too sophisticated for an organization to build for itself. The last two sections in this chapter summarize capabilities to ask for in these infrastructures.

8.1 Inquiry Requirement Pattern

Basic Details

Related patterns:	Report
Anticipated frequency:	2–15% of requirements
Pattern classifications:	Functional: Yes

Applicability

Use the inquiry pattern to define a screen display function that shows specified information to the user. The word "inquiry" implies that the information being displayed is not modified by this function.

Discussion

Inquiries are the pinnacle of a system, in the sense that you've gone to great trouble and expense to gather valuable information—and now you finally get to show it to people. Specifying a requirement for an inquiry is straightforward enough, though there's potentially quite a lot to say, which is described in the list of content that follows. But there's also the question of how to decide what inquiries we need. This is all too often a hit-and-miss affair, a wish-list of anything anyone can think of. A free-for-all can leave us with some inquiries that no one ever uses, while others that *are* needed are missed. Inquiry requirements are numerous, so it's hard to tell whether something's been forgotten. One way to be more systematic is to start with pervasive requirements demanding that every item of information be viewable on at least one inquiry (as described in the "Extra Requirements" section later in this pattern). This means we needn't worry about simple and mundane inquiries. We can then concentrate on inquiries for a specific business purpose. If we forget anything, there will be an inquiry of last resort to show us what we want, even if it's not ideally suited to the task at hand.

The bulk of inquiries are for *stored* information (data from the database), but they can also be for dynamic information about the state of the system's hardware and software components, or information from attached devices (card readers or credit card payment devices, for example) or any other source of information.

This book spells inquiry with an "i" consistently (rather than *enquiry*). This was an arbitrary choice, but having decided, it's useful to stick to it rigidly. It enables you search on "inquiry" and be reasonably confident of finding every one.

Content

A requirement that defines an inquiry should specify the following:

1.   **Inquiry name**   Give each inquiry an unambiguous name, so that separate inquiries don't get mixed up. Try to keep the name short, though this might not be possible if two similar inquiries must be distinguished from each other.

2.   **The business intent of the inquiry**   This is appropriate if the inquiry fulfills a specific purpose rather than being useful for a variety of reasons. An example of a multi-purpose inquiry might be a general customer details inquiry. The business intent can explain the **circumstances** in which the inquiry is intended to be used and **by whom**, which could be specific ("finance department") or general (any employee, customers). Properly capturing

the intent of an inquiry is more important than its details (the next item), especially if it allows developers the opportunity to build one inquiry function that satisfies more than one of the inquiry requirements.

3. **The information to show**   This refers to the values (fields) that are to be shown for each entity displayed (not to which *entities* are shown, which is covered by the selection criteria item that follows). Don't specify the inquiry's appearance, just its *content*. Make clear where this information comes from (typically the entity or entities it relates to) and what details to show about it. You don't always need to spell out every item of information. Describing it in general terms is often preferable ("full details" or "financial details," for instance), because it avoids the risk of missing something. A general description also remains correct if items are added later. If any item of information is to be calculated on the fly, explain how. If any items of information are to be highlighted (especially when they're in particular states), explain them. If totals and/or other summary information are to be shown for inquiries that show a list, specify them separately from the information for each item in the list itself.

    Occasionally, it's worthwhile to mention information that is *not* to be shown or to state explicitly that only the information indicated—nothing else—is to be shown. Otherwise, if a prominent piece of information is not indicated, a developer might regard it as an omission and show it anyway. If there is a sound reason why certain information is not to be shown, it's a good idea to state that reason.

4. **Sort sequence**   (Optional.) If more than one item can be shown, state the order in which they are to be shown. If the user can choose between two or more sequences, the requirement must say so. You might want to specify, as a desirable add-on, alternative sort sequences, in which one sort sequence could be specified in the requirement, and a refinement requirement (with a lower priority) added for the other(s).

5. **Selection criteria**   (Optional.) Selected criteria can be either chosen by the user, fixed, or a mixture of both. If the user can control which items will be shown, specify which values can be used as selection criteria. For fixed selection criteria, describe what they are, and take care that the selection doesn't appear arbitrary to the user or vary from one request to another; for example, if the inquiry shows historic data, the user might be confused if the length of time covered isn't always the same or items appear and disappear at the beginning or end, apparently at random.

6. **Navigation**   (Optional.) Describe any specific ways in which we allow the user to navigate around the inquiry (that is, internally within it) or to other functions (for example, to drill down to other inquiries or to invoke a maintenance function to edit the data). You can also describe how this inquiry is invoked—how users get to it—but only bother if there's something useful to say.

7. **Interactions**   (Optional.) If there are any special ways in which the user can interact with the inquiry, describe them clearly. Specify only what these interactions need to achieve; don't get embroiled in detailed aspects of the user interface (buttons, hyperlinks, and so on).

8. **Automatic refreshing**   (Optional.) If the inquiry is able to refresh the data it displays (without the user having to request it), specify how such refreshes are to be triggered. Typically, refreshes are triggered either by time (such as every 30 seconds) or when the underlying data itself changes—and it's important to specify which. If you suspect automatic refreshing might be difficult or costly (using the technology you expect, for instance), only demand it if it's really necessary. If this item is omitted, assume the display does not refresh itself.

This is quite a long list, with too many topics to cover in a single requirement—though few inquiry requirements involve more than half of them. As soon as an inquiry requirement grows unduly large, divest the rest into separate refinement requirements. Each of the last three topics often deserves its own refinement requirement if there is enough to say about it.

Template(s)

Summary	Definition
«*Inquiry name*» inquiry	There shall be an [«*Inquiry name*»] inquiry that shows «*Information to show*». Its purpose is «*Business intent*». For each «*Entity name*», the inquiry shall show the following: ■ «*Information item 1*» ■ «*Information item 2*» ■ … [The items to show shall be listed in «*Sort sequence details*» sequence.] [The items to show can be specified by entering any of the following selection criteria: ■ «*Selection criterion 1*» ■ «*Selection criterion 2*» ■ …] [The user shall be able to navigate «*User navigation details*».] [The user shall be able to interact with the inquiry «*User interaction details*».] [The information shown shall automatically refresh «*Automatic refresh details*».]

This summary form is preferred to a verb-phrase form such as "View «*Inquiry purpose summary*»." This is because each inquiry needs a name—which the latter form doesn't provide, thus leaving an unknown someone, later in the project, to name it, and leaving us with no tie between that name and this requirement.

Example(s)

Summary	Definition
Financial transaction inquiry	There shall be an inquiry that shows the financial transactions for a selected customer in a selected date range. It shall show a detail line for each financial transaction made by the customer in the time period, in reverse chronological order. Each detail line shall show ■ Transaction date and time ■ Transaction description ■ Transaction amount The inquiry shall also show the total number of transactions made by the customer in the period. The user shall be able to select any transaction shown and view its full details.

Summary	Definition
Recent orders inquiry	There shall be an order inquiry that enables a customer to view details about their recent and outstanding orders. "Recent" means all orders fulfilled or removed within a specified length of time. This length of time shall be a systemwide configuration parameter (set to, say, 30 days).
	This inquiry shall be accessible only by the customer who placed the order and by authorized employees. (In the latter case, the user shall select which customer to show orders for.)
	This inquiry is static; it does not refresh itself automatically.
Component status inquiry	There shall be an inquiry to allow an operator to view details of the current status of a single system component (such as a machine or server process). The details shown shall depend upon the type of component.
	This inquiry can be invoked either by selecting a component in some other inquiry or by entering its component name.

Here's a refinement requirement that defines the refresh characteristics of an inquiry:

Summary	Definition
Large order inquiry refresh	The large order inquiry shall redisplay itself, without user action with refreshed values, to maintain the timeliness of its content.
	This requirement does not state how this should happen (in particular, whether it redisplays periodically or values should be broadcast whenever they change), nor does it define what it means by "timeliness."
	If the inquiry refreshes periodically, rather than dynamically keeping itself up-to–date, then:
	■ The refresh rate shall be configurable (expected to be a time of the order of 30 seconds.)
	■ The user shall be able to manually request an immediate refresh.

Extra Requirements

A single requirement (plus any refinement requirements) usually suffices for an inquiry—which is just as well, because inquiries are numerous and we don't want the number of requirements about them to explode. But there are a couple of topics for which pervasive requirements can usefully be specified, and these are discussed in the following subsections:

1. **Comprehensive inquiries**   To prevent having to diligently specify an inquiry for every little piece of information, specify a few catch-all requirements to deal with everything you forget.

2. **Common inquiry characteristics**   If there are rules that you want to apply to all inquiries, specify them once, such that they apply across the whole system.

The aim in both cases is to specify *only once* something we want, in general terms, rather than lots of times for individual cases. This both saves considerable specification effort and leaves out no part of the system.

Comprehensive Inquiries   The premise of this section is that **all the information in the system should be viewable**, one way or another. This sounds like a sensible goal for every system, but it's rarely asked for. Who knows how many systems actually achieve it: not many, probably. A system having information that no one can get at—or which none of its users knows is there—can be dangerous. Once an omission of this sort is discovered, it's often resolved by means of an ad hoc addition, without normal validation and security controls. These requirements act as insurance if we fail to specify a comprehensive set of inquiries, and demand a comprehensiveness of inquiry coverage rarely found in requirements specifications. Here are a few sample pervasive requirements of this kind:

Summary	Definition
All information viewable in an inquiry	Every piece of information in the system shall be viewable in at least one inquiry. That is, there is to be no information that lurks inaccessible within the system.
	Pieces of information not to be displayed for security reasons (such as passwords, hashed data, or data encrypted using a key unknown to the user) or for other valid reasons are excluded from this requirement—but the *presence* of this information shall be indicated in at least one inquiry.
All information navigable for inquiry	There shall be a systematic way to navigate to every piece of information in the system and then to view it using an inquiry as per the previous requirement. That is, there is no information that lurks *unknown* in the system (even if the previous requirement provides some way to view it if only we knew how).
	The motivation for this requirement is to prevent a situation where we know something's in there somewhere, but we have no way to get to it. (For example, something that can only be displayed by entering its ID cannot be navigated to systematically if we don't know the ID.)
All user-accessible information viewable by that user	Every piece of information stored by the system that is **accessible to a user** shall be viewable in at least one inquiry **to which that user has access**. That is, there is to be no information that lurks invisible to a user who is authorized to view it.

Note that if you have access control, there's still the possibility the system contains data to which *no one* has access—but that's a separate question.

These requirements cover business information, but one could, in theory, write similar requirements covering other kinds of things that are amenable to display in an inquiry—such as the status of hardware and software components. But this book does not attempt to go beyond business information because it's impractical to figure out just what constitutes *all information* for them, let alone whether it's worthwhile.

Requirements of this sort have wide-ranging implications—for developers, testers, and when estimating overall development effort: roughly speaking, for each kind of information (that is, each database table), an inquiry must be built.

Common Inquiry Characteristics   Specify only once any characteristic that you want all inquiries (or all inquiries of a particular type) to share, rather than requesting it repeatedly for each one. It saves time and avoids the risk of individual requirements differing. Ask for characteristics that are good practice or that you want to standardize across all inquiries in the system. Here's an example that insists that every inquiry not only show information, but also make clear what information it shows:

Summary	Definition
Inquiry selection criteria displayed	Each inquiry shall make clear **what** it is currently showing. That is, it shall not merely display information; it shall also inform the user how the information was selected (in other words, what it means). In particular:
	■ If selection criteria are used, all selection criteria shall be displayed and be identifiable as the selection criteria.
	■ When displaying a single entity, its primary ID shall be displayed.
	■ If any or all of the selection criteria are fixed, they shall be explained in the inquiry's online help.
	Any variable information shall form part of the inquiry display (rather than being obtainable in some other way) to permit the inquiry to be printed and still be equally meaningful.

Considerations for Development

Check that the information is available.

Consider whether there are potential performance concerns.

If the display is to automatically refresh itself, how easy is it to achieve that in the prospective user interface environment?

Considerations for Testing

Testing that an inquiry requirement is satisfied must include displaying the inquiry to verify that it shows what it's supposed to.

Pay special attention to pervasive inquiry requirements, because they mean you must scour the system for all the inquiries they apply to—and then you must test that each inquiry complies. If there's a requirement that insists that every type of information in the system must be viewable by at least one inquiry, you have to go one step further and start by identifying all the types of information (which usually means all the database tables).

8.2 Report Requirement Pattern

Basic Details

Related patterns:	Inquiry
Anticipated frequency:	2–15% of requirements
Pattern classifications:	Functional: Yes

Applicability

Use the report requirement pattern to define a report that shows specified information to the user. The information being displayed is not modified by the report—although it might involve some background generation of data.

Discussion

A report is a way of presenting information—it's very much like an inquiry, in fact, so we must begin by explaining the distinction. Back in the old days, it was clear: an inquiry was something you looked at on the screen, and a report, something you printed on paper. But no longer. Scrolling lets us manipulate large quantities of information onscreen, and reports are viewed increasingly onscreen rather than printed out. This is a trend we should encourage, to reduce use of paper, wear and tear on printers, time waiting for printing, and the security risks of papers falling into the wrong hands.

When you need to show some information to a user, decide whether to specify it as an inquiry or as a report. Make that decision on a sound, rational basis, rather than arbitrarily just because someone had one or the other in mind. Factors to consider are:

- **Factor 1: How much information is to be shown?**   If it's a single item (such as details for one customer), an inquiry is more suitable; if it's an open-ended amount of information, a report is preferable. Also, if you need to show many columns of information, a report might be better.

- **Factor 2: How interactive do we want it to be?**   Reports are passive (using current technology, at least). If we want to be able to change what we're looking at or to navigate elsewhere (such as by clicking on things), we should use an inquiry. And if we need the information to automatically refresh itself on screen, an inquiry is the way to go.

- **Factor 3: How often do you need a hard copy?**   If printing frequently, make it a report.

- **Factor 4: How many people need to see it?**   You can run a report, send it to other people, and be confident that they'll be looking at what you are; instructing them to run an inquiry is less dependable. You can also send a report to someone who doesn't have online access to your system.

- **Factor 5: Do you need to be able to save the results?**   A report is more amenable to being stored than an inquiry is—though it depends partly on the nature of the underlying user interface infrastructure. (For example, an HTML page can be saved.)

- **Factor 6: Where does the information come from?**   If it's not from a database, a reporting product might be unable to read it.

- **Factor 7: How volatile is the information?**   If data changes frequently, a copy of a report will quickly become out-of-date.

- **Factor 8: Is an inquiry or a report cheaper to implement?**   You should also be aware of the answer to this question, so that if all other considerations balance out, you can specify a requirement for whichever option is cheaper. Ordinarily, one might expect a report to be cheaper, because a reporting product usually comes with a report design tool to make creating a new report easier.

If you get conflicting answers to these questions, consider specifying *both* an inquiry and a report for the same information.

The reporting needed for a serious business system is often—and perhaps nearly always—inadequately specified up front. It's hard enough to figure out the transactions that drive the system, so it's not surprising that there's little enthusiasm for working through lots of secondary and less frequent activities. With new views of the business wanted regularly, reporting for management, sales and marketing, and other areas remote from day-to-day operations is frequently the most volatile part of a system. So don't expect the requirements to be able capture them all. But the clearer the picture you can paint, the better: give it your best shot. At least eke out all the *sorts* of reporting that are needed, and get a reasonable idea of the number of reports. Ways to go about this are to examine the following:

1. **The people** who might be interested in receiving reports: this could be a significantly broader group that those who actually use the system: finance people, auditors, management at all levels, system administrators, project managers (for error and system performance statistics and such), and human resources people. It might include people outside the organization, such as government and industry bodies, customers, agents, suppliers, and other business partners. Ask yourself who could conceivably have a legitimate interest in some aspect of what goes on in your system.

2. **The activities** needed to keep the business running: for the purposes of reporting, don't worry about the every-hour, mainstream activities, because they'll never be neglected. Pay special attention to operational activities that involve decision-making, because all such decisions are based on information—so try to identify what information is needed and what form would be most effective for it.

3. **The strategic stratosphere:** what sorts of—predominantly statistical—information would help those involved in directing the business (chiefly senior management and sales and marketing)? It's important to gain a good grasp of the expectations of the people at this level, because the scale and complexity of reports for them could have a significant impact on the overall size of the system. Also, the processing needed to generate such reports could be so intensive that it will have a noticeable impact on overall system performance; if a separate reporting system is needed to avoid this, we need to identify this as early as possible and cover the implications in the requirements.

It's not acceptable to write a sweeping requirement that covers multiple reports, especially if it's open-ended. Something like "a full set of finance reports" or "all reports required by the government regulator" are at best a hint that a lot is missing and are useless as requirements. If the specific reports cannot be pinned down, say so in informal text, **not in a requirement**.

Pay attention to special occasions on which reporting is especially important (especially ends of month, quarter, calendar year, or financial year). Don't make the mistake of getting the day-to-day reporting right and neglecting infrequent reporting tasks. Specifying "obvious" needs in a cursory manner could lead to reports that are unwieldy in practice and impose too great a workload on users during these busy times. Also, attempting to add these reports just before they are needed could unearth other omissions in the underlying system that cannot be fixed in time.

When investigating what reports are needed, you will gather much valuable information about who should receive them, how often, how many copies, how long they should be retained, and so on. These details don't belong in requirements because they are liable to change—and you should demand a system in which they can be changed at any time. But retain all the reporting information that is gathered, and use it when configuring the initial system. Concrete decisions on report production and distribution should be made in the lead-up to the system being installed, probably while it's being tested. If possible, let users experiment with a test system, to familiarize themselves with it. They can refine the reporting set-up and decide operational matters at that time.

Some organizations regularly print reports and file them away, or file away electronic copies so they can refer to them later as a last resort. This suggests the system itself isn't properly and reliably retaining information—that it has holes in its database design, often relating to historic data. It can also be a sign that users lack confidence in the system. Designing better systems diminishes this role for reports, so fewer reports might be needed. If you're specifying a replacement for an existing system, keep your eyes open for reports being used in this way.

Data Warehouse Magic

"Ah, we've got a data warehouse. We don't need to worry about reports." A data warehouse—if you haven't encountered one—is a data repository, typically driven by a relational database and either using a specialized product or built in-house, that's intended for rich querying. It might do clever things, but just because you throw everything you've got into them doesn't mean you'll magically get out the pearls of wisdom you seek. At some point, someone has to figure out what information is needed for a particular purpose and what massaging of the available data must be done to provide it. The earlier this is done, the better, which means specifying the information in the requirements.

Specifying necessary reporting in the requirements means that potential performance implications of intensive reports will come to light earlier, and testers will know what reporting to test. Reports added ad hoc later on will be subject to less scrutiny and control.

A traditional report prints numeric and textual values in a formatted manner. But reporting products are typically able to produce various kinds of **charts**, so don't limit your thinking to conventional presentation. Equally important, though, don't introduce charts just because you can and they're pretty—constraining developers by mandating a chart when they might find a more effective way of achieving the goal. Concentrate on the purpose and content, not on the presentation.

An important factor to consider when specifying a report is *how many pages* it's likely to contain when it's run in practice. When you have a large database, it's easy to devise huge reports with more pages than anyone can ever wade through. (Sometimes users are interested only in the grand totals at the bottom.) Reports that allow the user to specify selection criteria can turn out to be unexpectedly large due to the selection values entered. It's useful to be able to specify the maximum number of pages that are allowed and to warn users beforehand of potentially long or slow reports.

Content

A requirement that defines a report should specify the following:

1. **Report name**
2. **The business intent of the report**
3. **The information to show**
4. **Sort sequence**
5. **Selection criteria**

6. **Automatic run details**   (Optional.) If the report is intended to be run automatically (without being requested by a user), state the frequency (for example, daily or monthly), describe who the report is to be distributed to, and indicate whether it can be run on request, too.

7. **Totaling levels**   For which values do we want totals? Consider each level in the sort sequence and ask whether totals would be helpful whenever that value changes (for example, per customer or per currency).

8. **Page throw levels**   Consider each level in the sort sequence and ask whether a new page should be started whenever the value changes.

The first five of these items are as described in the inquiry requirement pattern.

Template(s)

Summary	Definition
«Report name» report	There shall be a report that shows *«Information to show»* *«Selection criteria»* sorted by *«Sort sequence»*. The purpose of this report is to *«Business intent»*.
	For each *«Item type name»*, the report shall show the following:
	■ *«Value name 1»*
	■ *«Value name 2»*
	■ ...
	[The items to show can be specified by entering any of the following selection criteria:
	■ *«Selection criterion 1»*
	■ *«Selection criterion 2»*
	■ ...]
	Totals shall be shown for *«Totaling levels»*. [A new page shall be started for *«Page throw levels»*.]
	[The report is intended to be run automatically *«Automatic run details»*.]

Example(s)

Summary	Definition
Foreign exchange deal report	There shall be a report that lists all foreign exchange deals made in a selected time period (by the desk for whom the requester works).
	The report shall show the following information for each deal:
	■ Deal type
	■ Deal amount (including currency)
	■ Date and time
	■ Exchange rate
	■ Name of organization with which the deal was placed
	At the end the report shall show totals per organization and grand totals for the number of deals, and deal amount.

Extra Requirements

There are quite a few ways in which we might want to standardize all the reports created for a system. We can specify a pervasive requirement for each one we wish to insist upon. Here is a list of such requirements to consider including, some of which should be tailored to suit your environment:

Summary	Definition
Reports security and privacy	All reporting functions shall comply with all stated security and data privacy requirements.
	It should not be strictly necessary to state this requirement explicitly, but we do so to stress the following implications of those requirements:
	■ No user should be able to produce a report that contains data to which they have not been granted access.
	■ Tools used to develop new reports should cause all reports produced with them to comply with all stated security requirements.
Consistent report layout	All reports shall adhere to a standard layout, which includes headings and trailers (footers). This layout shall allow for branding by the company (logo, company name, and system name in headings).
Reports show date and time produced	Every report shall show, on each page, the date and time it was produced.
Reports show parameters	Every report shall show all parameters used to control its generation. That is, it shall be possible to see which selection criteria were used (without which it's not possible to know what the report means).
Reports show recipient	Every report shall show the name of the person for whom it was produced. For reports produced upon request, this shall be the name of the requester; for reports produced automatically, the recipient shall be specified beforehand.
	If there are multiple recipients, it shall be possible to assign a name to the group, in which case the group name is printed as the recipient name in all copies.
Reports show degree of confidentiality	Every report shall show, on each page, a statement of its degree of confidentiality. Each report for which no confidentiality level has been expressly decided shall by default be regarded as "company confidential."
	This requirement does not imply the presence of a list of allowed degrees of confidentiality. It shall be possible to draw up a special statement of confidentiality to suit circumstances of a particular report (for example, "finance department confidential").
Report subtotals and totals	All reports shall show subtotals and totals where applicable.

Summary	Definition
Highlight amount overflows on reports	Where values exceed the space available, a consistent mechanism shall be used to show this fact (for example, "##########"). The purpose of this requirement is to prevent a partial value being interpreted as the full value.
	(Reports should, however, be designed wherever possible with sufficient space to accommodate the largest realistic amounts to prevent such overflows in the first place.)
Report page number	All reports shall show, on each page, the page number.
Report page count	All reports shall show, on each page, the total number of pages in the report.
	The intent of this requirement is to allow the recipient to tell whether pages are missing (when read in conjunction with the page number).
End of report line	All reports shall show an "end of report" line at the bottom.
	The intent of this requirement is to allow the recipient of a report to tell whether it is incomplete.
Capped data line	If data is omitted from a report because its size has been capped to a maximum number of pages, a line shall be printed at the bottom of the report to make this clear.
	No totals shall be printed after capping has taken place, since such totals are liable to be incorrect.
Reports on A4 paper	All reports shall be designed for printing using a laser printer on A4 paper with landscape orientation.

A further pervasive requirement can serve as a catch-all, to avoid having to laboriously specify in the requirements lots of rarely-used reports while at the same time demanding the creation of reports for data not explicitly specified in the requirements (for example, derived data generated for performance reasons):

Summary	Definition
Comprehensive set of reports	All data stored within the system shall be accessible via the available reports (except data that should not be shown for security reasons). That is, if data exists, there must be the ability to view it on some report or another.

Considerations for Development

If a report writer product is used to deliver reports (which is usually the sensible thing to do), the development of each individual report is solely a matter of using the report writer's design tool. (If you're using an open source reporting product, the design tool—or tools—might come from different developers.)

Considerations for Testing

First, identify all the circumstances in which the report can be run, and then simulate all those cases. For example, different types of users might run a report in different ways, or a report might be run in a different way on the last day of the month or following a public holiday.

Testing that a report requirement is satisfied involves running the report for each identified test case to verify that it shows what it is supposed to.

Also test reports against the **pervasive** requirements that apply to all reports. This can be sometimes be simplified: if the reporting product used is able to *guarantee* that a pervasive requirement is always satisfied, then it doesn't need to be tested for each individual report.

For any report for which selection criteria can be specified, entry of those criteria should be tested in a similar manner to a data entry function. Test that each value is validated appropriately. Then test that the expected entities were actually selected.

Testing a report needs to go beyond verifying that it satisfies its original requirement. A report might achieve its business purpose but still be impractical to use. If it contains *extra* information, it'll probably still satisfy the requirement, but it might render it hard to read the important values. Selection criteria might add flexibility, but if users end up typing in the same values every time, it's inefficient. View the report from user's point of view. Does it fit well into their workflow?

Simulate all days on which additional reporting is performed (year-end, quarter-end, month-end, and so on).

8.3 Accessibility Requirement Pattern

Basic Details

Related patterns:	Refer-to-requirements, user authentication
Anticipated frequency:	Zero to eight requirements
Pattern classifications:	Functional: No; Pervasive: Maybe

Applicability

Use the accessibility requirement pattern to specify the extent to which the system (or part of it) must be accessible by people with a certain kind of disability or other specific need—that is, how convenient it must be for them to use. This requirement pattern takes such a broad view of "specific needs" that some apply to everyone, and it thus covers those aspects of *usability* (general user-friendliness) that are amenable to being defined in requirements.

Discussion

Accessibility is generally taken to mean providing access for people who have disabilities of various kinds and degrees of severity (ranging, for example, from color blindness through low vision to blindness). That's certainly the motivation for accessibility legislation and standards. The people affected are often regarded by businesses and by builders of systems as a small minority who can be safely ignored. But people who can benefit from accessibility features in systems constitute fully **60 percent** of adults of working age (according to studies cited at the end of the "Example(s)" section later in this pattern). And taking steps to help those who have difficulties or impairments can make such a difference to them that they deserve consideration out of proportion to their numbers. Providing accessibility for those who need it also improves usability for everyone. So this requirement pattern talks in terms of "**specific needs**" and takes an open and inclusive view of who has them. They go beyond people with disabilities to embrace people who aren't computer literate; people who lack linguistic skills (such as people with cognitive difficulties or speakers of English as a second language); people who could suffer eye, hand, or brain strain when using the system; people who have never used the system before; or people who are experienced "power users" of the system. In short, accessibility embraces everybody in one way or another. This is a novel way of looking at some of these situations.

When discussing disabilities, *terminology* is a very sensitive issue. It is easy to sound demeaning or patronizing even without realizing it. Terms for a particular disability, or for the subject in general, often acquire negative associations and new terms are then introduced. This book even introduces the term "specific need" to avoid the more common "special need," which is itself beginning to be regarded as condescending. When writing about this subject, take care to treat every group of people with respect.

The poor accessibility of the vast majority of systems is a powerful sign that there isn't a strong enough business case for doing better. Another factor is low awareness of the need for systems to be accessible—which means the case for accessibility isn't being made as well as it might, a situation that better requirements specifications can help remedy. There are several sound arguments for a business to make a system more accessible: (1) a law says you must; (2) it will attract more customers; (3) fewer people will raise customer service issues; (4) it will make employees more productive. Not all apply to every system. Getting management support can be a hard sell, and even then resources for accessibility might be the first to be cut when development is under pressure. Merely helping people isn't a motivation for a hard-nosed business—though I suspect it's likely to motivate developers more than any of these business reasons will, which is important because it will give them more interest in doing a good job.

There is no *usability* requirement pattern in this book: it is deemed not to deserve one. That's partly because our broad treatment of accessibility covers many aspects of usability, and partly because attempts at guaranteeing usability via requirements fail miserably. A couple of sensible steps are covered in the "Usability" subsection of the "Extra Requirements" section of this pattern, along with more on the drawbacks of usability requirements.

All accessibility-related requirements apply both to the software we develop and to the technology we use—most importantly, to third-party products that deliver parts of our user interface. If you specify requirements for any infrastructure that the system needs, include a requirement (as per the refer-to-requirements requirement pattern in Chapter 5, "Fundamental Requirement Patterns") that states that all our accessibility requirements apply to it, too. We can also ask that more fundamental technology (especially the operating system and Web browsers) offer accessibility features that help satisfy our accessibility goals (or, at least, don't render them unachievable).

Accessibility-related requirements can be specified at three levels:

■ **Level 1: A law or standard that must be adhered to**   Use the comply-with-standard requirement pattern for this. It is your responsibility to find out which laws apply to your system. Bear in mind that laws and regulations are liable to change.

   If you're under no obligation to satisfy a law or standard, you can ignore level 1 without ill effect. Don't write a requirement of this kind just for the sake of it.

■ **Level 2: A type of specific need the system must satisfy, and the extent to which the need must be satisfied**   This is what an accessibility requirement is for, as described in the content explanation at the end of this section and covered in the "Template(s)" and "Example(s)" sections later in this pattern. Requirements at this level have the major benefit of making readers aware of the *people* we're aiming to assist; requirements at levels 1 and 3 can be abstract, and their benefits can be harder for some readers to discern.

- **Level 3: Detailed features we want the system to have in order to satisfy the specific needs**   These are expressed in terms that developers can easily digest and that testers can test. They are covered in the "Extra Requirements" section of this pattern.

The second level is a more detailed picture of the implications of the first level, as the third level is of the second. You can therefore write as informal material (rather than requirements) any level that's spelled out in more detail. It saves everyone's time and avoids contention between the levels. For example, testers don't have to worry how to test against a type of specific need if all its implications are covered in specific requirements. Nevertheless, if a system must comply with a particular law, that, too, is a concrete requirement and should be presented as such—though you can indicate that it doesn't need to be tested in detail because its implications have their own requirements.

If a law has detailed stipulations, represent them at Level 3. You could therefore omit Level 2, but I suggest this equates to satisfying the letter of the law and ignoring its spirit. To me, Level 2 is important because it's the one concerned with the *people* we're trying to assist and thus motivates developers more than requirements whose purpose is less obvious.

Here are a few representative Level 1 requirements:

Summary	Definition
Section 508 of Rehabilitation Act	The system shall be accessible to people with disabilities in accordance with Section 508 of the U.S. Rehabilitation Act, as amended, 1998—commonly referred to simply as "Section 508."
	(Section 508 applies to all systems and Web sites developed, purchased, or run by any U.S. Federal government agency, though there are certain exceptions.)
	Source: *http://www.section508.gov*
Americans with Disabilities Act	The system shall be accessible to people with disabilities in accordance with the Americans with Disabilities Act, 1990.
	Source: *http://www.usdoj.gov/crt/ada/statute.html*
U.K. Disability Discrimination Act	The system shall be accessible to people with disabilities in accordance with the U.K. Disability Discrimination Act, 1995.
	Source: *http://www.opsi.gov.uk/acts/acts1995/1995050.htm*
Web content accessibility guidelines	All Web pages displayed by the system (including all static pages of documentation) shall comply with the Web Content Accessibility Guidelines, version 1.0, produced by the World Wide Web Consortium.
	Source: *http://www.w3.org/TR/WAI-WEBCONTENT*

Observe that each of these examples cites the year that the applicable law was enacted, or a version of a standard, to make it clear the system won't automatically be aware of subsequent amendments (if there were to be any).

Whenever we break down a requirement into lower level requirements that represent its implications, we want a systematic way to do it—to give us confidence that we haven't missed something. So how can we go about finding the kinds of specific needs we want to deal with? For this purpose—and stepping away from our gentle concern for people for a moment while still looking at a system from the user's point of view—we can treat a human being as a typical system with three main kinds of components: *input, processing,* and *output:*

1.	**Input**, via the senses—of which we only need to worry about the two appealed to by typical commercial systems.		
	1.1.	**Vision**, relating to information a system normally displays.	
		1.1.1.	Color blind.
		1.1.2.	Difficulty or impairment.
		1.1.3.	Complete blindness.
		1.1.4.	Flashing screen could cause a seizure.
		1.1.5.	Liable to eye strain (that is, everyone who uses their eyes).
	1.2.	**Hearing**, relating to the playing of audio by a system.	
		1.2.1.	Difficulty or impairment.
		1.2.2.	Complete deafness.
		1.2.3.	The user being in a loud environment in which sounds produced by their machine are hard to hear even with unimpaired hearing.
		1.2.4.	Sound not produced by the user's machine.
2.	**Processing**, performed by the user's brain—referred to as **cognitive abilities**. It means how easily a person interprets and understands the information that a computer system presents to them and how long it takes them to decide what their response will be. It doesn't equate to intelligence.		
	2.1.	Difficulty comprehending information presented by a computer (for example, people with dyslexia).	
	2.2.	Slow to make decisions.	
	2.3.	Limited knowledge of the language in which the system is presented. This might include speakers of English as a second language (if English is the language of the system) and children.	
	2.4.	Not computer literate.	
	2.5.	Unfamiliar with the system.	
	2.6.	Power user—someone who knows the system very well and doesn't want to be slowed down by being told things they already know (including prompts for individual fields).	
3.	**Output**, which means how you tell a computer what you want it to do. Systems normally rely on a user signaling their intentions by using one or more devices operated by the hands, typically a keyboard and mouse in combination.		
	3.1.	Limited manual dexterity, or pain while moving the hands.	
	3.2.	Being able to use one hand only.	
	3.3.	Unable to use hands at all.	
	3.4.	Liable to repetitive strain injury, such as carpal tunnel syndrome—which is a risk for everyone who uses their hands.	
	3.5.	Being unable to communicate vocally (with speech).	

We're interested in disabilities here only to the extent that they create distinctions that affect the steps that a system must take to assist. As a result, these categories are inexact and a little arbitrary. For example, a user might be slow to respond because of dexterity difficulties rather than because they're slow to make decisions. But if one response is for the system to give users as much time as they need, the reason is immaterial.

Some people with specific needs can only use computers with the aid of specialized devices and/or software products—called **assistive technology**—of which there's a wide and growing range, designed to help in diverse ways. We don't need to discuss them here, though analysts and developers concerned with accessibility will benefit from an understanding of the most significant types. (Information about types of assistive technology, products, and manufacturers can be found at *http://www.microsoft.com/enable/at.*) One of the most important aspects of making a system accessible is allowing assistive technology to work effectively. Anyone who uses assistive technology relies upon a chain of support that utilizes special features of the operating system, Web browser, and more. It would be a shame if that chain broke because the last link was an HTML page, from your system, that was written in a careless manner.

The first step in making a system accessible is *awareness*. Analysts, in particular, need to understand the issues in order to write good accessibility requirements. A company then needs to create accessibility-related guidelines and/or standards that suit its way of developing systems. Much of this requirement pattern is written as if achieving accessibility is an overhead, but if it becomes second nature, that overhead is significantly reduced. When software and other elements of the user interface are built with accessibility in mind from the outset, less extra work is needed.

Content

An accessibility requirement should contain the following.

1. **Type of specific need**   Each requirement must cover a *range* of needs of a particular kind, because it's impractical to write a requirement for each individual possibility. The best course is to write a separate requirement for each range that places its own distinct demands on the system. For example, the needs of a person with color blindness differ from those of someone with low vision, and the needs of a blind person are very different again. Having one requirement spanning all visual disabilities isn't helpful to developers or testers. Go into as much detail as it takes to make the range of specific needs clear.

2. **Which part(s) of the system must be accessible**   If you mean the whole system, say so. It is possible (but not desirable) to make some parts of the system accessible and in others take no steps towards accessibility, or to assign different priorities to the accessibility of different parts (for example, to prioritize the public parts used by customers above internal functions used by employees).

   In an ideal world, all parts of a system would be fully accessible from the start. But in practice, a company with a limited budget could be forced to make compromises. The trend towards tougher accessibility laws would leave such a company with fewer options for compromise.

3. **The extent of support**   How convenient should use of the system be for a person with this need? To what lengths are we prepared to go to make the system easier for them to use?

4. **Estimated percentage of users affected**   (If applicable and known.) This can bring home to readers of the requirement that accessibility isn't just for a tiny number of people. Having this information also enables us to determine how many will benefit from improvements in this area and helps us concentrate on features of greatest benefit to the most people.

5. **The clause in a law or standard to which this requirement pertains**   (If relevant.) It's better to say "pertains" rather than "satisfies" because a requirement at this level is too broad to be so categorical and warrants the writing of detailed requirements for the individual implications.

Separating accessibility into several Level 2 requirements allows those areas with the greatest impact to be prioritized higher if we don't have the resources to make the whole system fully accessible from the start. It might seem harsh to postpone accessibility for one class of users (say, employees), but if we have a thousand times as many customers as employees using the system and the organization can't afford to implement all accessibility requirements right away, it maximizes the benefit. On the other hand, if a law says our system must be accessible to employees, but the law doesn't apply to customers, we'd probably do the reverse. But again, legislative changes might impose higher accessibility demands throughout the system.

Template(s)

Summary	Definition
Accessible by people with specific «*Specific need name*» needs	The «*System part*» shall be accessible by people with specific «*Specific need description*» needs [to the extent that «*Extent of support*»]. [An estimated «*Percentage affected*»% of users are likely to benefit.] [This pertains to «*Clause in law*».]

This summary format is a little long-winded, but that's to make it clear that the purpose of such requirements is to benefit real people; a more concise "«*Specific need name*» accessibility" sounds too impersonal to me.

Example(s)

Summary	Definition

Accessible by people with specific vision needs	The system shall be accessible by people with specific vision needs, to the extent that a user shall be able to:
	
	  a. Display the whole user interface in a large font without truncating displayed text or other values.
	
	  b. Use a screen magnifier (to magnify a selected part of the screen).
	
	  c. Use a screen reader (to read aloud information displayed).
	
	An estimated 27% of working age adults have a vision difficulty or impairment (16% mild and 11% severe).
	
	This pertains to §1194.31 (a) and (b) in Section 508.

Accessible by color blind people	The system shall be accessible by people who are color blind, to the extent that they shall be able to discern all text and other information displayed by the system as easily as a person without color blindness. Any meaning conveyed through the use of color shall also be conveyed by other means discernable by a color blind person. An estimated 9% of men and 0.5% of women are color blind.

Summary	Definition
Prolonged use without eye strain	The system's user interface shall avoid visual constructs that are apt to cause eye strain after several hours of continuous use. Such constructs include flashing visual objects, low contrast between adjacent objects (such as text and its background), and bright colors.
Accessible by people who are hard of hearing	The system shall be accessible by people with special hearing needs, people in a loud environment that precludes their hearing sounds made by the computer, or people whose computer has no sound capability or has sound switched off. An estimated 21% of working-age adults have a hearing difficulty or impairment (19% mild and 3% severe). This pertains to §1194.31 (c) and (d) in Section 508.
Accessible by people with specific cognitive needs	The system shall be accessible by people with specific cognitive needs, including people with limited ability to read and write English, to the extent that the system shall a. Phrase all instructions clearly. b. Use terminology consistently. c. Avoid obscure words where there are more commonly-used alternatives. d. Provide context-sensitive help for all input-capable user interface components (such as buttons and entry fields). An estimated 20% of working age adults have a cognitive difficulty or impairment.
Accessible by people with specific dexterity needs	The system shall be accessible by people with specific manual dexterity needs, to the extent that it is fully usable by a user who lacks fine motor control, is unable to perform multiple physical actions simultaneously, or has limited reach or physical strength. An estimated 26% of working age adults have a manual dexterity difficulty or impairment (19% mild and 7% severe). This pertains to §1194.31 (f) in Section 508.
Prolonged use without hand strain	Any operation that a user is likely to perform many times in succession over a prolonged period shall not involve awkward movement of the hands or fingers and shall not expect the user to perform many actions (such as key presses) in a short time. Having to press two or more keyboard keys simultaneously is deemed to constitute an awkward movement.
Accessible without voice	A user shall be able to perform all functions of the system without using their voice. This pertains to §1194.31 (e) in Section 508.
Accessible by novice users	A person with basic computer literacy shall be able to figure out how to use every function in the system. It shall be possible to access any online help needed to achieve this shall be directly from any function for which it is needed. For the purpose of this requirement, "basic computer literacy" means being comfortable using a personal computer and common desktop applications.

Summary	Definition
Convenient for power user employees	Any function used repeatedly and often, by any employee, shall be performable with a minimum of steps (including a minimum of keystrokes and/or mouse actions), and shall not delay that user by displaying instructions they already know.

The specific need percentages cited in the preceding examples come from the following two research studies conducted by Forrester Research, Inc. on behalf of Microsoft Corporation:

- **"The Market for Accessible Technology–The Wide Range of Abilities and Its Impact on Computer Use,"** 2003, freely available from *http://www.microsoft.com/enable/research/phase1.aspx*

- **"Accessible Technology in Computing–Examining Awareness, Use, and Future Potential,"** 2004, freely available from *http://www.microsoft.com/enable/research/phase2.aspx*

Extra Requirements

The bulk of the requirements in this section are for features that contribute to satisfying one or more accessibility requirements; that is, they are requirements at Level 3 as described in the "Content" section earlier in this pattern. They are divided into the topics that follow, and each is dealt with in its own subsection that follows. ("Specific need steps," however, has a separate subsection for each of four types of specific need.)

1. **General accessibility**   Define steps to take that aren't limited to just one kind of specific need, and define accessibility etiquette to prevent our system from getting in the way of any kind of assistive technology.

2. **Specific need steps**   Specify detailed requirements for the types of specific need identified in the example "Discussion" section: *vision, sound, cognition,* and *dexterity.* (*Speech,* however, is not dealt with, because few commercial systems depend on voice input.) Note that user preferences and tailoring for all kinds of specific needs are covered in the next topic.

3. **Tailoring to an individual user**   Provide ways for an individual to adjust our system's user interface according to their user preferences.

4. **Documentation and support**   Make documentation accessible to people with specific needs, and give them access to further assistance (including customer service).

5. **Certifying compliance**   Describe the extent to which the system complies with an applicable law.

6. **Usability**

This section doesn't pretend to satisfy all the provisions of any particular accessibility law but uses the provisions of Section 508 of the U.S. Rehabilitation Act as its starting point, because that's the most prominent such law and the one whose stipulations go into the greatest detail (at the time of writing). This section addresses all the main demands as they apply to the software of a system. But **this section isn't comprehensive**: it ignores other clauses that don't affect typical commercial systems, such as the captioning of instructional videos, special environments (for instance, user interaction via a telephone), or embedded systems. Check what's relevant to your system, and write requirements on any additional topics that apply to it. The underlying principle is that everything that you present to your users should be accessible. Any requirement relating to a law or standard should identify which clause (and which law or standard) it satisfies or contributes to satisfying. If you're building a system for multiple jurisdictions, you might need to mention more than one law.

Many of the examples that follow contain a statement that they are "intended to satisfy" particular clauses of Section 508. These are indicative only; they represent only my (non-legal) opinion. When you specify real requirements yourself, however, you should make stronger statements: write that they are "deemed to satisfy" or that they "satisfy" the relevant clauses. But if you do so, you must verify thoroughly that each requirement does achieve what it claims. Whenever a system must comply with a law, the steps needed to achieve compliance must be identified, identified as early as possible, and seen by the widest possible audience. To achieve those goals, the requirements are the place to identify the steps, and the place to state categorically that you believe that each requirement is sufficient to satisfy the part of the law to which it relates.

All the examples that follow are, as all requirements should be, as technology-independent as possible. Even those stipulations of Section 508 that are specifically for HTML are expressed here in general terms. This section uses the term **presentation unit** to mean a self-contained set of information that is intended to be displayed together, such as an HTML page. However, where relevant, each example explains the implications when HTML is indeed the medium. Some technologies contain features that make it easier to implement accessibility, but this isn't the place to discuss them. If you're using a particular technology (say, a browser-based user interface), you can write requirements for specific ways in which it must be used to improve accessibility.

General Accessibility   In examples that are self-explanatory enough not to need further introduction, this section covers a few good practices and matters that apply to more than one kind of specific need.

Summary	Definition
Don't interfere with accessibility features	The system shall not interfere in any way with features of the operating system or other products that are identified as serving accessibility purposes (assistive technology). This includes external devices that might be present solely for accessibility purposes.
	This is intended to satisfy §1194.21 (b) in Section 508.
Synchronized multimedia alternatives	The system shall provide a semantically equivalent alternative for the video and/or audio parts of any multimedia presentation or animation that shall be synchronized with the main presentation. One alternative might suffice for both media. It is also acceptable to present the content of the presentation in the form of static information.
	This generally means providing an alternative stream using a different medium (usually text and/or audio) that is synchronized to the main stream, to help people who have difficulty perceiving either video or audio.
	This is intended to satisfy §1194.21 (h) and §1194.22 (b) in Section 508.

Summary	Definition
Readable without style sheet	It shall be possible to fully perceive and understand a presentation unit without any additional resource that defines aspects of its presentation style (a "style sheet"). The intent of this requirement is to bar style sheets from containing semantic information, because assistive technology might be unable to extract that information.
	This is intended to satisfy §1194.22 (d) in Section 508.
Downloadable by people with specific needs	Whenever software is available for download to the user's machine, instructions for downloading and installing shall themselves comply with all accessibility requirements in this specification, and downloading shall not begin until instructed by the user.
	This is intended to satisfy §1194.22 (m) in Section 508.
Avoid duplicate command components	Any presentation unit that ordinarily contains multiple user interface components to initiate the same command shall provide some way to avoid duplication of components that have the same purpose (in particular, in the case of HTML, duplicate navigation links).
	The intent of this requirement is to avoid unnecessarily burdening users of assistive technology and users who have difficulty reading the screen.
	This is intended to satisfy §1194.22 (o) in Section 508.

The following are two alternative ways of approaching the matter of users having to respond in a given length of time. Avoid the first whenever you can, because it involves a more complex user interface for the user and the building of additional functionality.

Summary	Definition
Control of timed responses	The user shall be informed whenever they are expected to respond within a fixed length of time and shall be given the opportunity to indicate that they need more time.
	This is intended to satisfy §1194.22 (p) in Section 508.
No timed responses	The system shall never expect the user to respond within a given fixed length of time. This does not preclude the system dealing with exceptionally slow responses in whatever manner is appropriate (for example, if the circumstances reflected in the original display no longer apply).
	This is intended to satisfy §1194.22 (p) in Section 508.

A related matter is screens that automatically refresh without the user asking:

Summary	Definition
Auto-refresh control	For any screen that auto-refreshes (that is, redisplays itself) spontaneously, the user shall have the option to switch auto-refreshing off. If auto-refreshing occurs after a given length of time, the user shall be able to modify that time.

People with specific needs must be able to authenticate themselves when biometric means are in use (that is, when a uniquely distinctive body part, such as a fingerprint, is used to identify the user). (See the user authentication requirement pattern in Chapter 11, "Access Control Requirement Patterns," for more.) The following example insists on that users who are unable to use a biometric reader must still be able to authenticate themselves:

Summary	Definition
Biometric identification alternative	If a biometric form of user identification is used (for example, a fingerprint reader), any person shall be able to be identified by other means if they do not possess the requisite biological characteristics (which includes missing that body part or not being physically able to present it to the reader).
	This is intended to satisfy §1194.26 (c) in Section 508.

Specific Vision Needs   The vast bulk of information presented by commercial systems is designed to be visual, which is why this subsection has the most subjects for requirements. Many of them are intended to help assistive technology to present information in an alternative way, which is difficult enough at the best of times. Take a look at the source of an HTML page and try to pick out the bits that a user is interested in: for a rich page, it's not easy, even without the myriad tricks that page writers use to get just the right appearance. Or imagine explaining the contents of a Web page to someone who can't see it, when at the same time you can't see any of the graphics in it.

Let's start with the biggest single driver of assistive technology, which affects the building of every part of the user interface:

Summary	Definition
User interface component semantics	Information about each user interface component shall be programmatically available, such that assistive technology can determine (and present to the user via other means) its type, state, content, and identity (name and description). When soliciting information from the user (via an "electronic form"), the semantic information shall be complete enough to allow the user to enter and submit data.
	When applied to an HTML page:
	1. A textual explanation shall be provided for every user-perceivable non-text element via "alt," "longdesc," or equivalent HTML attributes, or in element content.
	2. Each table column and row heading shall be a "th" HTML element.
	3. Each cell in a complex table shall be unambiguously associated with its column and row heading(s).
	4. Each frame shall have a textual title.
	This is intended to satisfy §1194.21 (d) and (l) and §1194.22 (a), (g), (h) and (i) in Section 508.

Don't be a nuisance when users with specific needs have less free screen space than other users:

Summary	Definition
Screen and window sizes	The system shall not make assumptions about a user's screen size (number of pixels wide or high) or the size or position of any of the windows within which the system's user interface is displayed.
	The intent of this requirement is to accommodate users with specific needs who could have a screen with lower resolution than most users or who have to devote some of their screen "real estate" to assistive technology (such as an onscreen keyboard).

The following two examples relate to the screen focus. You might think that you needn't worry about screen focus matters because standard user interface technologies take care of this themselves, and to a large extent they do. For example, a browser displaying HTML pages can be expected to do so. But these requirements are still important as instructions to developers not to break them (if there are ways to do so—for example, using scripts embedded scripts in HTML pages). In addition, when choosing a user interface infrastructure, add these to the requirements that it must satisfy.

Summary	Definition
Screen focus indicated	The user interface component that currently has focus (that is, will receive any input from the keyboard or equivalent device) shall be identified by a clear onscreen indication.
	This is intended to satisfy part of §1194.21 (c) in Section 508.
Screen focus programmatically exposed	The screen focus shall be programmatically exposed so that assistive technology can determine the current focus and be notified when focus changes.
	This is intended to satisfy part of §1194.21 (c) in Section 508.

If you have text to display, then display it as text; don't use graphics or anything else that assistive technology can't make sense of. Even attaching the text itself to an image of a piece of text is tedious to present non-visually.

Summary	Definition
Display text naturally	Text shall be presented through text-specific user interface infrastructure operations, such that assistive technology can retrieve at least the text content, text input caret location, and presentation style attributes.
	This is intended to satisfy §1194.21 (f) in Section 508.

Here's a rule to insist on universally:

Summary	Definition
Flashing frequency	Nothing presented visually by the system shall flash, blink, be perceivable as flashing or blinking, or cause the screen to flicker, at a frequency greater than two per second and lower than 55 per second. This includes text, blank areas of color, video, and animations.
	The primary motivation of this requirement is to avoid triggering a seizure in a susceptible person (for example, someone at risk of an epileptic seizure). Secondarily, avoid irritating everyone else.
	This is intended to satisfy §1194.21 (k) and §1194.22 (j) in Section 508.

Now for a few rules on using color responsibly:

Summary	Definition
User colors never overridden	The system shall not override any user-selected color, color contrast level, or other display-related attribute.
	This is intended to satisfy §1194.21 (g) in Section 508.
Information never via color only	Color coding shall never be the only means of conveying any information, indicating an action, prompting a response, or distinguishing a visual element. That is, if all color were removed, the system could be used equally as well.
	When applied to HTML, each page shall be designed so that all information conveyed with color is also conveyed in another way that does not depend on color (for example, using context or some other form of markup).
	This is intended to satisfy §1194.21 (i) and §1194.22 (c) in Section 508.
Choice of colors	Whenever a user is permitted to adjust color and contrast settings, a variety of color selections, representing a range of contrast levels, shall be provided.
	Note that some people cannot see white text on a black background, and others cannot tolerate a white or bright background and must have a black or dark background.
	This is intended to satisfy §1194.21 (j) in Section 508.

Presenting an **image** to a user and inviting them to interact with it is impossible in most cases if the user can't see it. Section 508 focuses on a specific case for which special provision *can* be made: what are called "image maps," where clicking on a nominated region initiates an action associated with that region. Situations where a user is asked to point to a position on the screen (such as on a geographical map or when using a graphics editor) are monumentally hard to present non-visually; either avoid them altogether, or recognize that this part of your system is not accessible. Here are a couple of alternatives to choose from:

Summary	Definition
Image interaction alternatives	Whenever a user is asked to select from a range of discrete options by selecting a location in a graphical area (in an image, typically), there shall be an alternative, non-graphical method of presenting the same options and letting the user select one.
	This is intended to satisfy §1194.22 (e) and (f) in Section 508.
No interaction with graphics	The system shall not ask a user to select from a range of discrete options by selecting a location in a graphical area (such as an image).
	This is intended to satisfy §1194.22 (e) and (f) in Section 508.

Whenever software dynamically generates what the user sees (as in a script embedded in an HTML page), assistive technology might not be able to keep track of what's going on—so neither will the user. A script is generally either purely cosmetic (to make the display prettier) or it does some real processing. In the first case, we can ask for a non-script textual alternative for users with a visual disability or impairment—most of whom won't benefit from the extra prettiness. It's unreasonable to ask for a non-script alternative in the second case, because that means duplicating the functionality; it's better to demand that the script use standard user interface components that accessible technology can detect and interact with. These complementary approaches are reflected in the following two requirements:

Summary	Definition
Text equivalent of cosmetic script	Any presentation unit that contains its own software to display content to the user (such as a script or applet in an HTML page) shall contain explanatory text, associated with the software, that conveys the same information.
	This is intended to partially satisfy §1194.21 (l) in Section 508.
Scripts to use only standard user interface components	Any presentation unit that contains its own software to display content (such as a script or applet in an HTML page) shall cause only standard user interface components to be used to display information and to accept input from the user.
	This is intended to partially satisfy §1194.21 (l) in Section 508.

Specific Sound Needs   Sound is very much a secondary output medium in most systems, especially commercial systems (except for sound produced by assistive technology such as screen readers). Making a system convenient for a person with hearing difficulties to use should therefore be easy enough. But bear in mind that removing sound outputs altogether can cause difficulties for other users (particularly those with visual impairments). Here are two alternative ways to deal with the use of sound for alerting the user:

Summary	Definition
Visual cue for audio alert	Whenever a sound is played for the purpose of alerting the user, a visual cue shall also be invoked.
	This is intended to satisfy §1194.22 (b) in Section 508.
No sound alerts	Sounds shall not be used for the purpose of alerting the user.
	This is intended to satisfy §1194.22 (b) in Section 508.

And here's one other method that gives users some control over sound:

Summary	Definition
Sound volume adjustable	Whenever sound is played, it shall be possible to adjust the volume.

Specific Cognition Needs   Our aim here is to make the system easier to understand. It's hard to demand this in requirements, because the most important aspects are subjective—such as to write all text in clear language (mentioned in the equivalent Level 2 requirement in the "Example(s)" section). Section 508 makes one narrow demand:

Summary	Definition
Consistent icon meaning	Any image used to identify a control, status indicator, or other programmatic element shall be used to mean the same thing wherever it is used.
	This is intended to satisfy §1194.21 (e) in Section 508.

One further aspect is covered in the preceding "General Accessibility" section: giving users all the time they need to respond.

Specific Dexterity Needs   Manual dexterity is relevant to us only as far as it relates to instructing the computer to do something. The contemporary devices of choice are a keyboard and a pointing device (typically a mouse). It's reasonable to assume that control over any assistive technology used to perceive computer output can be achieved using the keyboard, mouse, or a means built into the technology. Requirements need not be concerned with how assistive technology might achieve this (though analysts, developers, and testers would benefit from knowing). Here's a requirement to make input easier for some:

Summary	Definition
Keyboard only	It shall be possible to perform all input to the system (including all navigation and initiation of operations) by using the keyboard alone.
	An exception is granted for purely graphical operations in situations where using the keyboard is inherently impractical.
	This is intended to satisfy §1194.21 (a) in Section 508.

Tailoring to an Individual User   There are three ways to make a screen in a system accessible to users with specific needs:

1. **Incorporate accessibility into the definition of the screen directly.**   Technology like HTML has many accessibility features, and systems should be developed to take advantage of them. Proper use of common user interface elements lets assistive technology do its job. But even so, this approach can involve compromises: the sheer size and complexity of many pages detract from their accessibility. So it's a laudable approach, but not always enough.

2. **Create a second, accessible version.**   Sometimes an organization wants to include in a system's user interface features that are not accessible (say, scripts to display fancy animated menus). That's fine, according to Section 508, so long as an alternative is provided that is accessible. Of course this means that you have to maintain two implementations on an ongoing basis, and you have the headache of checking that they're consistent.

3. **Tailor it to suit each individual user.**   A library might have a big set of conventional books and another (inevitably smaller) set of Braille books for the blind, but a software system can be much smarter than that. Why not transform each page dynamically to suit each individual user? It's perfectly possible if we care to take the trouble. Almost all commercial Web-based systems already perform dynamic generation of output for many other purposes, so it's not a big step.

These three approaches are not mutually exclusive. The first way should always be implemented to its fullest extent, even if the second and/or third ways are needed, too.

Tailoring our system for each user gives us much flexibility. There are two parts: providing a way for a user to specify their preferences, and then taking those preferences into account when presenting the user interface to them. For a Web-based system, we can create lean HTML pages devoid of any baggage that the current user doesn't want. Here are a few things for which we could beneficially define user preferences:

- Frames: yes, no, or don't care.
- Whether to duplicate command components (such as buttons and navigation links).
- Preferred location of command components: top, left, right, or bottom of screen.
- Colors. At least two preferences must be supported: background and foreground. Consider having the software check for and warn against incompatible or unreadable choices (such as choosing identical or similar colors for background and foreground).
- Font sizes and styles.
- Screen auto-refresh: yes, no, or don't care.
- Minimum time needed for a response.

Alternatively, for some of these factors, you can use values that are chosen by the user and recorded as operating system settings (such as system colors and fonts). This saves users the trouble of having to express their preferences more than once.

Be sensitive in what you ask users. Don't ask about disabilities directly. Each item in this list is a way in which the system can be tailored, and if you ask in these terms, people are unlikely to be offended. Offer an "I don't care," "no preference," or "no response" option if the question is a matter of any sensitivity at all. Also, never ask for preferences that aren't implemented; it can be very frustrating.

Just for completeness, here's a requirement for the option that Section 508 permits to offer an accessible alternative for each part of the user interface that isn't accessible:

Summary	Definition
Text-only equivalent pages	For each presentation unit that does not comply with the accessibility requirements in this specification, there shall be an equivalent that *does* comply. The functionality of any such equivalent shall always be consistent with the original, even when changes are made.
	This is intended to satisfy §1194.22 (k) in Section 508.

Documentation and Support   There's no point in going to the trouble of making your system accessible if no one knows about it or no one knows how to take advantage of its accessibility features. More generally, users with specific needs should be able to obtain general assistance as well as anyone else. The following requirements convey these goals:

Summary	Definition
All documentation accessible	All documentation available to users shall be available in a form that is itself readily accessible to users with specific needs.
	This is intended to satisfy §1194.41 (a) in Section 508.
Accessibility documentation	Descriptions of all accessibility-related features shall be available.
	Note that the previous requirement demands that this documentation is itself accessible.
	This is intended to satisfy §1194.41 (b) in Section 508.
Accessible customer service	All services provided to assist users (customer service) shall be accessible by users with specific needs. In particular, all support services available via the user's computer shall satisfy all the accessibility requirements in this specification.
	This is intended to satisfy §1194.41 (c) in Section 508.

Certifying Compliance   It isn't always enough for a system to comply with a law. Sometimes, you have to document how well it complies. In the case of Section 508, companies wishing to sell electronic and IT products to the U.S. government must fill in a Voluntary Product Accessibility Template (VPAT). It's handy to know in advance whether a document of this nature is expected, because parts of it can then be written while the system is being built. As examples, completed VPATs for Microsoft products can be found at *http://www.microsoft.com/industry/government/section508.mspx.*

Here's an example requirement:

Summary	Definition
Complete a VPAT	A Voluntary Product Accessibility Template (VPAT) shall be completed for the system. The purpose of this is to describe how well the system satisfies Section 508 accessibility requirements, as a prerequisite to marketing the system to agencies of the U.S. government.
	Source: *http://www.access-star.org/ITI-VPAT-v1.2.html*

Usability   Usability is important, but it is a matter of good user interface *design* and not something that requirements can guarantee. No matter how hard the requirements might try, it's always possible to build an unfriendly system that satisfies them: there's no magic prescriptive way to prevent it. It depends on using good user interface designers and involving user representatives. Conducting usability studies with people with disabilities can also provide valuable insights on the practical usability of a system.

Usability requirements often ask for user interface characteristics that sound attractive, but which are define in such imprecise terms that they're meaningless to developers and testers. They ask for the user interface to be "easy to learn" or "intuitive," to have a "logical flow of input," to "use softly saturated colors," or to "group information by subject." They sometimes mandate particular user interface constructs—drag-and-drop, check boxes, drop-down lists, toolbars, for example—without indicating in what circumstances they should be used; these are all part of the design, and requirements have no business getting involved at this level. Leave the user interface designers and developers to pick the best user interface component and technique for each task. Unhelpful or unnecessarily constraining usability requirements do nothing but reduce developers' confidence in whoever specified them.

That leaves little for example usability requirements to say, but here are a couple of token efforts:

Summary	Definition
Sensible default values	The system shall assign the most sensible default value to each input-capable field, wherever practical.
Common operations convenient	It shall be convenient for the user to initiate each common operation within a particular function. This shall be taken to mean a single keyboard operation or a very small number of mouse clicks and little mouse movement.

Considerations for Development

To do a good job developing accessibility capabilities, there are three areas that a software engineer should as a starting point have a working knowledge of:

1. **The range of specific needs that computer users have**   This requirement pattern mentions the main categories, but it's only a start.

2. **The accessibility features built into the operating system and other products and technology you're using**   (Such as Web browsers and HTML.) Popular operating systems come bundled with various accessibility utilities that many people (including developers) are unaware of, including an onscreen keyboard, screen magnifier, and screen reader. The underlying accessibility features of popular operating systems are also very extensive. Learn what they can do for you.

3. **A few of the most important types of assistive technology and a rough idea how they work**   This can give you a feel for what you should do to allow these products to work properly—because you understand what you'd want if you were in their developers' shoes. For example, a screen reader for a blind person must interpret visually-oriented constructs (say, by looking at an HTML page, or—more tricky—by getting hold of the individual user interface components displayed by a desktop application), decide which bits the user's interested in, and then output its conclusions to a speech synthesizer. (If you want a challenging development job, here's a fertile field for you!)

Developing to help assistive technology, then, involves providing as much *semantic information* as possible—that is, to signal, as far as you can, the role and purpose of each item that you present on the user interface.

IBM's developer guidelines for accessibility—at *http://www.ibm.com/able*—contain implementation suggestions for popular technologies (including HTML, Java, Windows, and Unix). The guidelines themselves mirror Section 508 to a large extent.

Considerations for Testing

Before doing anything else, testers should gain an appreciation of accessibility issues and an understanding of all relevant laws and regulations (such as Section 508).

Some accessibility features are amenable to a certain degree of automated testing, and there are many available resources that can help you test the accessibility of a system. In fact, accessibility features built into the operating system itself and standard applications such as Web browsers can themselves drive automated testing. Get to know the tools that are most suitable. For a start, there are several (some of which are free) that analyze HTML pages and tell how accessible they are and how to improve them, including

- *http://webxact.watchfire.com*—a free service that judges the accessibility of any Web page
- *http://zing.ncsl.nist.gov/WebTools*—a range of "Web metrics" tools for testing usability and accessibility

In addition, some browsers allow you to see a text-only view of any Web page you visit.

Verify that user interface resources (such as HTML pages) adhere to guidelines and standards (for example, that they both use accessibility-friendly tags and do so in the correct manner). This is easier than testing the user interface's accessibility.

Try using the system with a few different types of assistive technology, both those built into the operating system (such as a screen magnifier and screen reader) and dedicated products. Use the system without the mouse for a day or two. Put yourself in the shoes of each type of user with specific needs. Ideally, involve people with disabilities in your testing; they will give you a better picture of your system's accessibility than anything else. Testing accessibility thoroughly is expensive and time-consuming.

One approach to putting yourself in various users' shoes is to invent a range of "personas." This is a concept that Alan Cooper describes in his book "The Inmates are Running the Asylum," 1999, and the idea is that you create a handful of fictitious people as realistically as you care to and then imagine how they would react when they use your system. In effect this takes the notion of "actors" one step further, so you create several personas for an actor. It's impractical to do this for more than one or two actors, so pick those that are the most important—say, a customer. Then devise a persona for each kind of specific need that you want to test, give them a name, a brief life history, and a personality: Chris is color-blind, Martine is hard-of-hearing, Nelson has one arm, Great-Uncle Augustus is computer illiterate, and so on.

IBM's developer guidelines for accessibility (mentioned in the "Considerations for Development" section) contain detailed testing advice for each guideline.

8.4 User Interface Infrastructure

Purpose

A user interface infrastructure is a coherent set of components that together enable a user to interact with the system, excluding anything developed as part of a specific system, general underlying software (such as an operating system), and hardware. That is, a user interface infrastructure is what's left if you take away the system and everything it needs to run that isn't wholly related to the user interface. For instance, the user interface infrastructure for a simple Web system might comprise a browser and a Web server. Unfortunately the pieces we're left with are usually tied to a particular technology, which we want to avoid as far as we can. A Web server is usually an implementation detail that requirements needn't worry about—but a Web browser is visible to our users, so we can't ignore it. This leads us into a dilemma about how much to say about a user interface infrastructure. Four possible approaches are as follows:

1. **Say very little.**   Leave it up to the development team to pick the most suitable technical solution.

2. **Describe only any technology that *must* be used.**   Otherwise, don't make technology statements. For example, we might require a browser-based user interface, and leave open how it's achieved. It can be hard to consider user interface matters without a general appreciation of prevalent technologies. Consequently, it is probably counterproductive to try being abstract when stating our requirements: if we have to support a specific technology, say so.

3. **Specify the user interface capabilities required.**   This is likely to become intricate and tied to particular kinds of user interface components, so go only as far into detail as you must. Avoid being drawn into defining the low-level characteristics of everything: drop-down lists, scroll bars, menus ... and on and on.

4. **A mixture of (2) and (3).**

The user interface is an area for which we might need *more than one instance* of an infrastructure. We might have different classes of users who have very different user interface demands. This is particularly true if we have specialized end-user devices—for example, in the case of a payment processing system with EFTPOS terminals for users in stores and PCs for internal users.

The subject of user interface infrastructures is often ignored completely in requirements specifications—usually without noticeable impact, no doubt because adopting a user interface technology is such an obvious need that projects take it in their stride. However, any area of functionality for which we have no explicit requirements is liable to be tackled in an ad hoc, unsystematic, and uncontrolled manner, perhaps according to the whims and prejudices of a senior member of our development team. As a result, the chosen solution might not be the most suitable for our problem—even if the person who makes the choice is competent to decide—because some important factors might be unknown to them at the time. A better solution might be overlooked.

Invocation Requirements

User interface invocation requirements do two things: first, they constrain the technology that can be used; and second, they state capabilities that the user interface must support (that is, things users can perceive when using the system's functions).

Technology constraints don't need to mention specific technologies or products but can include factors that influence the choice of technology. These can include salient characteristics of devices from which the system must be accessible. Here are a few examples:

Summary	Definition
Access via Web browser	It shall be possible to access every user interface function via common Web browsers. For the purpose of this requirement, a common Web browser is one that is used by at least 5% of Web users. For each such browser, all major versions that have been released in the past two years shall be actively supported.
Client software download unnecessary	Users shall not have to download and install client software.
Prevalent programming language	All software that runs on a client device shall be written in a prevalent programming language, which is one for which software can be run on a personal computer without having to download a supporting environment. This requirement does not preclude the use of more than one programming language, provided each one satisfies this requirement.

It's important to strike the right balance between a broad sweep and being too narrow—which is often not easy. For instance, the "Access via Web browser" requirement carefully avoids committing the system to working with every version of every browser every developed, while at the same time not mentioning specific products or version numbers. It introduces a "rolling window" that automatically keeps up with the latest releases. Write these requirements to be timeless: as far as possible, we want them to be valid in five years' time, and we can't predict what product versions will be in common use then (or even what products).

Here are a few examples of capabilities to be supported by a user interface:

Summary	Definition
Automatic screen refresh	It shall be possible for a function with a user interface to automatically refresh itself (for example, whenever any displayed data changes), without the user having to act. It is expected that few functions will need to refresh themselves.
Fixed graphical animations	It shall be possible to display fixed graphical animations. For the purpose of this requirement, "fixed" means the content of the animation is unaffected by the user's action: once it begins, it plays—like a video clip.
Interactive animated graphics	It shall be possible to display graphics that are animated and respond to user input under software control. That is, it shall be possible to develop client software that can display animated graphics.

Implementation Requirements

Commercial systems typically make use of user interface infrastructures built by someone else, outside the scope of the system. (That is untrue only for truly exceptional systems that require the building of their own specialized hardware devices, which we won't worry about here.) Usually, our user interface implementation requirements are limited to extensions to existing third-party products—if any. These requirements are typically relatively limited in their scope—for example, some special-purpose graphical widgets or an application programming interface (API) wrapper to make a product easier for developers to use or to mask implementation details. As a result, a user interface infrastructure is unusual in that its invocation requirements are usually more extensive than its implementation requirements.

We only need to consider detailed user interface implementation requirements if we want to undertake a rigorous process for the selection of a solution product (for a Web server, say), in which we want to perform detailed comparisons of alternative options.

8.5 Reporting Infrastructure

Purpose

A reporting infrastructure produces reports for us and usually lets us design new reports. You might decide to broaden this scope in various ways—such as to include matters relating to the database(s) on which the reports are produced, to add access control requirements not accommodated by off-the-shelf products, and to distribute and store reports after they have been produced.

The core of a reporting infrastructure is invariably a mainstream product built for the purpose. However, this might need to be augmented by extra capabilities we must build for ourselves, particularly if our infrastructure's scope goes beyond simply producing reports. Conceivably, our reporting requirements might be too onerous for a single reporting product to satisfy, and we might have to employ two or more products (for example, one for producing reports and one for designing them). If you specify requirements that cannot be satisfied by the known capabilities of commercial reporting products, be prepared for your reporting infrastructure to become a major undertaking.

Occasionally, organizations expect their reporting infrastructure to compensate for deficiencies in their database design, and therefore ask too much of it—especially its ability to cope with grotesquely complicated queries and joins. Be alert to this possibility. The result can be reports that are fragile and inefficient.

This section uses the term **report** to mean the definition of one type of report, and **report instance** to mean the results obtained by running a report at a particular time.

Invocation Requirements

A database usually acts as the primary interface between a system and the reporting infrastructure that produces its reports: the system places data in the database, and reports then read it. The first invocation requirements we must consider are those that give us all the database access capabilities we need. For example, if we have multiple databases, we might need to let our users choose which database to run a report on, or to run reports across more than one database. We might want to introduce a new database solely to run reports on, so they have no performance impact on the rest of the system. Requirements of this sort can become extensive and complex—

and could justify turning them into a separate infrastructure in its own right. Strictly speaking, the types of requirements cited for database access could be considered implementation requirements, since they are features internal to the reporting infrastructure. But databases certainly act as an interface, and if we regard any interface as invocation-related, it is correct to class these as invocation requirements.

Other types of invocation requirements to consider are as follows:

1. It shall be possible for other software to invoke a report.

2. It shall be possible to display to a user a list of all the reports they are authorized to run.

3. It shall be possible for a request to run a report to invoke special software to generate data before running the report itself.

4. Are there other sources of data (that is, other than databases—such as XML documents, flat files, or the contents of LDAP directories) from which we want to produce reports?

Implementation Requirements

The major areas to consider in the implementation requirements of a reporting infrastructure are:

1. A **report design tool**—it is easy to define requirements that no commercial design tool satisfies, so take particular care here. You might have to lower your (or your customer's) expectations.

2. **Delivery mechanisms** for the ways in which a report can be delivered to a recipient. This includes onscreen display, printing, and ability to save in various output formats (of which HTML, CSV, plain text, XML, and PDF are common these days). For printing, consider how the printer to use is chosen and what our reporting infrastructure needs to know about available printers to achieve that. Possibly, we would like a report recipient to be able to forward that report instance to someone else.

3. **Chronicle entries** (audit trails) that record when a report is run or is delivered to a recipient.

4. **Access control**, which we might want to apply to all reporting functions (running, viewing, designing, and so on). Do we need to worry about restricting access to selected data, too? The impact of access control requirements can be severe, because commercial reporting products are usually poor at supporting them—and your chances of finding one that fits with your access control infrastructure are slim at best.

5. Ways to **notify recipients** when a report has been produced for them.

6. **Report content and formatting**, which might include the extent of graphics capabilities, totaling, charting, and anything else we want to be able to include in our reports. Such requirements are most useful when deciding which reporting product is most suitable or to alert us that our chosen product does not provide all the capabilities that we would ideally include.

7. The **scheduling of reports**. Is it sufficient to be able to run a report on request, or do we need to be able to have certain reports run automatically at a specified frequency? If so, how fancy does the scheduling mechanism have to be, and what frequency options do we need?

8. **Reports on the usage of the reporting infrastructure**, such as a summary report of the number of reports produced in a given time period.

9. **Backing up** report definitions and report instances.

10. **Housekeeping**, to purge report instances no longer needed.

Chapter 9
Performance Requirement Patterns

In this chapter:

9.1 Response Time Requirement Pattern 195

9.2 Throughput Requirement Pattern 204

9.3 Dynamic Capacity Requirement Pattern 212

9.4 Static Capacity Requirement Pattern 215

9.5 Availability Requirement Pattern 217

By "performance" we mean the same as in the Olympic Games: how fast, how long, how big, how much. But there are no medals for success, only boos from the crowd for failure. Performance deals with factors that can be measured, though that doesn't mean performance requirements always specify goals using absolute numbers. In fact, it's best to *avoid* numbers if you can (for reasons discussed soon). It also helps to avoid stating performance requirements in terms that are hard to measure—in particular, in terms that would take an unreasonable length of time to test, such as mean time between failure. As with the rest of this book, we're talking here about typical commercial software systems, not anything life-critical such as aircraft or medical instruments.

This chapter contains requirement patterns for five types of performance encountered often in commercial systems, as shown in Figure 9-1. (Note that the dynamic and static capacity requirement patterns are separate because their characteristics are distinctly different.) You might come across others. When specifying a requirement for another performance factor, consider the issues that apply to all (or most) types of performance, which are discussed in the "Common Performance Issues" subsection that comes next.

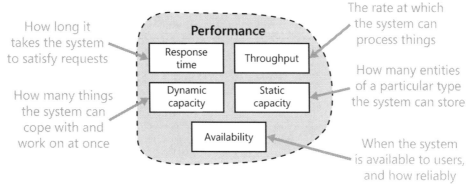

Figure 9-1 Requirement patterns in the performance domain

Unfortunately, there are no agreed definitions for the main terms used in this chapter, especially *performance*, *capacity*, and *quality*. I base the usage here upon the meanings we'd expect in a brochure for a new car: *performance* figures for top speed, acceleration, engine power, passenger *capacity*, load *capacity*, and so on. Its *quality* refers to intangibles: how well-built it is, how comfortable, what a pleasure to drive–which don't lend themselves to being quantified, the attributes the car company must convey with extravagant adjectives and flowery language. This chapter doesn't deal with *quality* requirements.

If an aspect of performance is worth specifying, it's worth specifying well, which demands thought and care. If it's not worth that effort, leave it out (or express it informally, not as requirements) because it will just waste everyone's time. Performance requirements are important because they can have a profound effect upon the architecture of the whole system; it's not always a matter of throwing in more hardware until it works well enough. We're faced with a dilemma of either specifying requirements in a way that's easy to write but a nightmare to build to and test, or having to formulate requirements that might look twisted and convoluted to a nontechnical audience. There are genuine difficulties to overcome; it's up to you whether you tackle them in the requirements or whether you brush them under the carpet, for the poor developers and testers to sort out.

Common Performance Issues

This section describes a number of issues that recur in the performance requirement patterns in this chapter. Some are likely to apply to *all* types of performance (not just those covered here), the rest just to *most* of them. These issues are important and can have a profound impact on how performance should be specified and whether a performance requirement you write is meaningful at all. They are presented in rough order of impact (highest impact first).

Issue 1: Easy to write equals hard to implement.   Most kinds of performance can be expressed very neatly—but when they are, they tend to be unhelpful. "The system shall be available 24×7, give users a one-second response time, handle 1,000 simultaneous users, process 200 orders per minute, and store 1,000,000 customers." A piece of cake to write! But for each performance target you set, ask yourself: what do you expect developers to do with it? Numerical performance targets like these are often so remote from the job of the software that it's reasonable to ask how developers are supposed to react to them: what should they do differently (assuming they code professionally as a matter of course)? If there are no obvious steps they can take, they can hardly be held responsible if the system fails to reach the target. Also, it's usually not possible to test whether a system achieves numerical performance targets until after it's been built (sometimes not until it's installed and running live), by which time it will take much fuss and rework to fix. Nevertheless, you should always get an early feel for the *order of magnitude* of each prospective performance target. For example, are we talking about hundreds of customers or millions?

Instead, if you can, specify requirements for steps to be taken to contribute to good performance in the area in question. All the performance requirement patterns in this chapter are "divertive" patterns—see Chapter 3, "Requirement Pattern Concepts"—that try to steer you away from the obvious. (But be aware that this is the opposite of what other authors advise. They like the precision and apparent certainty of numeric performance targets. I will present my arguments and leave it to you to decide.)

The situation might appear a little different when you intend to purchase a solution: any off-the-shelf product either satisfies quantitative performance requirements or it doesn't. But if a third party is building a solution just for you, it's just as unfair to present them with purely quantitative targets as it would be to your own developers. And are you prepared to take their word their solution performs as promised? Finally, it's untidy for the requirements to make assumptions about the nature of the solution.

Issue 2: Are we specifying a complete, running system or just the software?   To go anywhere, software needs hardware to drive it, and the performance of the whole system (hardware plus software) depends on the power of the hardware. Software is to hardware as a trailer is to a tractor. Setting performance targets for software in isolation is meaningless and silly, yet it happens (and is worth a quiet chuckle when you see it). If any component that affects a performance target is outside your control, you can't promise to achieve it, so don't make it a requirement. But you can state it informally in the requirements specification, if you like. One way out is to define an indicative hardware set-up and define performance requirements for it. (See the "Step 3: Choose Indicative Hardware Set-up" section in the throughput requirement pattern later in this chapter for further details.)

System performance can also depend on how third-party software products behave. If a particular call to such a product turns out to be slow, you could be unable to meet performance targets. If there is any third-party software, is it under your control or not? If it is, reassure yourself that it performs well enough. If it's not under your control—that is, it's outside the scope of the system as specified—don't hold your performance goals hostage to how well *it* performs.

Issue 3: Which part of the system does this performance target apply to?   For most kinds of performance, a performance requirement can apply to a single function, a group of functions, a single interface, and so on, or it can apply to *everything* (*all* functions). Always make clear what the requirement applies to. Also, don't make it apply to more than it needs to, because it could be difficult (that is, expensive) or impossible for some things, things we might not be bothered about anyway. For example, demanding user response time of a second for everything might be impossible to achieve for some processing-intensive functions and as soon as they're treated as exceptions, respect is lost for the whole requirement. (Developers also lose respect for anyone who writes unachievable requirements.)

Issue 4: Avoid arbitrary performance targets.   If someone gives you a performance goal, ask them where it came from and ask them to justify it. "Plucked out of thin air" isn't a good enough reason. Performance targets can result from a mixture of assumptions, reasoning, and calculations. If so, make all this background information available to your readers, either by including it in the requirements specification or by telling them where it can be found (for example, in a sizing model). Too many performance requirements are arbitrary. If there isn't a good enough reason for them, leave them out.

Issue 5: How critical is this performance factor to the business?   The severity of the damage done if an aspect of a system performs inadequately varies enormously: from disastrous to mildly irritating (or perhaps not even noticed). If the system runs out of free storage capacity (disk space), it could fail completely; if response times grow a little, it might not matter. So ask yourself how critical this performance factor is. What's the worst that could happen? If we risk serious damage, place extra stress on measuring and monitoring actual performance (which is the subject of the next issue). At the other end of the scale, if the potential damage is negligible, why bother to specify it at all?

If you have difficulty ascertaining from your customer how important this performance level is to them, ask how much extra they're prepared to pay to achieve it: an extra 10 percent of the *total system cost*? Fifty percent? One hundred percent? (These are the sorts of figures we could be talking about.) The answer doesn't translate directly into a priority or justify particular steps, but it does give a good idea of how seriously to treat it.

Issue 6: How can we measure actual performance?   Setting a target isn't much use unless you can tell how well you're doing against it. Who'd buy a car without a speedometer? Measuring actual performance is often left as a testing activity, with external tools wheeled in like the machines that monitor patients in a hospital. But it's much more convenient to have this ability built into the system itself. Then it can be used in a production system, and by developers. Some types of performance cannot be determined by the system itself (for example, the response time perceived by a remote user); other types of performance cannot easily be perceived externally (for example, how long an internal system process takes). Monitoring functions are a common subject of extra requirements in the performance requirement patterns in this chapter. Note that for some kinds of performance (such as response time), the act of measuring and recording performance could itself take time and effort and so affect the result a little—though we can be reassured that performance can only get better if such measuring is removed (or switched off).

Monitoring functions are always useful in letting a system administrator see how well a system is running, but they're not usually seen as contributing to the system's business goals, so they're usually given a low priority or dropped altogether (and perhaps built quietly by developers for their own use). Arguing that they play a key part in meeting performance targets provides the solid justification they need in order to earn their rightful place in the requirements.

Issue 7: By when does this performance target need to be met?   Some performance targets reflect planned business volumes that will take time (perhaps years) to achieve. Always state the timeframe in such cases. This allows optimizations to be made at the best time for the business and the development team. In particular it can save unwarranted effort being devoted to performance during the initial implementation phase, which is usually the busiest.

Issue 8: Put only one performance target in each requirement.   Don't lump several targets together. Separating them gives each target the prominence and respect it deserves, lets you give each one its own priority, and makes it easier (for testers in particular) to track each one.

Issue 9: What can be done if this performance target is not met?   Pondering this question can give you a useful insight into how seriously to treat this aspect of performance—that is, how much care it deserves and how big a mess we risk if we don't. Can it be improved by beefing up the hardware? Is tweaking the software likely to help? If the problem lies with a third-party product, are we stuck with it? If this aspect of performance isn't good enough, where does the responsibility lie: hardware, software, a bit of both—or will it be impossible to tell? Don't treat this issue as a way to assign blame (because blame comes into play only after a mess occurs and doesn't help prevent it) but as a way to understand the performance needs better so that there won't be a mess in the first place.

Sizing Model

The system aspects for which performance targets are commonly set aren't independent of one another: if your number of customers grows, you can expect a corresponding increase in transactions, disk storage used, and so on. It's useful to build a model of how these things relate to each other. A spreadsheet is the most convenient and flexible tool to use. Include explanations, state your assumptions, and generally make the whole model as transparent as possible.

The values in the sizing model can be divided into three types: *variables*, *parameters*, and *conclusions*. **Variables** are the key business numbers that drive everything else (such as how many customers we have). Keep the number of variables to a minimum—perhaps just one. **Parameters** reflect assumptions about how the business works in practice (such as the number of order inquiries for each order placed, how frequently an average customer visits our Web site, and how long they stay each time). **Conclusions** are values calculated by the model, which can be as numerous and sophisticated as you care to make them. The variables and parameters describe the volume of business, and the conclusions show the resulting load the system must carry—the basis for its performance goals.

A sizing model lets you play with the variables and parameters, which is especially fruitful when discussing projected business volumes with senior executives and sales and marketing wizards.

A sizing model created at requirements time can be transformed and refined after development to reflect how the actual system behaves. Extra knowledge is available then that can be incorporated into the model—to enable it to be used to calculate the actual size of machine(s) needed to accommodate a particular volume of business. This is particularly useful if you're building a product, because you can plug in each customer's business volumes and have the sizing model work out what hardware they need.

9.1 Response Time Requirement Pattern

Basic Details

Related patterns:	None
Anticipated frequency:	Between zero and three requirements, rarely more
Pattern classifications:	Pervasive: Maybe

Applicability

Use the response time requirement pattern to specify how much time the system may take to respond to a request. It is typically used where the time an operation takes is of interest to a person (normally a user) or another system.

Do not use the response time requirement pattern just for the sake of it. If a particular response time isn't vital, don't worry about it.

Discussion

Response time is the length of time between a request being submitted at a particular place to a system and a response being perceived at the same place. It is most popularly applied to **user response time**, which is the length of time between a user submitting a request (hitting the button) and the response being displayed on their screen. But this pattern can be used for other operations, for instance physical processes (such as the time to manufacture or physically deliver something) and processes involving multiple people (for example, if a step must be approved by a supervisor). Note, though, that it's especially hard to pin time targets to the system itself in such cases. It's especially important that, instead, you break it down into its parts and identify ways to make each part efficient.

Four distinct ways exist for stating a response time goal:

Approach 1: Define a quantitative requirement. This is the commonest way and the one usually suggested. The content of this type of requirement is described in the "Strategy 1" section that follows. This is an easy option—you can simply invent a figure if you like—but it's problematic to implement and test (as argued in "Issue 1: Easy to write equals hard to implement" earlier in this chapter). A requirement of this type is of most use when deciding what hardware configuration is needed, once the system has already been built.

Approach 2: State it informally. Explain it for the edification of developers about what we're after, but not as a requirement. State the same information as if you were writing a requirement according to Approach 1, but write it as casual guidance for developers. Since it's informal, it needn't be as rigorous as if you were writing a requirement—but still give some thought to each of the items of information mentioned.

Approach 3: Define requirements for steps to take to contribute to good response times. Rather than state a quantitative performance target, it's much more fruitful to dig deeper to identify and specify steps that can be taken to give the system the best possible response time. These steps are regarded as extra requirements in this requirement pattern and are discussed in the "Extra Requirements" subsection coming up. This is the hard option but the most helpful to developers.

Approach 4: Say nothing. Having thought about response times for some aspect of a system, a perfectly valid option is to decide not to mention it in the requirements specification. At several points, this requirement pattern suggests saying nothing. Positive inaction!

In addition to simply choosing one of these ways, they can be combined into richer strategies. Two suggest themselves:

- **Strategy 1: Break down end-to-end quantitative target.** The only response times for which we have a natural feel are those experienced by users, so this is a sensible starting point—but it's not helpful if part is outside the scope of the system. This strategy turns an end-to-end response time into one just for those parts within our control. Perform the following steps:

    a. Decide on a maximum acceptable response time to users (called end-to-end because it includes everything): for example, two seconds.

    b. Identify the constituent pieces involved in delivering the response. This need be done only at a very high level, for the purpose of allocating time to each piece. For example, everything between a Web user's PC and our back-end application could be regarded as one piece. Or you could treat the Internet as one piece and your router, firewall, Web server, and internal network as another piece. Any external system that must be called would be another piece. Some pieces might be outside the system's scope. Assume an indicative hardware set-up as necessary.

    c. Allocate a fraction of the end-to-end response time to each component (or group of components—for example, all those out of scope). This will involve some guesswork, but you probably won't go far wrong. In our example, we might allocate to our application system half a second of the overall two seconds.

    d. Specify a response time requirement for that portion that *is* within the scope of the system, using the amount of response time allocated to it. Alternatively, you can specify a separate requirement for each logical component within scope.

This strategy is especially important when dealing with processes that involve human intervention (such as manual approval by a supervisor), or other kinds of nonsystem delays.

■ **Strategy 2: Quantitative target and contributing steps.**   The aim is to get the benefit of both. Start by defining a quantitative performance target (Approach 1), and then study it and identify steps that help achieve it (Approach 3). Once you've identified these steps, you can demote the original performance target to an informal description (Approach 2).

If requirements are being specified at two levels—that is, business requirements first and detailed requirements afterwards—Approach 1 suits the business requirements and Approach 3 the detailed requirements.

These two strategies aren't mutually exclusive: you can use the first and *then* the second. All these ways and strategies have their place. Which one is best depends on how important the performance target is, the scope of the system being specified (is it the software only?), the nature of your development environment (how much do you trust your developers to do a good job?), and personal preference.

Content

The following list describes what a quantitative response time requirement (as per Approach 1) should contain. It's so lengthy because it explains how thinking about a particular item of information can steer you to framing the requirement in a different way.

1. **Type of operation**   What does this requirement apply to? Is it for a specific function, a collection of functions, all functions for a class of users, or something else? Don't impose a demand on all user functions; apply it only to those that genuinely need it. Limit its scope as much as possible. Exclude rarely used functions. Use a requirement of this type to inform developers of those areas whose performance they should worry about.

2. **Exceptional cases**   Is the response time target likely to be unachievable in some cases? For example, functions that involve intensive processing will be slower, so it's unfair to judge them against the same goal. However, it's difficult to know at requirements time which functions have lots of work to do—and yet we don't want to let developers get away with inefficiency by using intensive processing as an excuse. You must find the right balance.

3. **Timing boundaries**   What exactly are we measuring? That is, what causes the stopwatch to start and what causes it to stop? Be precise, because differences in interpretation could profoundly affect how well the system satisfies the requirement. For example, if you're requesting a Web page (say, containing many images), are you measuring to when the page begins to display, when its main structure is displayed, or when the whole page is fully displayed (with all the images)?

Pick boundaries such that everything from start to finish is within the scope of the system being specified. **Exclude anything over which you've got no control** (such as a potentially slow public network). In fact, set the boundaries so that they span as few variable factors as possible. If you can't do this, identify indicative hardware or assumed performance (such as Internet connection speed) for the parts that are outside the system's scope—though they are in themselves hard to specify and won't behave uniformly even then. If you end up setting a target for the system's internal response time, it won't be directly observable by a user, so you need a way for the software to measure and record it (which is described in the "Response Time Monitoring" subsection of the "Extra Requirements" section later in this pattern).

4. **Tolerable length of time**   This is the maximum acceptable response time itself. Ordinarily, this should be an absolute quantity (two seconds, or half an hour, say), because values such as *fast*, *quick*, and *imperceptible* are subjective and can't be verified definitively. (I say "ordinarily" because on a rare occasion it's preferable to use a subjective measure. I have in mind the situation where we merely want to prevent unusually slow response times, rather than insist on very good ones. In this case, it's advantageous to avoid defining "unusually slow" in case anything faster is regarded as fine even if it's still slow.) It is always possible to replace a subjective value by picking an absolute quantity to represent it. For example, *fast* might be defined as less than one second in this context, and *imperceptible* as less than a twentieth of a second—in rough accordance with the frames-per-second rate of human sight: the blink of an eye.

If we're pressured to include factors outside the system's scope, an alternative strategy is to define a unit of measurement to use as a datum and then to express a performance target in terms of this unit. For example, if we define one *boing* to be the time it takes to show a simple (reference) Web page, from request to completed display, then we could set the acceptable response time for some other function at four *boings*, or two *boings* plus half a second. This strategy has the advantage of taking into account the actual speed of variables outside our control. The value of a *boing* isn't fixed; it varies according to the environment. For a PC on a local network, a *boing* might be half a second; with a slow Internet connection, a *boing* might be five seconds. It's possible to phrase a requirement to avoid having to name your artificial unit of time. You can use the same unit in more than one requirement (in which case it's difficult to avoid naming it).

5. **Justification of length of time**   Where did the tolerable length of time figure come from? This could include a calculation and/or argument, or it could refer to an external source where the justification is given (such as a sizing model). If the figure is arbitrary, or you can't find a good reason for it, maybe it's not important.

6. **Indicative hardware set-up**   Try using this if your timing boundaries go beyond the scope of the system—especially if you're specifying software only. This must include every component that affects the response time: server machine, external services that are called, Web server, firewall, router, communications networks, client machine, and so on. Treat the unpleasantness of doing this as an incentive to push the timing boundaries as close to the system's scope as possible.

    Alternatively, you can refer to a description of indicative hardware given elsewhere.

7. **High load caveat**   When any system's very busy, response times are liable to degrade. You can't ignore this factor. It makes sense for a response time target to apply only up to a certain load. Don't attempt to predict at what load level it will start to degrade noticeably, but you could define a level of business activity (in terms of throughput or simultaneous users) that the system must be able to handle while still meeting response time targets.

    Something else to insist on is **graceful degrading** of performance under load: to not tolerate instant gridlock as soon as some threshold load is reached. It's unrealistic to specify this in precise terms, so the best approach is to ask that response times must degrade only incrementally (gradually) as load increases and that a sudden jump in response times must never occur.

8. **Motivation**   Why are you specifying this performance goal? Why do you need good response time? It could be so the user can get more work done (an employee), or it could be that if they're bored they'll go somewhere else (a casual Web visitor). The answer to this question might hint that a quantitative performance requirement is *not* the best approach: perhaps you should reformulate the requirement to tackle the motivation. For example, the motivation for a fast download of software by a Web visitor might be so that they don't give up impatiently halfway through. Since it's unreasonable to demand that a download of unknown size be done in a specified time, you could replace it by a requirement that the visitor be given an indication of progress or be sufficiently entertained while the download takes place. Displaying a progress bar might be enough. (This topic is revisited in the "Response Time Masking and Explaining" subsection.) You don't always need to state the motivation explicitly in the requirement itself, but always ask yourself what it is.

Template(s)

Summary	Definition
«Operation type» response time	Each *«Operation type»* shall have a response time of no more than *«Tolerable length of time»* from *«Timing boundary start»* to *«Timing boundary end»* [when using *«Indicative hardware set-up»*]. This figure is based on *«Justification»*. [This requirement does not apply to *«Exceptional cases»*.] [*«High load caveat»*.] [The motivation for this requirement is *«Motivation»*.]

Example(s)

Here are a few example response time requirements with quantitative targets:

Summary	Definition
Inquiry response time	Any inquiry shall complete the display of its results, from the time the user submits the request, in no longer than 4 seconds plus the display time of a simple reference page from the same location. This figure is based on anecdotal tests indicating that users begin to lose patience soon after this time. This requirement does not apply to inquiries across large volumes of data where arbitrary selection criteria are allowed.
Transaction switching time	The average time for the transaction switch to route a customer request to a service shall be less than 300 milliseconds. (This figure has been calculated as one twentieth of the time that a reasonable customer would consider acceptable to wait for a typical transaction. An acceptable wait for a typical transaction is taken as 6 seconds—based on timed figures for the processing of credit card transactions.)
Web page display time	Each Web page produced by the system shall be fully displayed in no longer than 10 seconds from the time the user requested it, when using a 56k bits per second modem connection. This requirement does not apply to pages containing one or more large images. This requirement does not apply when the number of users currently using the system exceeds 90% of the simultaneous user capacity (as stated in *«User capacity requirement ID»*). Above this level, it is acceptable for the display time to increase in rough proportion to the number of simultaneous users.
Data format error response time	Any error in the format of data entered by a user shall be pointed out to the user with a suitable error message no more than 1 second after they submit the information to the system. Note that this requirement need not rely upon network communications being fast enough: local validation on the user's machine would also satisfy it (although validation must in all cases be performed on the server side too, because not to do so would represent a security weakness).

Here are some example response time requirements that do not mention quantitative targets:

Summary	Definition
User response times never excessive	No user function shall have an average response time in normal system operation that a reasonable user would consider excessive for that type of function.
Timely identity card issuance	It shall be possible to issue an employee identity card on request sufficiently fast for "while-you-wait" delivery.
	Ten minutes is regarded as an acceptable wait time for the purposes of this requirement, though this should not be treated as a clear boundary between "good" and "bad." A quicker time would deliver increased user satisfaction with the system, and a longer time increased irritation.
Fast display of personal happiness calculator	A happiness club member shall get fast response when displaying the personal happiness calculator for the first time after entering the club's Web site.
	(This requirement makes no judgment on how the happiness calculator is implemented. It can be taken to mean that a long delay while waiting for an applet or other software to load is unacceptable. At the same time, it cannot be read as ruling out use of such software.)
	This requirement is not specified in terms of an absolute length of time, partly because display time is affected by factors outside the company's control (most notably the member's connection speed). To put it another way, to specify a time we would also need to specify the PC and communications to which it applies.
	It is recognized that this requirement is stated in subjective terms—but so is deciding whether response time is too slow. Thus, the person verifying the system is granted a degree of freedom in deciding whether it feels acceptable in practice. It was decided that this was preferable to setting arbitrary targets in advance.

Extra Requirements

They're diverse and deserve thought. That's the first thing to say about extra requirements that might be written about response time, either in addition to or instead of a quantitative response time requirement. Three categories of extra requirements are discussed here, each one in its own section that follows:

1. **Steps that contribute to good response times**   Things to be done to help the system perform well.

2. **Response time monitoring**   Functions for measuring response times and letting administrators see them.

3. **Response time masking and explaining**   Ways to lessen the chance of a user becoming impatient or confused while waiting for a response.

Steps that Contribute to Good Response Times   There are innumerable ways to improve response times. They depend upon the nature of your system and your environment, and this section doesn't attempt to identify them. It's up to you to find any major logical steps that suit your situation, where "logical" means it addresses *what* we need but not *how*. The development team is in a position to identify other ways to deliver the best possible response times. Here are a few token examples of requirements that contribute to good response times:

Summary	Definition
Reports not to impact external users	The running of internal reports and inquiries shall not perceptibly degrade response times for external users.
	The intent of this requirement is that database-intensive internal reports and inquiries should use different database tables from those used for external user functions and should run on different machines.
Frequent reports efficient	All reports and inquiries that are expected to be run frequently shall be designed so as to require few database accesses.
	The intent of this requirement is that summary tables should be used so as to avoid repeated reading of large numbers of records from transaction tables. Of course, generating such summary tables requires the same amount of processing, but this should be done only once (or as few times as possible) and preferably when users are not waiting.
Email processing not to impact main system	Processing related to the sending and receiving of emails shall have no performance impact on the processing of requests from customers.
	It is suggested that this be achieved by running the email server software on a separate machine from the rest of the system.

Observe that the first requirement here is likely to have a major impact on the architecture of the system: two databases, which involves significant additional functionality to maintain and update, functionality for which you might or might not choose to define requirements. Also observe that the intent paragraph in each of the first two examples is expressed in terms of its effect on an expected solution but that the requirements themselves do not mandate this solution.

Response Time Monitoring   Measuring response time sounds straightforward, but it seems that however you try to do it, little practical difficulties crop up. There are three main ways to measure response times:

1. **Using the system itself**   This is limited to the scope of the system itself, which means a server system can measure only internal response times—which is fine if this is how your response time targets are expressed. There are two difficulties with a response time measured by the system: first, what to do with the measurement—because storing it would take machine time and effort (it can't be done within any existing database update, since the response time clock is still ticking then)—and second, the act of measuring could add a little extra work and make the response time marginally longer, so you might want to be able to switch measuring on and off.

If the scope of your system includes software on each user's machine, that software could record response times. But you then also need means to gather that information centrally (that is, to send it back to base) and for the central system to be able to receive and store it.

2. **Using an external measurement tool**   There are products that do this, both commercial and free, to let you measure response times at any point in a network or on a user device. In a normal business environment, it's not sensible to consider building your own. To measure user response time, software must be installed on the user's machine, which can be restrictive. (You can't get response times for an arbitrary external visitor to your Web site, for example.)

3. **By hand**   Use a stopwatch to record how long something takes. This is tedious and subject to human error. The results must be recorded by hand, too. If the results are to take into account the circumstances, they must be recorded as well (date and time, network connection speed, and such like), which adds to the work. Then you have to collate the recorded results.

Often, response times are measured and checked only when testing the system, but being able to do so when the system is running live is valuable.

Once you have response time measurements, what do you want to do with them? The two main uses are to

- **Produce and present statistics**. They can show response times in a variety of ways, depending on the richness of the response time data that has been gathered: per function, per class of user, or according to the system load. But gathering enough data for statistics of this sort is a major commitment.

- **Raise an alarm** if response times are inadequate or grow slower.

Response Time Masking and Explaining   There are limits to how much we can reduce response times. Some types of operations are bound to take a relatively long time, such as downloading software. We have to live with it, and we must turn our attention to how we can make the user's experience as painless as possible. Even if it leads to a longer overall wait, it's probably worth it. Options include

1. **Warning the user before any possible wait**   This is common courtesy and should be universal, but plenty of Web sites don't do this. Also tell the user beforehand how big any download will be.

2. **Letting the user know what's happening**   This could be a simple message: "Download in progress." Better is a progress bar of some kind, although how hard this is to implement (or whether it's feasible at all) depends on the technology used, which you might not know at requirements time.

3. **Masking the delay**   So that the user doesn't perceive it or perceives it less. Perform the slow operation in the background while letting the user do something else—or keep them occupied in some other way. There are various tricks. Give the user something to read while they wait. Chop up the delay into more than one piece. Don't force a user to download parts of your software they might never use. They all involve extra work, so only insist on them if it's worth it. It might be worthwhile going to trouble for a visitor to your Web site (a potential customer) but not for a humble employee.

Some of these options might sound like solutions—that is, rightfully the preserve of the development team. If you want to leave them free to pick the best option, frame the requirement in terms of what you want to achieve (the motivation), though you can mention a *suggested* solution informally, too.

Here are a couple of representative example requirements:

Summary	Definition
Slow operation prewarning	At any point from which the user can initiate an operation that would take longer than 20 seconds (when using a 1-Mbps Internet connection), a warning to this effect shall be displayed.
Happiness calculator download progress bar	A progress bar shall be displayed to the user while the happiness calculator software is being downloaded to the user's PC, to show what percentage of the download has been done.

Considerations for Development

Consider what a developer is expected to do with each response time requirement.

If no requirements are present for features that contribute to good response time, consider what features might be appropriate.

Considerations for Testing

Consider whether a suitable hardware set-up will be available against which to test response time requirements.

If any high-load caveats are specified, consider how to simulate a suitably heavy load in a test environment.

How are you going to measure response times accurately? Does the system itself contain any ability to measure response times? If not, and that's the only way, insist on this capability being added.

9.2 Throughput Requirement Pattern

Basic Details

Related patterns:	Scalability, response time, inter-system interface
Anticipated frequency:	One requirement in a straightforward case, up to three or more per system and per inter-system interface (for one or more interfaces)
Pattern classifications:	None

Applicability

Use the throughput requirement pattern to specify a rate at which the system—or a particular inter-system interface—must be able to perform some type of input or output processing.

Discussion

How fast can we throw things at our system? This is the type of question most commonly answered by throughput requirements. Less frequently: how fast must our system churn things out? This sounds easy enough to specify: just say how many whatsits per whenever. But unfortunately it's not as simple as all that—and it can be downright difficult to write satisfactory throughput requirements, for several reasons. First, how do we work out what rate we need? It involves predicting the future, which is never spot-on at the best of times but might be little more than guesswork if this is a new business venture or if we're building a product for other businesses to use. Second, if critical pieces—particularly the main hardware and, for an interface, the communication lines—are outside the scope of the system, how can we set meaningful throughput targets for the software alone?

Before agonizing about how to work out a throughput target, ask yourself: what's it for? Can we do without it? Don't specify throughput just for the sake of it. For most systems, being *scalable* is more important than achieving a fixed throughput figure. If we specify strict scalability requirements, we can often either avoid specifying throughput at all or we can specify a relatively modest throughput target, confident that if we need more, we can scale up (normally by adding more hardware). If you don't have a sound basis for determining target throughput, it's often better not to try, rather than putting forward impressive-looking figures that are meaningless and perhaps dangerously misleading.

These days, throughput is mainly an issue for a commercial system only if there are a large number of users, which means either it's open to the world (typically via the Internet) or it's used by a large organization. This requirement pattern assumes we're dealing with a high throughput system—because with available technology, anything else can be handled comfortably simply by buying more hardware and using better underlying products (such as a database). There's nothing to be gained by writing a requirement that the system must cope with at least *two orders per day*.

You can't specify throughput just by asking people or by thinking about it, scratching your head a bit, and then writing it down. There are several things to figure out, and you're probably going to have to do some *calculations*. Here's a suggested approach, which chops the problem into several more manageable pieces:

- **Step 1: Decide what to measure.**   Pick something that's fundamental to the system. For a retail system, it could be *new orders* (how many we must be able to receive in a given time, that is). One system could have several throughput requirements for different measures, but don't worry about secondary activities whose volumes depend largely on something you've already chosen; they're taken care of in Step 2.

- **Step 2: Work out other relative volumes (if necessary).**   Devise formulae for working out the relative volume of secondary activities of interest based on the thing whose throughput we're measuring (for example, how many order inquiries per order). In effect, this is a little model of relative volumes, which can form part of an overall sizing model.

- **Step 3: Choose indicative hardware set-up (if necessary).**   If hardware is outside the scope of the system, define a rough hardware set-up for which to specify a throughput target.

- **Step 4: Determine average throughput.**   Organizations think of projected business in terms of relatively long timeframes: per month, per week, or perhaps per day (relatively long, that is, from the point of view of a computer rated in billions of cycles per second). Begin throughput calculations by thinking in the same way as the business, which gives us an *average* throughput over a relatively long period of time.

- **Step 5: Determine peak throughput.**   The load on the system won't stay constant: a conveniently average throughput won't be delivered every minute or every second. How much will it vary? What's the busiest it will get? It's the answer to the last question that gives us our target throughput—because **the system must cope with the *peak* load**.

Each of these steps is described in more detail in its own section that follows. Steps 4 and 5 need to be performed for each distinct measure identified in Step 1.

Step 1: Decide What To Measure   For the main throughput target, pick the thing most *important* to the organization. For a business this means the one that makes the money, which isn't necessarily the one with the highest volume. In most systems it's the business *transactions*. (That's why for a retail system, we'd pick *orders* rather than *inquiries*.) If you have several common things, pick the one that happens most frequently. It's best to pick only one thing for which to set an overall throughput target. Step 2 takes the system's secondary throughputs into account.

There could be several different types of the thing on which you've decided to base throughput—several different types of business transactions, for example. In this case, either pick one (the most important or the most numerous one) and treat the others as secondary (and deal with them in Step 2) or estimate what percentage of the total each type represents. The final results are the same.

In addition to the system's main throughput target you can set a separate throughput target for each inter-system interface for which this factor is important. This makes sense only if there's no direct relationship between the system throughput and that of the interface in question; if every transaction is sent down the interface, it doesn't need its own target.

Distinguish between incoming and outgoing throughput. Usually, it's the incoming throughput that constitutes the load on the system; the system can send things out with much less effort (invoices, emails—no matter what they are). The exception is systems whose main purpose is *producing* something. One incoming transaction could generate one or more outgoing transaction. The net effect, in terms of communications bandwidth, could be more than the consideration of just the incoming transactions would indicate. Communication pipes, however, aren't the same as physical pipes: a heavy flow one way doesn't necessarily mean there's no room for anything to go the other way, and the capacity one way might differ from the capacity the other way.

Step 2: Work Out Other Relative Volumes   In Step 1 we identified what requests to base our throughput measuring on. But handling them isn't the only work the system has to do. Step 2 aims to get an idea of the load imposed by everything else. However, the results of this step don't feed into the throughput requirement itself. It serves two purposes: first, to gain a better understanding of the overall load on the system, and second, to supply useful information to whoever will decide what size hardware is needed. (It's not possible to *size* the hardware at requirements time.)

Draw up a list of the other everyday activities of the system (or, for an inter-system interface, the other things the interface handles): important inquiries, registration of customers, and so on. Then estimate how many of each of these there will be on average for each one of the things the throughput measures. For a Web retail site, we might estimate that product inquiries outnumber orders fifty to one, the number of new customers registering is a third of the number of orders, and there are two order inquiries for each order.

A spreadsheet is the most convenient tool to use; it lets us easily change the primary volume and recalculate all the others. If you've already created an overall sizing model, add these factors to it.

One extra factor that's often useful to add is the *origin* of the things we're measuring. Where do they come from? What owns or produces them? For example, the origin of business transactions might be customers. Estimating the rate at which a single origin entity creates such transactions can then form the basis for our throughput calculations, in a way that people find more natural. Asking how many orders an average customer will place per month is easier to picture than an absolute total number of orders in isolation (though wherever you start, you ought to reach the same results).

There is a slight danger that the developers will take trouble to make sure the primary transaction type is handled lightning fast, to satisfy the throughput requirement. This might leave everything else disproportionately—and perhaps unacceptably—slow. It's hard for the requirements to protect against this: you can hardly *ban* or complain about the efficient execution of anything.

Step 3: Choose Indicative Hardware Set-Up   If we're building a system for a particular organization, we have only its projected business volume to worry about, so we can specify target throughput independently of hardware. The hardware can be chosen later, when we've built the software and know how well it performs. In this case, bypass Step 3.

On the other hand, if we're specifying only the software for a system without knowing the power of the machines it will run on, we can't just throw up our hands and announce that it's impossible to specify throughput requirements. That would render even the most inefficient software acceptable (as far as the requirements are concerned). This dilemma is particularly important when building a product because different customers might have enormous variations in their business volumes. One answer is to devise an indicative hardware set-up (such-and-such machine with a so-and-so processor running this operating system and that database, and so on) and to state the throughput *it* must achieve.

A slightly different approach is to focus on one aspect of hardware performance—the machine's CPU cycle rate is the obvious one—and specify target throughput against it. For example, we could demand one business transaction for every 10 million CPU cycles (so a 2 GHz machine would handle 200 business transactions per second). This is a rather simplistic alternative. It doesn't take into account any of the other factors that affect throughput, and it forces you to deal in unfamiliar quantities. (Can you feel the CPU cycles go by?)

It's distasteful for the requirements process to address hardware at all, but we have no alternative if we must address performance in the absence of a concrete underlying environment. A car maker couldn't tell you the top speed of a planned new car if its engine size isn't known yet.

Step 4: Determine Average Throughput   Now it's time to approach the gurus who can foretell the future of the business. This is the domain of sales and marketing and senior management; no one else possesses such powers. Arrange a session with them to discuss and set down business volume projections. The goal of Step 4 is to determine the volume of business in terms of the time period the business feels most comfortable with (per year, quarter, month, week, or day)—and thus average throughput.

Give your business gurus free reign to express their estimates of business volumes however they wish, but intervene if they start talking in terms that aren't measurable. Doing Steps 1 and 2 beforehand—or at least preparing a first version of your sizing model—lets you demonstrate and tinker with it during the session. It's usually most natural to start by discussing volumes in terms of whatever comes most naturally—often numbers of customers rather than transactions, and then how many transactions each customer will make in a given time period. That is, take a step back from the thing you'll actually base the throughput target on.

For an established business (if we're replacing an existing system, say), target throughput can usually be set with a reasonable degree of reliability. For a new venture it's largely guesswork. Be alert to the eternal optimism of sales predictions. ("In five years' time, 50 percent of the world's population will be buying their whatever-they-are online, and we intend to have 90 percent of that market.") If that happens, bring the discussion down to earth by asking what volumes will be in the shorter term. It's far better to cater for smaller initial volumes and require the system to be scalable than gear up for starry-eyed exaggerations. This demonstrates that it's important to **always associate a timeframe with every throughput target**—indeed, every performance target of any kind. If possible, do so relative to when the system goes live, rather than an absolute date. It's perfectly acceptable to specify two targets for the same thing, covering different timeframes—either putting both in the same requirement or writing two separate requirements. The latter allows the targets to be assigned different priorities.

Other factors you might want to take into account include budget (how much high-power hardware can the organization afford?) and the potential damage to the business if it cannot cope with demand. Also, if the business is subject to seasonal variation, base the target throughput on the busiest season (or time of year) or special busy dates. For example, a system for a florist can expect to be most busy on Valentine's Day.

Step 5: Determine Peak Throughput   Assuming we have an *average* throughput (from Step 4), how do we turn that into a real, immediate, here-and-now throughput? What's the greatest load we must be ready for? In a sense, our system must be a marathoner, a middle-distance runner, and a sprinter all in one—and the peak throughput says how fast it must be able to sprint. The aim of Step 5 is to determine a short-term peak throughput based on the long-term average.

The rest of this section applies to *incoming* throughput. *Outgoing* throughput is easier to determine because we typically have a lot more control over when it happens (for example, producing invoices or sending emails). Outgoing throughput also tends to be less important, because it usually imposes less of a processing load.

What's the ideal unit time period for which to set peak throughput? A day and an hour are too long because they provide plenty of time to satisfy the target while still having long periods with little (or even no) throughput. A second is too short because it implies that the target throughput must be achieved *every* second, which leaves little room for even fleeting hiccups. What's the point of such a tight requirement if it's not possible for any user to notice if it wasn't achieved? Indeed, no one would probably notice if the system did nothing at all for a second. Let's not split hairs and debate funny time periods like five minutes or thirty seconds. Keeping to nice round numbers, the most convenient time period is therefore a *minute*. The rest of this section assumes we're calculating throughput for the *peak minute*. If you have sound business reasons for a different time period, then use it.

The extent to which peak throughput varies from the average depends on numerous factors according to the nature of the system. Common factors are

Factor 1: The system's availability window   This means its normal hours of operation. For a company's internal system running from 9 to 5, a day's average throughput is crammed into eight hours. For an always-open Web system, it's spread over 24 hours.

Factor 2: Naturally popular times   At what times of day is a typical user most likely to use the system (according to their local time zone)? If you're offering a service to businesses, it's likely to be busiest during working hours. If it's recreational, it'll probably be in the evening and at weekends.

Factor 3: Geographic distribution   How widely spread are your users? Across different time zones? If your system is available worldwide, do you have a dominant region from which most of your business comes (such as North America)? This factor can lead to complex patterns of load through the day.

Factor 4: High activity triggers   Do you have any situations that are unusually busy? Is there anything that could cause peak throughput to be much higher than the average? For example, if you're selling concert tickets online, you can expect to be deluged the moment tickets for a popular artist become available.

Build a model as sophisticated as you like or as simple as you can get away with to calculate the peak throughput. In addition to these factors there will also always be *natural variations* from minute to minute. A statistician would be able to work this out properly, but in the absence of one, resort to guessing. If you have no meaningful data at all, you must assume the peak throughput will be appreciably higher than the average, but not massively so. A factor of double might be a reasonable assumption of last resort.

Content

Once we've figured out a throughput target, a requirement for it needs to contain the following:

1. **Throughput object type**. State the sort of thing whose throughput is to be measured (such as *new orders*).

2. **Target throughput quantity** and **unit time period** (for example, *10 per second*).

3. **A statement about contingency** (if you wish). In some circumstances, it's worth adding a contingency factor on top of the estimated throughput. (That factor is usually a semi-arbitrary percentage—say, 10 percent or 20 percent.) If you decide to do so, state the amount of contingency that's included in the target. Ordinarily you'd increase the contingency in line with your uncertainty, but that could prove expensive here (in extra hardware cost). If you include a contingency without saying so, the development team might add their own contingency as well, and no one will know what's going on: you could end up with an over-engineered system without realizing. If you *don't* include a contingency, say so, if there's a risk of anyone wondering.

4. **Part of system** (if relevant). A throughput requirement applies either to the system as a whole or just to a part (usually an inter-system interface). If this requirement is for a part, say which.

5. **Justification**. Where did the target figure come from? How was it calculated? What figures were used as the basis for the calculation? In only the simplest cases is a self-contained justification concise enough to fit within the requirement; otherwise, refer to a justification that resides elsewhere. Either include it as informal material in the specification or keep it externally. Referring to a sizing model is fine.

    The justification might contain sensitive information that you don't want all readers of the requirements specification to see. If so, omit it from the specification. Consider omitting reference to it altogether if you don't want some readers feeling like second-class citizens.

6. **Target achievement timeframe**. How far into the system's life does the target need to be achieved? It might be immediately after it's installed, after a year, or at some distant time in the future ("eventually").

7. **Indicative hardware description** (if relevant), from Step 3 of the preceding approach.

Template(s)

Summary	Definition
«Throughput type» rate	*«Part of system»* shall be able to handle *«Throughput object type»* transactions at a rate of at least *«Throughput quantity»* per *«Unit time period»* [when using *«Indicative hardware set-up»*]. [*«Target achievement timeframe statement»*.] [*«Contingency statement»*.] [*«Justification statement»*.]

Example(s)

Summary	Definition
Order entry rate	The initial system shall be able to handle the entry of orders by customers at a rate of at least 10 per second. No contingency has been added; this rate represents the actual demand expected. See the system sizing model for details of how this figure has been arrived at. It is located at *«Sizing model location»*.

Extra Requirements

Verifying whether the system achieves a throughput requirement can be difficult and tedious if the system itself doesn't help, so features for measuring throughput are the first candidates for extra requirements. Then we can think about steps to maximize throughput and how we want the system to react when it reaches its throughput limits. Here are some topics to consider writing extra requirements for:

1. **Monitoring throughput**   Monitoring can be divided into immediate and reflective: immediate tells us the throughput level *right now*; reflective provides statistics on throughput levels *over an extended period*, to highlight busy periods and throughput trends.

2. **Limiting throughput**   We can't stop incoming traffic directly (or, at least, it's usually too drastic to), but we can consider restricting the *causes* of traffic—such as limiting the number of active users, perhaps by preventing users logging in if the number already logged in has reached the limit. This could be refined to let in some users but not others—registered customers but not casual visitors, for example. Another step could be to disable resource-intensive secondary functions at times of high load.

3. **Maximizing throughput**   What steps can we take to squeeze the most through the system? One way is to "clear the decks" during times of peak throughput: arrange for some other processing to be done at other times. That depends on how much load is imposed by other processing. If it's not much, it's not worth bothering. Also consider insisting upon separate machines for background processing.

4. **High throughput characteristics**   Computer systems, like all complex and temperamental creatures, can behave differently when pushed to their limits. The response time requirement pattern recommends putting caveats on that aspect of performance when the system is experiencing high load, but there might be others that you want to apply only when the throughput is within its stated limit.

5. **Implementation sizing model**   It's sometimes useful to have a good sizing model to help determine the hardware needed to achieve a given throughput level, particularly if you're building a product. You can make this a requirement. State who will use this model: your customers or only representatives of your organization. A requirement of this kind effectively asks the development or testing team to extend any sizing model produced during the requirements process to take into account the software's actual performance.

Considerations for Development

Design to maximize the efficiency of high-volume transactions. For example, don't send information more than once. And keep interactions as simple as possible—don't use two request-response pairs when one would suffice.

Even if there is no requirement for throughput monitoring, it's useful to incorporate at least a rudimentary way of showing current throughput. Find out whether an automated throughput tester is going to be purchased or built for the testing team. If so, make sure it's available to the development team for their use, too.

Considerations for Testing

Attempting to manually make suitably large numbers of requests to a system is, in most cases, logistically impossible. To test throughput, you need an automated way to generate a high volume of requests. You might find a product to do this job, or you might have to build your own software for the purpose (in which case treat it as a serious development effort). Whichever way you go, a good automated throughput testing tool should let you do these things:

1. Define the requests to submit to the system (and the expected response to each one). The two basic ways are either to pregenerate large quantities of test data or to define rules by which test data can be generated on the fly.

2. Start submitting requests (and stop, when you've done enough).

3. Dynamically change the rate at which requests are submitted. This allows you simulate low, average, and heavy demand levels.

4. Monitor the response time of each request. This provides an external picture of how the system behaves.

5. Validate each response. This doesn't tell you about throughput per se, but being able to automatically check that large numbers of responses are as you expect is a valuable bonus.

6. Simulate the load on the system likely to be imposed by other activities, because it's not realistic to assume the system will be able to devote its full attention to one kind of request.

7. Generate reports on the system's performance. The accumulated response time data can be used to calculate throughput figures. It can also provide response time statistics: the shortest, average, and longest response times, and how response times vary with throughput.

The throughput that a system can handle doesn't vary proportionately with the power of its hardware, so it's hard to figure out just what testing using a hardware set-up different from that of the production environment tells you: extrapolations are likely to be difficult and unreliable. There are also many hardware factors that determine its overall power: the number and speed of CPUs, memory, disk drives, network bandwidth, and more. A sizing model helps, but it's still only a model and will have limited accuracy. Modify the sizing model based on observations from the real system.

9.3 Dynamic Capacity Requirement Pattern

Basic Details

Related patterns:	None
Anticipated frequency:	Up to two requirements
Pattern classifications:	None

Applicability

Use the dynamic capacity requirement pattern to specify the quantity of a particular type of entity for which the system must be able to perform processing at the same time. It is intended primarily for the number of simultaneous users a system must be capable of handling. It also suggests what do to when too many users come along at once.

Discussion

Specifying dynamic capacity is difficult, unless you have an existing system from which you can obtain figures. It doesn't help developers, except as a rough idea of scale. It comes into its own only when sizing hardware, after the system has been built. Demanding that a system be scalable is much more valuable and can be done *instead of* demanding a particular capacity level—see the scalability requirement pattern in Chapter 10, "Flexibility Requirement Patterns." Nevertheless, the topics discussed in the "Extra Requirements" subsection are well worth thinking about. Those requirements are often more useful than a dynamic capacity requirement itself—in particular, being able to exert control on the load imposed on your system. A Web site is open for the whole world to come and visit, but if even a *small* country turned up all at once, you'd be trampled underfoot unless you took precautions.

You can calculate an expected number of simultaneous users using a sizing model, but producing a decent estimate is tricky and takes a lot of care. You need to work out how an average user behaves: when they visit, how long they stay, which functions they use (and how many times). If your users are distributed across multiple time zones, take into account what percentage of users reside in each time zone—and adjust their visit times to the system's local time zone.

Content

A dynamic capacity requirement should contain these items:

1. **Type of entity**   What sort of thing are we stating capacity for? In the case of simultaneous user capacity, this is either all users or just one or more class of users (for example, *customer*). If two different user classes behave in very different ways (that is, place very different levels of demand on the system), treat them separately—or else we're adding apples and oranges. For a system driving a Web site, two fundamental classes of users exist: external (customers and casual visitors) and internal (employees, and perhaps employees of partner companies). An internal user might impose a smaller load on the system (per minute) than an external user to whom we might, say, display fancy graphics. And we might have fewer internal users logged in at any one time, although it is important for employee productivity that the system has adequate dynamic capacity for them.

    Note that a dynamic capacity requirement doesn't concern itself with the *duration* of user sessions.

2. **Number of entities**   How many must the system be able to handle at once?

3. **Entity condition**   In what state must an entity be in order to count? What must they be doing to be regarded as dynamically using the system? For example, we typically count users who are logged in, actively using the system, or both. Define this carefully and explain it precisely, or else users who aren't dynamically using the system are likely to be included. In particular, users might leave the system without telling us (logging out); this is the norm for visitors to Web sites. Write an entity condition clause to exclude departed visitors from the count of dynamic users. The subject of what to do about users who don't log out (what we might call "stale" user sessions) is dealt with in the "Extra Requirements" and "Considerations for Development" subsections of this pattern.

4. **Duration of peak, if relevant**   Some systems have peaks of activity that last only a relatively short time. If so, describe the nature of such peaks—what causes them, when, and for how long—because it might be possible to take steps to squeeze the best possible performance from the system while peaks last (by "clearing the decks" so that the system has as little other work as possible during these times). If this item is omitted, the system must be able to maintain this capacity level all the time it is running.

5. **Concessions during peak period**   If we're specifying dynamic capacity for a peak period (that is, short continuous duration), what concessions in other areas (in functionality and/or performance) can be made to help boost dynamic capacity?

6. **Achievement timeframe**   By when must the system be able to cater for this capacity level? If this isn't stated, it's reasonable to assume the system will cater for this capacity level from the moment it is installed and for ever thereafter.

Template(s)

Summary	Definition
Simultaneous «*Entity type*» capacity	The system shall be able satisfy «*Entity count*» simultaneous «*Entity type*»s «*Entity condition statement*» [«*Duration of peak statement*»]. [«*Achievement timeframe statement*».] [«*Peak period concession statement*»].

Example(s)

Summary	Definition
Simultaneous customer capacity	The system shall accommodate 100 customers logged in and active simultaneously. A user is deemed to be active if they have submitted a request to the system in the past five minutes.
Peak customer capacity	The system shall accommodate 200 customers logged in and active simultaneously when tickets for a popular concert go on sale—from half an hour before the published sale time until two hours afterwards. The definition of active customer is as given in the previous requirement.
	During a popular concert initial sale peak, it is acceptable for secondary services offered by the Web site (including any involving large downloads or the streaming of audio or video) to be shut down. It is also acceptable to prevent internal users from accessing any functions that involve intensive processing.

Extra Requirements

A dynamic capacity requirement could have the following kinds of extra requirements—though they are all useful in their own right, and they can be specified even if you decide not to specify a dynamic capacity requirement at all:

1. **Limit the number of users allowed in at once**. This is usually achieved by preventing someone logging in if there are already at least a certain number of users logged in. This scheme can be refined to treat classes of users (or specific users) in different ways. For example, when the system is busy, we could let in only high-priority users.

2. Consider ways to **reduce the load** on the system imposed by internal users at times when it's exceptionally busy. Perhaps we could arrange for intensive work to be done at times of low external load. You could require the ability to temporarily disable functions that cause intensive processing.

3. **A monitoring function** to show the number of users currently active is always useful. This could show how many users are being handled by each server machine, and how many users of each type. It could let you dig down and view information on a selected individual session (start time, time since last request, user type, functions accessed). But be careful what you ask for, because it could be costly in development effort and its potential impact on performance. System monitoring is discussed further, with an example requirement, in the "Attack Direction 6: Duration of Failures" section of the availability requirement pattern later in this chapter.

4. Add one or more **inquiry** or **report** to show the number of active users over time, and perhaps also according to time of day (in order to identify peaks).

5. To help achieve a dynamic capacity requirement, developers might **free up valuable system resources** used by users who appear to have gone away. This, of course, is an implementation matter that doesn't concern the requirements. But it could have consequences the user might notice if they do return. They might be forced to log in again, or details of what they had done in the session might be lost, or their first response might be a little slower than normal (while the system fetches the details of their session and allocates any resources the session needs). If these sorts of consequences are unacceptable, write requirements to prevent them. But bear in mind that by doing so, extra hardware (or other steps) might be needed to achieve the dynamic capacity goals.

6. Demand a function to **forcibly eject (log out) a selected user**. This could be accompanied by a related function to bar a selected user, to stop them coming back. Neither of these functions directly affect dynamic capacity, but they can help if a particular user's actions are imposing a significant load on the system (either by accident or maliciously).

7. **Raise an alarm if the number of simultaneous users exceeds a set number**. You could ask for the ability for several different thresholds, each with its own alarm severity.

8. A sophisticated system could let a system administrator tinker with **rules for allocating user sessions to machines**, to give certain users (or types of users) better performance. This can also allow the load on a machine to be reduced, preparatory to shutting it down (for example for maintenance or upgrading). However, features such as this stray close to prescribing solutions: they are hard to specify without making assumptions about the nature of the solution.

Most of these are features for observing how well the system is performing, and for controlling it in order to squeeze maximum performance from it. The scalability requirement pattern (in Chapter 10) discusses further measures that contribute to achieving high dynamic capacity, such as the ability to add resources (server machines, for example) dynamically.

Considerations for Development

Consider how to deal with "stale" user sessions (again, where the user has departed without logging out). If a user session takes up precious resources, there are two approaches to making the most of them. First, they can be freed up by forcibly ending the session, which could inconvenience the user if they attempt to return shortly after. Second, we could store the session details elsewhere (such as in the database) so that the session can be revived if the user does come back.

Make provision for processing load to be spread across multiple server machines so that the system's dynamic capacity isn't held hostage by the performance of a single machine and whether that one machine can satisfy a given dynamic capacity target. Again, this says that scalability is usually more valuable than being able to achieve a particular performance goal. What would happen, for instance, if the volume of business turned out to be larger than anticipated? It's better to be able to react positively than to throw up your hands and plead that the system performs as asked for.

Considerations for Testing

Any dynamic capacity target (such as the number of users logged in simultaneously) is likely to be so high that imposing this load manually will be difficult. After all, if the target is small, there's little point in the requirement being there. A test team (even if it conscripted extra volunteers) has better things to do than trying to manually replicate the activity of a collection of users twice its number. The only option is to use software to simulate this many users. There are products for this purpose, and it's easier to buy one of these than to embark on developing software in house to do the job.

9.4 Static Capacity Requirement Pattern

Basic Details

Related patterns:	Data longevity, data archiving, scalability
Anticipated frequency:	Between zero and two requirements, rarely more
Pattern classifications:	Affects database: Yes

Applicability

Use the static capacity requirement pattern to specify the quantity of a particular type of entity that the system must be able to store permanently (typically in a database).

Do not use the static capacity requirement pattern to specify for *how long* information must be retained; use the data longevity requirement pattern for that. Also do not use it to specify how much *disk space* the system needs.

Discussion

With storage being so cheap and databases able to handle vast quantities of data, static capacity itself isn't a critical issue per se: we're unlikely to have trouble finding enough disk space for whatever we need to store. The importance of a static capacity requirement is indirect: that all aspects of the system be designed and built so as to be practical and work well when the target number of entities are present. For example, an inquiry or report that shows every individual entity is impractical if we have more than a few hundred.

Most business systems have one type of entity that determines the quantity of most or all other high volume entities—one that drives everything else of note. *Customer* is typically the best type of entity to use. It determines the number of derivative entities—its extended family—such as (customer-initiated) transactions, a history of customer details changes, customer preferences, and so on. A system could have more than one type of driving entity that are independent of one another volumewise; if so, write (or consider writing) a static capacity requirement for each one.

A sizing model can be used to roughly estimate the disk space needed for a system's database, based on a target number of driving entities and the logical structure of this type of entity (see the data structure requirement pattern in Chapter 6, "Information Requirement Patterns") and its derivative entities, such as transactions. Add a large contingency (50 percent?) for extra overhead and columns added during the database design stage, plus a fixed chunk for configuration data (say, 20 Mb?) and space for chronicle data (which could itself be very large). Also add space for any multimedia resources (such as a picture of each customer, if you have them). But regard any such estimate as indicative only.

Content

A static capacity requirement should contain

1. **Type of entity**   What sort of thing are we guaranteeing enough room for (for example, *customer*)?

2. **Number of entities**   What's the minimum number the system must be able to store, and still work well?

3. **Entity inclusion criteria**   Which entities count for capacity purposes? If this item is omitted, *all* entities of the stated type are included. The purpose of this is to permit excluded entities to be removed (or moved somewhere else, where they have less impact on performance). For example, if we include only *active* customers—and we need to state precisely what that means—we are at liberty to take out all inactive ones, if that will help keep the system running smoothly. That's not to say excluded entities *must* be removed; if the system runs fine with them present, there's no performance reason why they can't stay. However, there must be a requirement for a function to remove the excluded entities (see the data longevity and data archiving requirement patterns in Chapter 6). This item has the effect of granting the development team a degree of leeway.

4. **Achievement timeframe**   By when must the system be ready for this capacity level? If omitted, the system must always support this capacity.

Template(s)

Summary	Definition
Total «*Entity type*» capacity	The system shall be able to handle a minimum of «*Entity count*» «*Entity type*»s. «*Entity inclusion criteria*». [«*Achievement timeframe statement*».]

Example(s)

Summary	Definition
Initial customer capacity	The system shall be able to handle a minimum of 50,000 customers upon initial installation.
Eventual customer capacity	The system shall eventually be able to handle a minimum of 1,000,000 customers. This figure covers only those customers who have accessed the Web site in the past three months or placed an order within the past twelve months. It is not expected that this level of business will be reached earlier than two years after initial implementation.

Extra Requirements

A static capacity requirement can prompt extra requirements for the following kind of functions:

1. **Remove inactive information**, to stop the system getting clogged up with data. (See the data longevity and data archiving requirement patterns.)

2. **Statistical inquiries or reports** to show changes in the number of entities over time. This reporting could be linked to changes in other performance measures over time (for example, how growth in business volume has affected average response times).

3. **Raise an alarm** if the number of entities reaches beyond a set number (or within a set limit of an actual capacity estimated by the system itself, perhaps based on available disk space).

Considerations for Development

Check that every specified function that accesses any type of entity whose volume is affected by a static capacity requirement will be practical to use and can be implemented with acceptable response time.

Considerations for Testing

A way is needed to generate a sufficient quantity of data. This involves either invoking the system's software or writing something to emulate what it does.

You can't simply extrapolate performance at one capacity level to deduce performance at a higher capacity. Or, rather, the greater the difference (ratio) between the two levels, the greater the risk the extrapolation will be wrong (due to performance degrading). A factor of two or maybe four isn't a risk; a factor of ten is just about tolerable; twenty or more isn't good enough. To test that a system caters for a stated capacity, you need to generate that many (or a number smaller by a factor whose risk you consider acceptable). And you need to generate a representative quantity of every other type of dependent entity: transactions, chronicle entries, and so on. To do this, you need software to manufacture artificial data.

9.5 Availability Requirement Pattern

Basic Details

Related patterns:	None
Anticipated frequency:	Usually no more than one requirement—though from it might flow dozens of extra requirements
Pattern classifications:	None

Applicability

Use the availability requirement pattern to define when the system is available to users: the system's "normal opening times" (which could be "open all hours") plus how dependably the system (or a part of the system) is available when it should be. This requirement pattern is written to fit systems that appear to have a life of their own, such as server type systems that sit waiting with a range of services for users to call upon whenever they wish. It is not meaningful to specify availability in the same way for desktop-type applications (such as a diagram editor) that you start up when you want.

This requirement pattern has **not** been written to satisfy the demands of **life-critical systems**. It is for normal business systems, where the most disastrous outcome is commercial (financial).

Discussion

It's easy to say "the system shall be available 24x7," but even the most bullet-proof, fail-safe, over-engineered system won't roll on for ever. Anyone who's aware of that should have qualms about such a blanket requirement. In any case, "24x7" has become cliché: it's often not intended to be taken literally when used in speech, so you can't rely on it being taken seriously when stated as a requirement. Fortunately, there's an easy answer to that too: add a percentage to it. "The system shall be available to users for 24 hours a day, every day, *99 percent of the time.*" That's better. But where has this figure of 99 percent come from? It sounds suspiciously arbitrary. And if I'm a software developer, what am I to do when I encounter such a requirement? What should I do differently if it said 99.9 percent? If I'm the project manager, how much will it cost to achieve this 99 percent? If I'm a tester, how can I test that the system satisfies this requirement? If I run it for a week nonstop without incident, is that good enough? No, requirements like this are unhelpful to everyone. It's time to go back to the drawing board.

A Sense of Percents

Availability percentages are quoted with apparently careless abandon, so let's spell out what they actually imply. For a system that aims to be available 24 hours a day, the following table shows for how long the system must run before it can acceptably accumulate one hour of downtime (time when the system is unavailable to users when it should be available):

Availability	equates to 1 hour's downtime every	and downtime in a year of ...
90%	10 hours	5.2 weeks
95%	20 hours	2.6 weeks
99%	4.2 days	3.7 days
99.9%	6 weeks	9 hours
99.99%	13.7 months	53 minutes

Bear in mind that these reflect unavailability *from all causes*, both planned and unplanned. These figures let us picture how much havoc would be wrought to our availability target by, say, a 12-hour shutdown to upgrade the software or by a six-hour shutdown after an attack by a hacker.

Let's look at availability rates in a different way and venture subjective judgments on how hard a few availability levels are to achieve (though they'll vary according to the nature of the system and the technology you use):

Downtime of	equates to availability of	and is how hard to achieve?
1 hour per day	95.833%	No problem.
1 hour per week	99.405%	Beginning to get tight.
1 hour per month	99.863%	Much care needed!
1 hour per year	99.989%	Very tough indeed!

System failures are a matter of luck: they might never happen. But if you want high availability without taking the necessary trouble, the odds of achieving it are stacked heavily against you.

Let's start by recognizing that our revised easy requirement is conveying two things. First, what I'll call the **availability window**, which is the times during which we *want* the system to be available (for example, 24 hours every day, or stated business hours). And second, *how dependably* it should be available during those times (the hard part!). The availability window is easy to specify and says a lot about the nature of the system, so begin by writing a requirement for it. It can be 24x7 if necessary, but making it less reduces the pressure on developers. The converse **unavailability window** (scheduled downtime) gives time for the various housekeeping and other extracurricular activities every system must perform—for which 24x7 allows no dedicated time at all. Doing these things during the unavailability window makes it easier to provide high availability the rest of the time. Define the bounds of the availability window according to what you *require*, not what sounds attractive.

The remainder of this section discusses an overall approach to specifying availability. For clarity, it leaves out the details of how to carry out each step and how to specify the resulting requirements; they are covered in the "Extra Requirements" subsection.

Before going any further, we must recognize that **our availability goals cover only components within the scope of our system**. We cannot be held responsible for the availability of anything that's outside our control. It's essential to state this clearly and prominently in the requirements specification—or everyone will naturally attribute to the system any downtime due to external causes. If the discussion and setting of availability goals must include external factors, separate the goals for the system from external goals. For example, if the customers of a Web-based service are to perceive less than *one hour's* downtime per month, we could allocate *ten minutes* of that to Internet communication unavailability (outside our control, but for which figures can be obtained), *five minutes* to Web server unavailability (assuming it to be outside scope) and *forty-five minutes* to unavailability of our system. The latter could then be sub-allocated into *five minutes* for hardware and operating system and *forty minutes* for our own application software. These allocations can be adjusted. For example, by choosing high-quality, replicated hardware and high-quality third-party products, we can reduce their allocations, leaving as much as possible for our own software. But this takes us into the technical realm that the requirements stage should eschew as far as possible.

Separate downtime allocations can be given to different parts of the system. If so, statistics should be gathered once the system goes live to see how well each part is going against its target. To do this, the duration of each failure must be correctly assigned to the correct cause—system or external—which isn't always easy to do. It's also liable to be contentious if different managers are responsible for different parts of the system. It's questionable whether a system can dependably work out when it's been available, but if you want it to, define requirements for what you want it to record. Otherwise, gathering these statistics is a manual process.

Our availability conundrum can be summed up as

a.   We don't know what we'd get if we ignored availability.

b.   We can't work out how much we need, or how much we're prepared to pay for it.

c.   We don't know how much we could improve it by if we tried, nor how much it would cost.

To produce requirements for those features that our system needs in order to achieve the business' availability goals, we must satisfactorily unravel all three parts of the conundrum. That's a tall order; in fact, it is literally impossible, and the following paragraphs point out why. But that doesn't mean we should give up; we just have to set our sights a bit lower.

Taking (a) first, every system has what we can call a **natural availability level**, which is what you get if your developers build the system without paying any special attention to availability. (Notice that I say *your* developers, because if they're highly skilled your system will have a higher natural availability level than if they were mediocre.) The trouble with *our system's* natural availability level is that we can't possibly know what it is until well after it's been built. We might have a gut feel, but any attempt to quantify it would be just a wild guess. Nevertheless, it's a useful concept for discussion purposes: it helps us tell when we're on shaky ground.

For (b), the news is better: we can paint a reasonably clear picture of how important availability of this system is to the business—by quizzing key stakeholders about the damage the business would suffer in various situations, and asking them how much they'd be prepared to invest to reduce the chances of it happening. The results are still not strictly systematic—because of our inability to determine the chances of such failures happening, nor how much it would actually cost to do better—but they give the project team a sense of how far to go to improve availability. They also give stakeholders a good understanding of the issues.

Moving on to (c), achieving anything higher than the natural availability level is going to cost money. You'll also quickly reach a point of rapidly diminishing returns, where each incremental increase in availability costs noticeably more. The following graph demonstrates the cost of increasing availability—though I stress it is indicative only and not based on real figures. Cost 1 is that of the natural availability system, which—we discover eventually—has 95 percent availability. Building a system with 99.5 percent availability would cost roughly twice as much—*double the whole system budget*, that is. This demonstrates how vital it is to get availability requirements right: few other aspects of a system can have such a large impact on its cost.

Figure 9-2 shows the whole y-axis down to zero to point out that 95 percent availability is actually quite a high figure. Also, being prepared to accept reduced availability in an effort to reduce cost is usually a waste of time.

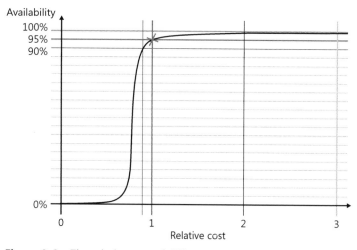

Figure 9-2   The relative cost of different availability levels

We run into further trouble when we try to specify ways to improve our system's availability: we can't know how much effect each possible precaution will have. If a system already exists, we can at least spot the most common failings and focus on them; but we can't do that for a system that's yet to be built. Hints can be found by looking at experiences with the organization's other systems, or systems previously built by the same development team, or similar systems.

The best way to achieve our availability goals is to specify requirements for a wide range of features that contribute. These requirements can be identified by investigating the three main causes of downtime (regular housekeeping, periodic upgrades and unexpected failure) and working out ways to reduce them. Each of these requirements can contain an estimate of its availability benefit. Give each one a low priority by default—though you can give a higher priority to any you feel deserves it (because many of these features will be worthwhile in their own right). Post-requirements planning can estimate the cost—in development effort and/or the financial cost of purchasing extra hardware or third-party products—of implementing each requirement. These benefit and cost estimates then let you make more informed choices of which of these requirements to implement: some requirements will emerge as more cost-effective than others.

The resulting requirements might not give stakeholders assurances in the terms they seek (or are used to seeing), but to do so would be misleading, because you couldn't guarantee the system will achieve them.

The steps to take are as follows (and the subsections referred to are within the "Extra Requirements" section later in this pattern):

Step 1:   Write a requirement for the availability window, as per the template and example in this pattern. If different chunks of the system can have different availability windows, write a requirement for each one.

Step 2:   Work out the seriousness of the impact on the business of downtime—as described in the section titled "The Business Impact of Downtime."

Step 3:   Specify what is to happen when the system is unavailable or not working properly, as described in the "Partial Availability" section.

Step 4:   Give a thought to surreptitious unavailability—which means bursts of poor response time when background work is being done by the system—if the unavailability window is small or nonexistent, as described in the "Surreptitious Unavailability" section.

Step 5:   Specify requirements for features to improve availability—by investigating the causes of downtime and working out ways to reduce them, as described in the "Requirements for Reducing Downtime" section.

All the preceding steps are undertaken as part of the requirements specification process. Further steps, which follow, can be done later, after cost estimates have been made for implementing the system—including specific estimates for all the requirements that contribute to increasing availability:

Step 6:   Estimate the cost of implementing each requirement for improving availability. This should be done as part of the project's main estimation process.

Step 7:   Calculate the cost effectiveness of each requirement for improving availability, based on its estimated cost and its estimated effectiveness. A spreadsheet is perhaps the most convenient vehicle for doing this. Use these cost effectiveness values to decide whether to implement any of these requirements immediately; adjust the priority of each requirement accordingly.

Content

A requirement to specify the availability window needs to contain the following:

1. **Normal availability extent**   The times during which the system is planned to be available. This could be "always" (24x7), or a start and end time each day—and perhaps which days of the week, too.

2. **Meaning of *available***   A definition of what is meant by *available* in the context of this requirement. This must not be stated in terms that depend on *how* the system is implemented (for example, the availability of an individual server machine). For a typical system, *available* means that users are able to log in and perform whatever functions they have access to. Assuming a system is either available or not is something of an over-simplification; see the "Partial Availability" subsection later in this pattern for a discussion of the possibilities in between.

3. **Tolerated downtime qualifier (optional)**   A caveat recognizing that perfect availability can't be guaranteed, and describing where more details are to be found about the amount of downtime that would be considered tolerable.

Template(s)

This template is for a requirement that defines the availability window of a system, with an optional clause for a tolerable level of unavailability (which needn't itself be in quantitative terms).

Summary	Definition
«*Extent*» availability	The system shall normally be available to users «*Availability extent description*» [, except in exceptional circumstances of a frequency and duration not to exceed «*Tolerated downtime qualifier*»]. "Normally available" shall be taken to mean «*Availability meaning*».

Example(s)

As for the template, these examples define the availability window. All other requirements related to availability are covered in the "Extra Requirements" section.

Summary	Definition
7 a.m. to 7 p.m. availability	The system shall be available to all users from 7 a.m. to 7 p.m. on business days (that is, weekdays that are not public holidays), except in exceptional circumstances of a frequency and duration not to exceed those defined in other requirements. "Available" shall be taken to mean that all user functions are operational.
Availability of dynamic Web functions	The dynamic functions of the company's Web site shall be available to visitors 24 hours per day, every day of the year, except for unscheduled downtime not to exceed 1 hour per week (averaged over each calendar quarter) plus scheduled downtime not to exceed one outage per calendar month of a maximum of 4 hours to be carried out at the time of a week's lowest Web site activity. "Dynamic functions" are those that require the active involvement of the Web shop system (for example, to place or inquire on orders).

Summary	Definition
Web site availability	The company's Web site shall be available to visitors 24 hours per day, every day of the year. "Available" shall be taken to mean that all static Web pages shall be viewable. In addition, if any dynamic function (as defined in the previous requirement) is unavailable, then a static page of explanation shall be presented in its place.
	It is recognized that constant availability with no interruption at all cannot be guaranteed, but only outages resulting from extraordinary causes that could not reasonably be prevented will be regarded as tolerable.

Extra Requirements

The proper specifying of availability can involve numerous extra requirements of diverse kinds; they might include many features that developers find desirable but which do not normally appear justified to the business. Typing them directly to the availability goals of the business provides that justification.

This section is divided into four in accordance with the approach described in the preceding "Discussion" section: the business impact of downtime, partial availability, surreptitious unavailability, and requirements for reducing downtime. The last of these is where the serious action is, and it is itself broken down into six separate areas, each covered in its own subsection.

The Business Impact of Downtime   The first questions to ask are: Just how vital is high availability? Why's it needed? What's it for? Does survival of the business depend on it—in which case you've got to go to enormous trouble and expense? Or is it just nice to have, like a company intranet outside office hours, where if it's down you'll try again later? Answers to these sorts of questions are your best guide to the most suitable way to frame availability goals.

You can work out the seriousness of the impact on the business of downtime (during the availability window) by presenting key stakeholders with a few scenarios. One might be: the system fails altogether at 9 a.m. on Monday morning. How much damage has the business suffered after half an hour of the system being down? After two hours? Six hours? Three days? Pick the point at which serious pain starts, and then ask: How much extra is the business prepared to invest to reduce the chances of suffering this much damage? (Recognize that there's a kind of backward connection here: longer failures do more damage but are easier to shorten, so it's necessary to find *shortest* downtime period that hurts.)

Write up the results of these exercises as informal narrative in the requirements specification. Don't simply record every remark that was made: distill the salient conclusions into a few punchy points. Where possible, identify the source of the statement (if it's a senior executive, say) to give it added weight. The aim is to guide anyone involved in planning or developing the system—to give them a feel for the lengths they should go to. Here are a couple of examples:

- "An outage of more than twenty-four hours would lead to a permanent loss of 25 percent of customers. (Source: marketing manager)."

- "We're prepared to pay an extra *«Amount of money»* if it means we can be up and running again two hours after a major incident. (Source: CEO)."

These are targets only: it's impossible to guarantee they'll be achieved, because nothing's going to force the gremlins in the machine to abide by them. So stating them as requirements—things the system is *required* to satisfy—is problematical and actually reduces their credibility. Statements like these carry more weight when they're *not* requirements.

If you still feel the urge to state an availability percentage (or, equivalently, a tolerable amount of downtime per given time period), go ahead. If so, it's preferable for this to be an informal statement too—because it can't be guaranteed either.

Partial Availability   What should happen when the system isn't fully or properly available to users but is still alive enough to do *something*? See if there's some fallback position that lets you deliver a reduced service to users or at least inform them that something's wrong. When one part of a system fails, most of the time the rest keeps on running. So treating all failures as all-or-nothing gives an exaggerated picture of their effect on availability. Still, because availability is already too complicated to calculate, you can, if you wish, ignore the subtleties of partial availability when confronting quantitative availability levels.

It can be worthwhile to divide a system into two or three chunks for the purpose of availability goals. These chunks could be according to their importance or the technology we know each uses. For example, if we're building a Web site and the system behind it, it would make sense to state higher availability goals for the static parts of the Web site than for the interactive parts (placing orders, say).

When the system is partially available, the working part might be able to adapt accordingly. For example, if the software behind our Web site fails (or is down for maintenance), we'd like to let our users know that certain functions are temporarily unavailable—perhaps by having fallback static Web pages to display in this situation. Here's an example requirement:

Summary	Definition
System unavailable page	When the system is unavailable to users, any attempt by a user to access the system shall result in the display of a page informing them that it is unavailable.
	This response is not expected if those parts of the system needed to provide such a display are themselves not running—though all practical steps shall be taken to make to the user that something is wrong.

The requirements can't state the reaction to every type of failure (and mustn't attempt to), but they may address a small number of salient ones. It's also possible to specify requirements for steps that are to be taken when appropriate to improve error handling; these can act as guidelines for developers.

Surreptitious Unavailability   If we don't give our system spare time to do its housekeeping (that is, no unavailability window), it is forced to do it while users are active. This can manifest itself as intermittent slow response time or possibly a disconcerting delay (say, 30 seconds or a minute) if it stops certain types of processing for users altogether. We can call this **surreptitious unavailability**, because the system is unavailable for this time but in such a way that the unavailability is difficult to notice.

If degraded performance is tolerable for a short while, adjust your performance requirements to allow it—and to say how much is acceptable—though at requirements time it's impossible to know how much time might be needed. You could also stipulate quiet times of day (or days of the week) to which such tasks are restricted. If degraded performance is *unacceptable*, make this clear, either in the relevant performance requirements themselves or in an additional requirement. Otherwise, developers are likely to argue that response time during housekeeping is a special case. Either way, bring this issue out into the open early.

Demanding both constant availability and consistently good response times is liable to create a squeeze that puts pressure on developers—and costs extra to deal with. (That this appears to happen rarely is perhaps due to surreptitious unavailability being ignored.) Relax this squeeze if you can: don't write onerous requirements unless there's a genuine need. If the goal is for the effect of background housekeeping not to be noticeable—which is usually perfectly acceptable—it's a good idea to permit a degrading of user response times small enough to fit the bill (say, by 10 percent).

Here are a few example requirements for alternative ways to prevent surreptitious unavailability getting out of hand (though they can be used in combination if need be):

Summary	Definition
Housekeeping response time increase maximum 10%	The running of system housekeeping processes while users are active shall not cause a perceptible increase in response time for any function of more than 10% over that when no housekeeping process is running. (That is, an increase in response time of up to 10% during housekeeping is tolerable.)
No housekeeping between 5 a.m. and midnight	No system housekeeping processes shall be run between the hours of 5 a.m. and midnight.
No housekeeping to run for more than 2 minutes	No system housekeeping process may run for more than two minutes in any ten if it might cause a perceptible increase in response time for any user function of more than 10% over that when no housekeeping process is running.

Requirements for Reducing Downtime   We can increase a system's availability by examining the three main causes of downtime—maintenance, periodic upgrades, and unexpected failure—and working out ways to reduce them. Some of these ways will be more cost-effective than others. Decisions on which ones to implement (and when) can be taken later in the project: it usually makes business sense to defer some in order to deliver the system faster. The role of the requirements here is to provide the information on which these decisions can be based: to demonstrate what precautions *can* be taken, what effect each is likely to have, and some idea of their complexity.

Requirements specifying features introduced to help achieve availability targets can be diverse and numerous (so there is a lot to work through in this section!). They span the duplication of hardware and software components and features needed by the products you use (such as the database). They also cover functions for monitoring, startup and shutdown, error diagnosis, software installation, security, and potentially other things that don't have an obvious connection to availability. Lots of these functions the system needs anyway, but improving availability might demand that they be better: more powerful, faster, easier to use—in general, built with more care and attention.

In lots of systems, many of these behind-the-scenes functions are often cobbled together as an afterthought, with little time allocated to developing them. Part of the reason is that most requirements specifications omit them altogether—because their connection to the system's business goals appears tenuous and normal users don't use them. **Connecting functions directly with availability goals that are in turn attached to business goals gives us solid justification for including those functions and for treating them with the same seriousness as the rest of the system.** This is an important point: well worth highlighting.

To identify extra requirements for functions that help us achieve our availability goals, we need to look at the reasons systems are unavailable. Anything that reduces any of these causes will increase our expected availability. Let's introduce a few straightforward formulae. The first one breaks the problem down into three constituent factors:

Formula 1:   **Total downtime** = **Maintenance** + **Upgrades** + **Failures**

where   **Total downtime** is the amount of time during any given period for which the system is unavailable to users during the planned availability window.

Maintenance is regular housekeeping that needs to be performed to keep the system operating smoothly—such as database backups—or business processing that cannot be done while users are accessing the system and which must be performed during the availability window. The stopping-and-restarting of any component counts as maintenance if it must be done periodically.

Upgrades are the installing of new software or hardware, and all related tasks.

Failures are anything that goes wrong that renders the system unavailable.

Assign every cause of downtime to one of these three factors. The dividing lines between them aren't always clear-cut. For example, if new software has to be rushed into production to forestall a looming failure known in advance, should that count as a normal upgrade or a failure? You could introduce an extra category for "preemptive corrections" and perhaps more for other boundary regions. They could be useful for management purposes, but they would only cloud the following discussion so they're omitted here.

A second formula can be applied either to all outages collectively or to one of the three factors at a time:

Formula 2:   **Downtime** = **Frequency of outages** × **Average outage duration**

(We talk about **average** duration here because we're making estimates for the future, not dealing with actual outages in the past.)

Maximizing availability is equivalent to minimizing frequency and duration for each of the three factors. Frequency needs to be treated separately from duration because reducing one involves different steps to reducing the other. Let's consider each of the three factors in turn and suggest ways to minimize their frequency and duration—giving us **six directions** from which to attack the problem and which are discussed in the following six subsections in the order indicated in this table:

	Frequency	Duration
Maintenance	1	2
Upgrades	3	4
Failures	5	6

But first observe that downtime for maintenance and upgrades will be zero if they can be undertaken wholly outside the availability window. Every serious system has various sorts of housekeeping tasks it must undertake. Many of these tasks are usually easier to do if nothing else is happening at the same time—especially real work by pesky users.

All of these six attack directions must be considered for **everything that is within the scope of the system**. This includes hardware—if that's in scope. It also includes all third-party products you need—if they're in scope. The implication is that the project team is free to choose all the products the system needs—in particular, to choose products that enable us to satisfy the availability requirements. A complication arises if product choices are forced on the project. If possible, treat these products as outside the system's scope and, accordingly, separate their availability goals from the availability goals of the system in scope. This isn't always possible, however, and you might have to accept responsibility for the availability of a product that's somewhat outside your control. There can also be cloudy areas. For example, if the choice of database has already been made, you might still be able to reconfigure it or purchase add-ons so as to increase its availability.

For each of the six attack directions, it's necessary to work through each of the types of constituent technical pieces in turn. The main ones are

1. **Hardware**. Consider the following:
    - ❑ The computer(s) on which the system will run.
    - ❑ Computers running other software: database, Web server, firewall, and so on.
    - ❑ Users' desktop machines (conceivably!).
    - ❑ Communications hardware, including internal networking devices, cabling and phone lines, and hardware.
    - ❑ Power supplies, both the normal and emergency uninterruptible supplies.
2. **Third-party software products**, such as database, Web server, and middleware.
3. **Our own software.**

Draw up a list of all those pieces relevant to your environment that have a bearing on the availability of your system. For each of the six attack directions, consider each item on your list and specify requirements for it as appropriate (as described in the following six attack direction subsections).

Again, worry about only those pieces that are *within the scope* of your system, as defined in the requirements specification. If the list you draw up includes things you believe shouldn't be the project's concern, you might have set the system's scope too broadly and need to reduce it. Nevertheless, it's useful to put in the requirements specification a list of all the pieces outside scope whose failure can affect the availability of your system—because your stakeholders might want to check their dependability and perhaps improve some of them.

Each requirement created to improve any of these attack directions should include a statement estimating the extent to which it contributes. Occasionally, it's possible to state the extent categorically (not as a mere estimate). This statement can be omitted if the requirement's definition already makes the effect obvious. A suggested template for such statements is

"It is estimated that this requirement reduces «*Factor*» by/to «*Extent*».

where   «*Factor*» is one of the six attack directions

and   «*Extent*» is the average amount by which it improves the factor."

An average is usually worked out by estimating in what percentage of failures this requirement will help, and by how much it helps on average then. For example, something that helps in five percent of failures but typically saves then 20 minutes will save an average of one minute per failure. Here are some examples:

- "It is estimated that this requirement reduces average duration of daily housekeeping by five minutes."
- "This requirement reduces frequency of upgrades by three per year."
- "It is estimated that this requirement reduces duration of each application software failure by 15 minutes on average."

Always stress when anything is just an estimate. At requirements time, we don't know how much the system is going to cost or what its "natural" availability will be. So we have little idea how much extra it'll cost to achieve stated availability goals. Even metrics determined from previous projects (if you have any) wouldn't tell us much. Too much depends on technology choices that (usually) have yet to be made. **It is therefore impossible for the requirements to make concrete judgments on what features our software needs in order to deliver acceptable availability.** And this is even before we begin to think about how much it would cost.

There is a risk that the total of the downtime savings indicated in these requirements might add up to more downtime than we anticipate—by overselling the benefit of some of the preventive steps. To prevent this happening, you could extract all these figures and, say, put them in a spreadsheet.

If availability demands aren't onerous or if you have confidence that the system's natural availability level will be good enough, you can leave out of the initial implementation *all* the requirements for increasing availability. They can be introduced selectively later once we see how good the system's actual availability is and the causes of any failures that do occur. It is, however, a good idea for developers to bear in mind all the availability-related requirements—to make provision for them so that it's straightforward to add them later. Also. choose third-party products that satisfy these requirements as far as possible: it would be disappointing to have to replace a third-party product later just because it's not reliable enough.

Now for the six attack directions themselves. Note that they're all written to cover hardware and third-party products as well as our own software.

Attack Direction 1: Frequency of Maintenance   Commercial systems historically do their regular maintenance once a day: the old end-of-day run. This is a convenient and natural cycle. There might be sound business or technical reasons for doing system maintenance several times a day—or less than once a day. These reasons should take precedence over the desire to reduce frequency of maintenance as part of our efforts to improve availability. But this section would be failing in its duty if it didn't point out that doing maintenance less often improves availability (if user access must be curtailed to perform maintenance). On the other hand, there might be a trade-off between maintenance frequency and maintenance duration: when doing it less often means it takes longer each time.

A system can have more than one type of maintenance—for example, daily and monthly. Moving some processing from a frequently run type to a one less frequently run would then reduce the total maintenance time—and improve availability. But it's rare that the requirements can effect changes like this; they are more a design matter.

Here's an example requirement for the record—but it does look rather old-fashioned:

Summary	Definition
Maintenance no more than daily	The system shall not be shut down for maintenance more than once per day.

Attack Direction 2: Duration of Maintenance   Duration of maintenance can be brought down to zero for most types of system through the use of suitable products (especially the database); it might take some extra development effort, too. Here are some sample requirements for a few things that contribute to reducing (or eliminating) maintenance time:

Summary	Definition
Database backups while system active	A database product shall be selected that permits backing up of the database while other database activities are going on.
	It is estimated that this requirement reduces duration for which the system would be unavailable to users for maintenance by fifteen minutes each day.
Product restarts unnecessary	Each product used (both software and hardware) shall be chosen on the basis that it can be depended upon to run for an extended duration without needing to be restarted.
	It is estimated that this requirement reduces duration for which the system would be unavailable to users for maintenance by thirty minutes each week.
Housekeeping while system active	All system housekeeping tasks that can be performed while the system is available to users (such as purging old data) shall be.
	It is estimated that this requirement reduces duration for which the system would be unavailable to users for maintenance by ten minutes each day.

Note that these requirements contribute to reducing both maintenance duration and *frequency*, so the estimates of their impact must reflect both.

Attack Direction 3: Frequency of Upgrades   The frequency with which the various components of the system are upgraded is determined primarily by the forces that motivate the upgrade: to introduce new features or other software improvements, fix defects, add faster hardware, and so on. Those forces will usually strike a sensible balance with the forces that don't want the system interrupted. Nevertheless, if it's important for availability reasons to limit the frequency of system shutdowns for upgrades, the requirements are the place to say so. Each type of component in the system (hardware, third-party products, our own software, and so on) has its own upgrade considerations, and therefore need to be treated separately in these requirements.

It's worth observing, though, that stable systems need upgrading less frequently—and because high-quality systems are stable, this implies that *quality* reduces frequency of upgrades. There's also a trend towards more iterative development methodologies (shorter development cycles with more frequent deliveries, that is), but it's not necessary to install every iteration live. Iterative approaches don't force us into more frequent upgrades.

Requirements that address upgrade frequency are more technical than requirements should be. But if you want to go further—to take steps to perform upgrades without interrupting user access—you'll have to get more technical still. It is possible to design systems in such a way that you can upgrade software components while the system is running, but it's very hard to do. Don't expect an average development team to be capable of tackling it. And expect it to be expensive, for both development and testing.

Here are a couple of example requirements:

Summary	Definition
Three-monthly software upgrades	An upgraded version of the system's application software shall ordinarily be installed no more frequently than once every three months. (This requirement is present solely to help facilitate calculating the estimated system downtime.)
Machine shutdown without interrupting system	It shall be possible to shut down a machine that runs application software without interrupting user access to the system as a whole.

Attack Direction 4: Duration of Upgrades   A typical system upgrade in many organizations is poorly planned and is of a duration that cannot be predicted in advance. It can drag on to be a thirty-six hour marathon of frequent coffee breaks and late night pizzas. The people involved might be lauded for their stamina and dedication, but their heroics shouldn't be necessary and involve risks.

The duration of an upgrade can be reduced by *preparation*, which costs time and money. The shorter the duration, the more preparation must be done (to cram all the work into the smallest possible window). As you make the window smaller, the preparation effort grows exponentially. Possible steps:

1. **Rehearse what needs to be done.**   This can include trying out the upgrade on a test system (or more than one).
2. **Automate as much as possible.**   Write scripts, or more substantial software. Often these aren't regarded as "real software," but they are, and they should be treated just as seriously as any other software. After all, if they do something wrong, they can do just as much damage.
3. **Prepare instructions for the work that needs to be done.**   Arrange for as many tasks to be performed in parallel as possible.
4. **Do as much as possible beforehand.**   Spend your precious downtime on only those tasks that must be done while the system is down.
5. **Bring in as many people as necessary.**   If minimizing the time it takes is the top priority, bring in as many people as it takes.

Some organizations omit some or even all of these steps—often out of sheer ignorance. While requirements cannot involve themselves in the conduct of a particular upgrade, they can indicate the lengths that should be taken to reduce the duration of each one. They're useful if they merely alert people responsible for upgrades to the fact that it's possible to make preparations.

If you have *multiple instances* of the system to upgrade, preparation becomes more cost-effective because it's shared across all those instances. Software for automating upgrades is particularly important if you're specifying a product. In this case, you definitely need to specify proper requirements for the upgrade software.

Avoid setting a time limit for upgrades unless there is a genuine business reason. Even for one system, upgrade durations will vary. We just want each one to take as little time as possible. If we set a limit of three hours, we'd still want a two-hours-by-hand upgrade to be done more quickly if possible.

Here are a couple of example requirements:

Summary	Definition
Minimize software upgrade duration	All reasonable steps shall be taken to minimize the length of time for which the system must be shut down when upgrading its software. "Reasonable steps" shall be taken to mean up to two person days of effort for each hour of downtime saved.
	It is estimated that this requirement reduces average software upgrade duration by two hours.
Upgrade instructions	Instructions shall be written for each system upgrade, to describe all the steps that must be taken to install it successfully.

Attack Direction 5: Frequency of Failures   What we're talking about here is **reliability**, in the sense of rarely going wrong. There are two types of failures: **accidental** (such as software defects, hardware breakages) and **deliberate** (primarily malicious attacks by someone either outside or inside the organization). We need to take steps to prevent both. Minimizing accidental failures is achieved by **quality**. For hardware and purchased software, this means buying reliable, high-quality products. For our own software, it means building with quality: primarily sound development to keep software defects to a minimum and good testing to find them. Hardware reliability can also be enhanced by replication: having more than one of everything (or some things).

Protecting against deliberate attempts to cause failures is a matter of security. It includes firewalls and antivirus software, as well as access control to prevent valid users doing things they shouldn't.

There's only one requirement here, because we don't have room to cover the other topics that contribute most to stopping failures: good development and testing practices, and security.

Summary	Definition
Replicate hardware	All hardware components of the system shall be replicated, such that failure of any one hardware component shall not render the system unavailable to users.
	It is acceptable for system performance to be poorer than normal after the failure of a piece of hardware.
	It is estimated that this requirement reduces the frequency of failures by two per year.

Attack Direction 6: Duration of Failures   A system that fails only once a year would appear to be of high quality. But that counts for nothing if it takes three weeks to recover from that one failure. Stopping failures from happening in the first place is usually given much higher priority than keeping the duration of each shutdown to a minimum. But according to our Formula 2 for total downtime, reducing their duration is just as important.

When a failure occurs, its duration is determined by the following formula:

Formula 3:   **Outage time = Time to detect + Time to react + Time to fix**

where   **Outage time** is the length of time from the moment the system became unavailable to users until it becomes available again.

Time to detect is the length of time it takes to detect the failure and to raise the alarm. It includes the time it takes to notify people.

Time to react is the length of time between people being notified until the first person can begin to work on the problem.

Time to fix is the length of time it takes to investigate and rectify the problem and make the system available to users.

Imagine your average system crashing at 2 a.m. The *time to detect* is the half-hour it took a dozing operator to spot the usual messages are missing from the screen; the *time to react* is the hour and a half it took to phone, wake, and drag into the office the on-call programmer; the *time to fix* is the three hours the programmer looked for subtle clues among paltry evidence before finding the cause (the thirty seconds spent rectifying the silly fault hardly registers), plus the half hour it took to restart everything. Minimizing outage time involves minimizing all three factors: it's little use having lightning-fast system monitoring detect a problem in a millisecond if it still takes hours to fix. It also means paying for a taxi to get the programmer to the office ten minutes faster is just as valuable as fixing it ten minutes quicker, which is something for expenses-conscious managers to bear in mind.

It's analogous to a house fire. The duration of the fire is how long it burns before someone raises the alarm, the time it takes for the fire brigade to arrive and put out the fire—oh, plus the time before you can repair the damage and move in again. The last point is worth noting: what we're interested in is how long it takes before everything's back to normal.

The preceding formula assumes human intervention is necessary, but it is possible for a system to deal with some types of problems automatically. For example, if a system monitor detects an expected process is not running, it could start it up. In such cases outage time equals time to detect plus time for automated reaction. It must be stressed, however, that it's hard to develop automated responses that properly rectify an identified problem, and such responses are possible for only a few kinds of fault. The system monitor in this example doesn't do that: it doesn't prevent the problem recurring, which it would do repeatedly if an error in the relevant process's software caused it to crash each time it starts up.

The remainder of this section deals with each of the three factors in Formula 3 in turn. It addresses only features that can be built into a system, although operational factors have an equally large (or larger) part to play. Requirements are not the place to deal with the details of operational matters.

Time to detect   Minimizing the time it takes to detect a failure involves spotting any problem as fast as possible and then notifying whoever should be notified, also as rapidly as can be.

In an office full of people, if one person suddenly collapses, others would notice and come to their assistance. In contrast, if one machine in a network (or one process in a machine) collapses, the natural reaction of its colleague machines is to do nothing or at most to complain that it's not doing its job. If we want machines to feign a little concern, we have to tell them how. For this, requirements should be specified, covering three aspects:

1.   Any piece of software that detects a serious error must raise an alarm.

2. Special system monitoring facilities are needed to check that all machines and processes that should be running are running and to raise an alarm if they're not. They need to run on more than one machine, if they are to detect the failure of a machine on which they run.

3. A notification mechanism is needed—something to *raise an alarm* on request—to tell nominated human beings there's a problem that someone needs to fix. This might provide some way for the people to acknowledge being notified. And if no one acknowledges the notification, the mechanism might notify more people.

The first two are types of problem detection, and the third covers what to do when a problem is detected. All involve investigating the specific needs of your system and its environment: one-size-fits-all requirements won't work here. Here are some questions to ask—and when answering them keep in mind that the primary concern is reducing response time:

- What constitutes a *serious error*? Don't attempt to identify them individually, but define criteria by which any type of error can be judged whether it counts as serious.

- Which people need to be notified when a serious error is detected? Does it depend on what kind of error? Does it change according to the time of day (especially outside normal office hours)?

- By what means should we notify people? A message on a screen, email, pager, SMS, instant message, ring a loud bell, tell some other system? Do we need to notify one person by multiple means? Should we use different means for different people or at different times of the day? Should the means to use vary depending on *how serious* the error is?

- Do we need acknowledgment that someone is taking responsibility for the problem? What if no one acknowledges doing so?

It's not necessary to ask what machines and processes need to be monitored, because that's too technical. It's possible to specify a requirement for this in general, technology-independent terms (as the second example requirement that follows does).

The detecting of an error or the raising of an alarm could take other actions too, if we want—say, for exceptionally serious errors. For example, if an attack by hackers was detected, we might want to shut down the system completely. This is within the scope of the subject of availability only insofar as it prevents further damage, but it demonstrates that the features being discussed here can be beneficial in ways beyond just reducing the duration of failures.

Software that checks a system's availability can also be a basis for *statistics* on its availability. Up to a point, that is, because the checker could itself fail and can tell us nothing when it's not running. It also needs to be built to cater for deliberate system downtime and, ideally, to have a way of distinguishing the three types of downtime, which means system shutdown lets the operator express *why* the system is being shut down.

Here are some requirements covering the three aspects listed:

Summary	Definition
Serious software error raises alarm	Any software that detects a serious error shall raise an alarm, by invoking the notification mechanism specified in the next requirement.
	A *serious error* for the purpose of this requirement is one that is deemed to require immediate human intervention.
	It is estimated that this requirement reduces the average duration of a failure detectable within software by 30 minutes.

Summary	Definition
Notification mechanism	There shall be a mechanism to notify designated people using designated means when a message is passed to it. The following means shall be supported: ■ Email ■ SMS ■ Pager *Designated people* means a list of users associated with the category to which the message belongs. Each user who wishes to be notified by pager must have a pager number set for them. *Designated means* are all those means on a list of means associated with an individual user. There shall also be a default list of means to use if a user to be notified has no list of their own.
System monitor	There shall be a system monitor that is able to detect within 30 seconds the perceived failure of any of the machines and processes that are expected to be running at all times. It is estimated that this requirement reduces the duration of each failure of a monitored machine or process by five minutes.

In practice, notification mechanisms deserve to be specified in more detail than in the second requirement here. You could even treat it as an infrastructure in its own right. Examples of various notification-related example requirements are given in the extendability requirement pattern in Chapter 10.

Time to react   Getting investigators working on a failure is largely an operational matter, which doesn't concern the requirements. Steps might include making provision for emergency access to the live system by people (mainly developers) who normally don't have it. It might be, though, that special features can be added to the system to enable quicker access by whoever is to investigate a failure. These could include

1. **Remote access facilities**, if the system doesn't otherwise need them. The intent here is to allow someone to dial in from home, especially after hours, to work on the problem.

2. **Access control extensions**, to allow an investigator to do more in an emergency situation than they would normally be allowed to.

Bear in mind, though, that some types of failures could also affect the working of these features too, if hardware on which they depend has failed. Insisting on replication of components used in combating a failure is worthwhile. Even if rarely needed, it is precisely at times of crisis that they will be called upon.

Observe, too, that these features give an investigator exceptional ability to do deliberate damage and they thereby constitute a risk (however small) of facilitating a worse incident. Lest you consider such a coincidence unlikely, a malicious developer could contrive a failure precisely to provide this opportunity.

Here are a couple of example requirements:

Summary	Definition
Emergency remote access	The system shall provide the ability for a personal computer to dial in and access it remotely. This facility shall ordinarily be disabled and enabled only in the event of a system failure that warrants immediate investigation.
	It is estimated that this requirement reduces the duration of each failure that occurs outside office hours by one hour.
Emergency extended access	It shall be possible to grant extended access to a nominated person, to bypass normal access control restrictions.
	This feature is intended to be used only when the person in question is investigating a system failure; extended access is to be revoked immediately afterwards. (It is recommended that for the duration of the emergency any person granted such access be closely supervised.)
	It is estimated that this requirement reduces the duration of each failure by 15 minutes.

Time to fix   Minimizing the time it takes to fix a failure involves providing investigators with as much information about the problem as possible and giving them the best tools for probing the state of the system. This is a subject that's often completely ignored when specifying and developing systems (beyond chronicling errors), but at the very least you should reflect on whether it deserves serious consideration. Another important way to getting a system up and running quickly is making provision for disaster recovery; this topic is discussed at the end of this section.

The information to help diagnose a failure needs to be gathered as a matter of course while the system is running normally—like an aircraft's black box flight recorder. Steps that can be taken to gather this information include:

1. Record everything that happens in the system that might be of interest, especially errors (even those not serious enough to constitute a system failure).

2. Insist that all error messages be clear, correct, and detailed. Considerable time can be wasted if a problem produced an error message that was uninformative or, worse, misleading. An investigator could be sent off on a wild goose chase.

Here's an example requirement for each of these two steps:

Summary	Definition
Record all errors	Every error detected by the system shall be recorded. At least the following shall be recorded: ■ Error ID ■ Message text ■ Date and time at which the error occurred ■ Machine name of the machine on which the error occurred For the purpose of this requirement, a minor exception condition that the software is designed to handle completely itself (such as invalid data entered by a user) does not constitute an error. It is estimated that this requirement reduces the average duration of each failure by two minutes.
Clear, detailed error message	Each error message shall be clear and self-explanatory and contain items of variable information as appropriate to isolate the cause. The variable information might be the name of a machine, the amount of free space on a disk, a customer ID. It is estimated that this requirement reduces the average duration of each failure by two minutes.

As for **diagnostic tools** to investigate a problem, steps to consider include:

1. **Identify a range of tools** likely to be useful for investigation, and install them on the system.

   If it is unacceptable to have the investigative tools permanently installed (for valid security reasons because they do constitute a security risk), have them readily at hand. There might be several ways to do this: having software ready to install, or having a separate machine containing the tools ready to connect to the live network.

2. **Document error messages**—not necessarily all, but those about which something extra can usefully be said. These explanations can tell an investigator what an error really means, what causes it, and how to respond to it. The set of error message explanations must be made available to investigators. While this step might appear to relate to the gathering of information, the set of error messages actually constitutes a diagnostic tool.

3. **Develop special software to examine the integrity of the system**, especially its data. Programmers sometimes create such software for their own use in testing, which then usually languishes unknown and unappreciated, which is a waste. Regarding such utilities as part of the mainstream system can make it available to help when a problem occurs.

Here's an example requirement for the second step:

Summary	Definition
Error message explanations	Each error message for which explanatory information is available (over and above its message text) shall be documented. The following information shall be provided for each such message: ■ Error ID ■ Message text ■ Explanation of each item of variable information: its origin and meaning ■ Extended explanation of error's meaning ■ Description of likely cause(s) ■ Description of suggested response(s) It is estimated that this requirement reduces the average duration of each failure by one minute.

Another way to get a system up and running again quickly is to invest in a **disaster recovery** system: a duplicate hardware and software environment, preferably in a different physical location. As its name suggests, such a set-up lets you get up and running again when anything up to and including a disaster befalls the main site. But it doesn't help if the reason for the failure was a major software fault that affects the second system, too. Disaster recovery involves a lot more than setting up a second environment, and it must be investigated—and later tested—thoroughly. Bear in mind that any upgrades performed on the production system must also be performed on the disaster recovery system. Here are some simple example requirements that suggest a few aspects to worry about but that in practice deserve to be specified in much more detail:

Summary	Definition
Disaster recovery site	There shall be a disaster recovery site at a physically separate location from that of the main production system. It shall duplicate all the features of the main site. It is acceptable for the disaster recovery system to have lower performance than the main system.
Disaster recovery data	There shall be a means of supplying the disaster recovery site with an up-to-date copy of all production data. There shall be a similar means to supply data to the production system, to allow it to start running again when the fault has been fixed.
Disaster recovery communications	There shall be a means of directing **all** communications intended for the production site to the disaster recovery site instead, in the event of a disaster. It shall also be possible to switch communications back to the production system when the fault has been fixed.
Disaster recovery procedures	There shall be written procedures to explain how to get the business operating from the disaster recovery site.

Considerations for Development

If you're faced with an unfriendly availability requirement, question it: "What am I supposed to do with that?" Should that get you nowhere, work your way through the suggestions in the "Extra Requirements" subsection in this pattern to come up with a swag of concrete steps to take. You can even formulate them as requirements if you like. Then implement them.

Too many kinds of extra requirements related to availability exist to discuss them here. But pay particular attention to the *availability window* specified for the system, because this affects whether housekeeping tasks must be performed while users are accessing the system.

Throughout the development process, document any problem you detect that could affect system availability and explain how to deal with it and recover when it occurs. Check with the testing team to see if they have discovered this problem already, as they might have valuable additional information and insights.

Considerations for Testing

A classic availability requirement (of the "24x7 availability 99.9 percent of the time" kind) is so hard to test that it's not even worth trying for a normal commercial system, which is the root of the argument against such requirements in the first place. The kind of starting-point availability requirement advocated by this pattern (that defines the availability window) is more practical to test: you need to simulate a small number of days' running (you might even consider that one day suffices) and check that there's nothing that prevents you running the system constantly during the specified hours. Whenever you encounter a primary availability requirement, first ask yourself how easy it is to test. Also be alert for the two nastiest kinds: those that are *impossible* to test, and those that are *feasible but impractical* to test.

No matter what form availability requirements take, testing should include running the system continuously for an extended period, which means for as long as you can but certainly for several days. Running for a month or more continuously is excellent. Keep a wary eye open for memory leaks: observe how much memory each process takes up, and check that it doesn't grow steadily the longer the process has been running. Any software that's expected to run for an extended period will surely lead to unhappiness if it has a memory leak. Pass it back to the development team smartly, but also let it keep on running to see what happens.

Requirements whose aim is to deliver availability (those covered in the "Extra Requirements" section earlier in this pattern) are too diverse to enumerate here. Treat each one individually on its own merits. If extra requirements of these kinds have not been formally specified, but developers have devised their own steps to achieve availability goals, you could find out what those steps are and test them as if they were requirements. It's impractical to *prove* that all the steps demanded to increase availability actually deliver a stated availability level. The best you can do is review any reasoning or calculations performed by the analyst or developers and ask yourself if their assumptions look reasonable.

Test for surreptitious unavailability. Find out if any housekeeping-type tasks are performed while users are active. If so, perform a range of user functions while this housekeeping is underway, and test its effect on response time.

Nearly all systems are installed containing known defects. Document well each known defect that has the potential to affect the availability of the system. Explain what causes it, how to diagnose whether it was the cause of a system failure, and how to respond when it happens. Make these explanations as easy to find as possible in the event of a failure. These steps can reduce the length of a system outage significantly.

Chapter 10
Flexibility Requirement Patterns

In this chapter:

10.1 Scalability Requirement Pattern.. 241

10.2 Extendability Requirement Pattern... 246

10.3 Unparochialness Requirement Pattern................................... 254

10.4 Multiness Requirement Pattern... 261

10.5 Multi-Lingual Requirement Pattern....................................... 272

10.6 Installability Requirement Pattern... 274

A flexible system is one that can adapt to suit changing circumstances. What sort of circumstances might they be? That's for you to decide: you need to write a specific requirement for each kind of flexibility you want. It's meaningless to try saying, "The system shall be flexible." Building flexibility into a system is done for longer term benefits; it usually doesn't make much (if any) difference to the system when it's first delivered, though it makes it easy to react to changes in requirements in the areas that are built flexibly. Flexibility requirements generally contribute to a "good," robust system, in addition to satisfying specific goals. But some kinds of flexibility are expensive to implement, so ask for them only if they're necessary.

The requirement patterns in this chapter cover those types of flexibility most commonly needed in commercial systems, as shown in Figure 10-1. Observe that *multi-lingual* is a specific kind of multiness, and so is *multi-organization unit* in the commercial domain. Also, *installability* isn't exactly flexibility in the same sense, but this is the most convenient place for it.

Software grows old. A new system is as pure as a newborn baby, but alterations accumulated during its life leave scars and cause its joints to creak. Each modification places a little extra stress on the system's architecture. Steadily they become harder to make, until eventually every tweak risks nasty side effects. Building flexibility into a system from the outset means it takes many kinds of changes in its stride, leaving less cause to interfere with its vital workings—so it grows older more slowly. **Refactoring**, a conscious effort to tidy up software, can be viewed as an attempt to remove symptoms of the aging process. It's more effective and less effort to lessen the deterioration in the first place. Flexible means *agile* in the dictionary sense of the word: supple and healthy. *Extendability* is perhaps the type of flexibility that contributes most to software longevity.

Always give flexibility requirements a high priority, because flexibility is not something that can just be bolted on afterwards: it's fundamental to the system design. Adding it later could involve so much effort you might as well not bother trying.

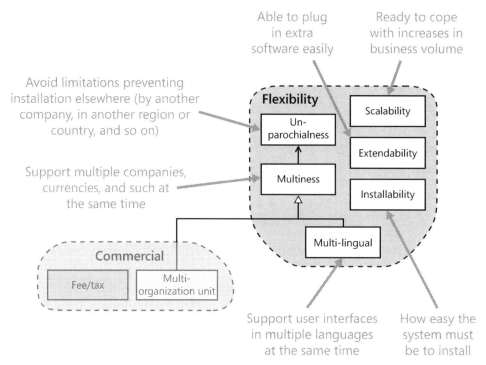

Figure 10-1 Requirement patterns in the flexibility domain

There's a complex relationship between flexibility requirements and performance requirements. Flexibility requirements primarily influence the nature of the software; performance requirements primarily affect the hardware needed. Used together, performance requirements can tell us just what sort of numbers we're talking about when contemplating scalability. Recognize that there's often a trade-off between flexibility and software efficiency (which translates into lower performance, assuming the same hardware), because flexibility prevents streamlining and tuning the software for just one thing. Pay serious attention to the short-term and long-term trade-offs between flexibility and performance. Unless squeezing the last smidgen of speed from the software is critical, opt for flexibility.

Flexibility is often difficult to test. One option is to talk to the development team: ask them what one would do to modify the system in a way specified in a flexibility requirement. Use their response to get a feel for whether they've actually thought about it properly and are ready for it. This theme is revisited in several of the flexibility requirement patterns in this chapter.

Regardless of whether you choose to use any of these flexibility requirement patterns, you can include the following requirement (or one like it) to spur developers to avoid one type of limitation that could lead to trouble in later life:

Summary	Definition
No artificial quantity limitations	The system shall impose no artificial limitations on how many entities of any particular type can exist (regardless of the quantity and power of the hardware). For example, it would be unacceptable if a maximum of 20 suppliers were allowed, or 100 types of product.
	This requirement does not apply to genuine limitations imposed for sound reasons (such as the biggest integer allowed by a programming language or the database, or the number of countries a 3-character code permits)—which are usually much larger than are ever likely to be needed in practice.
	This requirement also does not apply to external systems that are outside the company's control. (But encourage external suppliers to avoid or remove such limitations where possible.)

10.1 Scalability Requirement Pattern

Basic Details

Related patterns:	None
Anticipated frequency:	Zero or one requirement; rarely more
Pattern classifications:	Affects database: Yes

Applicability

Use the scalability requirement pattern to specify a way in which a system must be able to expand without undue pain, typically to accommodate growth in business volume.

Do not use the scalability requirement pattern to demand a particular level of performance; use one of the performance requirement patterns for that.

Discussion

Scalability means never having to say you're sorry that the system can't cope with more. Scalability means being prepared when the load on the system increases, having ways to react without resorting to drastic changes or redevelopment. Scalability doesn't happen by accident, and if you don't ask for this ability, don't be surprised if you don't get it. Scalability can be expensive, so if you want it, you'd better be prepared to pay for it. And if don't need it, don't ask for it; when you're building a system for a small environment and the chances of using it elsewhere are low, think twice about whether it's worth it.

A scalability requirement is an instruction to developers to design the system such that it can grow in a particular direction, with no obstacles in its way. It is a signal that the system must not be restricted to any stated business volume.

Scaling is often driven by an increase in a single factor only. In a commercial system, it's usually the number of customers (or, more generally, the number of users). Rarely are there are more factors whose growth independently causes a proportionate increase in load on the system (and, consequently, a need for a separate scalability requirement). For example, doubling the number of products a retail business offers for sale is unlikely to double the load directly. A single scalability requirement usually suffices.

Scaling a system's overall performance is of two main types. First is **scaling out**, the ability to spread the processing load across as more machines. Second is **scaling up**, by increasing the power of individual machines. Generally, requirements should be concerned only that the system can scale, without caring how. But an ability to scale out is sometimes worth demanding in requirements because it influences a system's basic software architecture and cannot be retrofitted, whereas scaling up typically doesn't affect the software at all. A system can accommodate a growing load only if the quantity and/or power of its hardware are increased accordingly, in proportion. A system isn't scalable if the hardware needed grows at a faster rate than the load; for instance, if doubling the load demands four times the hardware, we'd soon be unable to keep up with increasing load.

Performance requirements implicitly apply regardless of the extent to which the system has been scaled, unless otherwise stated in either the scalability or performance requirements. This is especially relevant to *response time* and *availability* requirements (because we can expect overall *throughput* and *capacity* to grow as the system grows): they must not become progressively worse as the system scales. In practice, performance measures are likely to change marginally with the system's load. This is acceptable if it's barely perceptible to users. Nevertheless, if you sense there's a risk that the importance of maintaining performance levels could be forgotten as the system grows, you could strengthen the relevant requirements to make it clear.

Consider flow-on scalability demands upon third parties—that is, all systems you interface to and all third-party products you use. Investigate whether they are all suitably scalable; if they're not, you're in trouble. This applies to products you are forced to use and any the project is at liberty to choose for itself. For the latter, impose our scalability requirements on them too, when evaluating their suitability.

Content

A scalability requirement should contain the following:

1. **Type of item to be scalable**   What aspect of the system needs to be scalable? For example, it could be the number of customers.

2. **Indicative high business volume**   Just how far might the system need to scale? Indicate only a rough order of magnitude: tens, hundreds, thousands, millions, or whatever it might be. Expressing it in vague terms is a positive advantage, because it prevents the development team building to accommodate a specific number (as if it were a performance requirement)— with the risk of that number representing an absolute limit.

    No system can be scaled without limit, so don't use words like "infinite" or "unlimited" to describe the extent of scalability. What we're saying is that we want the system to be capable of scaling as big as we're ever likely to need. I like the word "unrestricted," because it conveys that we want nothing in the way of expansion, without implying expanding for ever. At least, that's what it conveys to me; admittedly it's a fine distinction. Pick a different word if you wish.

3. **Ease of expansion**   How easy must it be to expand the system? How dynamically? In ideal circumstances, an extra machine could be added while the system's running. Is it worth it? If omitted, it is reasonable to assume that scalability can be achieved by shutting down the system, adding extra hardware, doing a bit of reconfiguration, and starting it up again. If you want more than this—or if less will suffice—then say so. (The upgradability aspects of the installability requirement pattern, which appears later in this chapter, cover these issues, too.)

4. **Motivation**   Why do we need this kind of scalability? The commonest motivation is to cater for growth in business.

Template(s)

Summary	Definition
«Scalability aspect» scalability	The system shall be scalable to accommodate an unrestricted number of *«Type of item to be scalable»*s. *«Indicative high business volume»*.
	[*«Ease of expansion statement»*.]
	[*«Motivation statement»*.]

Example(s)

Summary	Definition
Customer scalability	The system shall be scalable to accommodate unrestricted growth in the number of customers (prospectively to several hundred thousands).
	The motivation for this requirement is to cater for future growth in the business.
Distributed office scalability	The system shall be scalable to allow its use by an unrestricted number of distributed offices of the company. (Eventually there could be over one hundred offices.)
	The motivation for this requirement is to allow the system to be used across the whole company and all its subsidiaries (including future acquisitions).
Document library scalability	The document management system shall be scalable to manage an unrestricted number of electronic documents. (There could be millions of such documents, with a total size of several terabytes.)

Extra Requirements

Making a system scalable can (and usually does) have significant implications that go beyond simply being able to handle a bigger load. Consider the following topics, and write extra requirements as necessary:

1. **Characteristics that must not degrade as the system grows**   In what ways must the system keep performing just as well as it grows? This is covered in the "Characteristics That Must Not Degrade with Growth" subsection coming up.

2. **Steps to take to contribute to scalability**   Are there any specific features we want our system to have to help it be scalable? Or so it'll continue to be as easy to use as volumes grow? This topic is discussed in the "Steps That Contribute to Scalability" subsection.

3. **Scaling the number of sites**   If we achieve scalability by running the system in more and more sites, we need to consider how to co-ordinate them. See the "Scaling the Number of Sites" subsection.

4. **Monitoring functions**   We need functions to tell us how close to maximum load the system is, which will help us plan expansion. See the information about measuring and monitoring in the performance requirement patterns and in the introduction to the performance domain.

5. **Not wasting hardware**   If you're especially concerned to make the most of precious money spent on hardware, insist on being able to keep old hardware in service whenever new hardware is purchased. That is, you can write a requirement that it shall be possible to add hardware in order to expand the system.

Characteristics That Must Not Degrade with Growth   It's sometimes useful to specify that a particular characteristic of how the system behaves must not noticeably degrade as the system scales—that is, as the factor identified in the main scalability requirement increases. For example, regular downtime for housekeeping must not increase in proportion to volume. Do this if you're worried that this area is at risk of being left behind—of performing badly as business volume grows. Explicitly identifying things that shouldn't degrade as the system scales spells out the implications of a scalability requirement. These things can themselves then be examined to see if there are specific steps we can take to help achieve them, as described in the "Steps That Contribute to Scalability" subsection that follows.

Here are a few examples of requirements for this purpose:

Summary	Definition
Transaction data scalability	The time taken to produce any report or inquiry showing information about transactions shall depend predominantly upon the quantity of data to *show* (and not the total quantity of data *stored*).
	This requirement does not apply to any report or inquiry that allows the user to enter arbitrary selection criteria.
Non-growth in system operation effort	The effort needed to administer the system (as measured in hours per week of system administrators' time) shall not grow as the number of customers grows. That is, if there is any increase in system operation work, it shall be proportionately less than the increase in customers.
Availability unaffected by growth	Any increase in the number of customers shall not degrade system availability to an extent noticeable by any users.
No report size limits	There shall be no limit upon the size of a report. A report can be as large as necessary to show all the data it is asked to show. It shall be practical to manipulate very large reports.
	This requirement has significant implications for the reporting infrastructure. For a start, it implies that a large report should not be stored as a monolithic blob.

Observe that the first three are hard to test. They're intended mainly factors for developers to take into account.

Steps That Contribute to Scalability   When thinking about scalability, the emphasis is on performance factors: having enough sheer horsepower to cope with an increasing load, being able to process more transactions, being able to store more data, and so on. But that's not the whole story. All the system's functions must continue to be practical to use as the system scales. Scan all the specified functions to see which ones might involve more work for users as the system grows. Pay special attention to the following areas:

1. **Inquiries and reports**   Specify functions such that an increase in the quantity of data in the system is *not* accompanied by a similar increase in the amount a user must plough through. One way to do this is to allow the work to be shared among several users, perhaps by segregating the data so that each user is responsible for only part of the data.

2. **Maintaining and administering**   Tasks that are straightforward at low volumes can become time-consuming, tedious, increasingly liable to human error, and finally impractical as volumes grow. Making such functions just as easy to use as the system scales up means they must be more sophisticated and consequently more expensive to develop (though that might be justified by reduced operational costs).

   Consider the impact of a large number of configuration entities and of a large number of server machines. One way to reduce the problem is to arrange for some information to be shared by multiple configuration entities (so that one change affects them all)–that is, structuring data with the maintenance implications of scalability in mind. A more sophisticated approach is for maintenance functions to be able to apply a change to multiple entities at once.

3. **Installing and upgrading**   How frequently is extra hardware likely to be added? How much advance warning are we likely to get? Just how many machines might be end up with? The answers to these questions might justify special steps to make it as easy as possible to install the system on a machine, to upgrade the software on a machine, and to slot a new machine into the live environment. This topic builds on what a scalability requirement says about "ease of expansion." (See the installability requirement pattern for more.)

Scaling the Number of Sites   A system that scales by being installed in more sites has an extra kind of complexity: how to co-ordinate those sites, both technically and businesswise. A head office and a number of satellites is the most common situation (and the simplest, except for the case of no co-ordination at all). Investigate the relationships between sites and the extra functionality needed: functions used by head office only, data to be sent to head office, dissemination of data to satellites (for example, configuration information that embodies aspects of business rules or corporate policy), and possibly numerous other things.

Then, what kinds of corporate **restructuring** might happen (such as merging two satellites)? Does the system need to be ready for such eventualities? If no provision at all is made, achieving them later might be very difficult indeed–if, for example, different sites allocate the same customer number to different customers.

Complexity of this kind could go unnoticed if you concentrate on an initial implementation in a single site, so ask yourself whether you need to worry about it. It is important, is bound to have a major impact on how the system is implemented, and must be properly specified.

Considerations for Development

Scalability can be achieved by choosing underlying technology built to help spread processing load across multiple machines, or it can be achieved by our own software, or by a mixture of both. Distributing loads across machines is a lot more complicated to implement than it at first appears, so use a third-party product to do the hard work for you whenever possible.

Consider whether the scalability being asked for can be achieved by a single database. If not, work through the implications of having multiple databases. How closely do they need to work together?

What would need to be done to co-ordinate them? Can the overall system be divided into a number of islands that work largely independently of one another?

Take special care with the design of database tables that are directly or indirectly affected by the kind of scalability being demanded and with the design of functions that maintain this data. Avoid duplicating data for which many entities could share the same values, to save having to modify a value many times (a number of times that increases as the system scales up).

Considerations for Testing

Scalability is difficult to test at all. One exercise is to get the system running and verify that adding extra resources is as easy as it should be. Then test that the new configuration can cope with a proportionately increased load. Measure the actual performance gain as the resources scale. If you get that far, you've done well. But it doesn't prove that you can keep on adding hardware with the same effect. It's unrealistic to test that the system possesses "unrestricted" scalability.

You can probably get a subjective feel for how scalable the system is by talking to the developers about it. What steps have they taken? How did they approach the subject? Are there any design documents that deal with scalability? Have they discovered any potential problems? The depth to which they can answer these questions should give you an insight into how much faith you can place in the scalability of their work.

Scalability is an infinite area. You must determine when you have done enough and are satisfied with the results. Performance requirements can give you a feel for what is a reasonable point at which to stop.

10.2 Extendability Requirement Pattern

Basic Details

Related patterns:	Inter-system interface, documentation
Anticipated frequency:	For most systems no more than two requirements; for complex systems fewer than 10 requirements
Pattern classifications:	None

Applicability

Use the extendability requirement pattern to mandate that a specific aspect of the system be built to make it easy to extend by "plugging in" extra software. In particular, use it in situations where there are (or might be in the future) several different ways of doing things and we want to be able to add more without major disruption.

Do not use the extendability requirement pattern for alternatives that *cannot* be achieved by slotting in extra software. Common examples are differences achievable solely by configuration, including some multinesses (such as multi-lingual and multi-currency), and variations that affect the system as a whole, such as being able to run on multiple named operating systems (you can't just "plug in" the ability to run on Unix).

Discussion

An extendability requirement acts as a way to tell developers to build a particular part of the system in a flexible manner so that we can extend it by simply slotting in new software without revamping the underlying architecture each time. Some kinds of flexibility aren't amenable to being treated in this way—including anything that can be regarded as a multiness (according the multiness requirement pattern) and anything that can't be achieved simply by adding software to support it. If you have a fixed list of alternatives that *cannot* grow, you don't need extendability but it can still be good practice to apply it, because extendability promotes modularity: it's a subtle way of encouraging good design in one area. In any case, it's rash to assume something will *never, ever* change.

This requirement pattern calls a piece of software that is plugged in a **driver,** as in a *device driver* or a *printer driver*. This term is used only to make this discussion easier to read; requirements themselves don't need to use it. An extendability requirement is invariably followed by at least one requirement for a driver, because without it the ability to extend serves no immediate purpose.

An extendability requirement usually sits amid a sequence of requirements: first a requirement that defines an aspect of the system; second the requirement that this aspect be extendable; and finally one or more requirements for drivers and possibly other requirements (all of which are covered in the "Extra Requirements" section later in this pattern). The extendability of an aspect of the system can be combined with its definition, but separating them gives the need for extendability added weight and allows it to be given a different priority. This sequence is shown in Figure 10-2.

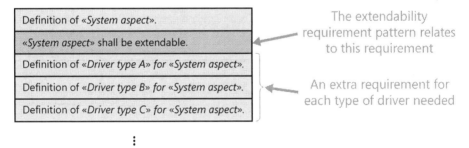

Figure 10-2   The sequence of extendability-related requirements

Here are a few typical examples of extendability:

- **Available payment methods**. (See the example requirement later in this pattern.)
- **Supported file formats**. Regard each circumstance in which files are accessed as a separate kind of extendability. For example, if one part of a system reads graphics files and another part reads text files, treat them separately. Also treat *input* and *output* as distinct.
- **External systems to interface to**—provided they all play the same role.
- **Types of notification methods**. (See the example requirement in this pattern and the driver requirements in the "Extra Requirements" section.)
- **Types of devices to control**—for example, printers or EFTPOS terminals.
- **Supported communication protocols**.
- **Allowed encryption algorithms**. Don't mix fundamentally different types of encryption though: a *public key* algorithm and a *symmetric* algorithm aren't interchangeable.

Extendability is much more important and valuable when building a software product to be sold to multiple organizations than when building for one organization only. It makes it easier to tailor each installation, without affecting the core product.

Sometimes building in the ability to easily extend in a certain way turns out to be harder than it appeared at requirements time. For example, the things on your list of alternatives might have less in common than they appear; they might vary a lot more. This might not become clear until design time. So there are limits to how much we can expect from extendability.

Content

An extendability requirement needs to cover:

1. **The aspect of the system that is to be extendable**   Which can be expressed in terms of the type of *driver* to slot in.

2. **Ease of extendability**   How easy should it be to slot in a new driver? Usually it's best to simply insist that a new driver be added without software changes to the core system. This is equivalent to being able to plug a new electrical device into the main grid's power without having to modifying the socket you plug it in. Occasionally you might need to demand more—some kind of plug-and-play capability, perhaps—so that a new driver can be added without shutting down the system.

3. **Configuration details**   In addition to its software, **configuration information** is needed for each driver so that the system knows it's there and how to call it. This too is largely a matter for the developers to sort out. The requirements need to worry only about anything that's visible to users, such as the name by which it's presented to them. If you want anything else to be visible—such as a help page—then say so.

Perhaps surprisingly, extendability requirements tend to be remarkably straightforward, simple even. The main reason is that they should ignore technical details. They merely need to state what we want; how it's achieved is the developers' responsibility.

Template(s)

Summary	Definition
«System aspect» extendable	It shall be possible to extend the *«System aspect»* by developing and "plugging in" an extra software module. The introduction of any such module shall not require fundamental changes to the core software of the system to allow its introduction. *«Ease of extendability»*. [*«Configuration details»*.]
«Subcomponent type» pluggable	It shall be possible to add a new *«Subcomponent type»* by developing and "plugging in" the software necessary to support it. A new *«Subcomponent type»* shall not require fundamental changes to the core software of the system to allow its introduction. *«Ease of extendability»*. [*«Configuration details»*.]

Example(s)

Summary	Definition
Notification methods pluggable	It shall be possible to add a new method for notifying users by developing and "plugging in" the software necessary to support that method. A new notification method shall not require changes to the core software of the system to allow its introduction.
Payment methods pluggable	It shall be possible to add a new method by which customers can pay by developing and "plugging in" the software necessary to support that method. A new payment method shall not require changes to the core software of the system to allow its introduction.

Extra Requirements

An extendability requirement can be followed by several extra requirements. There is usually at least one of first type from the list that follows; the others are topics you should give at least cursory thought to, although they're not often relevant:

1. **A type of driver**, one requirement for each.

2. **Installation**, to specify how easy it must be to install and configure a driver.

3. **Third-party driver development**, if people outside your development team will need to develop and test drivers.

Each of these is discussed in its own subsection that follows.

You might encounter extra dilemmas when specifying some types of drivers, but most turn out to be due to the nature of the driver rather than making this area extendable. Be alert to the distinction. Here are a few such situations:

4. **Driver security**   Convenient extendability can open security holes: making it easy to slot in new software makes it easy to slot in *malicious* software. If this is a concern, take steps to guard against it. Give driver security particular thought if third parties will develop drivers. (See the "Third-Party Driver Development Requirements" subsection later in this pattern).

5. **Switching from using one driver to another**   For example, if we can plug in encryption algorithms, we could decide to stop using one and start using another. This might be a hard thing to do (if we have to re-encrypt anything encrypted using the old algorithm), but any difficulty has nothing to do with extendability.

6. **Catering for multiple different versions of a driver**   Treat each version as a separate driver, but define the configuration information such that it recognizes the relationship between the two and perhaps their order (that is, which comes first). How to decide which version to use is nothing to do with extendability; neither are the complications you might face in gradually moving from an old version to a new version or in dropping an old version as soon as it's no longer needed. But these issues must be confronted.

7. **Distinguishing between multiple different drivers and multiple instances of the same driver**   Some drivers need *instances* to be created, and some drivers don't. For example, for printers you need a driver for each type, and then each physical printer is an instance (and you can have two printers that use the same driver). For output file formats you don't need to worry about this: once you have a driver for a particular format, you simply use it whenever you like.

Driver Type Requirements   Having a separate requirement for each type of unit to plug in lets us prioritize them individually and gives us space to say whatever's useful about each one. It also reduces the temptation to gloss over each one, which a simple list within another requirement encourages—and it denies us the opportunity to end such a list with an insidiously nasty and unacceptable "etc."

A requirement for a type of driver needs to contain these items:

1. **Driver description**, of what is to be slotted in, to whatever level of detail is needed—although a brief summary often suffices. Mention any special characteristics you think are relevant, especially things that might affect its complexity (and, consequently, any estimate of how much it will cost to implement). Say enough to make clear what needs to be done. For example, for a file format, state which version and give the location of the standard that defines it. For a payment method, don't just say "credit card"; consider the types you need to support and the financial institution(s) you need to clear transactions with.

2. **The system aspect** to which the driver relates—or the *type of driver* being plugged in—as per the parent extendability requirement. You can often express this in passing. You might think this is obvious from the context of the requirement (that is, because it follows its parent requirement), but it needs to be clear when read in isolation.

3. **Special information** (if any) needed by the driver each time it is invoked. For example, pager notification needs a pager number, email notification needs an email address, and credit card payment needs credit card details. Say where this information comes from.

   You might also need to specify special configuration details for a specific driver.

4. **Responsibility for underlying infrastructure**—a description of who is responsible for specifying and implementing it. If a driver is neatly self-contained (such as one for a file format), no more needs to be said. But a driver often involves considerable behind-the-scenes infrastructure functionality—for example, a credit card payment mechanism or pager notification service—functionality that must be properly specified and implemented. Who's responsible? Is it within the scope of this system? Is the necessary infrastructure already in place? You must answer these questions. If you're going to leave this until later, you must make that clear: **make it obvious that specification work is incomplete**. The easiest answer is to say it's outside the scope and that the necessary infrastructure must be properly specified before this requirement can be satisfied.

These requirements tend to be as straightforward as extendability requirements (although the *responsibility* part can be awkward to express and can end up looking like picky legalese). It's easy to see why: we're interested in only the extendability aspect here; everything needed to deliver it is omitted. That's why further requirements must be written—somewhere—if some kind of supporting infrastructure is needed. Implementing each infrastructure deserves to be a project (or subproject) in its own right, or it might not receive the attention it deserves. In any situation where a large amount of work hides behind one innocuous requirement, it's likely to be given an inadequate budget and to be rushed. Developers are apt to dash out and find the first open source product they lay their eyes on. An infrastructure could be used for other purposes, too.

Any driver whose real work is done by a separate component (such as a third-party product or an external system) acts as an **adapter**. See the inter-system interface requirement pattern's "Interface Adapters" sidebar (in Chapter 5, "Fundamental Requirement Patterns") for a description of what adapters are all about.

Here are a few example follow-on requirements that specify drivers for notification methods (and notice the stressing of the infrastructures that are needed):

Summary	Definition
Notify via system message inquiry	It shall be possible to notify users of relevant events via the system message inquiry (as specified in requirement XR8.2), if they have it running.
Notify via email	It shall be possible to notify users of relevant events via email.
	To notify a user, an email address must have been entered for them.
	This requirement assumes the presence of an infrastructure for sending emails. Specifying and implementing such an infrastructure is outside the scope of this system, but must be done in order to satisfy this requirement.
Notify via mobile phone instant message	It shall be possible to notify users of relevant events via instant messages to a mobile phone.
	To notify a user, a mobile phone number must have been set for them.
	This requirement assumes the presence of an instant messaging infrastructure. Specifying and implementing such an infrastructure is outside the scope of this system, but must be done in order to satisfy this requirement.
Notify via pager	It shall be possible to notify users of relevant events via pager.
	To notify a user, a pager number must have been set for them.
	This requirement assumes the presence of an infrastructure for sending messages to a pager service. Specifying and implementing such an infrastructure is outside the scope of this system but must be done in order to satisfy this requirement.

Driver Installation Requirements   Installing a driver takes two steps, both of which can be influenced by requirements if you want to:

1. **Install its software**   If nothing is said about this, it's reasonable for everyone to assume that driver software will be installed in exactly the same way as any other software. If it needs to be easier (and, technology permitting, it can be made easier), add requirements to say so. The technology might let you install driver software while the system is running—but press for that only if there's a sound business need behind it.

2. **Configure it**   Each type of driver needs a function for configuring it. The presence of such a function is often left unstated, but it's a good idea to specify it explicitly.

    A driver's configuration can also control its *availability*—that is, whether it's "switched on" or not. You could write a requirement asking for the ability to install a driver but not make it available immediately.

Here are a couple of example requirements related to the installation and control of drivers:

Summary	Definition
Notification method maintenance	There shall be a maintenance function to allow the entry of details about a new notification method and the editing of existing methods.
Notification method availability	It shall be possible to specify for each notification method whether it is available for use or not. When a new notification method is added, it shall by default be unavailable. It shall be possible to change this value by using the notification method maintenance function.

Third-Party Driver Development Requirements   Is anyone outside your development team likely to be developing software to slot in? If so, they'll need to know how to do it. At the very least we have to publish a definition of the interface they must build to, but it's better to insist that a "Driver Developer's Guide" be written for this type of driver. Here's an example of such a requirement:

Summary	Definition
Notification method development guide	A development guide shall be written containing sufficient information to allow a competent software engineer with suitable skills to develop a notification method driver.

Requirements very similar to this are also used to allow third-party development of inter-system interfaces, as described in the inter-system interface requirement pattern in Chapter 5. See also the documentation requirement pattern, also in Chapter 5, for more about what to say.

You also need to be alert to the **security implications** of adding software written by a third party into your system. How much do you trust them? What steps can you take to protect your system? Here are a few suggestions [which indicate, within square brackets, who the work is to be done by]:

1. Insist that the source code be supplied for all driver software written by third parties. Also insist on adequate documentation, including commenting of the source code. [To be done by the third party]

2. Examine the source code for suspicious activities. [To be done by a suitable member of the development team or the testing team]

3. Compile the source code, and install that object code (rather than object code supplied by the third party). If you've checked the source code, that'd be a waste of time if the supplied compiled code is different. [To be done by a member of the development team or a system administrator]

4. Test the driver thoroughly. [To be done by the development team and/or the testing team]

Requirements aren't necessarily the best place to state these things, but you could write a requirement saying that precautions along these lines be taken.

Considerations for Development

An extendability requirement is in effect an instruction to the development team saying, "Build this part in a flexible way; don't hard-code it." Development depends on the type of extendability and the technology being used, so little more can be said here. A few things to bear in mind are as follows:

1. **Configuration for drivers**   Every type of driver needs its own configuration. What does it need to contain? Possibilities include:

   - ❑ **Driver ID**, for internal use.
   - ❑ **Driver name**, for display to users.
   - ❑ **Driver software location**. This might be its main class name. (You will, of course, have to figure out how to invoke this software.)
   - ❑ **State**: is it available (switched on)?
   - ❑ **Version number**.
   - ❑ **Developed by**, especially if by a third party.
   - ❑ **Help page file name** and location.

   Also consider what effect changing any of this information would have. If it could cause damage, think of ways to prevent it.

2. **Switching from one driver to another**   For some types of driver, it is necessary to impose restrictions or to define guidelines for use. For example, you might be building a product that allows your customer to choose which encryption algorithm to use—but if letting them change their mind after going live is too hard, prevent them doing so.

3. **Upgrading a driver**   See the inter-system interface requirement pattern in Chapter 5, because similar issues apply in both situations.

Considerations for Testing

Treat the testing of a driver the same as the testing of any other software. Much depends on the nature of the driver: testing the saving of data in a pluggable file format is a different matter from testing credit card payments.

If there are multiple drivers, test that the results obtained from each one is compatible with the others. For example, if all drivers are expected to deliver identical results, do they? This doesn't apply to all types of driver. For instance, drivers for saving data in different formats will be expected to produce difference results.

Test adding a new driver. Is it as easy as it should be? When testing the initial system, begin with at least one driver of each type missing and then watch closely as they are installed. Because an extendability requirement is basically a message to developers, talk to the developers about what they've done about it; ask them what they'd have to do to add a new driver.

Test different versions of the same driver. Test upgrading from one version of a driver to the next version. These kinds of tests might not be possible if only one version of each driver exists, which is often true for a new system. If not, quiz the development team about the provisions they have made for upgrading drivers.

10.3 Unparochialness Requirement Pattern

Basic Details

Related patterns:	Multiness, data type, extendability
Anticipated frequency:	One requirement per aspect, with extra requirements for the implications
Pattern classifications:	None

Applicability

Use the unparochialness requirement pattern to specify a particular way in which the system must not be limited to one business environment. The unparochialness requirement pattern says how *a single installation* of the system needs to be able to adapt to the organization and the place where it is installed.

Do not use the unparochialness requirement pattern to specify that the system must support multiple instances of anything simultaneously (such as multiple currencies); use the multiness requirement pattern, the next pattern in this chapter, for that.

Discussion

Parochial: narrow in outlook or scope, merely local. So says the dictionary. If you build a system for one organization, that's what you'll get—no more, no less. Don't assume it'll suit any other organization, even one down the road that's in the same business. It's unreasonable to expect otherwise, unless you expressly insist. Yet companies sometimes do: executives impressed by their new system have the bright idea of making money by selling it. But they're probably in for an unpleasant surprise if suitable provisions weren't made in the first place—which is where unparochialness requirements come in.

When building a product or a system for multiple sites, it must suit each of the environments in which it will be installed—or, at least, the system will be much better received (and, for a product, more competitive) if it's not obviously been built for someone else, somewhere else, or for a different market. But also take sensible steps to make a system amenable to installation in other environments it *might* encounter, without lots of rework, because adding it all later is invariably much harder than incorporating it from the outset.

Look beyond the narrow confines of a single target environment. It's natural for analysts and developers to specify and build systems that they, the customer, and the people they know would like to use—systems for *us*—and in the main it makes systems more friendly, more complete, and more sensible. But we can't allow this inclination to be our only guide, because we'll then get a system built *just for us*. People aren't intentionally parochial; when they're parochial, they are without thinking about it. Requirements to make systems less parochial are scarcer than they should be, which probably contributes significantly to systems being harder to implement successfully outside their home environment. This requirement pattern aims to prompt analysts to write requirements on this topic when they otherwise wouldn't.

Specifying unparochialness is a two-stage process. First, identify everywhere the system might be installed—not as a detailed list of installations, but in broad terms. Second, figure out what sorts of variation from one installation to another is needed to accommodate them all. The rest of this section covers the first stage, and the second stage is dealt with in the "Extra Requirements" subsection coming up.

Write an unparochialness requirement to sum up the scope of prospective installations—a statement of what we have in mind (such as selling to other companies in the same business in the same country). Then, write more detailed requirements to spell out what that really means in terms of specific ways in which the system shouldn't be tied down. But once we have the detailed requirements, the original requirement can be dropped—or demoted to being an introductory statement rather than a formal requirement. In a two-level hierarchy of requirements, the original unparochialness requirement equates to a high-level business requirement, and the rest are detailed requirements.

The first step, then, is to consider where the system might be installed. The most common possibilities are these:

- **Single site**   If it's a system for one site only (say, for internal use), can you be *sure* it'll never be installed anywhere else? If you believe you are sure, state it explicitly as an assumption—both to spur any reader with grander ideas to speak up, and to defend against possible accusations of inflexibility in the future.

- **Different sites**   If it's to be installed in multiple sites—or departments or operating units—belonging to the same organization, how diverse are they? What differs from one to another?

- **Different organizations**   Is it possible that the system will be installed by other organizations? If so, in what ways could their business practices be different? Answering this question usually involves serious investigation. If you assume everyone does things the same way, you're likely to be wrong. Even an expert in this business area who assumes that is likely to be wrong.

- **Different industries**   If you're building a system for use in one industry but would like to extend its use to others, what do they do differently? Fundamentally the industries might be very similar yet still vary in minor details (such as terminology used).

- **Different countries and regions**   Even the most cubicle-bound recluse is aware that other countries speak different languages and use different currencies, but they also do lots of other things differently. What things must our system worry about? The "Extra Requirements" subsection discusses a few. But that doesn't mean the system needs to adapt to every local difference. An overseas subsidiary might be accustomed to working in our language and quite happy to use our system in its original language.

It's worth repeating that we're just talking about tailoring the *whole system* to suit its local environment—not catering for multiple variations at the same time, which is what the multiness requirement pattern is for. For example, one installation being able to support users from multiple countries at the same time—in multiple languages, multiple currencies, and so on—involves a lot more than just avoiding a parochial outlook. Variable single-thing is not the same as multi-thing. A system that allows its base currency to be configured is definitely not automatically multi-currency.

Don't go overboard, though. Don't demand things that are likely to be expensive to implement but have a low chance of being needed (because they're speculative or no more than a gleam in someone's eye). Also, some things. such as data types, are so fundamental that allowing them to vary from one installation to another is just too hard.

> ## Temporal Parochialness
>
> The rest of this requirement pattern deals with *where* a system is suitable to be used, but there's also the subject of *when*. Don't limit a system to working only during a certain time period.
>
> Y2K is the most blatant example of systems demonstrating temporal inflexibility—and it's hard not to regard this inexcusable short-sightedness as a case of mass parochialness. It's easy to view Y2K as a software *development* failure, but plainly there were no *requirements* specified to prevent it. It might be a long time before we need to worry about Y2100 (or Y2.1K or Y21C, or whatever it'll be called), but one or two opportunities might arise before then for systems to stumble upon an artificial date beyond which they won't work properly. The last example requirement in this pattern aims to be a catch-all against all potential problems of this kind; it should not be necessary for requirements to identify specific pitfalls.
>
> Beware! The people who brought us Y2K are still out there (or, at least, their next generation are), poised to inflict further parochialnesses upon us—in both space and time—if we let them.

Content

An unparochialness requirement should convey:

1. **Suitability conditions**   How broad (and how limited) is the set of environments for which the system should be suitable? Be as specific as you can. If it might be installed in other countries but only in one continent (say, Europe), point that out. It might help the developers to know it won't be installed anywhere with a language that needs a multi-byte character set (as in much of Asia).

2. **Motivation**   Why do we want the system to be installable in these different environments? For example, we might want to sell the system there, or perhaps the company has offices there. If these are only secondary goals and the first installation is what we're *really* building the system for, say so in order to put this requirement into perspective.

3. **Example variations**   What are the implications of needing to install the system in this range of environments? Give some examples of the sorts of variation from one installation to another that's needed (such a different base currency).

Template(s)

Summary	Definition
Not specific to «*Single environment name*»	The system shall be suitable for use by any organization that «*Suitability conditions*».
	«*Motivation statement*».
	For example, «*Aspect variation statement(s)*».

Example(s)

Summary	Definition
Not specific to Acme	The system shall be suitable for use by any company in the same line of business, following the same business practices and residing in the same state as Acme Corporation.
	The motivation is to permit the sale of this system to similar businesses, though it must be recognized that the system is primarily for internal use by Acme Corporation.
	For example, the name "Acme Corporation Inc." and similar text values must not be hard-coded anywhere.
Suitable for Acme offices worldwide	The system shall be suitable for use by any Acme Corporation office in any country in which Acme operates.
	It is assumed that all users of the system speak English, so translation into other languages of the system's user interface, reports, documentation, and other materials is not necessary.
	Acme has offices in North and South America, Europe, and Asia.
Not specific to U.S.	There shall be nothing in the system that ties its use to the United States.
	For example, the local currency must not be fixed to be U.S. Dollars.

The following requirement aims to be a guard against temporal parochialness for all time:

Summary	Definition
No time restrictions	There shall be nothing about the system to prevent it being used for an arbitrarily long period (decades) into the future. That is, there shall exist no date beyond which the system shall cease to work normally.
	The motivation of this requirement is to prevent anything equivalent to Y2K problems.

Extra Requirements

Assuming we've identified (as in the preceding sections) the range of environments in which our system is liable to be installed, we now come to stage two: specifying the implications, in the form of all the possible types of variation from one installation to another. How can we work out in which ways other places do things differently? This can involve considerable investigation. This general purpose requirement pattern can't delve into matters that are specific to a particular organization or industry. But it can mention a number of things that can vary from country to country and common ways in which organizations vary—and it does so in the following two subsections.

One last extra requirement that might be worthwhile is to demand that the system's documentation not be parochial. Here's an example of such a requirement:

Summary	Definition
Documentation suitable for all installations	All documentation produced for the system shall be suitable for use by and readily understandable by any organization and in any country in which the system is liable to be installed (as per requirement XR19). In particular, no documentation for the system shall contain confidential Acme information.
	This requirement does not, however, extend to foreign languages: documentation only in English is satisfactory (though it does not preclude other requirements stipulating documentation in other languages).

Differences between Countries   Here is a range of things that vary from one country to another, with some resulting complications mentioned:

1. **Currency**   Switching a system's base currency (the one all monetary amounts are taken to be denominated in) can take more than just nominating a different one to use. It can affect the number of decimal places to which to display monetary amounts: not all currencies use two. If you have both a company base currency and a local currency, you might need to worry which way round exchange rates are quoted (for example, it's Yen to the U.S. Dollar, but U.S. Dollars to the Pound).

2. **Numeric display format**   The primary differences are in the symbols used for decimal points and thousand separators. Also, the thousand separators aren't put between the thousands in all countries (viz India with its 99,99,99,999 format made up of lakhs and crores and so on).

3. **Date display formats**   Is 1/4 the 4th January or 1st April? Simply allowing the system to conform to the local convention might not be enough to avoid confusion. For example, a report for head office might use a format different to that used in a local office that produces it. If there's any risk of confusion, you could add a requirement that the date format be explained explicitly wherever dates are shown.

4. **Language**   It's a large undertaking to translate a whole system into another language. If you want to make the system amenable to being used in a place with a different language, some of the things to consider include:

    a. Ban the hard-coding of all language-specific text, including error messages, menu contents, and other fragments for display to users. If yours is a Web-based system, don't assume the whole user interface is defined in HTML pages themselves.

    b. Text isn't the only medium that can be language-specific: the content of images, audio, and video can be too.

    c. Some languages (such as Chinese) require a multi-byte character set.

    d. Some countries (such as Canada and Switzerland) have multiple official languages.

    e. Keyboard layouts can vary, often to accommodate characters with accents or different alphabets.

f. A user could be running their operating system and other products in another language, even if your system is monolingual. So, wherever possible, avoid making assumptions about the names, prompts, and message texts that other software presents to the user. This applies mainly to user guides, help pages, and other documentation.

5. **Dialect**   Just because another country speaks the same language as you do, don't assume they say or spell everything the same or will understand the same colloquialisms (say, from sports popular in your country but not in others). If possible, use words that are spelled the same in all dialects. For example, "bookmark" is preferable to "favorite" because it avoids inflicting the American spelling of the latter on speakers of British English. This book takes trouble to talk about "how systems behave" rather than "their behavior/behaviour" for the same reason (except when it's awkward to do so).

6. **Time zone**   Bear in mind that not all time zones vary from one another in whole-hour increments. Daylight saving time varies: it doesn't start or end on the same date everywhere; some countries don't have it at all; and when clocks go forward in the Northern hemisphere, they go back in the Southern (and vice versa).

7. **Financial year**   The date on which the financial year ends varies from country to country.

8. **Calendar**   The working days of the week aren't the same everywhere. Public holidays are not necessarily countrywide (and of course they vary from country to country). Public holidays can be for a full day or for a half-day only. The Gregorian calendar is in practice the international standard, and commercial systems rarely need to deal with any other, but it's not the only one in day-to-day use. Some businesses, especially in Europe, use the ISO calendar (defined by the ISO 8601 standard), which states the day number in the calendar year instead of the month and day-in-month.

9. **Geographic regions**   Countries divide themselves up in different ways: states, territories, provinces, counties (and those are just in English-speaking countries).

10. **Post codes**   Some countries use simple numbers; some use more complex schemes.

11. **Address formats**   Even beyond region and post code differences, countries vary in how they conventionally display addresses.

12. **Telephone numbers**   The number of digits and the usual placement of separators vary.

13. **Measurement system**   Metric or that other one, whose very name varies between countries. In the U.S., it's called U.S. or English; in England, it's called Imperial. Plus, a country might use metric for some units but not for others.

14. **Punctuation**   Which characters should be used for quotes, question marks, exclamation marks, and so on?

15. **Cultural differences**   For example, images that are acceptable (even innocuous) in one culture might not be tolerated in another.

16. **The country itself**   We don't want the name of the local country itself to be fixed—or for the system to assume, in some hard-coded way, that it knows which country it's in.

This isn't a comprehensive list. It ignores areas that differ *functionally* from one place to another, such as tax, regulatory, and legal regimes. (Some of these differences can be dealt with by using the extendability requirement pattern we saw earlier in this chapter.) Ways of doing calculations could also vary—for example, bank interest calculations. (See the fee/tax requirement pattern in

Chapter 12, "Commercial Requirement Patterns," and the calculation formula requirement pattern in Chapter 6, "Information Requirement Patterns.") It also ignores variations that are usually of no concern to systems but that just might affect yours, such as national flag, continent, and hemisphere.

You're unlikely to need to worry about all of these things, but run through this list asking yourself whether each one is relevant.

Differences between Organizations   Organizations differ from one another in numerous ways, even in the same industry, and it's impossible to do more than scratch the surface here. But you might want to consider these few common topics:

1. **Data types**   Our company might use numeric codes for something; another company might use 3-character strings. It's usually impractical to switch from one data type to another, so avoid writing a requirement for the system to be able to. But you could consider adopting data types that are more flexible, such as strings rather than numbers.

2. **Organization structure**   Our company might have a two-level hierarchy of operational units; another company might have four. Take steps to accommodate the more complicated structures the system is likely to encounter. (See the multi-organization unit requirement pattern in Chapter 12 for more.)

3. **Employee roles**   It's always good practice to make employee roles configurable—if nothing else, to cater for change in our own organization. But it's more important if the system's going to be installed elsewhere. (See the access control requirement patterns in Chapter 11 for more.)

4. **Accounting entries**   If your system generates information for use by an accounting system, consider whether it's tied too closely to how your own organization performs its accounting.

5. **External systems**   For each external system our system connects to (via an inter-system interface), another organization might be running a different system. Make it as easy as possible to slot in a different inter-system interface (as per the extendability requirement pattern discussed previously in this chapter). If you interface to an external system for more than one purpose, another organization might use separate systems for each of them. In this case, it's better to treat each *purpose* as a distinct inter-system interface.

6. **Terminology**   One company might use different names for certain things.

Considerations for Development

Treat an unparochialness requirement like an instruction not to hard-code this area. That advice doesn't apply in every case: some things need different code to be called in different installations, which means allowing code to be plugged in (as described in the extendability requirement pattern covered earlier).

Considerations for Testing

Properly testing that a system is suitable for installation in the range of places demanded is a major undertaking. A reasonable simplification is to envisage two installations that differ from each other in every possible way. If we have a primary installation, it will be one; make the other as different as you can. This simplification still means we need two full test implementations of the system. If you don't want to go that far, perhaps because secondary installations are a low priority, perform one full pass plus a targeted set of spot checks for selected alternative values. Or try "anecdotal" checking: ask developers what they've done to satisfy the unparochialness requirements, read the documentation for signs that variations are catered for, and run configuration functions to see whether they allow the relevant base values to be changed.

10.4 Multiness Requirement Pattern

Basic Details

Related patterns:	Unparochialness, extendability, multi-lingual, multi-currency, multi-organization unit
Anticipated frequency:	Up to three requirements, rarely more
Pattern classifications:	Pervasive: Maybe; Affects database: Yes

Applicability

Use the multiness requirement pattern to specify that the system must accommodate multiple something-or-others at the same time, each of which has its own fundamentally distinct user interface or whose data must be kept rigorously apart from that of the others. (See the sections that follow for more detailed explanation of the suitability criteria.)

Do not use the multiness requirement pattern when the system need support *only one* from a range of alternatives; use the unparochialness requirement pattern in that case. The difference is that unparochialness allows an aspect to vary but the same variant is used systemwide; multiness allows multiple instances of an aspect to coexist at once. Also, do not use the multiness requirement pattern when support for multiple things is natural or built-in.

(Relative simplicity is the reason "multiness" was coined for this pattern's name. "Multiplicability" might be a more logical word to use, but what a mouthful it is.)

Discussion

A multi-lingual user interface, for instance, is obviously a major undertaking and one that deserves to be dealt with seriously in the requirements (if you need it). It adds an extra *dimension* to the system, and it is for adding this kind of richness that the multiness requirement pattern is intended. We could say our system is multi-customer, multi-product and so on (multi-anything-with-a-database-table, in fact)—but nothing is gained by doing so, and the multiness requirement pattern is not for them. There are other cases that are less clear-cut. How, then, can we decide whether something is significant enough to warrant a multiness requirement? It must satisfy one or more of the following criteria:

- **Criterion 1: Distinct user experiences**, where each alternative instance has its own version of much of what the user sees, such as a separate set of Web pages for each alternative. (For multi-lingual support, for example, everything language-dependent the user sees must be duplicated in each supported language.)

- **Criterion 2: Segregated data**, where the data associated with one alternative instance must be presented on its own, separately from the data of the others. A user might be able to see data for one alternative only, and users who can see more mustn't see them mixed up. (For example, if we're running a multi-department system, a user might be able to see the activities of their own department.) Each alternative in effect has its own little world, which operates to a greater or lesser extent as if it had its own system. There might be people, however, who can span several or all of them. The degree of separation can vary; it's not all-or-nothing.

- **Criterion 3: Unaddable data**, where data is incompatible, and is meaningless if added together. This occurs in any system that has amounts in multiple different units. And that's the test for this criterion: are they like apples and oranges that can't be added together? (For example, in a multi-currency system we cannot simply add an amount denominated in U.S. Dollars to an amount in Euros.) By this test, amounts belonging to different companies **can** be added together, so their data *can* be aggregated (though, depending on how rigorously their data must be segregated, it might never *actually* be aggregated).

It is possible for something to satisfy more than one of these criteria. For example, a system that supports multiple companies could fall into both of the first two: each company might have its own Web pages, and their data must be segregated. If something satisfies *none* of these criteria, it's not a multiness. What do we do then? The system still needs to support multiple of them in some way or another—but don't apply this requirement pattern to it. Examine its characteristics and define requirements for them. I suggest reserving the prefix "multi" in a requirements specification for things that *are* multinesses.

A multiness requirement is not necessary if an **extendability** requirement will suffice (which it will if we're able to support multiple things by plugging in extra software for them). Sometimes multiness goes hand in hand with extendability and you might need both—for example, in a system that supports multiple companies, each of which can slot in its own special software in certain areas.

No kind of multiness is trivial to implement. You can never say "The system shall be multi-whatsit" and leave it at that. You must spell out precisely what you mean: how much multi-whatsit support you need, and how far you want to take it. Different systems might treat multi-whatsit in very different ways—and quite right too, if they have different circumstances. Sometimes we have just a *façade* of multiness, not the real thing. That's good, because it means there's less work to do. For example, if a Web retail site wants to display indicative prices in a customer's currency of choice, that could be merely a little candy on the user interface that doesn't affect the main processing or the database—so it doesn't count as multi-currency because the difficult bits are missing (even though we need a few of the easier bits, such as knowing exchange rates).

This book contains specific requirement patterns for two types of multiness that are commonly encountered: **multi-lingual** and **multi-organization unit** (for multi-company, multi-office, multi-department, and such like). The latter resides in the commercial domain (that is, in Chapter 12). These requirement patterns make it easier to specify these topics without the distractions of the broader discussions in this base multiness requirement pattern itself.

Making *Provision* for Multiness

Implementing any kind of multiness is a lot of work, but adding it to an *existing* system is extra difficult (perhaps prohibitively so). However, it's more straightforward if the system was built from the outset with that kind of multiness in mind.

If there is even a slim chance of a multiness being added at any time during a system's life, consider making some kind of provision for it. Identify specific "hooks" that can be built in, and judge which ones are sufficiently cost effective (based on how easy they are to include and how much unpleasantness they might save later). The commonest types of hooks—with an indication of each one's cost of provision and potential saving later [shown in square brackets at the end]—are as follows:

1. **Provision in entity definitions (in the database)**   Add whatever data items (columns) the multiness would need—for example, for multi-currency, the currency of monetary amounts. In particular, add them to indexes (IDs) because revamping indexes later is likely to cause disruption and risk. For example, for multi-company, add the company ID as the first data item in an index. [Cost: low; saving: high]

2. **Configuration**   Catering for a multiness from the outset in configuration data and maintenance functions often takes little effort. One option is to grant developers the freedom to make provision for the multiness if they can do so easily. [Cost: low to moderate; saving: limited]

3. **ID allocation**   Introducing a multiness can affect how IDs allocated by the system itself (such as order numbers or account numbers) are generated. Think about what the impact would be, and if it sounds potentially nasty take steps to avoid the problem. [Cost: moderate; saving: potentially high, if relevant]

4. **Inquiries and reports**   A significant fraction of the effort of implementing a multiness is adding support for it to inquiries and reports—for example, segregating data or showing separate totals for unaddable values (such as for each currency). It's probably not worth building these things into individual inquiries and reports, but if you're acquiring a third-party reporting product, choose one that supports complex totaling of this kind. [Cost: high; saving: limited]

Check that whatever is done is coherent. Some of these hooks depend on others. For example, an inquiry can't cater for multiness if the data it shows doesn't. And support for the multiness in one place but not another could cause trouble.

If a multiness has been suggested (or there is any chance that someone might want it) but you've decided to make not even provision for it, state this explicitly in the requirements specification to avoid any chance of a misunderstanding.

More is said about making provision for multiness in the "Extra Requirements" subsection in this pattern and in the requirement patterns for specific types of multiness.

The multinesses in a system can be found and specified using the following process (each step of which is spelled out in its own subsection immediately following):

1. Identify candidate multinesses.

2. Decide whether something is a multiness.

3. Specify a multiness requirement.

4. Investigate the implications, and specify extra requirements for them.

Perform Steps 2 to 4 for each multiness you identify in Step 1. If you're using this requirement pattern to help specify a kind of multiness you've already identified, skip the first two steps.

Step 1: Identify Candidate Multinesses   There are three places to fish for possible multinesses:

- **Place 1: Definitions of data entities**   (We assume these exist already, so specify their requirements before tackling multinesses.) You don't need to scour every entity: concentrate on the important **living entities** (such as *customer* and *employee*) and **transactions** (such as *customer order*). For each candidate entity, run through its data items. Any data item that has one of the following characteristics is potentially a multiness:

  i.   **The data item identifies a configuration entity**. For example, in a customer entity we might unearth *country* and *region of residence*, *preferred language*, *owning company*, and *club membership type*.

  ii.   **The data item could be used to determine how to treat that entity**. For example, for customer we might stumble upon *date of birth*, and thus implicitly their *age*, which would let us give teenagers a different experience at our Web site if we want.

  iii.   **The data item is an amount that has a unit of measure**, whether or not the unit is explicitly present. For example, a monetary amount always has a currency as a unit of measure (even if in a parochial single-currency system the same currency is assumed everywhere).

  Pay special attention to data items used for identification (or indexing).

- **Place 2: The structure of the organization**   Or the structure of all the organizations involved, if there are more than one. Use the multi-organization unit requirement pattern both to specify organizational structure and to decide whether any kind of organization unit needs to be segregated enough to count as a multiness.

- **Place 3: Types of extendability**   Each type lets us plug in software for a particular purpose and often involves database tables shared by all the extensions of that type. We need a multiness if each extension's data must be segregated from that of the others or if they are mutually unaddable. For example, if our system provides an environment for multiple service providers (each able to slot in its own software), we probably need to isolate each service provider's data from the others.

This exercise isn't as daunting as it looks, and it can, in fact, be conducted quickly. Discard as many candidate multinesses as you can the moment they come to light. Drop without further ado any multiness that's clearly not needed. If in doubt, leave it out.

Figure 10-3 is a magical representation of how several candidate multinesses might be discovered in a few important logical entities.

The three examples on the left all use the multi-organization unit requirement pattern. Multi-lingual has its own requirement pattern, too.

Looking for candidate multinesses can be a creative activity. It can unearth possibilities you never thought of (such as separate user interfaces for different age groups, I imagine). But don't get carried away. Don't include some wild capability just because you can: make sure you can justify the cost it will surely add.

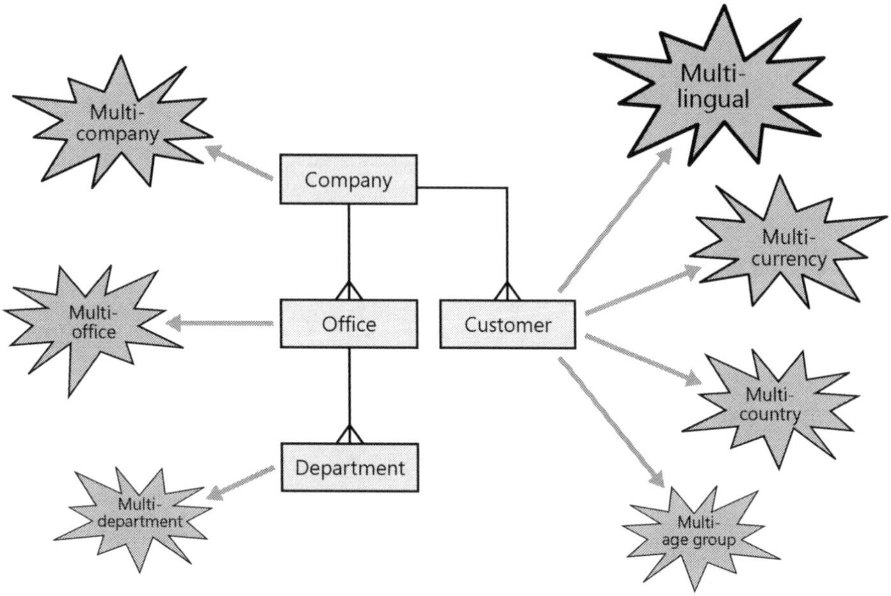

Figure 10-3   Identifying multinesses from logical entities

Be alarmed if your system has more than one multiness that has a need for multiple user experiences—multi-multinesses—because they lead to a multiplicative explosion. For example, if you need a set of Web pages for each of five companies and also for each of three languages, you need fifteen sets of Web pages altogether. This sounds like a nightmare in the making. Each multiness truly does behave like an independent dimension in this respect.

Step 2: Decide Whether Something Is a Multiness   Having identified a candidate multiness, work out how much support the system must provide for it. Do you need rich functionality, or will a superficial façade suffice? Consider what variations there might be in how we handle each of these things. We need multiness if there is sufficient difference between the possibilities—if they need different processing, or if they must be kept separate (for example, if they can't be added together, which applies to amounts in different currencies). Then test what's needed against the three criteria stated previously: distinct user experiences, segregated data, and unaddable data. If it matches any of these three, it is a multiness.

Asking whether putting "multi-" as a prefix in front of the name can sometimes give you a sense of whether it's suitable. If the result sounds over the top, maybe it's not important enough to be a multiness. If it sounds right and it deserves such grandeur, it's a vote in favor of treating it as a multiness.

Step 3: Specify a Multiness Requirement   Write a requirement that defines the extent of support you need for a particular type of multiness, as per the "Content" section coming up.

Step 4: Investigate Implications and Specify Extra Requirements   What must the system do to deliver this kind of multiness? Look at the effects it has on entity definitions and then on user functions such as inquiries and reports. Refer to the "Extra Requirements" subsection for the details. If the type of multiness in question has its own requirement pattern, refer to its "Extra Requirements" section too.

Content

A multiness requirement should contain the following:

1. **Multiness type**   What kind of thing are we asking the system to support multiple of? (For example, multiple languages.)

2. **Extent of support**   Give a summary of what level of support is expected from the system. For example, only our external Web site might need to be multi-lingual (not internal functions). Don't go into great detail; use extra requirements to spell out specific aspects.

3. **Expected number of instances**   When we say *multiple*, how many are we talking about? This is only significant when a distinct user interface must be constructed for each one–for example, for each supported language–and then it's very important. Either express it as a number (or range), or describe a condition that determines how many (for example, one for each company configured in the system).

   This raises the question of whether we're just specifying a system with an inherent multiness capability (say, multi-lingual), or whether in addition we expect the system to be delivered with support for a specific set of instances (say, English, French, and German). The main multiness requirement should limit itself to the former. If you need the latter, write extra requirements for them–one for each instance, if they are small in number, so that each can be assigned its own priority.

4. **Limitations**   What simplifications are acceptable? Don't force the developers to confront difficult aspects if they're unnecessary.

A requirement demanding that provision be made to implement this multiness in the future is similar but can be less detailed. The extent and limitations clauses should describe how much provision to make (and not to make), rather than how much multiness support. The expected number of instances can be omitted.

Template(s)

Summary	Definition
Multi-«*Multiness name*»	The system shall support multiple «*Multiness type description*». «*Statement of extent*».
	[«*Number of instances statement*».]
	[«*Limitations statement*».]
Provision to be multi-«*Multiness name*» [in future]	The system shall make provision for the future introduction of support for multiple «*Multiness type description*». «*Statement of extent*».
	[«*Limitations statement*».]

Example(s)

If most of the examples here look somewhat obscure, it's because the more obvious subjects reside in their respective requirement patterns (multi-lingual in this chapter and multi-organization unit in Chapter 12).

Summary	Definition
Multi-age group	The system shall allow distinct customer user interfaces to be provided for different age groups. Whenever a user interface "resource" is to be displayed, if an age-specific version is present, it shall be used; otherwise, a default (age-independent resource) shall be used. The types of "resources" to which this applies include Web pages, messages, images, audio, and video.
	It is anticipated that no more than three age groups will be supported.
	This requirement does not apply to the user interface of functions used only by employees.
Multi-marketing campaign	The marketing management system shall allow multiple independent marketing campaigns to be conducted. Information about campaigns shall be rigorously separated from each other, and no person shall be able to view or otherwise access information about a campaign with which they are not connected.
Multi-currency	The system shall be able to process transactions in multiple different currencies.
	This requirement does **not** include the ability to perform currency *conversions*.
Multi-fruit tree type	The fruit tree management system shall cater for multiple types of fruit tree. Whenever numbers of trees or quantity of fruit are shown, totals for different fruits shall always be shown separately (for example, no adding of apples and oranges).
	There shall be no artificial limit on the number of types of fruit tree.

Each of these four requirements matches one of the three criteria for multiness: the first requirement involves multiple user interfaces, the second has segregated data, and the third and fourth have unaddable data.

Extra Requirements

A multiness requirement tells us the system must cater for multiple whatever-they-are. But that's not enough. We need to spell out *how much* support the system must provide, for which we need extra requirements. The topics to cover depend on which of the three multiness criteria are satisfied. These are discussed in the following three subsections.

Distinct User Experiences   Providing multiple distinct user interfaces (such as one for each of several languages) takes more than creating multiple sets of Web pages. Other kinds of resources vary from one instance to another: snippets of text (such as error messages), images, audio, video, animations, and bundles to download, among others. Some of these could themselves contain text, or their content could vary in its own right (for example, company logos, legal terms, and conditions). Examine every kind of resource the system uses, and for each one ask whether it could vary from one multiness instance to another.

Other things might vary from one instance to another too, including the visual space needed to display a piece of text and the order in which words and clauses should be presented (especially if you're assembling text containing variables). The size (and shape) of an image might vary from one instance to another. If you want developers to take these variations properly into account, you have to write requirements for them.

Extra requirements might be needed for the following:

1. **Instances to implement**   Write requirements that identify specific multiness instances that are to be implemented. Avoid this if you can—because it smacks of specifying data rather than the system itself. How unclean this is depends on the nature of the multiness: naming particular languages is more acceptable than naming companies.

2. **Default instance**   Allow one instance to be nominated as the default, the datum. This is the one to use in the absence of any guidance to the contrary. Its implementation needs to be complete, with no resources missing. It is advisable for this to be the first instance implemented, to constitute the reference instance.

3. **Choosing instance**   If there are several instances available, how does the system decide which one to use for a particular user? Typically a user session continues to use one instance until told to change. There are four common ways to choose an instance other than the default: 1. The user visits a specific address (URL); 2. Temporary selection by the user; 3. Permanent selection by the user (as a user preference); 4. Derive from other known information (such as the customer's country). A system could use more than one of these ways.

4. **Substituting if a resource is missing**   What happens when something is missing for a particular instance (either a piece of text or a "resource" such as a Web page)? The smart—and resilient—answer is to use instead the equivalent resource for another instance. The easiest approach is to always use the resource belonging to the default instance, but there are more sophisticated possibilities, such as nominating for each instance the substitution instance to use, which makes it relatively easy to create "dialects" that contain few resources of their own.

   If each instance's resources are owned by its own legal entity (for example, if we're supporting multiple companies), check whether it's acceptable to substitute resources belonging to someone else. The system might need to accommodate rules determining what's allowed. If there's no instance that can be used as a default of last resort, the substitution mechanism might find itself without a resource it can use.

5. **Input interpretation**   Does the system ask the user to enter values from which it interprets meaning? If so, are any of those values tied to a particular instance of a multiness? For example, if the user typing Yes or No into a certain field conveys special meaning, a multi-lingual system should accept the equivalent words in the user's chosen language. A user interface can't be considered multi-lingual if you force the user to speak to you in a single language.

6. **Customer support**   If you're offering a customer support service, you might want different contact addresses for each multiness instance (phone numbers or email addresses, or both), which means telling customers what they are (perhaps via an instance-specific help page). Then you need customer service operators prepared to deal with each multiness instance (for example, who speak different languages or represent different companies). It also helps if the customer service operator is able to "see what the customer sees, which means being able to display the same function for the same multiness instance (even if not the same data).

7. **Resource editing function(s)**   Creating one set of resources is hard enough. Creating another set that's exactly equivalent but different in some respect (such as in a different language) is harder, unless you provide functions that help. For snippets of text (including error messages and so on), a function that displays one version and asks you to enter another version makes life a lot easier. It also helps if you show each one's context, because it's sometimes impossible to make an appropriate translation without it. You could keep track of a change to any resource, because it might signal that its equivalent instances need to be changed too. These are just some of the ways to help with the creation and managing of multiple sets of resources. Deciding which ones are worthwhile depends on how many user interface instances and how many different resources you have, how often they are likely to change, and how important the best possible user interface is to you—that is, how much you're willing to spend.

8. **Missing resource checker**   It's tedious, time-consuming, and unreliable to check by hand whether all the resources needed for an instance of a multiness are present. A utility can do this job a lot more dependably.

Here are sample requirements for a couple of these kinds of extra requirements:

Summary	Definition
Default «*Multiness name*»	The system shall have a default «*Multiness name*». The user interface shall be displayed according to this «*Multiness name*» unless and until an alternative is chosen.
	Every element of the user interface shall be present in the default «*Multiness name*».
Substitute missing «*Multiness name*» resources	If a «*Multiness name*»-specific resource is missing (not present) for a particular «*Multiness name*», the equivalent resource for the default «*Multiness name*» shall be used instead. This shall apply for any type of "resource" displayed in a user interface, including (but not limited to): Web pages, messages, pieces of text, images, and multimedia resources.
	An error shall be logged (with low severity) whenever a substitution of this kind is made.
	The motivation for this requirement is resilience: to display the best user interface even when resources it needs are missing.

For good measure here's a universal requirement to prevent developers burying text in code where it can't be modified and isn't amenable to multiple user interfaces:

Summary	Definition
No hard-coding of user-visible text	No piece of text that might be displayed to a user shall reside in source code. That is, every piece of text that a user might see must be modifiable without changing source code.

Segregated Data   The purpose of segregated data is to divide a single system into a number of distinct compartments so that a user who works in one compartment cannot access other compartments. This can be summed up like so: inaccessible instances of a multiness shall be invisible.

The primary aim of extra requirements is to prevent a few likely kinds of holes in the compartments, but that's not all:

1. **Prevent cross-instance access**   Don't allow a user associated with one instance to access data belonging to another. This is straightforward enough to build into specific functions, but care needs to be taken whenever flexible selection criteria are allowed. In particular, no normal user should be able to run SQL queries, nor to use any product that permits free queries (such as a report writer product).

2. **Give users access to instances**   Each user must be granted access to the multiness instances they should be able to work with. That raises the interesting question of who is allowed to grant this access. For example, in a system supporting multiple companies, each company will want only its own employees granting authority to its precious data—but there must be some kind of overall controlling body. The answer is for each company to have users who are able to set up other users for their company only, and for a "system manager" to create each company's special users in the first place. Extra checks can be put in place to restrict what a system manager can do, especially to prevent them accessing companies' data and to prevent them creating other users. Everything's possible—but it can get fiddly.

Don't let the brevity of this subsection fool you: this subject is not to be taken lightly. It deserves serious investigation, or you might find your system doesn't properly segregate its data.

Unaddable Data   When we have multiple kinds of data that can't be added together, extra requirements could be needed for the following:

1. **Cross-instance conversion**   Is there some way to convert an amount belonging to one instance into an equivalent amount belonging to another instance? For example, an amount in one currency can be converted to an equivalent amount in another currency. If cross-instance conversion is possible (and in some cases it isn't), specify how to perform it. Where do the conversion "rates" come from? The rates are likely to change over time. How? How frequently? Do you need different rates for different purposes? Consider specifying a "base" instance of the multiness to use as a datum for conversions—both to have a standard in which to report (for example, your local currency) and to save having to manage a "rate" for every permutation of instances.

2. **Never simply add values for different instances**   You could write a requirement stating that two or more incompatible amounts shall never be added together, although it might sound too obvious to warrant saying and often is.

3. **Distinct totals for each instance**   Any inquiry or report that lists data belonging to multiple instances and shows totals should show separate totals for each instance for which data is listed. For example, if an inquiry lists a number of transactions that are denominated in several currencies, totals should be shown for each currency. You could write a pervasive requirement that insists on this rule being applied across the whole system, which saves having to say it for each function to which it applies and it also covers those that might be added in future.

4. **Don't sort on unaddable amounts**   Presenting a list of customer bank accounts in descending order of balances is meaningless if they're in several different currencies and that wasn't taken into account. That's common sense, and it's reasonable to assume a developer will come up with a sensible solution. But if a general purpose tool (perhaps a third-party product) is used, it won't understand the data and might produce silly results. If you're worried that something like this might happen, write a requirement to prevent it.

Considerations for Development

Check that the *extent* of the multiness is clear. Can you tell how much the system must do?

Verify that third-party products are capable of satisfying the multiness requirements—both products you already have and those you need to acquire.

Considerations for Testing

Testing a multiness involves testing every function that might be affected, which is often many of them. First prepare a full range of representative data for more than one instance of the multiness. Then execute each of these functions, and visually scrutinize the results according to each of the multiness criteria this type of multiness satisfies. Each of the three multiness criteria that's satisfied has its own considerations:

- **Criterion 1: Distinct user experiences**   First decide whether you're testing an inherent ability to support multiple user interfaces or whether you're testing support for a specific set of instances, or both. This determines how many instances you need to test: in the first case, two is probably enough. It also affects how seriously to treat the omission of specific "resources" for an instance; in the first case, this might be unimportant. If testing an inherent ability to support multiple user experiences, consider what is called **pseudo-localization** (or **pseudo-loc**) testing, in which a set of resources is created automatically for a second user experience based on a full set for the first—typically by adding a fixed character (say, X) at the start and end of each value. This saves a large amount of manual effort creating a new version of everything. It also makes it easy to spot if a value from the wrong instance is being displayed, and it's understandable by everyone on the project (unlike if the second instance were in a different language).

  If the system's smart enough to use a substitute resource when one is missing for a particular instance, test an instance for which all resources are missing. Check that the user interface for every function looks satisfactory.

  If there's a "missing resource checker" utility, run it.

- **Criterion 2: Segregated data**   Test that a user restricted to data belonging to one instance of the multiness cannot access data (or other resources) belonging to any other. Pay special attention to any function that offers flexible selection criteria: is it possible to do a query, for example, that delves into forbidden data? Check whether there are any interfaces or other "unusual" ways to access the system. If so, verify that they enforce the same restrictions as the rest of the system. Third-party products are at particular risk of falling foul here, because they're unlikely to understand the need for segregation.

- **Criterion 3: Unaddable data**   Test that values for multiple instances of a multiness are never simply added together: they must either be shown separately or converted as specified in the requirements (for example, currency conversion using the correct exchange rates). Look especially at totals shown in inquiries and reports. Again, watch out for functions offering flexible selection criteria and for third-party products that are unaware when data is unaddable.

The multiness requirement pattern assumes that each instance is handled in exactly the same way by the software, so there is no need to test variations in logic. If there is a need for different software for a particular instance, see the extendability requirement (covered earlier).

Provision for something in the future can't be tested directly, because it hasn't been implemented yet. To tell whether some provision has actually been made, first look at the structure of database tables: are the necessary columns there? Second, look at configuration to see if this area is at least handled in an unparochial way. Third, look at inquiries and reports to see if their total lines look like they are amenable to separate totals for each multiness entity (for example, each currency).

10.5 Multi-Lingual Requirement Pattern

Basic Details

Related patterns:	Extends multiness
Anticipated frequency:	Zero or one requirement
Pattern classifications:	Pervasive: Maybe

Applicability

Use the multi-lingual requirement pattern to specify that the system is capable of displaying its user interface in more than one alternative natural language (for at least one class of user, though not necessarily all). Also use it to specify that the system can produce output (for example, printing letters or generating stock emails) or accept input in more than one language.

Discussion

Most of what's involved in specifying multi-lingualness is said in general terms in the multiness requirement pattern, which this pattern extends. This pattern is here to make specifying multi-lingual requirements easier and to point out some specific considerations.

Decent support for more than one language is a lot of work; it's not just a matter of creating an extra set of Web pages for each language. Don't ask for it just because it sounds impressive. Only require it if it's essential.

Other variations often go hand in hand with language differences, such as date and number formats. Some of these differences have a geographical element rather being than simply language dependent, and the word **locale** is used for a geographical region for which specific characteristics of this kind can be defined. Multi-locale is therefore perhaps a more accurate name for this requirement pattern, but multi-lingual makes more sense because this meaning of "locale" is unfamiliar to nontechnical readers and because the multi-lingual aspect is usually by far the most complicated. See the unparochialness requirement pattern earlier in this chapter for a list of factors that vary geographically in this way.

Multi-lingualness can be used for "dialects" as well as distinct languages—for example, American/British English and phraseology for different age groups. Having the system use substitutes for missing resources is especially effective in such cases, because for a dialect you need create only those resources you genuinely want to be different. Everything else works fine and can be expected to make sense to the user.

Consider cultural differences and national sensitivities, too. Is each language version simply a direct translation of another, or should we do more? What's acceptable in the home culture of people who speak one language can differ from what's acceptable somewhere else. This applies to text and images and other kinds of resources.

The international standard that defines codes to use for languages is ISO 639.

Content

A multi-lingual requirement should contain:

1. **Extent of support**   How much multi-lingual support do we need from the system? Asking for a multi-lingual user interface for only one class of users can dramatically cut the amount of work. Consider each class of users separately. Typically a multi-lingual support is delivered to customers only, and poor employees must make do with one language only.

2. **Expected number of instances**   How many languages are we likely to support? If we're planning to support dialects, state a separate number for them because they're less work and less risk.

3. **Limitations**   How can we make implementing multi-lingualness less onerous? If we can do without support for languages with multi-byte character sets (such as Chinese and Japanese), say so. Similarly, say so if we don't need to worry about languages that are read right-to-left (such as Arabic).

(This is a tailoring of the content described in the multiness requirement pattern just described.)

Template(s)

Summary	Definition
Multi-lingual [«*Scope qualifier*»]	The system shall support multiple languages. «*Statement of extent*».
	[«*Number of instances statement*».]
	[«*Limitations statement*».]
Provision [for «*Scope qualifier*»] to become multi-lingual	The system shall make provision for the future introduction of support for multiple languages. «*Statement of extent*».
	[«*Limitations statement*».]

Example(s)

Summary	Definition
Multi-lingual customer user interface	The system shall allow the customer user interface to be available in multiple languages. Each customer shall nominate which of a range of supported languages they wish to use, and then every piece of information displayed to them by the system shall be in that language. This shall include screen prompts, messages, and graphics, audio, and video that contain language-specific content.
	It is anticipated that no more than three languages will be supported. Languages that use a multi-byte character set need not be supported.
	This requirement does not apply to the user interface of functions used only by employees (which is needed in one language only).
Provision to be multi-lingual	The system shall make provision for the future introduction of support for multiple languages. Provision shall include at least the following:
	1. The structure of the database shall be such that multi-lingual support shall not necessitate the addition of columns to tables or the replacement of any table by one or more others.
	2. A user shall be able to nominate their preferred language when entering their personal details.

Extra Requirements

All the types of extra requirements in the "Distinct User Experiences" subsection of the multiness requirement pattern apply to multi-lingualness.

Here are a couple of specific examples:

Summary	Definition
Default language	The system shall have a default language. The user interface shall be displayed in this language unless and until a user chooses an alternative preferred language from among those supported. A Web address can have a language associated with it, and visiting such an address shall constitute choosing that language. (For example, visiting "*«Home URL»*/fr" might choose French.)
	Every element of the user interface shall be present in the default language.
Substitute missing language resources	If a language-specific resource is missing (not present) for a particular language, the equivalent resource for the default language shall be used instead. This shall apply for any type of "resource" displayed in a user interface: Web pages, messages, pieces of text, images, and multimedia resources.
	An error shall be logged (with low severity) whenever a substitution of this kind is made.
	The motivation for this requirement is resilience: to display the best user interface even when some of the resources it needs are missing.

Considerations for Development

Take inherent multi-lingual capabilities into account when deciding which technologies to use, especially if you must support languages that use multi-byte character sets.

There are also a small number of considerations in the multiness requirement pattern.

Considerations for Testing

Involve someone who can speak each language being tested. For proper independent testing, don't use a person who participated in translating or otherwise producing the resources for that language.

See also the considerations in the multiness requirement pattern.

10.6 Installability Requirement Pattern

Basic Details

Related patterns:	None
Anticipated frequency:	Between zero and two requirements
Pattern classifications:	Affects database: Yes

Applicability

Use the installability requirement pattern to specify how easy it must be to install or upgrade the system (or a part of the system).

Discussion

Whenever you go to the trouble of building a system, it's handy to be able to install it. You can always rely on the developers to install it ad hoc somehow, and that can be acceptable if you're installing it in only one or two places. Something better is called for if (a) you want other people to be able to install it, (b) you'll have more than a handful of installations, (c) you can't afford an installation to go wrong, or (d) you don't want to give developers unfettered access to production machines. That's where installability requirements come in—to impose order on installation, to indicate how important installation is and how much trouble we're prepared to take, and as a reminder to allocate adequate resources to it.

The subject of installation is rarely mentioned in requirements. When it isn't, it's as if there were an implicit requirement that says "There shall be a way to install the system. It doesn't matter how unpleasant, time-consuming, unreliable, or insecure it is." Installation is often considered at all only when the (first) installation date draws near, but it deserves to be "on the radar" from the beginning. A common sentiment is, let's worry about installation when we've got a system to install. But that's not good enough. It often involves developing installation software and instructions, which should be treated just like any other software and documentation—and as an integral part of the system. Otherwise they'll be uncontrolled and under-scrutinized—and probably unbudgeted too.

The importance of good installability depends on how many installations there'll be (both discrete sites and number of machines in each site), which organization(s) will be doing them (yours or, if it's a product, a customer), the skills possessed by the installer, the complexity of the system, and the cost if it goes wrong. Installation is often the first a customer sees of a system in the flesh, and if it's awkward or frustrating it can create a negative impression that's very difficult to correct. They might even give up and decide not to install your system at all.

Write an installability requirement for each part of the system that will be installed independently—for example, server software and client software separately.

If you like, you can omit a requirement of this kind and specify only those specific installation features you want, as covered in the "Extra Requirements" subsection coming up.

Content

An installability requirement should contain:

1. **Which part of the system (or all of it)**   Different parts of a system might be installed in different ways and at different times, although every part must be installed somehow (otherwise there's no point in having it). Write an installation requirement for each *installable unit*, and check that every piece of software belongs to one unit or another.

2. **Who can install**   Who should be able to install this part of the system? What minimum level of skill should they need?

3. **Ease of installation**   How easy must the software be to install? How smart should installation software be? Don't stray over the line into how the installation itself will happen—that is, its design. Don't go over the top either.

4. **Installation medium (optionally)**   How do we put the stuff to install into the installer's hands? This is separate from preparing the installation bundle, and it can itself involve a reasonable amount of work. For example, if the software will be downloaded, we must set up a place from which to download it; if we're going to supply the software on CD, we must prepare installation CDs. Avoid mentioning particular media technologies as far as possible.

Template(s)

Summary	Definition
«*System part*» installability	It shall be possible for the «*System part*» to be installed by a «*Person who will install*». «*Ease of installation statement*». [«*Installation medium statement*».]

Example(s)

Summary	Definition
Client application installability	It shall be possible for the Web Shop client application to be installed by a typical customer who has no special expertise. The installation process shall be convenient and involve the entry of little information by the user. The client application shall be downloaded from the service's Web site.
Main system installability	It shall be possible for the system's main (server) software to be installed by a competent system administrator who has no previous knowledge of the system or of the third-party products it uses (but who is familiar with the operating system of the machines on which it is to be installed). The software shall be installed from a popular portable medium (such as a CD).

Extra Requirements

Installing a system is a complex business, especially if we don't want it to *look* complex. Consider the following additional aspects, and ask yourself whether they deserve their own requirements:

1. **Installation instructions**   Even the simplest and easiest installation needs some instructions to tell an installer what to do. This constitutes documentation, so refer to the documentation requirement pattern (in Chapter 5), which has an example requirement for installation instructions.

2. **Authorization to install**   Is possession of the installable software enough to install the system? If you're selling a product, you might want additional control, such as asking the installer to register the software or enter a license key allocated to them. Even if you allow anyone to install it, you might want to be notified each time it is installed.

3. **Upgrading**   This is a special case of installing the system when a previous version is already installed. It has its own complications—and they tend to be neglected. See the "Upgrading" subsection in this pattern for further details.

4. **Troubleshooting**   If something goes wrong during installation, provide ways for the installer (a person) to determine what the problem is and to fix it in as many cases as possible. If not, provide information they can pass on to an expert to assist them. Don't expect installation software to be able to figure out every difficulty, but ask for it to handle anything that has a reasonable chance of going wrong.

5. **Security risks**   Sloppy installation can have security implications. Consider what they might be for your system, and write requirements to guard against them. For example, you might not want installation software lying around after it's been run (especially powerful general-purpose utilities). Or you could restrict an installer's access to sensitive data.

6. **Training**   You might need to organize training for the people who will carry out installations, if you have enough of them.

7. **Uninstalling**   Any piece of software that gets installed might one day need to be uninstalled. How easy it must be to uninstall a piece of software varies greatly depending on its nature. One usually expects a client or desktop application to have a properly packaged uninstall routine that will completely remove it at the click of a button. Expectations of server software are lower and typically nil for systems developed in-house. Write requirements for any uninstall demands you have. Write a separate requirement for each part of the system that has its own uninstall needs—for example, one for a client application and another for server software.

   Uninstalling an upgrade can be particularly troublesome (to the extent that it is sometimes impractical), so don't impose unreasonable requirements. For instance, if an upgrade involves converting data, it is normally not necessary to demand a reverse conversion process (because normally no one would need it).

Upgrading   We can expect a system to have several upgrades in its lifetime. (It better had—or it'll have a short life expectancy!) When specifying requirements for upgrading, we're not dealing with a particular upgrade but setting rules to be followed by all future upgrades.

The biggest question, when releasing a new version of a system, is: from which previous versions we must be able to upgrade to it? The answer depends on which versions are out there being used. Make sure the system is ready for every likely eventuality but don't go to the trouble of making provision for situations that, while conceivable, will never occur in practice in your environment. If you can, operationally, arrange for every site to upgrade whenever a new version is released; life will be simpler for everyone. Here's an example requirement to let us upgrade from any previous version:

Summary	Definition
Upgrade from any previous version	When a new version of the main system is released, it shall be possible to upgrade to it from any previous version.

Instructions and software for upgrading are likely to be different from installing from scratch. They could be so different as to warrant separate instructions and software.

If an upgrade fails, do your utmost to allow the previous release to be still usable. Insist that the system be backed up before starting an upgrade.

It can be irritating when you've gone to a lot of trouble to tweak a system to suit you, only for an upgrade to set them all back to their defaults. If you want to avoid upsetting your users in this way, write a requirement to prevent it, such as this one:

Summary	Definition
Upgrade not to affect configuration	Installing an upgrade shall not modify existing configuration values. An exception is made for any values that the new version uses in different ways from the previous version.
	The motivation for this requirement is to avoid wasting the time of users who have spent considerable time configuring the system to suit themselves.

Considerations for Development

Treat installation software as seriously as any other software, and treat it as a proper part of the system. Even if it's unsexy, it's still important. Automate as much as is cost-effective.

Create one or more utilities to check if a machine is ready to have the system installed: is there enough space, does it have the right operating system, are all required third-party products installed already, and are any other prerequisites met? Clearly explain every problem discovered.

Provide a reliable way of determining which version of the system is installed on each machine.

If you need to be able to upgrade to the latest version from any previous version, this can be achieved by a series of upgrades. For example, upgrading from version 1 to version 4 can be achieved by upgrading to 2 then 3 then 4. It's not necessary to properly install the *software* for in-between versions. We're talking mainly about information-related steps: creating database tables, converting data, and such like. This might be the easiest way to achieve upgrades from old versions, but it does mean that no installation software is ever short-lived; it's needed until *every site* has upgraded to a later version. But beware that upgrading via intermediate versions isn't always ideal. For example, if version 2 simplified some data (say, for performance) and version 3 restored the original complexity (because too much functionality was lost), upgrading from 1 to 3 via might cause loss of data that can be avoided if we go directly from 1 to 3. This might seem like a trivial matter to you, but it won't to users of the system.

If the system is installed on multiple machines, consider what might happen if some run one version of the system and some run another. If they reside in different locations, it might be impractical to upgrade them all at the same time, so you must arrange for old and new versions to run smoothly together.

Considerations for Testing

If installability is important enough to deserve requirements, it deserves to be tested properly, and that means going to the trouble of installing it from scratch purely to test how easy it is.

Test upgrades separately. Test the upgrading to a new version of the system from each previous version that is likely to happen in practice.

Ask the development team for a list of all the files that are loaded or created during the installation process and all the changes that are made to the environment of each machine by the installation. Check that installation makes the expected changes. See if you can detect any additional changes beyond those expected.

Beware of combinatorial explosion if you have several old versions, several machine environments (say, operating systems and/or databases), and several software components installed separately. Do all combinations work together? Does installation of the system work equally well in all cases? It's impossible to test all permutations, but you should prepare several different installation scenarios that together span every individual product and version that must be supported.

Test installation instructions at the same time as performing an installation—if there are instructions. If not, expect the installation to be self-explanatory. Do the same for an upgrade. Check that the instructions do this:

1. Describe prerequisites. These should explain everything you need before starting the installation and should list everything that should already be installed beforehand.
2. Adequately explain what the person installing needs to do.

3. Warn you against things you could easily do wrong during the installation.

4. State prompts and messages exactly as the installation itself presents them. If the instructions include sample screens, do they look the same as those displayed during the installation? Instructions that are even slightly incompatible can cause confusion.

5. Describe all the steps in the installation, in the same sequence.

Comprehensively testing installation also involves making mistakes. Draw a flow chart of the steps in the installation process and possible missteps. Consider things that could go wrong. What happens if an installation is abandoned before it finishes? Is it possible to restart it or to remove everything and try again? What happens if you try to install the system in an incorrect environment (for example, trying to use an unsupported version of the database, or with an essential third-party product missing)? Is the installation software smart enough to spot problems?

Test uninstalling the system. If there are requirements that cover uninstallation, test that it works to the degree and level of convenience demanded. If there are no such requirements, test whether uninstallation is practical. After uninstalling the system, verify that no traces of it remain (such as odd configuration files). Then reinstall the system as an extra check that the uninstall didn't leave anything behind.

Chapter 11
Access Control Requirement Patterns

In this chapter:

11.1 User Registration Requirement Pattern 284
11.2 User Authentication Requirement Pattern. 295
11.3 User Authorization Requirement Patterns 305
11.4 Specific Authorization Requirement Pattern 308
11.5 Configurable Authorization Requirement Pattern 313
11.6 Approval Requirement Pattern. 318

Access control lets us nominate all the people we're prepared to let in, check each one's identity when they visit, limit their access to only what they should see and do, and see who did what—so we needn't trust anyone more than we have to. These are essential features of almost every serious commercial system, and few do it well.

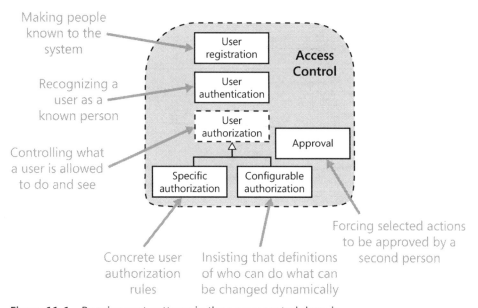

Figure 11-1   Requirement patterns in the access control domain

Access control comprises three main activities, which are the subjects of the following requirement patterns (as shown in Figure 11-1):

1. Making people known to the system (**user registration**).
2. Recognizing a user as a known person (**user authentication**).

3.   Controlling what a user is allowed to do and see (**user authorization**). This is divided into two requirement patterns, because there are two different types of requirement: the first is for stating a concrete access control rule (**specific authorization**); the second says that the definitions of who can do what can be changed dynamically (**configurable authorization**), so you can avoid the nitty-gritty in the requirements.

In summary, registration decides which people we'll let in; authentication lets them in; authorization decides what they can do when they're in. The third is the goal, and the first two merely prerequisites.

There's one further requirement pattern in this domain: **approval**, for situations where one user needs to approve the action of another before the action is allowed to proceed. This takes us a little beyond strict access control, but it's so closely related that it fits comfortably within this domain.

Another important aspect of access control is recording who did what ("audit trails"). This topic is covered in the chronicle requirement pattern in Chapter 7, "Data Entity Requirement Patterns," which includes several example requirements that relate to access control-related activities. Write requirements to demand that the use of all functions related to access control be recorded: it's hard to envisage reasons why you wouldn't.

User Accountability

Once a user has been authenticated (has logged in), it's possible to tie them to—that is, make them accountable for—all the actions they perform, which is very useful in its own right. It's the basis of **non-repudiation**, which is the ability to prove a user did something they deny doing (particularly of a financial nature). Associating an action with the user who initiated it is usually covered by other requirements (such as for functions and chronicle entries).

If you're serious about user accountability, decide which user (if any) is responsible for *background processing*—so that there's always a *person* who is ultimately responsible for each thing a system does and who has a strong incentive to see that it is performed properly. For example, if a background process calculates monthly fees for all customers, was it, in some sense, performed by whoever initiated it? Or if it's kicked off automatically at a certain time each month, is the person who originally set up the schedule responsible ever after? Define what you decide in suitable requirements. If you don't, the system might do things for which no one has responsibility. That happens by default in almost all systems, but it's probably not a good thing. After all, shouldn't the buck stop *somewhere*?

Access control is the only aspect of security for which this book has requirement patterns, though there are many other aspects. The reason is that it's the only aspect that needs to be specified in detail in requirements, because access control forms an integral part of a software system itself. The recording of important "audit trails" in chronicles does, too, for the same reason. But most other forms of security can be implemented externally, like a cocoon around our precious software: a secure physical environment, firewalls, vetting of trusted employees, security procedures, and so on. You need to specify whichever of these things are within your scope—but little more than a straightforward statement of its necessity often suffices (for example, "The system shall be protected from external attack by a respected firewall product"). You can go into more detail if you like, but you must determine for yourself what else to say; that's beyond the scope of this book.

Access Control Infrastructure Considerations

Access control is important, applicable to all serious systems, and tricky to implement, so it deserves an infrastructure of its own. But this is easier said than done. First of all, what's its scope? If we stick to the basics, we don't get the full benefit. If we make it richer, it quickly becomes very intricate—with all sorts of interfaces needed between various parts, in part because we'll want to control access to the tools used to configure access control.

The following diagram shows the main areas of functionality (plus responsibility for approving actions) and some of the logical interactions between them:

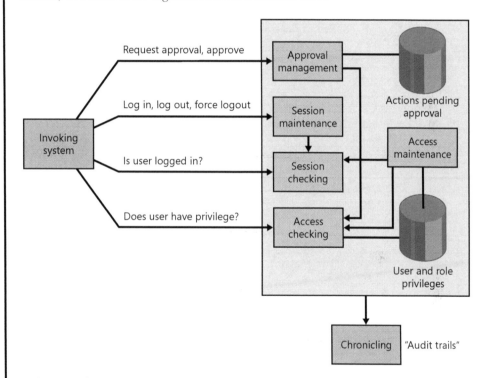

Other complications are that an access control infrastructure has maintenance functions that need to be integrated with the main system's user interface. It's also essential that the access control functions be secure; we don't want rogue software to trick the infrastructure into logging someone in, for instance, so the actual interactions could involve intricate protocols.

So while an access control infrastructure is an attractive idea, it's not possible to describe one here that would suit a wide variety of environments. This also explains why it's so hard to get third-party products to integrate with an access control regime, and why so many systems are disjointed as a result.

Access control-related requirements are necessarily often written by people who don't know a lot about security, because few organizations have a security expert on hand or can justify the expense of engaging one just to help write a few requirements. Fortunately, the requirements don't need to grapple with the intricacies of the subject or worry about the implementation challenges, which are considerable. As a result, neither do the requirement patterns here: they don't attempt to say what to do to make a system secure. So if you're going to bring in an expert, it can be more effective to do so *after* specifying the requirements. Anything to do with security is harder to achieve than it appears—because it doesn't merely have to function; it must also remain steadfast under attack, leaving no holes. Any bricklayer can build a wall, but one that resists determined assault is another matter.

11.1 User Registration Requirement Pattern

Basic Details

Related patterns:	User authentication, user authorization, data structure
Anticipated frequency:	One or two requirements
Pattern classifications:	Functional: Yes; Affects database: Yes

Applicability

Use the user registration requirement pattern to specify how new users are registered (set up in the system), with emphasis on capturing those details by which a user can later be authenticated (log in).

Discussion

Users are special. They are people, and they drive the bulk of what happens in a typical commercial system, so it's critical to know who each user is—to a greater or lesser degree of confidence depending on what we let them do. User registration, then, is more important than just another data maintenance activity. The primary aim of user registration is to record enough information to facilitate user authentication (login); everything else is secondary, though there could be quite a lot else to record.

Letting a user perform their own registration is the most convenient way, but anything they enter must be regarded as suspect (untrusted). They could supply false details (such as lying about their age), or they could enter details about someone else (which is, in some circumstances, a form of identify fraud). Alternatively, a user could be registered by a person who's already trusted, which is usually done when that person is in a position to attest to the prospective user's identity (such as if they're physically present). This is inherently much more dependable, so use it whenever it's practical (for example, for registering new employees). There is scope for more complex registration processes: to have some details entered by the user and some by someone else, or to check the veracity of certain information supplied by the user (against electoral rolls, credit reference agencies, the telephone directory, and such). This might sound invasive, but it depends on the nature of your system, the type of user, and how much faith you need in the accuracy of what the user tells you about their identity. These steps can raise the trustworthiness of the information in question, but they involve extra effort—both in operation and in development.

Content

A user registration requirement should contain:

1. **Class of users**   This identifies the type of user that is created by the registration process described by this requirement. If all users are registered in the same way, but the system treats different classes of users in different ways, explain how the user class is determined.

2. **User details**   What information do we want to record about each user? You can either list every item individually, or refer to a data structure (as per the data structure requirement pattern) that defines them, or a mixture of both. Alternatively, some details can be defined in extra requirements. Indicate which information is mandatory and which is optional. Not all information about a user needs to be entered when they register: concentrate on what information the system must be able to handle, rather than on which items must be entered during registration. It's useful to divide this information into the following five categories:

   a. **Identification details,** such as user ID, name, and email address—things used to distinguish this person from someone else. Sometimes other facts about a person are used to *assist* identification (for example date of birth), but they should be regarded as identification details in their own right only if they are essential to uniquely identify a particular person.

   b. **Authentication information,** most commonly a password. It might be augmented by further information that's called upon if the user forgets their password (such as a "secret phrase" or a few questions and answers that an impostor is unlikely to know). These details indicate that a person who knows them when logging in is the same person who registered.

   Criteria for an acceptable password can be stated here, or they can be the subject of a separate requirement. See the "Password Format" subsection of the "Extra Requirements" section of this pattern for suggestions on what to say.

   c. **Facts** about the person (that aren't used for identification), such as date of birth, title, gender, address, and phone number(s).

   If you use a biometric reader when authenticating a user, allow anyone who's physically incapable of using such a reader to be identified. (See the "Accessibility" point in the "Extra Requirements" section of the user authentication requirement pattern for more explanation.)

   d. **Preferences**. Define a user preference for each aspect of how the system behaves that the user is able to control. We needn't force a user to express their preferences when they register, but it's a good opportunity to let them do so.

   e. **Access privileges**, that define what this user is permitted to do and see. One way is for the user registration requirement to mention that one or more "roles" can be assigned to a user. This subject is covered in greater depth in the user authorization requirement patterns—though it is the registration process that assigns at least some initial access privileges to the user.

3. **Registration process**   This can be as simple as entering information about the user, or it can involve additional steps. The latter are typically to check the correctness of what we know about this user, including obtaining evidence that the user who wants to be registered is actually the person whose details have been provided. (That is, they're not an impostor.)

Extra registration steps usually involve interacting with external systems (such as a credit reference agency) or manual activities (such as examining a faxed copy of an identity document). A commonly-used step is to send an email to the user's email address and ask for a response; this merely proves that this person receives the mail sent to that address. Describe whatever you need in your case.

Even one class of users could have more than one **level** of registration. You might have rudimentary registration for basic access, but ask for more (and check more thoroughly) if a user wants to do more (that is, to be trusted more). A user's access privileges can thus be affected by which stage a non-trivial registration process has reached.

Template(s)

Summary	Definition
«*User class*» self-registration	A person shall be able to self-register as a «*User class*», by «*Registration process description*». They shall be asked to enter the following personal information: ■ «*User detail 1*». ■ «*User detail 2*». ■ ...
«*User class*» registration	It shall be possible to register a person as a «*User class*», by «*Registration process description*». The following information shall be entered about them: ■ «*User detail 1*». ■ «*User detail 2*». ■ ...

Example(s)

Summary	Definition
Customer registration	A visitor to the Web site shall be able to self-register as a customer, by entering the following details: ■ Chosen user ID * ■ Chosen password (to be entered twice) * ■ Name details, as described in requirement «*Req't ID*» * ■ Address * ■ Email address * ■ Contact telephone number ■ Gender ■ Preferred language * All items flagged with an asterisk are mandatory.

Summary	Definition
Employee registration	It shall be possible for an authorized user to register a person as an employee, by entering the following details about them:

- Full name (first, middle, and family names)
- Diminutive name (for example, "Bill")
- Job title
- Company email address
- Company telephone extension number
- Home address
- Home telephone number *
- Mobile telephone number *
- Gender
- Role(s) the employee is authorized to perform

All this information is mandatory except those flagged with an asterisk (*).

The employee shall automatically be allocated the next available employee number, which shall be displayed to the user.

An initial password shall be generated for the new employee based on the details known about them (including their employee number). The *form* of this password shall be sufficiently simple to be easily communicated to the employee without divulging its actual value, though a specific actual form is not mandated by this requirement. (For example, it could be "family name plus employee number.") When logging in for the first time, the employee shall be forced to change their password.

Extra Requirements

A user registration requirement can be accompanied by various kinds of extra requirements, most of which relate to the ongoing protection and maintenance of information initially provided at user registration. Consider which of the following areas you feel warrant requirements. Each area is discussed further in its own subsection that follows:

1. **Password format**   What criteria must a password satisfy to be acceptable?
2. **Changing password**   How and when?
3. **User de-registration**   If users can be created, it must also be possible to remove them.
4. **User data protection**   How well must we protect personal and private information about people? Are there any data protection laws we must comply with?
5. **Good security practices**   Are there any steps we want taken to encourage protecting user information? Are there any particular bad practices that we want to guard against?
6. **Special processes for new users**   Is there any more to be said about the user registration process? Are there any situations that arise with new users (such as how to tell them their initial password)?
7. **Day one considerations**   Who'll be able to use the system when it's first installed? Make sure *someone* can—and that in doing so, no security hole is left open.

Any of these things that affect users should be documented, so they can read what they're supposed to do. The documentation requirement pattern has an example requirement for a security procedures manual.

Password Format   Settling on criteria for an acceptable password involves making compromises. The best balance depends on the nature of your environment: how frequently users log in (and thus how likely they are to forget their password and need to write it down), the potential damage if a password is discovered, how likely an interested party is to discover a password that's written down, and so on. It can make sense to have separate rules for different classes of users: one for employees who use a system all day, every day, and another for visitors to a Web site. Making passwords convoluted makes them harder to guess, but also much harder to remember—and thus makes it much more likely that users will write them down. (*Long* passwords aren't necessarily unmemorable, though: a password made up of several words can be hard to crack, especially when accompanied by deviant spelling and with an unusual symbol or two thrown in.) Many apparently sensible steps that look like they improve security can actually have the opposite effect, especially when taken to extremes. Specify whatever password criteria you wish, but don't go overboard.

Summary	Definition
Customer password format	Customer passwords shall:

Customer passwords shall:

- Be at least six characters long.
- Contain at least one character from each of at least three of the following four categories:
    i.   Lowercase alphabetic (for example, a-z, ä, θ). All characters in languages that do not recognize case shall be regarded as lowercase for the purposes of this requirement.
    ii. Uppercase alphabetic (for example, A-Z, Ě, Ф).
    iii. Numeric (0-9).
    iv. Any other character (not in the first three categories).
- Not contain a string of three or more consecutive characters that can be found in any part of the user's name or user ID (when considered case-insensitively).

All passwords shall be regarded as being case-sensitive. Thus typing "open1sesame" isn't good enough if the password is "Open1Sesame."

These criteria apply to every function that can set or change a password.

This requirement is based on the Windows Vista password complexity requirements as stated at *http://www.microsoft.com/technet/windowsvista/security/security_group_policy_settings.mspx.*

Summary	Definition
Passwords difficult to guess	There shall be a table of values (dictionary of words) that may not be used as passwords. Any complete string in a password (that is, any complete sequence of alphabetic characters, but not substrings within an alphabetic sequence) that is an entry in this table shall not be allowed.

For good measure, you could ask for a utility to hunt for poorly-chosen passwords:

Summary	Definition
Password guesser	There shall be a "password guesser" utility that can be run periodically to create a list of all users whose password it was able to guess.

Changing Password   Users should be able to change their password whenever they want—for example, if they suspect that it's been compromised (because someone else might have discovered it). But unless you specify a requirement to this effect, the system is acceptable if delivered without a change password function. You might also want to force users to change their password from time to time or to restrict what they can change it to (such as not allowing the same value every time). The situation by which a user forgetting their password eventually leads to the password being changed is discussed in the user authentication requirement pattern's "Extra Requirements" section.

Summary	Definition
Change password	A user shall be able to change their own password. When changing their password, the user must enter: ■ Their current password. ■ Their new password, twice. (The second time is to guard against mis-keying, resulting in a password the user does not know.)
User password expiration	A user shall be forced to change their password the next time they log in if they have not changed it for a (configurable) given length of time.
Force user password change	There shall be a means to force a nominated user to change their password, such that the next time they attempt to log in, they shall be unable to do so until they successfully change their password to a different value.
Employee cannot reuse password	When changing their password, an employee cannot choose a password that is the same as one of their last few passwords (where the actual number is configurable). Use of this feature shall be configurable; that is, it shall be possible to switch it off.
Change employee password	There shall be a function that permits an employee to change the password of another employee. It is strongly recommended that access to this function be restricted to a very small number of users.

User De-Registration   For each function that creates users, there needs to be at least one function that removes them. Normally it should be possible to de-register them in the same manner as they were registered—which means that if a user can self-register, they can de-register on their own initiative; and if a user is added by someone else, then someone else must be able to de-register them. It might be worth writing a separate de-registration requirement for each relevant class of user, as in the following two examples:

Summary	Definition
Customer de-registration	A customer shall, provided they have no outstanding business, be able to de-register, after which they shall never be able to use the system again (unless they re-register). A customer is deemed to have outstanding business if their account has a non-zero balance or if they have one or more incomplete orders.
	When a customer is de-registered, all information of a personal nature held about them shall be deleted (except insofar as it is needed in order to comply with other legal or regulatory demands). Contact details (such as physical address or email address) and transaction details shall not be regarded as being of a personal nature for the purposes of this requirement.
Employee de-registration	It shall be possible to de-register an employee, after which they shall never be able to use the system again (unless they are re-registered).

User Data Protection   We return to the theme of users being special, this time not because they drive the system, but because they are people who are sensitive about what is known about them and about how information about them is used (and not abused). A well-specified system (and a responsibly-run business) will provide reasonable protection for user information, but that might not be enough. You need to worry about data protection and privacy laws that make further demands. These vary considerably around the world, so don't assume that what's acceptable where you live is good enough everywhere. Europe is generally stricter than the rest of the world, for instance.

Data protection is a large topic in its own right, deserving of more than this backwater subsection. But there isn't space in this book to do it justice, so we'll confine ourselves to suggestions on how to tackle this subject, list a few general guidelines, and give a few example requirements.

Here's a basic high-level process for specifying data protection requirements:

1. Find out which countries' data protection laws apply to the system. Obviously this includes the country (or all countries) in which the system is to be installed, but that might not be all. For instance, European Union data protection provisions extend to data recorded about EU residents by systems outside the EU.

2. Investigate the implications of all the applicable data protection laws, and write requirements for them. It's not good enough simply to write requirements that say, "such-and-such a

law shall be complied with"—because that encumbers someone else with figuring out what it means. (See the comply-with-standard requirement pattern in Chapter 5, "Fundamental Requirement Patterns," for more.)

3. Ask whether all demands of all data protection laws must apply from the first day the system operates, or you can obtain some leeway and postpone delivery of some features. Assign priorities to requirements accordingly.

4. Think beyond strict legal demands. Are there any practices that could cause your company embarrassment or loss of business if they became known? If so, write requirements that prevent these practices or render them unacceptable by the system. Laws that are tougher than any you need to comply with can be a source of ideas: they do, after all, exist to protect people. A list of a few key provisions follows. What's popularly regarded as acceptable can (and does) vary from one country to another, too.

5. If, along the way, you spot that a business activity that your organization is contemplating (or conceivably might contemplate in the future) could be illegal in some jurisdiction, don't let it pass. For example, you might be concerned that your company could be tempted to earn extra revenue by selling customer data. Deal with it either via a requirement, an informal note in the specification, or by bringing it the attention of senior management (depending on how likely or unlikely you feel it is to happen).

Some of the key data protection provisions are:

A. Capture only those personal details that you actually need and use.

B. Don't capture sensitive data about any person (unless it's vital to that person's use of the system, and they agree to it).

C. Don't use personal information for any other purpose than that for which it was gathered.

D. Let people know how information about them is used. In general, when a person supplies personal information, they are implicitly giving their approval for it to be used thus. But it might be appropriate for you to go further and ask them to express their consent. If the information is to be used in multiple ways, consider whether to let the user to choose which they accept. For example, you could let them opt out of receiving emails of various kinds.

E. Delete personal information as soon as it's no longer needed (including out-of-date and incorrect—and subsequently corrected—information). Because there could be other laws that mandate that we retain financial information for several years, there might be some data that we **must** keep and some that we **must not**.

F. Make provision for a person to see what information is held about them.

G. Store information about people only in the country in which the main system resides; don't move it to any other country.

A system that's built sensibly shouldn't have difficulty complying with these provisions. Don't regard this list as complete, though. Here are example requirements covering a few of these steps:

Summary	Definition
No sensitive information about any person	The system shall not record any sensitive information about any person. For the purposes of this requirement, "sensitive information" shall include all of the following:
	a. Racial or ethnic origin
	b. Political opinions
	c. Religious beliefs or other beliefs of a similar nature
	d. Membership of a trade union
	e. Physical or mental health or condition
	f. Sexual life
	g. The commission or alleged commission of any offense
	h. Proceedings for any offense committed or alleged to have been committed, the disposal of such proceedings, or the sentence of any court in such proceedings
	These provisions are in accordance with the U.K. Data Protection Act (1998), which is in line with European Union Directive 96/46/EC on data privacy. See *http://www.dataprotection.gov.uk*.
Explain use of personal information	There shall be a Web page that describes how the system uses the information it knows about a person, and the ways in which personal information is protected.
Let a person see information about them	It shall be possible to print out all the information the system stores about a selected person (except secret items used expressly for authentication, such as their password).
	The motivation for this requirement is to be able to respond to a person's request to see what information is held about them. Manual processes are needed to verify that the request comes from that person and to then furnish the print-out to them.

Good Security Practices   First of all, we want passwords to be handled securely. Requirements can't guarantee this, but you might want to force developers to make some basic precautions, as these two examples do:

Summary	Definition
Passwords never displayed	Passwords shall never be displayed on the screen when they are entered or at any other time.
Passwords undecipherable	Passwords shall be translated into an undecipherable form as close as technically possible to the point in the system at which they are entered. Any occurrence of the clear password shall be discarded immediately and never recorded in any kind of permanent storage.
	This requirement applies to every function that asks for entry of a password.
	It is strongly recommended that a one-way hashing algorithm be used for translation into an undecipherable form, because there is then no technical way to retrieve the original password from it.

Then you might want to outlaw a few bad practices such as loopholes, ways to bypass security precautions, and proliferation of software that asks users to enter secret information (such as their password). There are situations in which developers might be tempted—for honest reasons—to do something that weakens security. A few examples are:

Summary	Definition
No special user IDs	There shall be no user IDs that are treated differently by the software itself. That is, it is unacceptable for any piece of software to condition any action on the value of the user ID itself or any other user information (such as their name or address).
	The intent of this requirement is to prevent "back door" access of any kind, for any reason. This includes (but is certainly not limited to): user accounts for "demonstration" purposes; features to assist testing, debugging, problem investigation, or administration; and different handling of this user at login (such as use of a fixed password or other differences in authentication).
No access via system-generated passwords	No user shall be allowed to use a system-generated password as their normal password. The only acceptable use of a system-generated password is to give the user first-time access to the system; the user must be forced to change the password the first time they log in.
	A system-generated password is any password computed by the system itself or hard-coded within its software (though use of the latter in any circumstances is frowned upon).
Application software must not ask for password	No application software itself shall ask a user to enter their password unless that part of the software has been explicitly designated as being for security purposes.
	The intent of this requirement is to keep to a minimum the number of pieces of software that ask a user for their password, because each represents a risk—something that could be subverted to capture the password and pass it on for improper use.

Special Processes for New Users   Whenever a user is set up by someone else, we have the pesky problem of how to assign a password that only the new user knows, without the risk of someone else logging in as that new user first. Options include:

Option 1   Have the system automatically generate a password for the new user, which is then told to them. One way is to use a simple algorithm for the new password (as in the second preceding example user registration requirement), and for the new user to be told that algorithm. Always insist that a different password be generated for each user, rather than a standard password being used for everyone—because of the risk of the latter becoming widely-known. A second way to tell the user their password is to display the new password to the person setting up the account, who then tells the new user.

Option 2   Ask the new user to choose a password and type it in when their account is being set up. This insists that they be physically present, and runs the risk of the other person watching them enter their password—but at no time is it possible to log in as the new user with an artificial password.

Option 3   Ask the user to type their chosen password into a special preregistration function, which makes it available for the registration function to pick up later. Such a function must comply with all requirements for the secure handling of passwords (such as storing them in an undecipherable form).

The second option doesn't need extra requirements. Here are a couple for the first option:

Summary	Definition
New employee must change password	The first time a new employee uses the system, they must change their password.
Block inactive new employee	If a new employee has not logged in within a given length of time (say, three hours) after being set up, their access to the system shall be blocked.
	The purpose of this requirement is to limit the risk of another person discovering the absence of the new employee, being able to guess the initial password generated for them, and effectively taking over the new employee's account.

Day One Considerations   More than a few systems have been installed and started up on their first day—only for the project team's pride to be replaced by red faces when it's realized that no one can log in and no one can register a new user. Since it's a one-off occurrence, this might sound like it doesn't deserve a place in the requirements. But solving it might leave an ongoing security flaw, so it's best that everyone be made aware of the potential risk. We don't want a surreptitious utility to be built that can set up new users and then hangs around in the hands of one or two developers or systems administrators. If such a utility is needed, make sure it's known about and kept under strict control. Here's an example requirement to prevent one cause of a bad first day:

Summary	Definition
New system usable	When the system is freshly installed, it shall be usable by someone, at least to the extent that they can set up a new user and grant them access to system functions.
	The purpose of this requirement is to prevent a newly-installed system from being unusable by anyone.
	Any special processing needed to render the system usable before any real users have been registered shall be permanently disabled or removed from the system as soon as at least one real user has been registered.

Considerations for Development

The range of topics raised in this requirement pattern makes it clear that there is much to think about. The best advice is simply to take user registration seriously and not to cut corners. Always handle secret values (such as passwords) securely: at the first opportunity, render them indecipherable, and destroy the clear form.

Considerations for Testing

A user registration function is basically a data entry function and should be tested as such. Test the entry and validation of all values. Test that validation is not performed only on an untrusted client device (a remote user's PC). Test that any values that are intended to be secret (such as passwords) are treated as such, and cannot be viewed using the system (such as via inquiries or reports or obtained from logs or from querying the database).

Testing that a user registration process is secure cannot be done solely by *using* the system. It's a specialized activity (as discussed in the user authentication requirement pattern).

11.2 User Authentication Requirement Pattern

Basic Details

Related patterns:	Accessibility
Anticipated frequency:	One or two requirements
Pattern classifications:	Functional: Yes

Applicability

Use the user authentication requirement pattern to specify that a person must make their identity known to the system before they can access anything non-public or anything for which they cannot remain anonymous (in short, anything for which they must log in).

Discussion

Authentication is the process by which a registered user declares who they are and proves this assertion to the system's satisfaction. This requirement pattern says little on the subject beyond what is of interest to requirements; it doesn't worry about the considerable challenges of implementing a secure system. The most widespread form of authentication in commercial systems is just asking the user to enter their user ID and password, and that's what this requirement pattern concentrates on. The common name for user authentication is "logging in." (This book prefers logging *in* to logging *on*—on the basis that *entering* a system is a better metaphor than *climbing atop* it. Let's also point out that, as a verb, to "log in" is two words: "to log someone in" sounds fine, and is only possible if there is a gap in which to squeeze "someone.")

There are three accepted ways to check that a person is who they claim to be: something they **know** (such as a password), something they **have** (such as an ID card), and something they **are** (using a part of their body that can be distinguished from that of everyone else—such as a finger or an eye). Depending on how secure you want your authentication process to be, you can ask for more than one (a password *and* an ID card *and* a fingerprint, if you insist). There are various factors that affect what's best in a particular situation, including:

Factor 1: The potential damage that an impostor could cause   This depends on what the user has access to—not just which functions but also other assets (for example, a customer who has a large sum of money in their account), so you might want to consider stronger authentication for users who have the greatest powers (or valuables) in the system. Also consider possible *indirect* damage, such as to the company's reputation if unauthorized access became public knowledge.

Factor 2: The type of device on which the user self-authenticates   This could preclude certain kinds of authentication. For example, you can't expect the average Internet user to have a card reader attached to their PC (at least, not at the time of writing).

Factor 3: The local environment of the user   How trusted or untrusted is the user's device by virtue of where it resides? Is it snug inside a company office, or in the wilds outside? Is the user likely to have someone looking over their shoulder when self-authenticating? (Note that when using an ATM, you *don't* enter both a user ID and PIN; your bank card—which a spy can't see—says *who* you are.)

Authentication can be regarded as creating a **user session**, which grants the user access until the session ends. This might sound like an implementation contrivance, but it's not—and it makes some aspects easier to discuss (especially a few of the extra requirements that follow). It appears a good idea to prevent a user from having more than one session at the same time, but it can be problematic, due to technical unreliability (especially with communications). A user is liable to get frustrated if they "return" after a failure, attempt to log in, and are refused because they already have a session (which they cannot use). On the other hand, letting a user have many active sessions can cause problems, too. If you allow a user to have more than one session simultaneously, a history of their actions only makes sense if you show each session separately. One option is for logging in to terminate all previous sessions—but there are circumstances where that's awkward, too (for example, if a user is active and someone who has purloined their password then logs in).

Content

A user authentication requirement should contain:

1. **Class of users**   Which users does this requirement apply to? "All users" is an acceptable class.

2. **Authentication mechanism(s)**   How do you expect the users to identify themselves? You could be specific (entry of a user ID and password, for example), or you could just describe the level of security needed and leave the details up to the development team. Avoid mention of specific technologies as far as possible.

    You could also keep the login function for one class of user separate from that for other classes of users. For instance, you might not want Web customers anywhere near the login function used by employees.

3. **Initiated by**   When do users need to authenticate themselves? You could force users to log in to gain *any* access, or you could let them wander around anonymously and invite them to log in only if they want to do something that demands it. Both approaches have their place, and you might choose to treat different classes of users differently. For example, force employees to log in before they can do anything, but let Web site visitors log in when they want to. Another factor to bear in mind is that knowing who someone is as early as possible lets you record their actions, though you might irritate users if you insist on them logging in earlier than strictly necessary.

    Alternatively, you could leave the matter open—though for completeness, you could state that users must have authenticated themselves before doing anything that depends on their identities being known.

Template(s)

Summary	Definition
«User class» authentication/ login	A *«User class»* shall be able to self-authenticate (log in) by *«Authentication step(s)»*. [*«Initiated by description»*.]

Example(s)

Don't simply copy any of the requirements given here or in the "Extra Requirements" section. None of them suits all situations.

Summary	Definition
User authentication	A user shall be able to self-authenticate (log in), and must do so before they can access any function or information that is not publicly or anonymously accessible.
	The level of security offered by the mechanism used to authenticate a particular user (or class of users) shall be appropriate to the extent and sensitivity of the access they have (that is, the amount of damage that a malicious impostor could inflict). It is acceptable to use different login mechanisms for different classes of users.
	Customers and employees shall be kept apart to the extent that a customer shall not be able to log in as an employee simply by entering an employee's user ID and password into a customer login screen.
Customer authentication	A customer shall be able to self-authenticate (log in) by entering their user ID and password. They can choose to log in at any time (by visiting the login page)—but if they have not logged in when they attempt an action for which their identity must be known, they shall be prompted to log in and not allowed to proceed with the action until they have done so.
	The identity of each customer must be determined before they may initiate or view transactions. This shall be achieved by the customer entering their user ID and password.

Observe that the first example doesn't mention any particular authentication mechanism.

Extra Requirements

A user authentication requirement looks straightforward and self-contained, but there are various related matters you can specify in extra requirements, mostly to limit the misuse of user accounts. These include the following (each of which is covered in its own subsection that follows—except accessibility, which is covered in the accessibility requirement pattern in Chapter 8, "User Function Requirement Patterns").

1. **Forgotten password handling**   People forget things. They forget their passwords, especially if you force them to be long or to use strange combinations of characters. What happens then?

2. **User de-authentication**   (Logging out.) If you let someone in, you should let them out again—to tell you they've finished for now.

3. **Ending user sessions**   We can't allow a user session to last forever, so we need at least one way to bring it to an end. First, limit the duration of each session. It's also useful to let an operator terminate a selected user session (if a user appears to be up to no good, for instance) or all—or nearly all—sessions prior to shutting the system down.

4. **Absent user protection**   If a user's done nothing for a while, they might have stepped away from their machine, so we might want to try to stop someone else nipping in and doing things in that user's name.

5. **Helping users spot breaches**   Users themselves represent an army of people with a strong interest in discovering any abuse of their own accounts. So why not help them do it? Help them detect whether someone else has logged in with their user ID, and give them a way of signaling security breaches.

6. **Blocking users**   (So they can't log in.) There are several reasons for denying a user access to the system, including repeated entry of the wrong password, because they're going away (an employee taking a vacation, say), or simply because they've misbehaved. If users can be blocked, we need a way to unblock them. Finally, the ability to prevent *anybody* from logging in is handy—shortly before shutting down the system, if at no other time.

7. **Viewing user sessions**   Looking at current user sessions can tell you about what's going on in the system *now*. Storing session information and being able to study it *later* can help you investigate a breach of security and is a good source of statistics.

8. **Accessibility**   If you're using biometrics to check a person's identity, you should provide an alternative for people who are unable to offer the required body part to the device that reads it (because they don't possess it, lack mobility, or some other reason). This is a provision of Section 508 of the U.S. Rehabilitation Act. See the accessibility requirement pattern in Chapter 8 for more, including an example requirement (in the "General Accessibility" subsection of its "Extra Requirements" section). Beware of opening a security gap if you allow biometric authentication to be bypassed. Don't allow just anyone to say they're incapable of using a biometric reader; only allow nominated users to do so.

Forgotten Password Handling   We must be able to get a user back on track when they forget their password, for which occasion, we need another way for them to prove their identity. This is straightforward enough in an environment where the user is known personally to someone who can vouch for their identity (such as colleagues in an office): a trusted user can run a function into which the hapless user can enter a new password.

In the absence of a trusted second person who can verify a user's identity (for instance, when a customer wishes to use our Web site), we're likely to be forced to resort to more dubious means. A common stratagem is to ask the user for additional "secret" information when they register—either a "secret phrase" or one or more questions along with their answers. (Registration can suggest questions: what was the name of you first pet? The make of your first car?) This typically results in values that are easier to guess than a password, and often not secret at all. In recognition of this, it's best not to depend solely on this "secret" information to identify the user. Two extra steps are as follows. First, to ask the user to speak on the telephone to an operator, who can bring to bear their personal judgment about whether the user is genuine (and ask extra questions). Second, test whether this person is able to receive communications sent to the user (which can use any of the user's contact details—such as their home address or telephone number, but most often their email address, because it's quick and the sending of an email can be automated). Both these steps are weak from a security standpoint.

Whenever you're thinking about involving an operator in the forgotten password process, consider the potential operational cost, especially if the number of users is large. For systems that don't handle forgotten passwords automatically, this is one of the most numerous types of calls to help desks.

Summary	Definition
Customer forgets password	If a customer forgets their password, they shall be able to log in by entering the "secret phrase" they supplied when they registered plus a verification code sent to their email address.
	This shall be achieved by using the following process:
	1. The customer indicates via the login screen that they have forgotten their password.
	2. The system emails a one-off verification code to their registered email address (to prove this person can receive emails sent to it).
	3. Upon receipt of the verification code, the customer can log in by entering it plus their secret phrase. They are forced to change their password before they can proceed.
Customer forgets secret phrase	If a customer forgets both their password and secret phrase, there shall be a means of last resort whereby they can prove their identity and have a new password assigned to them.
	This shall be achieved by using the following process (or one equivalent to it):
	1. The customer is asked to phone a customer support number to speak to a helpdesk operator.
	2. The helpdesk operator establishes the customer's identity by asking questions about their registration information and recent transactions.
	3. The operator unblocks the customer's account and tells the customer a new (computer generated) one-off password.
	4. The system emails a new verification code to the customer.
	5. The customer uses the new password and verification code to log in and is forced to change their password and secret phrase (so the helpdesk operator doesn't know them).

User De-Authentication (Logging Out)   Give users the opportunity to log out explicitly, so they can prevent someone else from slipping into their seat after they've gone and performing actions in their guise. Do this even in environments where users rarely log out. For example, visitors usually leave a Web site simply by moving on to another one, or by exiting their browser— but someone in an Internet café won't want a complete stranger to be able to carry on where they left off. Logging out has the effect of ending the user's session. If you allow a user to have multiple sessions simultaneously, you must decide whether logging out applies to all of them or just to the one in which the logout was performed (both of which have their down sides)—or you could let the user choose.

Summary	Definition
User de-authentication	A user shall be able to de-authenticate (log out). After de-authentication, the system shall treat them just as if they had not been authenticated in the first place and shall regard all subsequent actions as being performed by an unknown user.

Ending User Sessions   It's good practice to limit the duration of a user session, to force a user to prove it's really them from time to time. Without such a limit, a user could log in once and continue to use the system indefinitely. When a session is about to end, ask the user to establish their identity again, and don't permit them to continue to use the system until they do so. If possible, do this in a natural break in what the user is doing (at the end of a transaction, say): be polite. It also helps to let the user know that we're doing this for their own security. The duration of a session should be somewhat longer than users are typically continuously active, so we might set it at twelve hours for an employee, or three hours for a Web site customer. Logging out also ends a user session (as described in the previous subsection). If you can reliably discern that a user is leaving, you can end their session; this depends on the technology being used.

Summary	Definition
User session timeout	Every user session shall automatically end (time out) a length of time after it began. The length of time shall be configurable per class of user.
	When a timeout is imminent, the user shall be invited to reauthenticate (log in again), which shall allow them to continue using the system without interrupting any functions they happen to be using at the time. If they do not reauthenticate, the system shall reject any further requests from this session.
Exiting client application ends user session	When a user exits the client application, any user session opened by that application shall be terminated.

Notice that the first preceding example carefully sidesteps the question of whether it *extends* the existing user session or *creates a new one*. Developers might have strong views on the subject, but it's solely a matter for them: it doesn't concern the requirements, so steer clear of it here.

Next, it's useful for an operator to be able to peremptorily terminate a selected user session: without it, you'd be hamstrung in halting a user who's discovered performing nefarious activities. Taking this one small step further gives us the ability to terminate all active user sessions (or all sessions for a particular class of users—such as all customers), which can be useful if we want to shut the system down. Oh, and remember not to terminate the killer operator's own session!

Summary	Definition
Terminate user session(s)	An employee shall be able to terminate a selected active user session, all active sessions for a selected class of users, or all active user sessions. They shall not be able to terminate *their own* user session.

If we can give a user advance notice that their session will end shortly, it's polite to do so. For example, if their session is nearing its time-out time, we could notify them, so they can log out and log in again with minimal inconvenience.

Absent User Protection   If an active user suddenly stops doing anything, it could be because they've walked off and left their machine all alone. A Web site customer who simply goes to another site (or shuts down their browser) without logging out can leave an open session. In these situations, we don't want someone else to be able to wander up (metaphorically in the case of an Internet attacker) and, as far as the system's concerned, impersonate the original user. If you want to prevent this, you can either write a requirement that expresses this intent, or write one for a specific way to prevent it—the commonest being an inactivity time-out, after which we ask the user to type in their password upon their return before they are allowed to proceed. We can then take this one stage further and let the user tell the system they're leaving their machine temporarily: that is, effectively to trigger the inactivity time-out immediately.

One awkward feature of locking a session can be (depending on the technology used) that it prevents anyone else from using the machine—which can be irritating. One way around this is to allow someone else to break the lock (though not to take over the original user's session, nor to see what they were doing). A further refinement is to let a user locking their session to say whether they're prepared to let it be broken.

Summary	Definition
User inactivity time-out	If a user with an active session has had no interaction with the system for longer than a configurable length of time, then the next time they make a request, they shall be asked to enter their password before they can proceed.
	The motivation for this requirement is to protect against someone attempting to take over a user's session when the user has walked away from their machine.
Lock user session	A user shall be able lock their current session, to indicate that they are about to leave their machine unattended. They must enter their password before they can proceed.
	When initiating the session lock, the user shall be able to indicate whether another user can break the lock. (Ordinarily, they should allow it to be broken, but might want to prevent it if they're in the middle of an important task.)
Break locked session	It shall be possible to break a user session that has been locked as a result of an inactivity time-out or an explicit lock. The person wishing to break the lock must enter their user ID and password, which terminates the original user's session and creates a session for the new user.

Helping Users Spot Breaches   A system cannot tell the difference between a legitimate user and someone else who's discovered their user ID and password, so a system can never detect a security breach of this kind. But if we tell the user a little about their last session (typically, the time they last logged in), they're in a position to judge whether someone else has been impersonating them in the meantime. Here's a requirement for the commonest way:

Summary	Definition
Show last login time at login	When a user has been successfully authenticated, the time at which they last logged in shall be displayed. The purpose of this requirement is to give them the opportunity to discover whether an imposter has been acting in their name since they last used the system.

If we help users detect misuse of their account, we should provide them with a way to tell us about it. You might think existing means of communication suffice, but it can be worth doing a little more. Here's one suggestion:

Summary	Definition
Notify operator of security breach	A user shall have a way to notify an operator of a security breach. If a standard notification method is used, it shall distinguish security breaches from other communications, to facilitate dealing with it as a matter of high priority. If email is the notification medium, a special email address shall be used for notifying security breaches, and users shall have a way of discovering this email address.

Think about what an operator should do when notified of a suspected breach of this kind. Have you specified requirements for tools that enable them to investigate (such as to view user sessions—discussed shortly)? Bear in mind that false alarms will probably greatly outnumber genuine misuses.

Blocking Users   By "blocking" a user, we mean preventing them from logging in to the system. There several situations in which we might want to block a user, including:

A.   The user enters their password incorrectly too many times in a row when logging in—because this might suggest someone else guessing and trying to impersonate them. It might be convenient for everyone for such a block to last for a short period of time only (an hour, say). We can afford to be relatively generous in the number of attempts to give a user to enter their password (25 or 50, say), because the chances of an attacker guessing the password in this way is still tiny (despite what Hollywood might have you believe). Systems that give a user only three attempts merely irritate the user and lead to more requests to whoever looks after unblocking user accounts (plus, for employees, loss of productivity until it's done).

B.   A user might wish to block their own access for a certain length of time, if they know they're going to be away (such as before leaving on vacation).

C.   An operator might wish to block a user who has been acting improperly or suspiciously.

If user accounts can become blocked, we need a way to unblock them. A useful related function is the ability to prevent all users (or a whole class of users—such as all customers) from logging in. This can be invoked prior to shutting down the system, to avoid frustrating users by kicking them out soon after they log in.

Summary	Definition
Block after successive invalid passwords	If a user enters their password incorrectly a given number of times in a row in one session, their account shall be blocked. The tolerable number of times shall be configurable per user class. (Suggested values are 50 for customers and 20 for employees—on the basis that impersonation of an employee is likely to have more serious consequences, and the far higher number of customers makes unblocking them a much bigger burden.)
Block own access	An employee shall be able to block their own access to the system for a specified length of time.
	The motivation for this requirement is to prevent improper access to an employee's account during known absences (such as vacations). If they return earlier than expected, they must ask an authorized other user to remove the block.
Block/unblock selected user	An authorized employee shall be able to block or unblock a selected user.
Disable/enable login	It shall be possible to switch off and on the ability of all users of a selected class to log in.

Viewing User Sessions   User sessions contain valuable information—both about what's currently happening in the system and about which users accessed the system when. It's wasteful to simply discard or ignore this potential treasure. So store it, and let it be exploited. It might help identify a breach of security (after the fact), if nothing else.

Summary	Definition
Active sessions inquiry	It shall be possible to list all user sessions that are currently active and then to display all details about a selected session.
Own session inquiry	A user shall be able to view details about their current session and previous recent sessions.
	The motivation for this requirement is to let a user see whether someone else has been accessing their account—by spotting sessions they don't know about.

Summary	Definition
Store user sessions	All details about each user session shall be recorded in some form of persistent storage (such as a database). These details shall include: ■ User ID. ■ Start date and time. ■ Identity of machine or terminal from which the user is accessing the system. The identity to record is liable to depend on the connection mechanism (for example, the machine name if over a local network or the IP address if via the Internet). ■ Authentication method (for example, password, secret phrase, or smartcard). ■ End date and time. ■ Limit date and time: when the session would time out. ■ Cause of session end. Causes include logging out, timing out, and termination by operator. Session details shall be stored at the time the session starts and be updated whenever any item of information changes.
Old sessions inquiry	It shall be possible to list all user sessions that were active at a nominated point in time and to display all details about a selected session.
User session statistics report	There shall be a report that shows, for each day in a selected date range, the number of user sessions that began in each hour during that day and their average duration. Separate figures shall be shown for each class of users (customers and employees).

Considerations for Development

Requirements related to user authentication merely specify necessary features; they don't worry about the complexities, of which there are many—too many to relate here.

Coding a login function is almost as easy as a "Hello World" program. But doing it securely is considerably more difficult. Take into account all the good practices described in this requirement pattern, even if they're not formally required. Turn the password entered by the user into an undecipherable form as soon as possible, and overwrite the clear form in memory.

Considerations for Testing

The testing of user authentication needs to be performed at two very different levels:

■ **Functional**   Does the authentication process work properly in all circumstances normally encountered in the running of the system? Test it just as you would any user function: the entry and validation of values, expected responses, and so on. Test that a user who has not logged in has no non-public privileges. Test that after a user logs in, they can access whatever they are authorized to.

Similarly, test all features discussed in the "Extra Requirements" section: the action and effect of logging out, session time-out, and so on.

- **Security**   Not only must user authentication work, it must also do so in a secure manner. It must prevent anyone else from learning sensitive information (especially user passwords). It must prevent the authentication process from being bypassed, subverted, or otherwise tricked. This is a specialized field. It involves replicating the wide variety of techniques that potential attackers could exploit, most of which are very sophisticated and highly technical. For example, someone listening to traffic between a user's machine and a central system can attempt a "replay" attack; this can only be tested by undertaking this kind of attack. This subject is beyond the scope of this requirement pattern; refer to specialized resources and consider bringing in an expert.

Ask for features that will assist testing. These include a way to view details about user sessions (especially when they end, so you can test that they time-out properly). To achieve this, we need the beginning and end of every user session to be recorded.

11.3 User Authorization Requirement Patterns

The purpose of access control is to restrict users to doing and seeing only what they should. This section talks about "what a user can do and see" as a concise way of referring respectively to the functions and the information they can access. Collectively they are referred to as **privileges** that they confer upon a user (or "access rights" or "permissions," though this book calls them privileges throughout). It's also worth recognizing that as far as a system is concerned, a user never does anything directly, so we mean what various parts of the system do on a user's behalf.

Access control is used most widely to control which **functions** someone can use. For example, a customer service operator could be granted access to all customer service functions, but little else. Functional access control can be extended to individual actions within a function (such as the ability to *change*, but not to *add*)—and while greater granularity gives more control, it takes more work both to develop and to maintain. Access control requirements can also restrict the **information** a user can see and can be used for other purposes (the commonest of which are spelled out in the specific authorization requirement pattern). These ways can be applied in combination. For example, a user might be granted access to one set of functions for one company and a different set of functions for another company. But this can get complicated: if you get away with authorizing access to functions and to information *independently*, life is much simpler.

There are two types of user authorization requirements: the first defines **specific privileges** (according to some access rule, such as for a named set of users); the second demands a **general ability to configure** who can do what. Each has its own requirement pattern. You can use both in a specification, in which case a configurable authorization requirement guides the capabilities of the system, and to guide its configuration, you can use specific authorization requirements (acting as a useful place to put knowledge gathered, to make setting up the system easier). A configurable authorization requirement is in effect an instruction to implement an access control infrastructure.

Regardless of how you choose to define who can do what, you should start by stating what access is allowed in absence of any guidance to the contrary. After all, a requirement saying that "A can do X" has little force if there's nothing to prevent everyone else from doing X. The most sensible approach to take is **denial by default**. That is, *everything* is to be inaccessible to every user, unless permission is granted to them either explicitly or by defining some things as publicly accessible.

The denial by default rule can either be specified as a special kind of specific authorization requirement, or it can be incorporated within the main configurable authorization requirements (as the first two example requirements in the configurable authorization requirement pattern do).

Bring as much of the system's activities within the ambit of access control as possible. Many system administrators, database administrators, and developers believe they're exempt from controls that apply to mere mortals. This mentality permeates many products, unfortunately, which can make it difficult to control them. Another difficulty with products is that they're unlikely to be amenable to cooperating with any access control regime you put in place. This could influence product selection decisions if you're serious about security.

Extra Requirements

Regardless of how you choose to specify user authorization, there are a few extra topics worth considering:

1. **Presentation and usability**   To bring *navigation* of the system into line with what the user can actually do and see, rather than wasting their time by showing functions they're not allowed to use.

2. **Delegating authority**   To let one person act on another's behalf.

3. **Preventing loopholes**   To prevent our efforts at access control being circumvented.

Each of these topics has it own subsection that follows. One more does not, because it's covered in its own requirement pattern:

4. **Approval**   Some activities might warrant approval by a second person (or even a third) before they can proceed. This topic is discussed in the approval requirement pattern.

Presentation and Usability   Systems have a natural inclination to appear stupid unless special steps are taken to prevent it. Denying access is one thing; not looking stupid in the process is something else—and one worth treating carefully, because it can save much time, effort, and frustration during the life a system. Don't clog menus with functions that the user isn't authorized to use; don't let them choose values that they're not allowed to, only to slap them in the face if they try.

How much should we tell users about the existence of things to which they're not allowed access? It's naïve to assume they'll not be aware of most of them in one way or another. (It's impractical to produce lots of different sets of user documentation, for instance—though online documentation attached to each function suffers less from this difficulty.) It's counterproductive to hide the existence of some functions, because a user might need to ask someone with extra privileges to do something for them—so they must be aware that other person can do more than they can. Awareness of inaccessible data is a different matter; in a multi-company system, for example, it might be essential to hide other companies completely.

Here are a few example requirements that aim to make access control more friendly in various ways:

Summary	Definition
Hide inaccessible functions	Places from which functions are normally selected (for example, in menus and as buttons or hyperlinks) shall not display functions to which the current user does not have access.
Disable controls for inaccessible functions	Places from which functions are normally selected (for example, in menus and as buttons or hyperlinks) shall display in a disabled manner those functions to which the current user does not have access.

Summary	Definition
Selection criteria omit inaccessible values	Selection criteria displayed by functions (such as inquiries and reports) shall not display values associated with data the user is not authorized to see (for example, in drop-down lists from which values can be chosen).
Let start only if can finish	The system shall not allow a user to begin an activity if they are not authorized to complete it.
	The motivation for this requirement is to avoid frustrating users.

Delegating Authority   Real businesses are intricate beasts whose managers quite reasonably want to decide who performs what tasks. If managers need a system to offer a particular kind of operational flexibility, it must be expressly built into the system. One kind of operational flexibility involving access control is the ability to delegate authority to someone else, as in this example:

Summary	Definition
Delegate authority	An employee shall be able to grant authority to another employee to act on their behalf.
	The delegator shall be able to nominate which privileges the delegatee can exercise in their name, including setting access-related limits.
	The motivation for this requirement is to allow a personal assistant to perform administrative tasks in place of the manager for which they work.
Assume delegated authority	An employee who has the authority to act on another employee's behalf shall be able to indicate to the system that they wish to do so. Any action they take thereafter shall carry the imprimatur of both users (done by B on behalf of A). When they have finished, they shall be able to indicate they have stopped acting on the other employee's behalf.
	Note that assuming delegated authority can grant a user privileges they do not normally have.

Preventing Loopholes   It's possible to implement access control as a thin veneer around a system that, once punctured, leaves the system completely unprotected. It's not the responsibility of requirements to figure out every kind of attack and the provisions needed to guard against it, but we can write requirements that point out potential loopholes we want to guard against, like this one:

Summary	Definition
Cannot bypass authentication	It shall not be possible to cause any part of the system to take any action on behalf of a user unless that part of the system has evidence that user has been authenticated.
	The intent of this requirement is to guard against being able to bypass normal controls to ask a system component to do something directly. This applies in particular to server processes (for example, where one process checks the user's identity and another process does whatever it's told).

11.4 Specific Authorization Requirement Pattern

Basic Details

Related patterns:	Extends user authorization; refers to configurable authorization
Anticipated frequency:	Up to a dozen requirements
Pattern classifications:	None

Applicability

Use the specific authorization requirement pattern to specify that a set of users is authorized (or is not authorized) to do or see certain things.

Do not use the specific authorization requirement pattern to specify that user authorization is to be configurable; use the configurable authorization requirement pattern for that.

Discussion

A specific authorization requirement makes a statement—of any kind—that affects what a certain set of users can see and do. These requirements can vary considerably, but they generally fall into one of the following categories (or possibly more than one—which is most frequently seen in combinations of Categories 2 and 4):

Category 1: Universal denial-by-default rule   To assert that nothing of value in the system is accessible unless permission is expressly granted.

Category 2: Functions   Functions that certain kinds of people are authorized to use. A requirement can either name an individual function or a class of functions.

Category 3: Actions within functions   For example, a user might be authorized to change details but not add or delete something or other.

Category 4: Data   To restrict access to certain information.

Category 5: Limits   Limits on values a user is allowed to work with—such as a monetary amount up to which they are authorized to perform a certain action (for example, a refund to a customer).

Category 6: Time   To restrict *when* certain privileges can be used (what times of day and/or days of the week).

Category 7: Environment   To apply restrictions to certain environments (such as remote access).

Category 8: Strength of authentication   To allow a user to do more if they logged in using a strong authentication mechanism (such as a smartcard) than they could do if they used a weaker mechanism (such as when they have mislaid the card and just entered their password).

Category 9: Transference   Where a restriction applied in one situation is transferred to apply in the same way to something else (such as data copied into a chronicle being subject to the same protection as the original data).

Category 10: Operational rules   To achieve such things as division of responsibility (so that the same person can't both perform and then approve a transaction, for instance).

Category 11: Blanket bans   Things that *no one* may have access to—mainly functions that are present anyway but which it's bad practice to use day-to-day in a commercial system (such as unrestricted access to the database or operating system).

Category 12: Blanket permission   Things that *everyone* can access without restriction. Publicly available things normally don't warrant a separate requirement to say so, but you might encounter a situation that deserves it.

Use this list to help identify what you need: go through each point in turn. Each one can be regarded as an **access rule** that the organization wishes to apply to the operation of its system. (If you'd like to apply certain rules more widely than just within one system, pull them out into a separate requirements specification—"common requirements"—and then refer to them in the requirements for each system to which they apply, as per the refer-to-requirements requirement pattern.) Recognize the bounds of what the system can realistically restrict access to—and don't waste your time trying to control anything beyond those bounds. That might include hardware, other systems, and third-party software used to implement part of the system. You might be forced to make unpleasant compromises.

Content

A specific authorization requirement needs to convey two things: **who** and **what**. The preceding list is of various kinds of *what*. As for *who*, express it in whatever terms are appropriate—but be clear. Don't name particular users (people). Mention roles or job titles, if you like, but if you do, define them either within the requirement or elsewhere (as informal material). This is important, because if you don't, readers are apt to interpret them differently. (Someone else's picture of a "systems administrator" might not accord with yours, for example, aside from theirs having green hair and yours purple.) If you're building a system to be used in multiple places, they might be organized very differently; make it as easy as possible for everyone to see how your system would fit their environment.

A specific authorization requirement should contain:

1. **Privilege description**   (*What.*) It can be anything to which access can be granted (or denied), but is most commonly the name of a function.

2. **Access rule**   (*Who*, and in which circumstances.) Most commonly, it identifies a **type of user**, and at its simplest, it says that such users are granted the relevant privilege. But put whatever you want into a rule—including conditions and other logic.

Template(s)

Summary	Definition
«Privilege summary» access	*«Privilege description»* shall [not] be accessible *«Access rule description»*.
«Privilege summary» access	A *«Type of user»* shall [not] be able to *«Privilege description»*.

Example(s)

The examples here are presented according to the categories listed in this pattern's "Discussion" section (along with a few that are combinations of Categories 2 and 4).

Category 1, a universal denial-by-default rule:

Summary	Definition
Denial of access by default	A user shall have no access to any function or information or other system resource unless they have been explicitly been granted permission, or unless it has been designated publicly accessible. In the case of information designated as publicly accessible, this shall be taken to mean only the ability to *view* the information, unless explicitly specified otherwise.

Category 2, functions (starting with one you might regard as so obvious that it goes without saying, although a stickler could argue that without it, unrestricted access is acceptable):

Summary	Definition
Access only when logged in	A user shall not have access to non-public functions or information if they have not logged in or have logged out.
Limited casual visitor access	A casual visitor to the Web site (who has not been authenticated as a customer) shall have only limited access. They shall not be able to even initiate any function that involves money (such as placing an order).
Employee maintenance access	The ability to maintain information about an employee (add, change, and remove) shall be limited to members of the human resources department.
Employee access to customer inquiries	A customer service operator shall be able to access all inquiries accessible by customers, to view exactly what any selected customer would. The operator shall be able to do this only for customers of the company for whom the operator works. It is not acceptable to achieve this by having an operator log in as the customer. The purpose of this is to allow an operator to explain to the customer any information they have difficulty understanding, and to see exactly what the customer sees: identical data in an identical format.

Category 3, actions within functions:

Summary	Definition
Customer maintenance	Each type of action that can be performed within the customer maintenance function shall be subject to separate access privileges. "Type of action" shall include changes to address and credit limit.

Category 4, data:

Summary	Definition
Service bureau has access to client companies	Employees of the service bureau shall have the same access to each of its client companies as the employees of those companies themselves have.

Summary	Definition
Company financial information access	Company financial information shall be accessible only by members of the finance department and senior managers. For the purpose of this requirement, "company financial information" means figures pertaining to the overall performance of the company, and other information of an accounting nature; customer order and payment information are not classed as company financial information.
Inquiries and reports not to show inaccessible data	No inquiry or report shall show data to which the current user does not have access. Where appropriate, inaccessible data shall be "filtered out." This shall be done in such a manner that summary information (totals, averages, and so on) are consistent with the data that is shown.

Categories 2 and 4 combined, both functions and data:

Summary	Definition
Configuration maintenance access	Only nominated employees shall be allowed to modify configuration parameters, and then only in areas expressly designated. For example, a finance manager might be allowed to modify only finance-related parameters.
Company can run agents' reports	The company shall be able to run for its own use all the reports available to its sales agents, to show information for any selected agent.

Category 5, limits:

Summary	Definition
Customer refund limit	An employee shall be able to approve a refund to a customer up to (and including) the refund limit set for them.

Category 6, time:

Summary	Definition
Initiate transactions only during nominated hours	An employee shall be able to initiate transactions during nominated hours of the day. It shall be possible to specify these hours of the day for each employee, but if they have not been set for an employee, a configurable default range of hours shall be used.

Category 7, environment:

Summary	Definition
Employee remote access	An employee shall be able to access the system from outside company premises if authorized to do so (and not otherwise).

Category 8, strength of authentication:

Summary	Definition
Reduced access by employee without smartcard	An employee who has been issued a smartcard but who logs in without it shall not during that session be able to initiate or approve financial transactions.

Category 9, transference:

Summary	Definition
Log data access as per original data	Access to data stored in a log shall be restricted to at least the same degree as access to the original data itself.
	For example, if a user is allowed to see customer details only for one company, they shall not be able to view details of a log entry about a customer associated with another company.
Query information access	Information that satisfies a query by a user shall be filtered to exclude anything the user does not have permission to view.
Document comments access	Access to comments made on any document shall be subject to the same controls as the document itself.

Category 10, operational rules (of which there is a further example in the "Cannot Approve Own Action" section in the approval requirement pattern):

Summary	Definition
Cannot extend own authority	No user shall be able to modify their own access privileges. In particular, no user shall be able to extend their own privileges.
View own orders only	The system shall permit a customer to view only orders that they placed, not orders placed by other customers.

Category 11, blanket bans:

Summary	Definition
No unauthenticated, uncontrolled, or blanket access	Every activity required for the normal commercial operation of the system shall be subject to all the access control requirements in this document. This requirement demands in particular:
	1. Low-level access to any database shall not be required. This includes SQL queries and any application that permits access equivalent to SQL queries.
	2. Command line access shall be restricted as per the next requirement.
	If or when this requirement is satisfied by all systems running on a particular server machine, then any of the above types of access described as "shall not be needed" can and should be toughened to "shall not be permitted."
	(Even if, for the operation of other systems, users must be granted uncontrolled access of the sorts this requirement is intended to prevent, policies should insist that those mechanisms not be used in relation to *this* system.)
	This requirement does not apply to steps necessary to rectify serious system problems, reconfiguration, or installation. Nevertheless, in those cases, this requirement should be relaxed only as far as is necessary to get those jobs done. (To compensate for the reduction in security in such situations, it is recommended that additional manual controls be applied—such as closely supervising staff when they undertake these tasks.)

Summary	Definition
No command line access	No command line access to the operating system of any server on which the system runs shall be granted to anyone involved in the day-to-day operation of the system. This includes anything equivalent to command line access, such as uncontrolled applications and the copying in of arbitrary programs, scripts, or other files.
	The motivation for this requirement is to force every action needed to operate the system to be available via a function whose use can be controlled and recorded, and to minimize the number of people who need command line access.
	This requirement does not apply to steps necessary to rectify serious system problems, or to install, upgrade, or reconfigure the system. (Nevertheless, in those cases, this requirement should be relaxed only as far as is necessary to get those jobs done).

Extra Requirements

None, beyond those common to both types of user authorization requirement.

Considerations for Development

Specific authorization requirements can be varied, and the ways to implement them can be equally varied. Deal with each one on its merits. Don't seek a grand mechanism that can solve them all: they might be too diverse.

The biggest decision is whether configurable access control is worth implementing, even if there's no explicit requirement for it. You can't expect a requirements specification to specify every little detail of who's allowed to access what. Judge for yourself how big the gaps are. Maybe there's an unspoken expectation of configurable access control; if so, bring it out into the open and resolve it quickly.

Considerations for Testing

Testing a specific authorization requirement is reasonably straightforward: can that kind of user access whatever it refers to? Are all other kinds of users prevented from accessing it? If a user is able to delegate their authority to another user, test that a delegatee is authorized whenever the delegator is. Change the kind of a user (if that's possible, for example by assigning them a different role), and test that their authorizations change accordingly.

An invaluable tool when testing authorizations is for all rejected authorization requests to be chronicled (logged). When reviewing requirements, check that this feature is included. If not, insist on it.

11.5 Configurable Authorization Requirement Pattern

Basic Details

Related patterns:	Extends user authorization; refers to specific authorization, chronicle
Anticipated frequency:	Up to two requirements
Pattern classifications:	Affects database: Yes

Applicability

Use the configurable authorization requirement pattern to specify that the definition of which users can do what is to be configurable (that is, can be changed dynamically).

Do not use the configurable authorization requirement pattern to specify what a set of users is authorized to do or see; use the specific authorization requirement pattern for that.

Discussion

Configurable authorization control is wonderful: it lets you change who can do what, whenever you like. An employee needs more authority to do their job properly? No problem! A company restructure? Bring it on! At the same time, it's a millstone, with major drawbacks: it's difficult and expensive to implement; it can incur performance penalties; it's time-consuming to set up and subsequently to maintain; ill-considered (or malicious) changes can have major consequences; and it introduces security risks of its own. So ask for access control to be configurable only if it's worth it; even then, keep it as simple as possible and use it only in those areas that justify it. (That is, don't use it everywhere just because it's there.) Also, take care to make clear what's needed and what isn't, so you don't inadvertently end up with an over-fancy solution.

Configurable authorization is most fruitful when used to control access to *functions*, because in any serious system, the functions are too numerous to fix their access correctly up front, for all time. Configurable authorization to *data* is rarely called for, because a normal system simply doesn't need the ability to partition data in arbitrary ways; the cases that do occur are usually isolated and best dealt with using specific authorization requirements. (Note that even without requirements for configurable authorization to data, the system might still be implemented with access control at the database level, on tables and SQL procedures and so on. That doesn't concern us here.) Sometimes, though, several sets of access configuration to functions are needed—one for each of a set of data values. For example, a multi-company system might allow permissions to be defined differently for each company within it—such that one user can access one collection of functions for one company and other functions for a different company. This renders configurable authorization more complex to implement and to manage, so avoid it if you can.

Give configurable authorization requirements a high priority, because if you need access control, you can't very well live without it for an extended period until it's delivered in a later phase—and any attempt at an interim solution could be a mess. In any case, its priority must be at least as high as any specific authorization requirements that depend on configurability.

Content

A configurable authorization requirement should contain:

1. **Class of users**   For which users do we want to make access configurable? Do it only for classes of users that need flexibility. Avoid it for classes of users that have largely fixed privileges—which, in most systems, includes *customers*. If possible, avoid it for high-volume classes of users (again, customers)—because of the likely performance impact.

2. **Nature of access**   Are we asking for configurable access to functions, or to data, or to a combination of both? Describe what's needed in as much detail as you can. Make clear the significance of what you're asking for; don't let a massive undertaking look innocuous.

3. **Motivation**   Why do we want this to be configurable?

Template(s)

Summary	Definition
«User class» access to *«Nature of access»*	A *«User class»* shall be able to access only *«Nature of access description»* to which they have been granted permission [(by virtue of the roles assigned to them)].
	The motivation for this requirement is *«Motivation statement»*.

Example(s)

Summary	Definition
Employee access to functions	An employee shall be able to access only those internal functions in the system to which they have been granted permission (by virtue of the roles assigned to them). An internal function, for the purpose of this requirement, is one that is not intended to be available to customers.
	Within each function, the ability to perform each distinct type of action (view, create, modify, delete, approve, and so on) shall also be restricted in the same manner.
	The motivation for this requirement is to allow the system to adapt to the skills of the workforce that uses it and to be able to react to reorganization of the company.
Employee access to data	An employee shall be able to access only those classes of data to which they have been granted permission (by virtue of the roles assigned to them). For the purpose of this requirement, "class of data" means any body of data that can be defined precisely such that no item of data shall belong to more than one body of data.
	This is not to say that explicit access must be granted to every item of data; it means control can be given for specific things that warrant it.
	A user shall have no access to data that is subject to such control, unless permission is explicitly granted to them. (That is, a **denial by default** approach shall be taken.)
	The motivation for this requirement is to allow data to be segregated in various ways so that a range of powerful inquiries can be made available to any user while still permitting them to view only the data relevant to them.
Employee access to functions per company	An employee shall be able to access only those internal functions for a particular company to which they have been granted permission (by virtue of the roles assigned to them) for that company. "Internal function" shall be taken to have the same meaning as in the requirement before last.
	The motivation for this requirement is to allow the operation of each company to be defined separately, while still permitting employees to do work for more than one company.

The first two examples spell out the two main "natures" of access control (functions and data). A more common way to express these sentiments might be, "A user shall be able to access only those functions and that information to which they have been granted permission," but that fails to address what information it might apply to, and it hides the enormity of what it's asking for to such an extent that only an eagle-eyed reader would spot it.

Extra Requirements

A configurable authorization requirement can have the following kinds of extra requirements, in addition to those common to both types of user authorization requirement (each of which is discussed in its own subsection that follows):

1. **Defining user roles**   We need a way to set up user roles and define what privileges each role has.

2. **Authorization inquiries**   Access configuration is hard enough to manage at the best of times, so provide inquiries to make it as easy to understand as possible: what each person is allowed to do, which people have each privilege, and so on.

3. **Chronicle authorization changes**   Keep track of changes to any of the configuration that controls who can do what.

Defining User Roles   It's most convenient to discuss roles in a reasonably abstract way (because it avoids repetition), which makes sense only if we assume that a user can assume several such roles. A role, then, doesn't necessarily equate to a job description—nor to an "actor" or "class of user." (Roles are likely to be more numerous than any of these other things.) Even if roles are to be configurable, it's useful for the requirements specification to list candidate roles informally; it gives readers a better idea of what we're talking about and can give the configuration a head start.

We need to specify a tool for defining user roles:

Summary	Definition
User role maintenance	There shall be a function for the creation and editing of user roles. Each role shall have a name and a description of its purpose. It shall be possible to maintain a list of the access privileges granted to any user with this role.

If we're defining roles, we could be picky and make sure the software actually uses the roles when deciding what a user is allowed to do:

Summary	Definition
Access control per role	The privileges a user has shall be determined by the roles to which the user is assigned. Privileges shall not be given directly to each user.

Authorization Inquiries   Why systems act as they do is always shrouded in mystery—invariably far more than necessary. The workings of serious access control can be equally mysterious if it doesn't let you see what's going on. A set of inquiries for this purpose is invaluable. The two most important ways in which authorizations should be viewable are **by user** (to see what each user can do) and **by privilege** (to see everyone who can access each thing). The latter can also point out anything to which *no one* has access, which means parts of the system are lying idle. Here are a couple of basic examples:

Summary	Definition
User authorization inquiry	There shall be an inquiry that lists all the access privileges granted to a selected user. For each privilege, it shall indicate which of the user's role grants it.
	Every user (except customers) shall be able to inquire on *their own* access privileges.
Privilege types inquiry	There shall be an inquiry that lists all the types of access privilege known to the system. For each privilege, it shall name all the user roles that grant it (and, in so doing, identify privileges granted to no one).

The second example leaves open the question of where the information about privileges "known to the system" comes from and how it gets there. The most obvious answer is that it's stored somewhere and there's a way to edit it. If you want to make that explicit, write a requirement to that effect; something like this:

Summary	Definition
Privilege type maintenance	There shall be a function for the creation and editing of information about access privileges. Each privilege shall have a name and a description of its purpose.

Chronicling Authorization Changes   Changes to the configuration of access control can have major consequences, so insist that all changes to access control are chronicled (as per the chronicle requirement pattern in Chapter 7). If a malicious user granted their own access to an extra function, used it, and then revoked access, chronicle entries could be essential in piecing together what happened. Refer to the chronicle requirement pattern for more.

Summary	Definition
Record changes to access control	Every change that affects the access privileges of any user in any way shall be recorded, including at least:
	■ Date and time.
	■ User ID of the person who made the change.
	■ Full details of the change.
Record authorization check	Each check of whether a user is authorized to perform a particular function or action shall be recorded. This record shall include the *context* of the check, which means that if several functions invoke the same subfunction, the record shall indicate which function invoked the subfunction.
	It shall be possible to turn the recording of authorization checks on and off. (It is normally unnecessary to record checks in a production environment, but it's useful when performing certain kinds of testing on the system and when diagnosing problems.)

Considerations for Development

If access control logic is simple and fixed, you can hard-code it. If it's not simple, or if it's liable to change, it's better to build a general, configurable mechanism—regardless of whether the requirements say you should. However, developing an underlying mechanism for access control is difficult and not for the faint-hearted. Apparently sensible and logical approaches can turn out to be a nightmare to manage in practice, because of the sheer quantity of configuration data. If you think a general access control mechanism will be worthwhile, bite the bullet early. Trying to retrofit it later is likely to be unpleasant.

Considerations for Testing

First of all, recognize that you're testing the requirements, not the privileges of whatever roles might have been set up: testing isn't responsible for checking that every user can do what they need to do their job. Having said that, it's always sensible to configure a test system as closely as possible to the live environment—which means defining roles and their privileges as realistically as possible.

When testing access to functions, for each function, test two things: first, that access to the function is controlled; and second, that the correct privilege is checked. This is exceedingly tedious to do manually. It helps if the system lets you observe each authorization check (down to the name of the privilege being checked); then you can see directly whether the correct privilege is used for each function. One way to observe authorization checks is to record them in a chronicle, and there is an example requirement for doing this in the "Chronicling Authorization Changes" subsection of the "Extra Requirements" section in this pattern.

A simpler test is to create a user role that can do everything, and verify that a user with that role can indeed do everything. Also create a user role that can do nothing, and verify that a user with that role can do nothing but publicly-accessible things.

One difficulty is that the number of privileges could keep growing. You'd have to be inhumanly diligent to insist on trying to test every new one that comes along.

11.6 Approval Requirement Pattern

Basic Details

Related patterns:	None
Anticipated frequency:	Often no requirements; rarely more than half a dozen requirements
Pattern classifications:	Functional: Yes; Affects database: Yes

Applicability

Use the approval requirement pattern to specify that a particular action (or set of actions) must be approved (or, in *some circumstances* approved) by a second person before it takes place.

Discussion

Any function in a system can be constructed so as to require approval before it takes effect. We usually think of one person approving an action requested by another, but it is also possible to allow a person to approve actions suggested by the system itself. ("An upgrade is available for the Whizzo Happiness Calculator. Would you like to download it now?" is an example.)

Imagine a bank in which a teller must have any large cash withdrawal approved by a supervisor. This sounds straightforward enough. But what constitutes *large*? Does it vary from teller to teller: are some more trusted than others? What is meant by *supervisor*? Can any supervisor approve it, or just the teller's direct superior? If a supervisor performs a withdrawal, must it be approved by another supervisor—and does that mean someone more senior still? Approving an action is invariably significantly trickier than it at first appears (or if you imagine that it will be tricky, you'll be proven right). It's also commonly neglected in both requirements specifications and software.

And when a *system* has to handle approval of actions, there are further complexities, because every system lacks the common sense possessed by every human being. How do we bring something needing approval to the attention of someone who can approve it? What if more than one person is able to approve it: do we bring it to the attention of *all* of them? If not, how do we decide which? What if a usual approver is absent? What if someone else wants to perform an action that affects the pending action (for example, if we're waiting for approval to debit a bank account, and another debit to the same account comes along); there are no easy answers to this one. Every little detail must be figured out and specified—and commonly they aren't, resulting in systems that don't behave sensibly and are awkward to use.

Content

The approval of an action is best specified as an extra requirement following that for the function that carries out the action. Approval requirements should answer some or all of the following questions, as appropriate:

1. **Which action(s) require approval?**   That is, to what does this approval requirement apply? This is what happens when approval is granted. If it's not simply a matter of performing an action specified somewhere else, explain what else is involved.

2. **Under what circumstances is approval needed?**   It could be *always*. If not, specify the conditions—such as up to some limit set for the user, or class of user (up to a specified monetary value, say).

3. **Who can approve, and under what circumstances?**   Answering this question involves several steps:

   ❑ Step 1: Identify all the users (or classes of users) who can approve this particular type of action. Also identify the circumstances under which they can approve—which can involve similar conditions to those in the previous question (on when approval is needed). For example, we might need some sort of limit up to which a user (or class of user) can *approve* a particular action (distinct from the limit up to which the user can *perform* the action without approval).

   ❑ Step 2: Identify the prospective approver (or approvers) for each user, or a way of working out who they are. For example, only people in the same department might be eligible. And we could nominate a supervisor for each user and state that they're to be the approver of first resort. When a bank teller needs approval for a large withdrawal, confine approval to the same bank branch (or havoc will reign!).

   ❑ Step 3: Consider what happens if a prospective approver is absent. If you identify only one person as approver, you're in trouble. You need some fallback position. If someone else is performing this job temporarily, how does the system know? Getting a system to behave smartly based on the information already at its disposal (such as it knowing who is logged in at the moment) takes a lot of thought.

❑   Step 4: Prevent a user from approving *their own* actions. This is covered in the "Extra Requirements" section in this pattern.

4.   **How promptly is approval needed?**   An approval requirement doesn't itself need to answer to this question, although it has a major bearing on the best way of bringing something needing approval to a potential approver's attention (which is the next question). If approvals are only needed by the end of the day, a relatively simple implementation will suffice; if an action must be approved within two minutes, it's a very different matter.

5.   **How is something awaiting approval to be brought to an approver's attention?**   There's no universal answer to this question: every way has its drawbacks. Which is the most suitable depends on the answers to the previous two questions. Decide how prescriptive you wish to be: either choose a specific mechanism, or merely specify the characteristics you want. Possible approval mechanisms (along with a few strengths and weaknesses) include:

a.   **An approve subfunction within the data entry function itself**   Where the user calls an approver over to their machine, who then self-authenticates and signifies approval (or rejection). This is the easiest mechanism to implement—and perhaps the most reliable, too, because it can take advantage of the user's human common sense. But it involves people walking around (how low tech!), and the risk of the approver's password being observed (plus the temptation for an approver to give their password to someone else to save all this trouble).

b.   **A stand-alone approval function**   This deserves a requirement of its own, which is why it's described in the "Extra Requirements" section of this pattern.

c.   **An electronic communication medium**   Email, SMS, or pager—or some other way of getting a message to a prospective approver. But that's just half the story: we still need a function by which they can grant approval. Use this sort of messaging mechanism only if the number of approval requests received by one person is relatively small.

The last two mechanisms need us to decide which approver(s) are to be informed of something awaiting approval. Typically just a subset of the people authorized to approve are informed. If using a notification mechanism that expects the recipient to respond, send a message to only one person: it would be frustrating to respond only to find that someone else has already approved the action.

6.   **What happens if an approver denies approval?**   You must always ask this question. It's surprising how often specifications fail to say what is to happen in this case, and as a result, systems sometimes struggle to deal with rejection (a surprisingly human trait for a system!). Actually, there are three distinct situations here:

a.   An approver says, "**I reject this. It must not be approved.**" Usually rejection is the end of the matter, but you might want to consider providing a way for the original user to challenge it: to let them pass it to someone else who might approve it.

b.   An approver says, "**I can neither approve nor reject this.**" This represents a firm and final decision on their part. They would do this if, for example, they believe they're not in a position to decide. The item needs to be passed on to another prospective approver for their consideration. You might decide that in your system, this situation will never arise—that every approver will always know what to do—but if so, you should make this a conscious decision; otherwise a user might be forced into making a judgment they don't want to.

   c. An approver says, "**I need more information before I can decide.**" In this case, consider whether the system needs to provide the prospective approver with the ability to explain what else they need. If so, specify that feature.

This assumes that just a single extra person needs to give their approval. It can be extended to cover two (or even more) people needing to approve. Sometimes this is best done as a "chain" of approvals (one person after another); sometimes they can each approve independently in any order. An example of the latter might be a system that allows the members of a committee to sign off on documents.

Template(s)

Summary	Definition
«Action name» approval	A *«Action description»* must *«Approval circumstances»* be approved by *«Approver description»*. [*«Approval promptness statement»*.] [*«Approval mechanism statement»*.] [If approval is denied *«Rejection action description»*.]

Example(s)

Summary	Definition
Large cash withdrawal approval	Any cash withdrawal larger than a teller's withdrawal limit must be approved by another employee within whose withdrawal limit it falls. Approval is granted by the withdrawal function on the teller's machine allowing the second employee to enter their user ID and password and then signify approval. The second employee shall also have the ability to reject the withdrawal, which results in it being canceled.
Employee vacation subject to approval	Every request for vacation of more than two days must be approved by the human resources department.

These examples demonstrate that while there's a large number of aspects to consider when specifying approval, the end result can be straightforward.

Extra Requirements

By now it should be clear that the business of approval is tricky and complicated. (That's why you still see bank tellers running around looking for supervisors to approve things, despite banks automating almost everything else in sight. Go and watch them before they end up in a museum.) Properly defining your approval workflow could take a variety of extra requirements, a couple of topics for which are:

1. Preventing a user from approving an action that they have initiated.

2. An approval function—either a special one for a particular kind of approval, or a general approval mechanism for managing *anything* that's waiting to be approved.

Each of these is discussed in its own section that follows.

Cannot Approve Own Action   It is unacceptable to allow a user to approve an action that they have performed. Apply this rule to every kind of approval. There is nothing to be gained by not having it: simply let users perform the action without approval being necessary if that's what you want. But it's important to state this restriction explicitly in a requirement—or be prepared for it to be forgotten. Note that an approval step is sometimes used simply to involve a second person, who could be at the same level as the first user (not a supervisor)—hence the elegantly descriptive German term *Vieraugen*, four eyes. In such a case, both users might have the same permissions, and an explicit restriction of this sort is the only way to prevent one person from both entering and approving. Insisting that a user be unable to approve their own action is an example of an operational rule as per the specific authorization requirement pattern.

Summary	Definition
Cannot approve own action	A user shall not be able to approve an action that they initiated. For any action that requires more than one approval, a user shall not be able to approve an action they have already approved.
	This requirement applies to every type of action that is subject to approval. It does not, however, preclude one user from being granted the ability to perform a function without approval (even if another user must obtain approval).

Approval Mechanism   An approval mechanism lets you see and pick items awaiting approval and go ahead and act on them. The simplest case looks after just a single kind of item (or a small number of fixed kinds).

If your system has more than one or two functions for which approval is needed, it could be worthwhile building or buying (and hence specifying) a *general* approval mechanism that can manage everything that's awaiting approval, to save duplicating the messy parts. This might include, for example, a function to display all items pending approval by the current user, regardless of what sorts they are. It could incorporate some kind of *workflow* support, and it could involve an infrastructure deserving of its own requirements specification. You would need to specify requirements for the pieces that make up a general mechanism of this sort. Such requirements could be wide-ranging and complex.

If prompt approval is needed, approvers must have an approval mechanism running all the time (or utilize some kind of notification mechanism). But what if they don't have it running? To work well for prompt response, this function must refresh itself (which is harder with some technologies than others).

Here's an example of a specific approval function:

Summary	Definition
Employee vacation request approval	There shall be a function (intended to be used by the human resources department) that lists all pending vacation requests by employees in departments that are the responsibility of the current user.
	This function shall allow the user to select and view the details of any vacation request (as well as the employee's accrued vacation) and to approve or reject the request.

Considerations for Development

If more than a couple of types of action need approval (or might in the future), consider building a generalized mechanism for storing any kind of unapproved action. This must be able to store anything that's yet to be approved, for which it needs to be flexible. Depending how sophisticated you want this mechanism to be, it could also provide a means for other functions to find out whether anything of interest to them is awaiting approval. For example, if a large bank account debit is awaiting approval, another function that wishes to know the balance of that account probably needs to take the pending debit into account. Also take care to protect this pending-action store against tampering.

Note that if we build a place to store pending (yet-to-be-approved) actions, this can also be used as the basis for handling timed and co-ordinated changes, as described in the introduction to the "Data Entity Requirement Patterns" chapter. So if you build a mechanism for one, you have a head start towards the other.

Considerations for Testing

Concentrate on what sorts of things could happen between the action being initiated and its being approved. Has someone already figured out all the extra actions that users could take that could interfere with the action awaiting approval? A workflow (or equivalent) diagram is a particularly helpful form. If not, produce one—and be suspicious that the system might be incomplete. Identify all the possible states an approval request can be in, and the ways it can change state. Figure out all the actions that any of the people involved could take at any stage. Then test these possibilities and verify that the system handles them satisfactorily.

Chapter 12
Commercial Requirement Patterns

In this chapter:

12.1 Multi-Organization Unit Requirement Pattern 325

12.2 Fee/Tax Requirement Pattern... 330

The commercial domain is for features pertaining to systems used to run a business, of which there are two here, as shown in Figure 12-1.

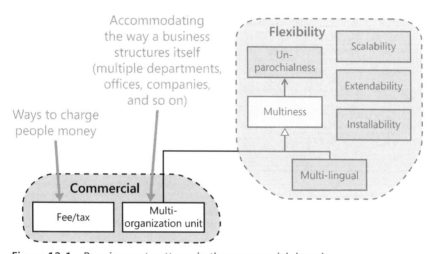

Figure 12-1   Requirement patterns in the commercial domain

12.1 Multi-Organization Unit Requirement Pattern

Basic Details

Related patterns:	Extends multiness; refers to user authorization
Anticipated frequency:	Zero or one requirement
Pattern classifications:	Affects database: Yes

Applicability

Use the multi-organization unit requirement pattern to specify a type of organizational construct that the system must be able to support, whether that be units of a specific type or a more complex structure (such as a hierarchy).

Do not use the multi-organization unit requirement pattern to enumerate the organization units themselves (such as listing actual companies or departments).

Discussion

A typical business is a much more complex organism than a typical system gives it credit for. A system is often regarded as merely a mass of functions used by a mass of users: flat and amorphous. But those users must be properly organized along the lines of the business itself, and the ways in which that's done has a significant impact on the functions themselves. Neglecting organizational structure during the specification of a system is likely to lead to unsatisfactory results and ongoing operational difficulties, which might never be traced to their ultimate cause. Note that we're talking here only about the organization structure as it affects the system when it's in production; the structure of the team that builds the system is irrelevant.

An **organization unit** is any subset of an organization that makes it easier to manage. It is a flesh-and-blood collection of people you can go and visit, such as "the finance department." An **organization unit type** is an abstract organizational concept—such as "department"—of which organization units are instances. Here are a few common examples of organization unit types: company, office, branch, department, subsidiary, and region. Relationships between organization unit types define the structure of the organization as a whole. Organization unit requirements concern themselves with organization unit *types*.

Organization units known to the system needn't be limited to the organization(s) whose business the system handles directly. Occasionally, a system must represent units of other organizations (such as agents, subcontractors, and other business partners), especially if their employees use the system. If so, bear in mind that each organization is likely to have its own structure. Consider all the organizations that might use the system and work out what structural variations are needed to suit them.

Working out an accurate model of the structure of the organization(s) in which the system is likely to be installed is important, and it's invariably neglected. A system that doesn't properly represent its business environment can run into various problems, some of which are never tracked back to this as the reason. Whenever a fundamental feature is not properly built in to a system, there's a temptation to deal with any resulting difficulty by using a half-baked fix (because it's too late and too daunting to do it properly)—like a mechanic who mends a broken down car but who's not in a position to rectify basic flaws in its design. Over time, the system becomes riddled with ugly workarounds and grows old prematurely.

Organizational structure isn't properly studied and specified for several reasons, and they're all unjustified. First, it might be regarded as simple and obvious—in which case it'll be easy to describe, so there's no excuse not to do it (though it often turns out to be less simple than it seemed). Second, at the opposite extreme, it might look too hard: convoluted and illogical, which is all the more reason to figure it out. If you can't cope, how are the poor users going to cope with a system not built to fit in with the structure they have to work within? Third, if the system is a product that will be installed in a wide variety of organizations, their structures will be unknown, giving yet more reason to work out how much variation they're likely to have and to accommodate it. If you don't, you're likely to lose sales, no matter how great the system is—probably without even knowing why. Fourth, structure isn't functional: everyone worries too much about what systems *do* and not enough about *how they're organized*. Fifth, no one thinks to bother. Systems will improve if they take organizational structure more seriously.

The structure of an organization isn't always uniform or consistent. A company might have several offices that organize themselves very differently. A nice neat hierarchy, with a fixed number of levels everywhere, often isn't good enough. We might encounter complex reporting lines too, or multiple departments with the same purpose in different offices. If you aspire to build a system that fits the way a company works, you need to understand what constituent parts it has.

If the system will be installed in multiple places, specify what types of organization unit *each installation* must cater for, even if there is a higher level of organization above them all. Alternatively, making the system aware of the higher level of organization can give you the flexibility to decide how many installations to have, thereby allowing the business to choose based on operational and cost considerations, rather than being dictated to by the system's design.

Content

There are two kinds of multi-organization unit requirement. The first kind defines a particular type of unit and should contain:

1. **Unit type name**. Identify the specific type of unit (for example, "department" or "branch").
2. **Unit type definition**. Define precisely what is meant by this type of unit. (For example, what is a "branch"?)
3. **Parent unit type** (if any). Include this if it's not a top-level organization unit.
4. **Characteristics**. What purpose does this type of organization unit serve? What impact does it have on the system? Concentrate on aspects that affect individual functions—especially access restrictions, and information display and selection criteria.
5. **Expected number of instances**. For a type of organization unit at the top level, give an absolute number (such as how many companies); for lower-level units, indicate how many per higher unit (such as how many departments *per company*).

The second kind of multi-organization unit requirement asks for the ability to define an organizational structure dynamically (by configuring it in the system). This kind of requirement should contain:

1. **Structure**   Describe what sort of abstract arrangement of units we want (for instance, a hierarchy, the most common). If something more complicated is needed (such as being able to set up a different structure for each company, or dual reporting lines), explain how it fits together and what it's for.
2. **Characteristics**   This is as in the first kind of requirement. It's sensible, when allowing the structure to be configurable, to accept that all types of units have the same characteristics as far as the system is concerned (such as the items of information held about each unit type: ID, name, manager's name, and so on).

    One characteristic we should ask for is the ability to define a **name** for each type of organization unit. For example, if we support any three-level hierarchy, what does each level represent? Without names, there's no way to display any of these things in the terms users are familiar with.

Template(s)

The first template here is for specifying a particular type of organization unit. The second template is for specifying the ability to configure an organizational structure in a flexible manner; it's deceptively sparse because the intricacies of what you want must be expressed in the *«Structure description»*.

Summary	Definition
Multi-*«Unit type name»*	The system shall support multiple *«Unit type name»*s [per *«Parent unit type name»*]. [For the purpose of this specification, a *«Unit type name»* is *«Unit type definition»*.]
	[*«Characteristics statement»*.]
	[*«Number of instances statement»*.]
«Structure summary» organizational structure	It shall be possible to define an organizational structure *«Structure description»*.
	[*«Characteristics statement»*.]

Unlike the base multiness requirement pattern, there is no separate template for a requirement that makes *provision* for multi-organization unit—because by the time you've made provision for it, you've done the bulk of the work.

Example(s)

Summary	Definition
Multi-company	The system shall be able to support multiple companies simultaneously in the same running installation. For the purpose of this specification, a company is an independent legal business on whose behalf the system conducts processing.
	Each company will have its own employees who use the system; they are to be aware only of the company for whom they work. (The specifics of this are covered in other requirements.)
	One installation of the system might be asked to accommodate up to a dozen companies.
Multi-department	The system shall support multiple departments per company.
	Each employee is primarily concerned with the activities of the department in which they work but might have reason to deal with the work of other departments.
	A company is likely to have between four and ten departments.
Three-level organizational hierarchy	It shall be possible to define a hierarchy of organization units of up to three levels, such that each employee works directly in one particular unit (at any level in the hierarchy).
	The name of the type of organization unit at each level in the hierarchy shall be configurable (for example, "company," "office," and "department").
	The purpose of this hierarchy is to allow functions to tailor what they display according to the organization unit the current user works in.

Extra Requirements

An organization unit requirement could deserve extra requirements on the following topics:

1. **Access control**   See the user authorization requirement patterns (in Chapter 11, "Access Control Requirement Patterns"), including their "Extra Requirements" subsections, which point out various extra topics to make life more interesting.

2. **Bureau for multiple companies**   Running a bureau service for multiple independent companies can involve its own complications, such as the activities of one company degrading the performance of another, calculating each organization's system resource usage, and software introduced by one interfering with (or even spying on) another. If any of these apply to your system, investigate and write requirements for them.

3. **Reorganizing**   Does the system need to worry about the structure of an organization changing? See the "Reorganizing" subsection that follows.

4. **Unit IDs**   Uniquely identifying an organization unit can be fiddly, especially if the whole structure is configurable. If you don't want to run the risk of the development team devising some logical-but-hideous solution that users will hate, write a requirement for something friendlier. You could also consider a requirement that bans the hard-coded interpreting of unit IDs, because that effectively renders them unchangeable and creates a fragile state of system atrophy. (And don't be so naïve as to assume such practices aren't widespread.)

Reorganizing   An organization is apt to change its structure from time to time, and the larger it is, the more scope it has to rearrange its parts. Also, the more levels of management, the more often a unit at the bottom is affected by new management initiatives. Systems typically make no provision whatsoever for such changes, for several reasons: reorganizations are assumed to be rarer than they actually are, they're something for the future, no one gives them a thought, and they're just too hard. Start by considering how likely future structural change is. How frequently has it happened in the past? What sorts of reorganizations are likely? How drastic? Might the company acquire or shed or merge operating units? How easy should it be for the system to react? What sorts of change are worth worrying about?

Finally, if our system supports configurable organization structure but doesn't have a miraculous in-built ability to bring everything into line when that configuration is changed, then we should prevent it from being changed. The following example requirement does just that:

Summary	Definition
Organization structure non-modifiable	It shall not be possible to reconfigure the structure of the organization within the system after it has been set up initially.
	The purpose of this requirement is to prevent changes for which the system is incapable of properly handling the implications.

Considerations for Development

Bear future changes in organization structure in mind, and do what you can in the design to make the impact less traumatic. Often there's not much that can be done. The area to bear most in mind is the database design so that data is tied to a particular organization structure as loosely as possible.

If you're going to cater for flexible organizational structures, decide how to identify each one: a suitable ID scheme.

Martin Fowler's *Analysis Patterns* book (1996) has analysis patterns for organization hierarchies and organization structure.

Considerations for Testing

Multi-organization unit support doesn't manifest itself directly: there's no single place where you can find it. It might affect many functions, so you must work out what they are and check that they all work as the multi-organization unit requirements say they should. (It can save time if you test all the multi-organization unit requirements together.) Here are some topics to look out for:

1. Inquiries, reports, and other functions show only information pertaining to relevant unit(s).

2. Access control: that a user can't see units they shouldn't. (See the user authorization requirement patterns in Chapter 11 for further information.)

3. Selection criteria default to the user's own organization unit(s).

12.2 Fee/Tax Requirement Pattern

Basic Details

Related patterns:	Inter-system interface, inter-system interaction, extendability, configuration, calculation formula
Anticipated frequency:	From one to upwards of a dozen requirements. A commercial system with no fees or taxes specified is likely to be incomplete.
Pattern classifications:	None

Applicability

Use the fee/tax requirement pattern to specify any fee or tax the system must calculate, report on, or levy. This requirement pattern can also be used (with only slight variations) to specify a *discount* on an amount a party is charged.

Do not use the fee/tax requirement pattern for any fee or tax for which the system does not contain the information on which the fee is based (such as charges for software development work). Such fees can be described informally in a requirements specification but not as formal requirements the system must satisfy.

Discussion

Sales tax, annual subscriptions, postage and delivery charges, transaction fees, agent commissions: few serious commercial systems don't involve a fee or tax of some kind. Fees are the sole source of revenue for many businesses. Taxes are a necessary evil, but getting them wrong is potentially disastrous if a company has to pay for mistakes out of its own pocket. Taxation authorities are not renowned for their compassion and flexibility. So calculating and levying fees and taxes deserve to be treated seriously, starting with their requirements.

A **fee** is any amount that one party charges to another for providing some kind of service. Underlying fundamental amounts, such as the purchase price of an item being bought, are not fees. A **tax** is any amount a taxation authority charges to a party (while providing no service directly in return!). As far as system specifications and software are concerned, a tax behaves so much like a fee there's nothing to be gained by treating them separately. In this requirement pattern the term "fee" should be taken to include tax too, unless it is clearly not appropriate. **Fee rate** means either a fixed monetary amount or a percentage.

Include requirements for *all* fees and taxes levied on the business for which the system is responsible. Do this even if fees are managed, collected, and even calculated by some other system (such as an accounting system, a dedicated billing system, or a spreadsheet). This makes developers aware of the information needed to calculate the fees so that they can take steps to provide it. For each other system involved here, specify requirements for an inter-system interface to it and requirements for the information to be passed across it. They make clear the responsibilities of each system; without them, it's hard to apportion responsibility for any difficulty that results. (See the inter-system interface and inter-system interaction requirement patterns in Chapter 5, "Fundamental Requirement Patterns," for further details.) If no such external system is in place but you *assume* there will be or should be one, state your assumption explicitly–and work through the consequences.

Revenue Model

If a system has more than two or three fees and taxes–or if the financial workings of the business aren't self-evident, which means nearly all businesses–it's worth tackling financial flows in a more systematic manner than just writing requirements for each fee and tax you can think of. A diagram is the best way. Show each kind of party who can pay or receive money, and then show all the possible flows of money between them that the system cares about. (Don't worry about flows *between* third parties.) Here's an example:

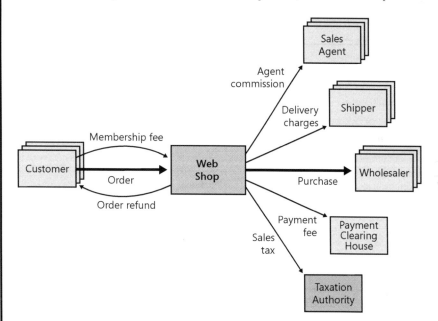

It's hard to show relationships between flows (such as how the revenue from one order is shared among several parties), but that's a secondary matter. What's important is to capture all the flows, so that none are forgotten–though for simplicity it's usually best to omit corrections and adjustments. Observe that multiple boxes are shown for some of the parties; this signifies that there could be many of them. Sometimes it's worth going into more detail to show the main *accounts* into which money is placed. Diagrams like this can be surprisingly difficult to draw, which is a sign that you don't fully understand how the business works.

Sometimes fees are omitted from the requirements specification on the assumption that all the raw information is there so it'll be easy to add them later. But if it's easy, it'll be easy to specify now. If it's not easy to specify now, that's even more reason to do so. Until you specify a fee, you don't know how tricky it might be. Don't leave loose ends here: they might become very frayed indeed. And just because the system has the raw data at some point doesn't mean it *stores* it; and even if it does, it might not be in a form that's convenient for calculating the fee. The details could contain all sorts of little complexities, some of which might be discovered only during development, but the analyst should aim to pin down everything they can and leave nothing unresolved.

Accountants as Programmers

Finance departments responsible for levying fees and for paying taxes often use spreadsheets to juggle the requisite figures; spreadsheets are powerful for this purpose and provide flexibility to modify the results that's hard to match. But if the data provided to them is in an inconvenient form, spreadsheets of mind-boggling complexity can be the result, and accountants are remarkably adept at concocting them. This is very bad practice. If we look at such production spreadsheets as software (which they are), they are software built in the worst possible way: unspecified, unstructured, full of repetition, with changes untracked, undocumented, and untested (indeed, virtually untestable—and unauditable), and usable and modifiable only by the author. Often their very existence is known only to the person responsible, and the (considerable) expense of producing and tending them goes unseen.

Frankenstein spreadsheets are a sign that the data in the system that spawned them is inadequate and badly designed. The answer is to properly investigate the financial and accounting needs up front—and to bring them fully within the scope of the system. Spreadsheets might well play their part in the solution, but if properly planned they will be a lot simpler and their role will be clear. Reducing dependence on uncontrolled mammoth spreadsheets also makes auditing easier, which assists in compliance with financial regulations (such as SOX in the U.S.).

Content

The five key factors in any fee or tax are: **how**, **on what**, **when**, **from whom**, and **to whom**. A requirement for a fee or tax needs to convey the following information:

1. **Name**   What is this fee or tax called? Be clear, precise, and unambiguous.
2. **Basis**   The nature of the calculation (*how*). The most common bases are:
    a. Fixed monetary amount (for example, a flat $0.20).
    b. Percentage of some other monetary value (for example, five percent of the purchase price).
    c. Monetary amount per time period (for example, $0.50 per month).

More complex kinds of calculation are possible, such as tiered or threshold rates. **Tiered rates** are divided into bands with a different rate applicable to each band (for example, $0.20 each for the first 20 Web pages viewed, $0.15 for each of the next 20, and $0.10 each thereafter). **Threshold rates** are similar, but just the rate belonging to the band into which the amount falls is used (for example, up to $100 shipping is 15 percent, between $100.01 and $200 it is 10 percent, $200.01 and over it is free). If you use such rates, explain exactly how they work.

Cite fee rates as indicative only; make them configurable.

3. **Origin**   What is the thing that is being charged for (*on what*)? A fee is usually charged either **on an event** or **over time**. Typical *events* on which a fee is charged are:

    a. **A transaction** (for example, an order).

    b. **An event in the life of a living entity** (for example, the registering of a new customer).

    c. **An action within the system** (for example, the running of a report). It is useful (and in practice usually necessary) to record every action on which a fee is charged.

    Charging *over time* is typically applied to a living entity, either directly to its life (for example, an annual fee for the life of a credit card) or via a subsidiary living entity created just for this purpose (such as a customer's subscription to a magazine, which continues for as long as the customer pays the fee).

    When multiple different fees are applied on the same thing, make clear the order in which they are applied and take care to precisely identify the amount that each fee is calculated on. For example, is sales tax calculated on postage?

4. **Condition (if relevant)**   Is this fee always charged or only in certain circumstances? For example, a bank might charge for account statements only if the account is overdrawn or might charge sales tax only to domestic residents. Describe the conditions under which the fee applies.

5. **When levied**   Describe at what point the fee is charged to the payer—that is, when the *liability to pay* is incurred. This is either when they are actually debited or when they are sent the bill and asked to pay. Note that fee amounts are not necessarily credited to the receiver immediately the payer pays (for example, taxes collected might be paid quarterly).

6. **Payer**   Who pays the fee (*from whom*)? In most cases the payer and/or receiver are obvious and can be omitted. But first ask yourself where the money is going from and to. If it's not clear or if the answer is "It depends," nail it down and state the answer explicitly.

7. **Receiver**   Who receives the fee (*to whom*)? In some cases, a fee might be shared among more than one receiver—for example, when part of a fee is paid as commission to an agent. Situations like this can be treated as two fees, one based on the amount of the other.

8. **Fee rate determinants**   What determines what the fee rate is? Often the same fee rate is always used (though even then it might change periodically). But other factors could come into play, such as where the payer or receiver resides (geographically—such as shipping charges depending on country), or who the payer and/or receiver are (that is, special rates for a specific party or specific combination of parties), or the currency of the amount to which the fee applies (it might look slicker to define a nice round number for each currency, rather than convert a single value into another currency), or the type of a transaction.

    If this isn't stated, developers should assume the rate to be a systemwide configurable value (that is, the same rate is used in every case).

9. **The system's responsibility**   How much of the work does the system need to do? The main possibilities:

   a.   Calculate the fee and automatically debit the payer and/or credit the receiver. Debiting means either taking money directly (such as via their credit card) or debiting an account that represents real money (such as an account or "electronic purse" we maintain on their behalf).

   b.   Calculate and automatically inform the payer and/or the receiver (in effect, send them an invoice).

   c.   Calculate and pass the details on to another system (such as an accounting or billing system or export for use by a spreadsheet).

   d.   Make sure the raw information is present, ready to be passed on to another system.

10. **Reference**   If the fee is defined in more detail elsewhere, state where this further information can be found. This is most applicable to taxes, for which truckloads of supporting material are usually available.

This list looks more daunting than it is in practice. However, it does explain only the basics of the fee. Many—perhaps most—fees involve various special cases and complications. Each of these should be specified in an extra requirement—first, so that they attract the attention they deserve, and second, because the fee's main requirement is likely to be large enough already.

A **discount** (such as 10 percent off) can be specified in a similar manner to a fee: it is, in effect, a negative fee based on another monetary amount. Use the preceding list as a guide for the information to include in a requirement for a discount, but identify what the discount is based upon, and note that the payer and receiver can be omitted.

Template(s)

Summary	Definition
«*Fee/tax name*» fee/tax	The system shall calculate a «*Fee/tax name*» fee/tax as a «*Basis*» on «*Origin*» provided that «*Condition*». It is paid by «*Payer*» to «*Receiver*» «*When levied*». The [fee]/[tax] rate shall be determined by «*Fee/tax rate determinants*».
	The system is responsible for «*System responsibility*».
	Source: «*Reference*».

Example(s)

Summary	Definition
Transaction fee	The system shall calculate and automatically levy a fee on each customer transaction of a type for which a transaction fee is defined as payable. The fee rate shall be defined for each transaction type.
Sales commission	The system shall calculate the sales commission payable to each agent for sales they make. It is calculated as a percentage of the value of each sale (excluding postage/delivery and insurance amounts).
	Sales commission is paid by the system operator to agents. The system shall *not* automatically generate payments to agents.

Summary	Definition
Report fee	It shall be possible to charge for each report delivered to an external party (for example, to charge an agent for each monthly statement). The fee rate shall be defined for each type of report.
Device rental	The system shall calculate **and automatically levy** the rental fee to be paid by each customer for the devices they have rented. It shall be charged monthly, at the end of the month. It is calculated as a fixed amount per month for each device the customer had installed during the month.
	The per-month fee amount can vary from one customer to another.
Device installation fee	There shall be a fee payable to the rental service operator for each device installed by them at a customer site. It shall be charged monthly, at the end of the **last but one** working day of the month. It shall be a configurable fixed amount (intended to cover travel) plus an amount per hour. It is the responsibility of the system to calculate the number of device installation visits and the time spent on each one.
	The minimum chargeable time for an installation is one hour.
	It shall be possible to specify different fee amounts for each type of device.
General sales tax	It shall be possible to calculate and levy General Sales Tax (GST) on all amounts liable to it, including fees. GST is to be calculated as a fixed percentage (currently 10%) of the total value of any order from a domestic customer.
	The GST rate shall be configurable. Any change shall be effective from a nominated date. A complete history of old rates shall be retained indefinitely.

Extra Requirements

The main requirement for a fee gives a good idea of what the fee is all about, but it is rarely enough by itself. Here are some common extra topics to consider, the first five of which are dealt with in more detail in their own subsections:

1. **More detail**, to specify the fee more precisely. What else must be said to be able to calculate the fee correctly and unambiguously? For example, it might be necessary to introduce it at a precise date and time, especially if it's a new tax being introduced.

2. **Special cases and complications**. Are there any oddities you need to worry about? If there are, you mustn't simply ignore them.

3. **Consolidation**. Some fees—especially some types of taxes—are not just a lot of individual amounts lumped together: they involve further processing on the consolidated amounts.

4. **Manual intervention**. Do we need someone to review and approve a fee before levying it, or to approve a tax amount before reporting it to the relevant authority? What about providing the ability to **waive** a fee if appropriate? Functions to manually apply a fee, or to make a manual adjustment, are always useful—unless you can guarantee the system caters for every conceivable eventuality and will never make a mistake (which you can't). They're a kind of insurance policy.

5. **Justify fee amount**. What if a customer complains a fee is too high, and you can't tell why? Might someone want to be able to look at a fee amount and ask where it came from? It'd be useful to understand how was it calculated without a major investigation or having to call upon a developer.

6. **Tracking unpaid fees**. If the system *asks* the payer to pay a fee but doesn't debit them directly, how do we track whether they've paid? Is it the system's responsibility? If so, what must it do? (Consider requirements for producing statements, a function to record payments received, and internal reporting.) If not, who or what system is responsible? If it's an external system, have we defined an interface to it? If there are no requirements on our system, say so—to stop anyone wondering if we've forgotten them.

7. **Fee rate changes**. Fee rates are likely to change, and any good system can take them in its stride. We want a fee rate change to take effect at a precise time, and we need to know what the fee rate was at any moment in time. This topic is covered in detail in the configuration requirement pattern in Chapter 7, "Data Entity Requirement Patterns" (which is directly relevant because fee rates are part of the system's configuration).

8. **Eliminate fee**. Do we need to be able to stop levying this fee at some point in the future, without modifying the software?

9. **Extendability**. From time to time organizations change how they charge fees, add new ones, and replace one with another. Governments fiddle with tax regimes when they see fit. So it's wise to demand that this area be built flexibly so that future changes involve as little pain as possible—especially if you're building a system to run in multiple countries or a product to be used by various organizations. See the extendability requirement pattern in Chapter 10, "Flexibility Requirement Patterns," for further details.

Many of these extra requirements can be written to apply to only one type of fee or to apply to *all* types, or anything in between, as necessary.

More Detail   A quick description of how to calculate a fee often contains ambiguities; it can raise more questions than it answers. Write extra requirements to resolve these ambiguities. (Most of this subsection relates only to fees that must be *calculated*, rather than to fixed fee amounts, although one or two points apply to the latter.)

First comes the nitty-gritty of the calculation. To how many decimal places should the fee rate be held? To how many decimal places should the fee amount be calculated? Should any rounding be applied to the calculated fee amount, and if so, how? These might seem like trivial questions, but tax regulations are often definite and intolerant about such things. It's also important to adhere to stated definitions of fees if they have been agreed to and published to customers or if we're building a system that must be consistent with some other system.

Fees levied over time are particularly fiddly. Resolve the following matters:

1. What does the time period really mean? For any time period of a month or more there are at least two answers, which we can call **calendar** or **lapsed**. A calendar month (or quarter or year) is exactly as per the calendar: paying for January means up to the 31st January, so if we start on 14th January we don't pay the full month. A lapsed month is an actual month from the start: from 14th January to 14th February.

For time periods measured in quarters and years, make clear what you mean. Are quarters three-month periods starting on 1st January? Are years calendar years or financial years? If financial years, on what date do they start? Might this vary, if the system will be used in different countries?

Be aware of minor anomalies with lapsed time periods. Does a lapsed month from the 31st January end on 28th February? Then might a customer who pays for another month feel short-changed when told it ends on 28th March? The problem is that two months doesn't always equal one month plus one month.

2. How do we charge for a partial time period? For half a month, do we charge for that fraction of a month, for a full month, or nothing at all?

3. When do we start charging the fee? When do we stop? What events constitute the start and end?

Last, do we have any multi-currency issues to worry about? Can the amounts on which a fee is calculated be in different currencies? If so, we must either convert the fee amount into that currency (resulting in a funny-looking fee amount) or define the fee amount in each currency we support (which means a lower fee in some currencies than others, if we use nice round numbers).

Here are a few representative extra requirements for some of the details just described:

Summary	Definition
Fee monetary amounts to at least 4 decimal places	Any fee that is specified as a monetary amount shall be definable to at least 4 decimal places of cents (for example $0.0025).
Fee percentages to at least 2 decimal places	Any fee that is specified as a percentage shall be definable to at least 2 decimal places (for example 0.05%).
Device rental for partial month	If a device is rented only for part of a month, a proportion of the monthly rental fee shall be charged according to the number of days in the month during which the device was installed. For example, for a device activated on 9th May, $(31 - 9 + 1)/31$, or $23/31$, of the normal monthly device rental fee will be charged for May. (See the requirements that follow on start and end of device rental.)
Start of device rental	Device rental shall start at the moment the device is installed at the customer's site, for the purpose of device rental fees.
End of device rental	Device rental shall end at the moment the device is removed from the customer's site, for the purpose of device rental fees.

Special Cases and Complications   Don't assume that working out a basic fee amount is the end of the story. Here are a few situations you might encounter that affect the result:

1. **Minimum and maximum fees.** Don't bill for silly amounts—either ridiculously low or high. Stories keep on popping up about computer systems chasing people for $0.01. Don't be guilty of perpetrating professional embarrassments like this. More sophistication can be added by comparing a fee amount with previous amounts charged to the same payer, or by asking for suspiciously large (or small) amounts to be manually approved before they are charged. The latter is likely to need its own threshold values defined.

2. **Fee-free period,** such as first month free.

3. **Odd fee periods.** Some organizations are forced to calculate periodic fees according to odd periods, because manual processes take several days at the end of the month. It's unfortunate that this happens, but when it does, all systems that provide billing-related information are forced to adhere to it. (Also bear in mind that this situation might improve in the future, which means that the system might be expected to switch to a more natural way of working. It's easy for such a switch to go wrong.)

4. **Rates that vary over time,** such as different rates at off-peak or busy times, or an annual subscription that becomes cheaper each year to reward loyal customers.

This section mentions things that are relatively common. Always properly investigate the complexities that apply in your own situation. Fees are invariably more complex than they appear, and failing to deal with the complexities can result in incorrectly calculated fees.

Here are a few example requirements for some of these things:

Summary	Definition
Free period for fee over time	For each fee charged over time, it shall be possible to specify an initial period for which no fee is payable.
	For example, an annual fee might be charged but the first year could be free.
Fee rate varies according to time	It shall be possible for different fee rates to be applied depending on the time of day and/or day of the week.
	The intent of this requirement is to facilitate peak and off-peak fees.
Fee over time changes over time	For each fee charged over time, it shall be possible to specify that a different fee rate be used after different lengths of time.
	For example, an annual fee might be $15 in the first year, $10 in the second year, and $5 per annum thereafter.

Consolidation   For some fees and taxes, the amount that's actually charged isn't just a matter of adding up amounts from the things on which it's charged: extra processing might be needed. Minimum or maximum fee amounts might apply to the total, not just individual fee amounts. Investigate what's needed. Here's an example:

Summary	Definition
Netting of sales tax	Where one organization passes on to another organization part of an amount received (such as a fee), sales tax shall be payable only on the net of the two amounts.
	For example, if the system operator receives $2.00 from a customer and pays $0.50 of that to an agent, the system operator pays sales tax only on the $1.50 difference.

Manual Intervention   Leaving a system to calculate and levy fees all by itself can be a risky business, given how sensitive people and organizations are about paying money and how many questionable situations can occur. Useful features for which to consider writing requirements can be divided into those that prevent mistakes and those that correct them.

Preventing mistakes means allowing someone to review what the system proposes to charge before it is allowed to go ahead. Review is useful only if something can be done about those the reviewer's not happy with—which means both the ability to approve the fee and to make an adjustment to it (including to waive the fee altogether). Manual review is practical only if the number of fees to be approved is of manageable proportions; if there are too many, you can still consider reviewing *large amounts* and letting the rest through automatically.

Correcting a mistake involves the ability to enter a fee amount in order to credit or debit the affected party. It helps if you can enter an explanation to make the adjustment's purpose clear. Here are a couple of simple examples:

Summary	Definition
Manual fee entry	It shall be possible for a user to enter details for a one-off fee.
Manual fee adjustment	It shall be possible for a user to make a manual adjustment to an existing fee amount that has been levied.

Justify Fee Amount   Computer systems are good at making masses of calculations, but they're awful at explaining what they did and why. Unless you expressly ask for accountability from software, you are most definitely not going to get it—and if you do ask, you'll only get it with a fight, because it's very difficult to implement properly. Even a spreadsheet will tell you only the formula it used, not where its data came from. Still, justification of how a fee was calculated can be valuable and a system feature worth paying for. If a taxation authority questions how you arrived at your tax amount and you can't tell them, you could find yourself in trouble.

Here's an example that's all-embracing (and, as a result, to be used only if you appreciate the consequences):

Summary	Definition
Justify fee amount	For each fee amount calculated, it shall be possible to obtain justification of how the amount came about. For example, when a fee amount is displayed to a user, that user shall be able to ask to see justification of that amount. Justification shall be taken to mean display of the formula used plus an explanation of the origin of each value supplied to it.

Considerations for Development

If a system involves several types of fees and taxes and might need to accommodate more in future, it's worth building this area in an extendable manner. This is especially true if you're building a product that is liable to be used in different countries, with different tax regimes.

Considerations for Testing

When reviewing requirements, check each fee requirement for precision: does it make clear what's meant to happen in all circumstances?

Testing fees can be divided into two parts. First, test that each fee is charged when it should, and only then. Second, test that each fee amount is calculated correctly (as per the calculation formula requirement pattern in Chapter 6, "Information Requirement Patterns"). If there are multiple types of fees, both parts must test that different fees interact as they should—that is, that you're not charging fees on fees (or taxes on taxes).

View fees from the perspective of each of the interested parties: the payer, the receiver (especially if it's a government taxation agency), a user involved in administering the fee, and an auditor. Is each party given all the information they might reasonably expect?

Test all manual actions involved in levying a tax, and check that they are practical. If unusual fee amounts must be approved, is the approval action efficient? Does it tell the user everything they need to decide whether to approve it?

Glossary

This glossary gives definitions of terms and acronyms used in this book. It is in the form suggested in the "Glossary" section in Chapter 2, "The Contents of a Requirements Specification." This book introduces no acronyms of its own.

Term	Definition
ACID	Properties possessed by any reliable database, in order to provide information integrity: **Atomic**—any change is made either completely or not at all; **Consistent**—whichever way you look at the data you get the same picture; **Isolated**—no change is affected by any other change that's in progress but not yet completed; and **Durable**—any completed change stays there.
Actor	A role that a person (or other autonomous entity) plays in a system. One person can play several actors (contrary to any preconceptions you might have from watching theatrical actors). An actor is portrayed as a stick figure (again, unlike thespians). "Actor" is a UML term used primarily with use cases.
Administrative data	Data used to keep a system running smoothly. Examples are counters such as the last-used customer number, and the time that month-end processing was last performed. Administrative data is either global or associated with a type of living entity (such as a customer's last order number).
Agile	1. A software development outlook that aims to be lean and flexible by valuing people over processes, software over documentation, collaboration over contracts, and responsiveness over plans.
	2. Being adept at reacting to the unexpected, an ability especially prized if one doesn't take the trouble to find out what to expect.
Analyst	A person responsible for gathering, analyzing, specifying, and managing changes to requirements. This book uses "analyst" to mean exclusively a requirements analyst (also sometimes called a requirements engineer).
	Analysts are sometimes divided into *business analysts* and *systems analysts*, mainly depending on whether or not they come from a technical background.
Archive	To archive is to move or copy a body of data from one medium of permanent storage to another. The "body of data" archived can be any subset of the available data. The backing up of a whole database is expressly excluded: it is not archiving.
Assumption	A statement that something can safely be treated as fact, as an axiom that can be depended upon (in the context of the system).

Term	Definition
ATM	Automated Teller Machine. An example of a device that authenticates a user by means of both something they have (a bank card) and something they know (a PIN).
Authentication	The process by which a registered user says who they are and proves it to a system's satisfaction.
Authorization	An authorization grants a user or class of users permission to perform a particular action or set of actions or to access particular resources.
Availability window	A system's normal hours of operation. For a company internal system running from 9 a.m. to 5 p.m., a day's average throughput is crammed into eight hours; for an always-open Web system, it is spread over 24 hours per day. (See the availability requirement pattern in Chapter 9, "Performance Requirement Patterns.")
Back office	The behind-the-scenes people and activities of a business (unsung heroes).
Business rule	A definition of an aspect of how a business operates. For example, a business rule could define how the business should act in a particular situation (such as when a customer credit card payment is rejected) or define a constraint (such as a limit on the size of payments an employee can approve).
Check digit	A digit calculated from a number and then appended to the number. It is used as a simple way to spot most errors when the number is typed in. If any digit is keyed in wrongly, there is roughly a 90 percent chance that the check digit calculated for the number keyed in will be wrong—so the user can be prompted to correct the number.
Configuration	Parameters that control how a system behaves. Examples are sales tax rates and bank account types. See the configuration requirement pattern in Chapter 7, "Data Entity Requirement Patterns."
Constraint	A restriction on how a system can be implemented. A constraint can restrict either the way the system can be built (for example, the programming language to use) or it can restrict some aspect of the delivered system itself (such as the technology it can use in production).
Co-ordinated change	One of a collection of related changes to information that all need to be applied at exactly the same time.
	For example, when a retail business changes its pricing schedule—raising some prices, lowering others, modifying discount rates, introducing a range of special offers—it will want them all to happen at once in a big bang, not in dribs and drabs.
CPU	Central Processing Unit. That part of a computer that performs the real computational work and where all the worst mistakes happen.
CRUD	**C**reate, **R**ead, **U**pdate, **D**elete: the fundamental operations performed on a unit of data in a database.

Term	Definition
CSV	Comma Separated Value. A simple file format in which a comma is used to distinguish individual values from one another, convenient for loading into a spreadsheet.
Customer	1. A person or organization who commissions a system. (In this context, they are the customer of the team that delivers the system.) 2. A person who makes purchases using the system; a type of user. (In this context, they are the customer of the organization that operates the system.)
Dependency	1. A reliance that one requirement has upon another requirement. 2. See "external dependency."
Derived data	Data computed from other kinds of data. Examples are daily order totals and total balances for each account type. Derived data can be identified by asking the question, "If I lost it, would I be able to regenerate it from the other data available?" In theory, you can regenerate all derived data from the data it is based on, though in practice it demands a sound database design (so there's some risk!). See the introduction to Chapter 7.
Divertive requirement pattern	A requirement pattern that attempts to divert the analyst away from an obvious—but bad or inappropriate—way of framing a requirement and towards a better way.
Domain	See "Requirement pattern domain."
Downtime	Time during which the system is unavailable to users when it is scheduled to be available. (Also a time when some users can feel down, while others nip out for a coffee or cigarette.) Note that according to this definition, scheduled routine maintenance does not count as downtime, even though users might want to use the system while scheduled maintenance is being performed.
EFTPOS	Electronic Funds Transfer at Point of Sale. A big name for a little box that lets a retailer debit a customer's credit or debit card. A candidate for the ugliest acronym widely inflicted on the general public.
External dependency	A factor that a system depends upon but which is outside the system's control. (See the "Major Assumptions" section in Chapter 2.)
Extreme programming	A lean, agile approach to software development in which "user stories" and detailed test cases take the place of traditional specifications. See the "An Extreme Requirements Process" section in Chapter 1, "Crash Course in Specifying Requirements."

Term	Definition
Fee	An amount of money charged by one party to another for some kind of service.
Follow-on requirement	A requirement that specifies additional details for an original requirement that it follows.
Functional requirement	A requirement that defines a function that the system must possess (an activity it must be able to perform, something it must be able to *do*).
Gold-plating	1. Features that confer no practical benefit 2. Features that a particular person wants excluded and which they wish to denigrate The second usage is the more common.
Historic data	Old, inactive data that is no longer affects current business, but needs to be retained for legal or future investigative reasons.
HTML	HyperText Markup Language. A language designed to let nuclear physicists share their research papers and that is later pumped full of steroids to carry all the information in the world.
ID	A unique identifier for some type of entity.
Infrastructure	An underlying set of capabilities needed to support one or more types of requirements.
Invisible ID	An ID that is used internally by the system in order to function, but which is not normally visible to users. For example, if we wanted to give customers the option of changing their customer ID, we could assign them a second, invisible customer ID that never changes.
ISO	International Organization for Standardization. An international standards organization. You have to pay money for copies of its standards. It lives at *http://www.iso.org*.
IT	Information Technology. The wide range of expertise, hardware, and software needed to manage (or to mess up or lose) large quantities of information.
JAD	Joint Application Development. An approach to specifying the requirements, user interface, and other high-level aspects of a new system through dedicated sessions involving executives, users, and developers.
LDAP	Lightweight Directory Access Protocol. A standard for components used to enable computers to find things, typically used to find organizations, people, and other computers using addresses of various kinds (such as names, email addresses, and phone numbers). The standard itself resides at *http://www.ietf.org/rfc/rfc1487.txt*. It is called "lightweight" because its parent, the X.500 standard, is even bigger.

Term	Definition
Living entity	An entity that has a lifespan: it is created, might be modified many times, and is eventually terminated. Examples are a bank account and a shop customer. (Termination means purely as far as a system is concerned; physical assassination is not involved.)
	Any entity that is for configuration purposes should be categorized as configuration rather than as a living entity, though it can enjoy a lifespan in the same way.
	See the living entity requirement pattern in Chapter 7.
Middleware	Software of indeterminate extent used to tie the major components of a system together—in particular, allowing the parts of a distributed system to communicate with each other.
Nonfunctional requirement	A requirement that defines some characteristic that a system must possess, but which is not something the system must be able to *do* (a function).
	Requirements do not divide neatly into functional and nonfunctional. A high-level nonfunctional requirement could lead to the defining of functions to deliver parts of it. (For example, a performance goal might lead to functions that help to achieve it). Similarly, a requirement for a function might have a follow-on requirement that defines a nonfunctional characteristic that the function must possess (restricting access to it, say).
ODBC	Open DataBase Connectivity. A standard for an application programming interface (API) produced by Microsoft for accessing a database.
Offline storage	A permanent storage medium that can be removed from a device that produces and/or reads it and that can be placed in a secure physical container (for example, a tape that can be locked in a safe).
Organization unit	Any subset of an organization that makes it easier to manage. It is a concrete collection of people you can go and visit (such as "the finance department"). See the multi-organization unit requirement pattern in Chapter 12, "Commercial Requirement Patterns."
Organization unit type	An abstract organizational concept (such as "department") of which organization units are instances. See the multi-organization unit requirement pattern in Chapter 12.
Outage	A single continuous period of time for which a system is unavailable to users. (Not to be confused with *outrage*, though the two can occur at the same time.)
PDF	A file format developed by Adobe Corporation for textual-oriented documents, which are produced by the Adobe Acrobat application.
Permanent storage	A place that can be relied on to store data for long periods of time and that doesn't lose it when the power is switched off. Examples are disk drives, magnetic tapes, CDs, and DVDs.

Term	Definition
Pervasive requirement	A requirement that applies systemwide for the purpose of defining something that applies to all requirements of a particular type.
	For example, "All reports shall show the date on which they were printed" is a pervasive requirement that implicitly applies to all requirements for reports.
PIN	Personal Identification Number. A numeric equivalent of a password.
	"PIN number" is the most widespread case of what *New Scientist* magazine has dubbed "RAS syndrome," where RAS stands for Redundant Acronym Syndrome.
Project	The mobilizing of a team for a temporary duration to achieve a set of stated objectives. For a system development project, its requirements define the objectives.
Recovery	The act of bringing up to date the data loaded into a database by means of a restore after a failure, by using an update log of changes made since the backup was taken.
Refactoring	1. The act of tidying up a piece of software that has grown untidy due to accumulated changes that were never envisaged when it was first written. (This is a term heard more in environments where comprehensive requirements are not specified.)
	2. The time and money allocated to the same.
Requirement	A single, measurable objective that a system must satisfy.
Requirement pattern	An approach to specifying a particular type of requirement.
Requirement pattern domain	A convenient grouping of related requirement patterns.
Requirement pattern group	A description of the features that a set of requirement patterns has in common.
	In object-oriented terms, a requirement pattern group can be regarded as an *abstract base class* for all the requirement patterns that choose to extend it.
Requirements specification	A requirements specification for a system is a document that states all the requirements the system must satisfy, plus any background material needed to make it readable and understandable.
	Note that this book spells it consistently as requirements specification (for "requirements" in the plural).
Requirements time	The phase in a project at which requirements are being specified. This expression is usually used when pointing out something that might not be known this early in the project. A happy, carefree time.
Response time	The length of time between a request being submitted to a system at a particular place and a response being perceived at the same place. (See the response time requirement pattern in Chapter 9.)
Restore	The act of copying reloading data into a database from a back-up when the main data is lost.

Term	Definition
SMS	Short Message Service. The cool way to notify a techo that a system has crashed and they must curtail their weekend to fix it.
SOX	Sarbanes-Oxley Act, 2002. Also known as the Public Company Accounting Reform and Investor Protection Act. A U.S. law enacted to enforce a high standard of financial propriety in public companies. See the SOX example requirement in the comply-with-standard requirement pattern in Chapter 5, "Fundamental Requirement Patterns."
SQL	Structured Query Language. A specialized programming language dedicated to interacting with a database (for reading and writing data and for other activities, too). SQL is the de facto universal standard for relational database products.
Surreptitious unavailability	A fleeting amount of time for which the system is unavailable to users while it performs a background housekeeping task. It typically manifests itself as slower-than-normal response time, but usually no one notices. (See the availability requirement pattern in Chapter 9.)
System	1. A cooperating collection of software components and (optionally) the hardware on which it runs that achieves a useful purpose or allows people who use it to achieve a useful purpose. (A computer system.) 2. The operational components of a business or part of a business, including computer systems, people, policies, and procedures, and all the other resources the business needs. (A business system in the broadest sense.) This book uses only the first definition.
Technology	Any externally-produced hardware or software that is used in the building, installing, and running of a system.
Tester	A person responsible for testing a software system—specifically, in this book, testing that the system complies with its requirements.
Testing	The process of finding out the extent to which a system deviates from what it should be doing.
Timed change	A change to information that needs to occur at a precise, predetermined moment in time. For example, switching to or from summer time has to happen at precisely 2 a.m. on a designated Sunday morning. Moving the Ruthenian Dinar across to the Euro must be done at midnight on a published date.
Timestamp	The date and time at which an event occurred.
Transaction	An event in the life of a living entity.
UML	Unified Modeling Language. A universally popular standard that can model every aspect of systems (and much else besides), resulting from a grand alliance between (that is, unification of— hence the name) the most revered system specification methodologists of the late twentieth and early twenty-first centuries. UML's official residence is *http://www.uml.org*.

Term	Definition
URL	Uniform Resource Locator. A way of representing the location of a resource, most commonly a Web page.
Use case	A main scenario and (optionally) variants that describe the steps involved in achieving a particular user goal. Each use case is initiated by an actor (or by another use case).
Use case diagram	A high level diagram showing one user goal or more, along with relationships with actors and other use cases. See the "A Traditional Requirements Process" section in the full version of Chapter 1 for a couple of inexcusably irreverent examples.
User	A person who uses a computer system.
User interface infrastructure	A coherent set of components that together allow a user to interact with the system, excluding anything developed as part of a specific system, general underlying software (such as an operating system), and hardware. That is, a user interface infrastructure is what's left if you take away the system and everything it needs to run that isn't wholly user interfacial.
User preference	An item of information that is set by a user to indicate one aspect of how they wish the system to behave.
User response time	The length of time between a user submitting a request (hitting the button) and the response being displayed on their screen. (See the response time requirement pattern in Chapter 9.)
UTC	Universal Time Co-ordinated. The datum time zone against which all others are defined. It has no daylight saving time. It is effectively what was formerly known as Greenwich Mean Time, and is what pilots call "Zulu."
Waterfall	A way of organizing a complex task in which one phase of the work is largely completed before beginning the next phase. See the "Waterfall and Whirlpools" section in the full version of Chapter 1.
XML	Extensible Markup Language. A miraculous format for information that's capable of storing absolutely anything at all.
XP	Extreme Programming.
XSLT	Extensible Stylesheet Language Transformations. A way of specifying how to magically transform an XML document into something else even more magnificent.

References

Ambler, Scott. 2002. *Agile Modeling*. Wiley. ISBN 0-471-20282-7.

Ash, Lydia. 2003. *The Web Testing Companion*. Wiley. ISBN 0-471-43021-8.

Booch, Grady, James Rumbaugh, and Ivar Jacobson. 1999. *The Unified Modeling Language User Guide*. Addison-Wesley. ISBN 0-201-57168-4.

Carroll, Lewis. *Alice's Adventures in Wonderland and Through the Looking Glass*. Instructive examples of the sorts of bizarre logic employed by the diverse characters encountered in software development projects, especially reviewers of documents.

Coad, Peter and Edward Yourdon. 1991. *Object-Oriented Analysis*. Yourdon Press. ISBN 0-13-629981-4.

Conan Doyle, Arthur. *The Celebrated Cases of Sherlock Holmes*. A readable primer on the application of logic to real world problems, and various analytical techniques. With case studies. (It's also worth observing that Sherlock Holmes was killed falling over a waterfall.)

Cooper, Alan. 1999. *The Inmates Are Running the Asylum*. SAMS. ISBN 0-672-31649-8. For insights into why products (and especially computer systems) are so often infuriatingly difficult to use.

Davis, Alan M. 1993. *Software Requirements: Objects, Functions and States*. Prentice Hall. ISBN 0-13-805763-X.

_____. 2005. *Just Enough Requirements Management*. Dorset House. ISBN 0-932633-64-1.

Eriksson, Hans-Erik and Magnus Penker. 2000. *Business Modeling with UML*. Wiley. ISBN 0-471-29551-5.

Ferdinandi, Patricia L. 2002. *A Requirements Pattern: Succeeding in the Internet Economy*. Addison-Wesley. ISBN 0-201-73826-0.

Fowler, Martin. 1996. *Analysis Patterns: Reusable Object Models*. Addison-Wesley. ISBN 0-201-89542-0.

Gamma, Erich, Richard Helm, Ralph Johnson, and John Vlissides. 1995. *Design Patterns– Elements of Reusable Object-Oriented Software*. Addison-Wesley. ISBN 0-201-63361-2.

Gilb, Tom. 2005. *Competitive Engineering: A Handbook for Systems Engineering, Requirements Engineering, and Software Engineering Using Planguage*. Elsevier Butterworth-Heinemann. ISBN 0-7506-6507-6.

Graham, Ian. 1998. *Requirements Engineering and Rapid Development*. Addison-Wesley. ISBN 0-201-36047-0.

Herzum, Peter and Oliver Sims. 2002. *Business Component Factory*. Wiley. ISBN 0-471-32760-3.

Hohmann, Luke. 2003. *Beyond Software Architecture*. Addison-Wesley. ISBN 0-201-77594-8.

Hooks, Ivy F. and Kristin A. Farry. 2001. *Customer-Centered Products: Creating Successful Products Through Smart Requirements Management*. Amacom. ISBN 0-8144-0568-1.

International Institute of Business Analysts (IIBA). *Business Analysis Body of Knowledge (BABOK)*. Available online from *http://www.theiiba.org*.

Jackson, Michael. 1995. *Software Requirements & Specifications*. Addison-Wesley. ISBN 0-201-87712-0.

_____. 2001. *Problem Frames*. Addison-Wesley. ISBN 0-201-59626-X.

Kulak, Daryl and Eamonn Guiney. 2000. *Use Cases: Requirements in Context*. Addison-Wesley. ISBN 0-201-65767-8.

Leffingwell, Dean and Don Widrig. 2000. *Managing Software Requirements*. Addison-Wesley. ISBN 0-201-61593-2.

McConnell, Steve. 1993. *Code Complete*. Microsoft Press. ISBN 1-55615-484-4.

_____. 1996. *Rapid Development*. Microsoft Press. ISBN 1-55615-900-5.

Morgan, Tony. 2002. *Business Rules and Information Systems*. Addison-Wesley. ISBN 0-201-74391-4.

Mowbray, Thomas J. and Raphael C. Malveau. 1997. *CORBA Design Patterns*. Wiley. ISBN 0-471-15882-8.

Mueller, John Paul. 2003. *Accessibility for Everybody: Understanding the Section 508 Accessibility Requirements*. Apress. ISBN 1-59059-086-4.

Robertson, Suzanne and James. 2006. *Mastering the Requirements Process*, Second Edition. Addison-Wesley. ISBN 0-321-41949-9.

Smith, Richard E. 2002. *Authentication–From Passwords to Public Keys*. Addison-Wesley. ISBN 0-201-61599-1. A good reference when considering an access control infrastructure.

von Halle, Barbara. 2002. *Business Rules Applied*. Wiley. ISBN 0-471-41293-7. Supporting material is available at *http://www.wiley.com/compbooks/vonhalle*.

Wiegers, Karl E. 2003. *Software Requirements*, Second Edition. Microsoft Press. ISBN 0-7356-1879-8.

_____. 2006. *More on Software Requirements*. Microsoft Press. ISBN 0-7356-2267-1.

Index

All page numbers that begin with "F-" refer to the full versions of Chapters 1 and 2. These are not in the printed book, but are available for download from *http://www.microsoft.com/ mspress/companion/9780735623989.*

A

acceptance of requirements, F-21–F-22
acceptance tests, 9, F-25
access control
  chronicle, 149, 150–151
  configuration, 140
  for data archiving, 115
  described, 281
  infrastructure considerations, 283
  integral to a software system, 282–283
  making more friendly, 306
  for organization units, 329
  recording changes in, 317
  for reporting, 190
  underlying mechanism for, 318
access control domain, 29–30, 281
access control extensions, 234–235
Access Controller, F-57
access control requirement pattern, 281–323
access only when logged in requirement, 310
access privileges for users, 285
access rights. *See* privileges
access rules, applying, 308–309
accessibility
  authentication alternatives, 298
  as a source of nonfunctional system aspects, F-70
  specific needs for, 168, 169, 172, 174–175, 178–182, 183–184
accessibility requirement pattern, 168–186
accountants, as programmers, 332
accounting entries, 260
accounting system interface, 56
ACID properties, 123, 154
acknowledgement of receipt, 58, 59
acronyms, use of, F-47–F-48
actions
  approving, 318
  authorizing within functions, 308, 310
  not approving own, 322
  pending, storage of, 129
active attack, 60, 61
active user sessions, terminating, 300
active users, number of, 149
activity peaks, 213
activity triggers, 209
actors, F-13, F-69

adapters, 53, 54, 250
address formats, unparochialness and, 259
"Affects Database" pattern classification, 35
agile manifesto, 8, F-22
agile outlook, adopting, F-22
agile requirements processes, 8–10, F-22–F-28
alarm monitor interface, 56
alarms, 214, 233
alphabetic characters, 87
alphabetic mnemonic, F-37
alphanumeric characters, 87
alternative templates, 25
ambiguities of fee calculation, 336–337
Americans with Disabilities Act, 170
analysis paralysis, F-4
analysis patterns, 20
analyst, F-8, F-16
anecdotal checking, 261
animated graphics, 188
Apache Web server, 69
Applicability section, 21, 23–24, 45
approval, 321–322, 323
approval mechanisms, 322
approval requirement pattern, 281, 282, 318–323
"approved" version, determining, F-52–F-53
architecture, infrastructures contributing to, F-64
archiving
  chronicles, 150
  data. *See* data archiving
artifacts in agile development, F-23
assistive technology, 172, 176, 178–179, 185
assumptions, 16, F-59, F-60
atomic changes, 123
atomic nature of requirements, 20–21
attachments, email, 123
attributes, defining, 34
audience, identifying, 13, 34, F-33
audio alert, visual cue for, 182
audit trails, 121, 190
Australian Privacy Act of 1988, 75
authentication
  biometric, 178
  defined, 295
  information for users, 285
  mechanisms, 296
  strength of, 308, 311

authors
    for each reference, F-50
    listing in the document history, F-52
    of a requirement pattern, 23
authority, ability to delegate, 307
authorization
    chronicling changes, 317
    example requirements, 309–313
authorization checks, 317, 318
authorization inquiries, 316–317
automatic refreshing of inquiries, 157, 159, 177, 188
availability
    of an interface, 57, 58
    lack of. *See* downtime
    scalability and, 242, 244
availability requirement pattern, 217–238
availability window, 208, 219, 221, 222–223

B

back door access, preventing, 293
background processing, responsibility for, 282
backups. *See also* data archiving
    database, 110
    information, 123
    reports, 190
    system, 229
Basic details section of requirement pattern, 21,
        22–23, 45
basis of a fee or tax, 332–333
binary numbers, 87
binding part. *See* formal part
biometric authentication, 178
biometric reader, 285
blanket bans, 309, 312–313
blanket permission, 309
blocking users, 298, 302–303
Boolean operators, 88
brackets, double-angled and square, 25, 46
break locked session, 301
bureau service, 329
business entities, identifying, 16, F-61
business hours, availability during, 222
business intent of inquiry, 156–157
business motivation behind a system, F-31
business purposes, data types for, 86
business rule patterns, 20
business rules, 38
business significance, 147
business systems, data categories in, 120–122
business volume, growth in, 241

C

calculations, 102–107
calculation formula, subcalculations, 103, 106
calculation formula requirement pattern, 102–107

calendar date, 88, 259
calendar time period, 336–337
candidate glossary terms, 14, F-45
candidate infrastructures, building a list of, F-64
candidate multinesses, 264–265
candidate patterns, multiple variants of, 44
candidate requirement pattern, 43
candidate solutions, F-10
capacity, patterns for, 47
capitalization, F-41, F-48
capped data line in reports, 167
card number format, 92
case of alphabetic characters, 87
case-sensitive identifiers, 98
cash withdrawal limit, 142
catch-alls, pervasive requirements as, 27
categorization of data entities, 119–120
certification authority (CA) interface, 56
change history for living entities, 131
changes, listing in the document history, F-52
changing passwords, 287, 289
characters, 87, 88
character sets, allowing, 87
charging fees over time, 333
charts in reports, 164
check digits, 89
chronicles, 121, 144–153
        chronicle entries for reports, 190
chronicle requirement pattern, 144–153
circumstances of approval, 319
classes of users, 285
classification lists, format of, 23
classification of requirement patterns, 23, 33–35
codes of conduct, as standards, 71
coding standards, compliance with, 76
cognitive abilities (accessibility), 171, 174, 182
collaboration over contracts, F-23
collaborative approach, 8, F-17, F-18, F-19
color, use of, 180, 183
commenting, of source code, 83
commercial domain, 29–30, 325
commercial requirement pattern, 325–340
commercial systems
    availability of, 217
    detailed requirements specification for, 79
    importance of transactions in, 134
    performance types in, 191
common data for living entities, 131
common inquiry characteristics, 159, 161
common requirements, 10, F-26
communication links, F-56
communication medium, 60
communications, disaster recovery, 237
communications mechanism, interfaces involving, 58
company coding standards, compliance with, 76
company financial information, restricting access to, 311

company standards, 71
company Web style guidelines, compliance with, 76
company-specific requirement patterns, 43
compatible technology, 70
completeness
    of chronicles, 145
    of requirements, 40
complex transactions, 134–135, 138
compliance
    with accessibility standards, 169, 170, 175, 184
    with data longevity regulations, 107
    demands for a standard, 73
comply-with-standard requirement pattern, 26, 71–79
component status inquiry, 159
components of a system, 15, F-55
compound data item, 95
compound data types, 88
comprehensive inquiries, 159, 160
computer literacy, accessibility and, 171, 174
conciseness of identifiers, 97
conciseness of requirement IDs, 13, F-37
confidentiality of reports, 166
configurable authorization, 47, 281, 282, 313–318
configurable authorization requirement
        pattern, 313–318
configuration, 120
    of drivers, 248, 251–252, 253
    multiness requirements and, 263, 264
configuration entities, 138, 141, 142
configuration files, 123
configuration requirement pattern, 37, 138–144
configuration values
    changing, 139–140, 143, 144, 149
    content requirements, 141
    defining, 140
    examples of, 142
    flexibility of, 138
    hard-coded, avoidance of, 138–139, 143
    representative, 141
    storing, 140
    systemwide, 138, 139
    templates for, 142
Considerations for development section, 21, 28–29,
        40, 48
Considerations for testing section, 21, 29, 40, 48
consistency
    of data, 123
    of glossary terms, F-49
    maintaining, 14, F-48
    promoted by requirement patterns, 19
consolidation of fees/taxes, 338
constraints, F-54
contact details, 96
Content section, 21, 24, 47
context diagrams
    advantages of, F-57

comparing for old and new systems, F-58
defined, F-54–F-55
in every requirements specification, 52
kinds of information on, 15–16, F-55–F-56
notable points about, F-57
samples, 52, 53
context of data types, 92
Context section of a requirements specification, 15–17,
        F-30, F-53–F-68
continuity of IDs, 99, 101
contradictions, resolving, F-43
core database, 124
core terms in a glossary, F-48
corporate restructuring, 245
cosmetic script, 181
cost-benefit analysis, 45
countries
    differences between, 258–260
    installing systems in different, 255
    ISO 3166 standard, 76
CPU cycle rate, throughput targets and, 207
cross-instance access, 270
cross-instance conversion, 270
CRUD operations, 154
cultural differences, unparochialness and, 259
currency details
    configuration values for, 142
    ISO 4, 217
    multiness in, 267
    number types for, 87
    unparochialness and, 258
customers
    putting in control, F-5
    using requirements, F-3
customer agreement, F-26
customer capacity, 216
customer details, storing, 130
customer number, 100
customer orders, archiving of, 113
customer password format requirement, 288
customer scalability, 243
customer service, accessible, 184
customer support for multiness instances, 268

D

data. *See also* information
    backdated, 109
    backing up, 123
    configurable authorization to, 314
    derived, 121
    disaster recovery, 237
    historic, 121
    restricting access to, 308, 310–311
    segregated, 261–262
    unaddable, 262
data access, recording unsuccessful, 148

data archiving requirement pattern, 110–117
data consistency, 123
data description for archiving, 112
data display, types of, 86
data durability, 123
data entities. *See also* living entities
   categorization of, 119–120
   naming, 122, 130
data entity domain, 29
data entity requirement pattern, 119–154
data entry function, testing user registration as, 295
data format error response time, 200
data husbandry, 85
data longevity requirement pattern, 107–110
data loss, 123, 124
data modification, archiving and, 115
data protection, 123, 287, 290–292
data recovery, 123, 124
data storage, 107, 108. *See also* data archiving
data stores, 122, 126–127, F-56
data structure, 136
data structure requirement pattern, 94–96
data type requirement pattern, 86–94
data types
   in calculation formulas, 103
   for different organizations, 260
data warehouse, 164
database
   ACID properties of, 123, 154
   backing up of, 110
   CRUD operations, 154
   estimating disk space needed for, 216
   recording events in, 151
   specifying a widely used, 68
   as storage mechanism, 120, 154
dates, 88, 89–90
   of each version released, F-52
   event, 151
   report, 166
   systemwide aspects of, 93
   unparochialness and, 259
date display formats, 90
day one considerations for user
     registration, 287, 294
Daylight Saving Time, 90
de-authentication of users, 298, 299–300
default language of a system, 274
default multiness instances, 268
definitions
   in a glossary, 14, F-44, F-45, F-46
   of requirements. *See* requirement definitions
delays, warning users about, 203
deliberate shutdowns, 231
delivery mechanisms for reports, 190
denial-by-default rule, 305–306, 308, 310
dependencies, 16, 45, F-59
de-registration of users, 287, 290

derived data, 121
descriptive placeholders, 46
design patterns, 20, 21, 42
designers, constraining, F-9
destination of archived data, 112–113
detailed requirements, 4, F-3, F-27
details in a requirement definition, F-42
developers
   constraining, F-9
   guidance to, 47, 48
   using requirements, F-3
   writing in the language of, 28–29
development
   approaches, 5–6, F-6
   facilities, 69
   splitting between multiple teams, 54
   technology, 66, 70
devolution of information, 135
dexterity, accessibility and, 171, 174, 182
dialects, 259, 272
diminishing returns, availability increases and, 220
disabilities, people with, 168, 169
disaster recovery systems, 237
disclaimers
   regarding the glossary, F-44
   stating, 13, F-33
discounts, specifying, 334
Discussion section in requirement pattern, 21, 24
disk space needed, estimating, 216
display format, 91, 99
display of data, 86
distinct user experiences, 261, 267–269, 271
distinctive requirement IDs, 13, F-37
distributed office scalability, 243
divertive performance patterns, 192
divertive requirement pattern, 32, 36
Document history section of requirements
     specification, 15, F-51–F-53
document library scalability, 243
document management system, 154
document purpose, F-30
Document purpose section, 12–13, F-32–F-33
document templates, 123
documentary efficiency, 9
documentation
   accessibility of, 175, 184
   of interfaces, 57, 61
   purpose of, F-24
   unparochial, 258
documentation requirement pattern, 81–84
domains
   assigning requirement patterns to, 29–31
   compared to requirement pattern groups, 32
   creating new, 44–45
   infrastructures in, 30
   as a source of candidate infrastructures, F-64
   specifying, 22

domain expert, F-15
domain specification, 37
downtime
    business impact of, 221, 223–224
    causes of, 221, 225
    levels of, 218
    reducing, 225–235
    scheduled, 219
    tolerated, 222
draft requirements specification, writing, 8, F-18–F-19
drivers
    configuration information for, 248, 249–250
    extendability requirements and, 247, 249
    installation requirements for, 251–252, 253
    switching between, 253
    system requirements for, 250–251
    third-party, development requirements, 252
    upgrading, 253
driving entity, 215–216
durability of data, 123
duration start trigger, 108
dynamic capacity, 47
dynamic capacity requirement pattern, 212–215
dynamic users, counting, 213
dynamic Web functions, 222

E

effort estimation, F-26
ejecting users, 214
electronic communication medium for approval, 320
email, 91, 123
emergency extended access, 235
emergency remote access, 235
employee ID, 100
employee roles, 260
end of report line, 167
end-to-end response time, 196–197
English as a second language, accessibility and, 171
entity life history diagram. *See* state transition diagram
errors, 148, 233, 236. *See also* failures
error messages, 83, 236, 237
essence of a requirement, F-42
European Union, data protection provisions, 290
events, 144–145, 148–149, 333
event date, recording, 151
event record, 151, 152
event severity levels. *See* severity level
evolution of requirements, F-38
example requirements, 45–46
examples in a requirement definition, F-42
Examples section in a requirement pattern, 21, 26
excluded entities, determining, 216
exclusions, 16, F-61
executive summaries, avoiding acronyms in, F-48
explanatory text, displaying, 181
explicit interaction requirements, 62

extendability, 239
    of fees, 336
    of an interface, 57
    multiness requirements and, 262
    requirement pattern, 52, 73, 246–253
    types of, 264
extendability requirement pattern, 52, 73,
        246–253
extended access, 234–235
extends requirement pattern relationship, 32, 33
external dependencies, F-54
external interfaces, standards affecting, 72
external requirements specification, 79
external sources, allocating IDs from, 99
external systems, 127, 260
external users, 212
extra requirements, 27, 47
Extra requirements section
    considering during requirements definition, 39
    example requirements in, 28
    in a requirement pattern, 21, 26–28
    writing, 47–48
extreme programming (XP), 9, F-6, F-24
extreme requirements process, 9–10, F-24–F-26

F

failures, 231–237
faithful nature of chronicles, 145
federation of systems, 54
fee rates, determinants of, 333
feedback on requirements specification, dealing
        with, F-21
fee/tax requirement pattern, 330–340
financial data, storage of, 109
financial flows, diagramming, 331–332
financial transaction, 137–138, 158
financial year, 259
flat files, 123, 124
flexibility, 135
    of configuration values, 138
    described, 239
    domain, 29–30
    of identifiers, 98
    importance of, 239
    performance requirements and, 240
    as a source of nonfunctional system aspects, F-70
    testing, 240
flexibility requirement pattern, 239–279
follow-on requirements, 20, 27, 28, 47, 132
forgotten passwords, handling, 297, 298–299
formal part of a requirements specification, 6–7,
        F-11–F-12
formal statement of a requirement, F-42
formats
    for documentation, 82
    for requirement IDs, F-37

framework, compared to infrastructure, F-64
freezing requirement IDs, F-38
frequencies for requirement patterns, 23
full year, storing dates for, 90
functions
  authorizing access to, 308, 310, 311
  availability goals related to, 225
  compared to use cases, F-13
  controlling access to, 314
  controlling use of, 305
  recording, 145
  testing access to, 318
  user. *See* user function requirement pattern
  for viewing chronicles, 152
functional areas, 41, F-68–F-69
functional area sections in a requirements specification,
    12, 17–18, F-30, F-68–F-70
"Functional" requirement pattern classification, 34–35
functional requirements, 4, F-3
functional testing of user authentication, 304
fundamental domain, 29, 51
fundamental requirement patterns, 51–84

G

gaps in a domain, 45
Gather information requirements process step, 8, F-17
generalizations, use cases as, 37
general-purpose glossary, writing, F-49
geographic distribution of users, 209, 259
geographic variations for calculations, 103
glossary, 14, F-44–F-49
government regulations as standards, 71
graceful degrading of response time, 199
graphics, 180–181, 188. *See also* images
Greenwich Mean Time, 90
groupable requirement IDs, 13, F-37
guidance, provided by requirement patterns, 19

H

hand strain, accessibility and, 171, 174, 182
happen time for a transaction, 136
hard-coded configuration values, avoidance of,
    138–139, 143
hard-coding language-specific text, banning, 258
hardware
  availability issues related to, 226
  power of, 193
  replication of, 231
  scalability requirements and, 244, 245
hardware setup
  response time and, 199
  for throughput, 205, 206–207
Have specification reviewed step, 8, F-19–F-20
hearing, accessibility and, 171, 174, 181–182
hexadecimal numbers, 87

high load caveat, response time and, 199
high-level requirements, 4, F-3
HIPAA standard requirements, 75
historic data, 110, 121
housekeeping. *See* maintenance

I

IBM, accessibility guidelines, 186
icons, consistent meanings of, 182
identification details for users, 285
identifier. *See also* IDs
  unique for each requirement, 13, F-33
identity card issuance, 201
ID requirement pattern, 97–101
IDs, allocation of, 99, 263
IEEE (Institute of Electrical and Electronics Engineers)
    technical standards, 74
IETF (Internet Engineering Task Force), 74
images, 123, 180–181, 188. *See also* graphics
implementation, 40, F-43
implicit interactions, 62
inaccessible data, filtering, 311
inaccessible functions, hiding or disabling, 306
inactive information, removal of, 217
inactivity time-out, 301
incorrect password entry, recording, 149
incremental approach to requirements, 3, 10, F-2,
    F-6, F-26, F-28
independent reviews, approach to, 8, F-19
indexes of data archives, 114
industry-specific codes of practice, 71
industry-specific patterns, 43
industry-specific regulations, 71
industry-specific standards, 75
inflexibility
  system, 135, 138
  temporal, 256
informal elements in a requirement definition, 13,
    F-42–F-43
informal part of a requirements specification, 6–7,
    F-11–F-12
information. *See also* data
  backing up, 123
  changes, 122
  described, 85
  devolution of, 135
  domain, 29
  entry, multi-part, 122, 124–125
  flowing in an interaction, 64
  form of, 86
  gathering, F-17
  gathering from people, 8
  infrastructure, 154
  inquiries for, 123
  integrity, 122, 123

restricting access to, 305
retrieval mechanisms, 154
standards, 71
storage, 120, 124, 154
types of, 123
information requirement pattern, 85–117
infrastructures
defined, 17, F-63
disentangling from business functions, F-67
extendability requirements and, 250
fewer distinct actors, F-69
identifying, 30
improving the boundary of each, F-67
for information storage, 120, 154
for a new domain, 45
numbered list of, F-65
overviews, 30, 31
process for identifying and specifying, F-64–F-68
relationships with domains and requirement
patterns, 30, 31
reporting, 155, 189–190
in a requirement pattern diagram, 33
requirements, 27, F-67, F-68
requiring technical analysis, F-67
treating a business rule product as, 38
user interface, 155, 187–189
using from other domains, 30
Infrastructures section in a requirements specification,
17, F-54, F-63–F-68
inheritance relationship between requirement
patterns, 32, 33
initial customer capacity, 216
input, 171. See also throughput
input interpretation by multiness instances, 268
inquiry
automatic refreshing of, 157, 159, 177, 188
dynamic use, 214
for information, 123
for living entities, 131
multiness requirements and, 263
from offline storage, 117
versus report, 162
response time, 200
scalability requirements and, 245
static capacity, 217
inquiry requirement pattern, 156–161
inspection of a requirements specification, F-19
installability requirement pattern, 274–279
installation requirements for drivers, 251–252
installing
driver software, 251–252
scalability requirements and, 245
instances, giving users access to, 270
Institute of Electrical and Electronics Engineers (IEEE)
technical standards, 74

integers, data type, 87
integrity, 122, 123, 126, 140
intent of a requirement, F-42
interactions
across an interface, 57, 62, 63
describing an activity across the interface, 52
with inquiries, 157
specifying types of, 63, 64
interactive documentation, 84
interactive tutorial, 83–84
interest calculations, 104–106
interfaces
defining, 15–16, 54, 55, F-55
describing within other systems, F-57
development considerations, 62
documentation of, 61
examples, 56, F-58
indeterminate number of, 53
influencing the design of, 63
of an infrastructure, 31
interactions in requirements, 63
to multiple systems for the same purpose, 52, 54
ownership of, 63
passport control for, 58
positioning in a context diagram, F-57
security requirements for, 60–61
specifying between systems, 52
standards defining, 79
switching to new versions of, 59
templates, 56, 64
testing, 62, 65
upgrading, 59–61
as weak links, 52
interface adapters, 53–54
Interface Developer's Guide, writing, 61
interface ID, 55, 64
interface name, 55, 64
interface ownership, 54–55
interface resilience requirements, 58
internal interactions, 52
internal users, 212, F-57
international dimension, unparochialness and, 258–260
International Organization for Standardization (ISO), 74
International Standard Book Number (ISBN), F-51
Internet Engineering Task Force (IETF), 74
Internet Explorer Web browser, 68
Internet-based retail system, F-35–F-36
inter-system interaction requirement pattern, 47, 62–65
inter-system interface requirement pattern, 51–62
inter-system interfaces, 15–16, 65, 206, F-55
interview approach to gathering information, F-17, F-18
introduction of the glossary, F-44
Introduction section of a requirements specification,
12–15, F-30, F-31–F-53
invalid interactions, testing for an interface, 65

invisible ID scheme, 101
invocation requirements
    information infrastructure, 154
    for an infrastructure, F-67, F-68
    in an infrastructure overview, 31
    reporting infrastructure, 189–190
    user interface infrastructure, 187–188
"is-a-kind-of" relationship, 37
ISBN (International Standard Book Number), F-51
ISO (International Organization for Standardization), 74
ISO 639 standard for natural languages, 76, 272
ISO 3166 standard for countries and regions, 76
ISO 4217 standard for currencies, 76, 142
isolated changes, 123
iterative development, F-6

J

Java programming language, 69
Javadoc, 81
Joint Application Development (JAD), F-17
Joint Requirements Planning (JRP), F-17
justification
    for a requirement's existence, F-42–F-43
    for the requirement's form, F-42
    stating for every exclusion, F-60

K

Key Business Entities section of a requirements
    specification, 16–17, F-54, F-61–F-63
keyboards, accessibility and, 171, 174, 182

L

lack of confidence in requirements, F-4
languages
    accessibility and, 171
    displaying user interface in more than one
        alternative, 272
    of documentation, 82
    ISO 639, 76, 272
    multiness requirements and, 262
    unparochialness and, 258–259
language-specific resources, substituting for missing, 274
language-specific text, banning hard-coding of, 258
lapsed time period, 336–337
layouts, consistent for reports, 166
levels of registration, 286
liability to pay a fee, 333
life support mechanisms for a system, 17, F-63
life-critical systems, 217
lifespan of a data entity, 120, 129
list of allowed values, 88
living entity
    event in life of, 120, 133
    lifespan of, 120, 129
    multiness of, 264

naming, 122, 130
    testing considerations, 133, 144
living entity requirement pattern, 129–133
load on a system, reducing, 214, 215, 245
loan approval decision rule ID, 100
local context diagram, F-56
local currency, configuration values for, 142
local scope, F-46
locale, 272
logging in, 295
logging messages, 58
logging out, 298, 299–300
logical data types, 86, 264–265
logical pattern for requirement IDs, F-37
logical remove only, 131
logical view of a system, F-56
login function, coding, 304
logs, 121, 123
longevity of transactions, 136
loopholes in access control, 307
lowest-priority requirements, including, F-40

M

machines, distributing loads across, 214, 215, 245
machine shutdown, user access and, 230
maintenance, 190, 225, 228–229
Major assumptions section in a requirements
    specification, 16, F-54, F-59–F-60
Major exclusions section in a requirements
    specification, 16, F-54, F-60–F-61
Major nonfunctional capabilities section in a
    requirements specification, 18, F-30, F-70–F-71
manifestations
    of a domain specification, 37
    of an infrastructure, F-65
    of a requirement pattern, 22, 42
manual dexterity, accessibility and, 171, 174, 182
marketing campaigns, multiness in, 267
masking wait times, 203
maximum acceptable response time, 198–199
meaningfulness of identifiers, 97
medium for documentation, 82
memorability of identifiers, 97
memory leaks, testing for, 238
messages, recording, 58, 59
metrics, attaching to a requirement pattern, 40
Microsoft Windows operating system, 69
missing resources, substituting for, 268
mistakes, correcting for fees/taxes, 339
modification rules for transactions, 137–138
modularity, extendability and, 247
monetary amounts, 87
month basis for interest calculation, 105
morsel sizes for different development approaches,
    5–6, F-6
multibyte characters, allowing, 87

multilevel numbers as version numbers, F-52
multilingual organization, 262
multilingual requirement pattern, 272–279
multi-locale, 272
multimedia resources, 123, 176
multiness requirement pattern, 261–272
multi-organization unit, 262, 328
multi-organization unit requirement pattern, 325–330
multi-part information entry, 122, 124–125
multiple data stores, 122, 126–127
multiple instances of a particular interface, 52
multiple parts, IDs comprising, 97, 99
multiple sites, 254, 255
multi-release deliveries, F-40

N

names, data structure for personal, 96
naming
    configuration values, 141
    data entities, 122, 130
    data types, 90
    identifiers, 98
    inquiries, 156
    transactions, 135
natural availability level, 220
natural languages, ISO 639 standard, 76, 272
navigation among inquiries, 157, 160
negative numbers, 87
new users, processes for, 287, 293–294
nonbinding part. *See* informal part
nonfunctional requirements, 4, 69, F-3, F-40
Nonfunctional requirements section of requirements
        specification, F-71
noninterference archiving, 110
non-repudiation, 282
normal opening times, 217
notification methods
    customer preferences for, 133
    for driver requirements, 251
    for report recipients, 190
    for system failures, 233, 234
novice users, accessibility and, 171, 174
numeric display formats, unparochialness and, 258

O

Object Management Group (OMG), 74
objectives of requirements, F-36
objects of a system, F-10
occurrence. *See* events
offline transactions, 117
off-the-shelf products, implementing infrastructures, F-68
OMG (Object Management Group), 74
online data storage, 107, 108
online documentation, testing, 84
open issues in a requirements specification, F-54
operating systems, 69, 185

operational rules, 308, 312
opportunistic approach to capturing requirement
        patterns, 43–44
optional parts of a requirement template, 25
Oracle database, 68
order events, storing, 147
order ID, 100
organization units, 264, 326, 327
organizational construct, 325
organizational structure, 260, 327
organizations, system building for different, 255, 260
origin
    of a term, F-47
    of transactions, 206
outages, 225, 232–237. *See also* failures
output, 171. *See also* throughput
outsourcing, tailoring documentation for, 84
over time, charging a fee, 333
overall processing state, specifying, 143
overflows, highlighting on reports, 167
owner
    of a glossary, F-49
    of transactions, 136
owner entity name, 98
ownership shyness, F-50

P

page count on a report, 164, 167
page throw levels on a report, 165
paper type for a report, 167
parameter values, 138, 195
parent entity, 130
parochial data type definition, 89
parochialness, 256, 257. *See also* unparochialness
participants in the requirements process, F-15
passive attack on an interface, 60–61
passive reviewers of a requirements specification, F-19
passwords
    changing, 287, 289
    criteria for acceptable, 288–289
    generating initial, 287
    system-generated, 293
password entry, recording incorrect, 149
password format, criteria for, 287, 288–289
password guesser utility, 289
pattern author, 23
"Pattern classifications" in a requirement pattern, 23
pattern manifestation, 22
pattern name, 21
patterns, 20, 43. *See also* requirement patterns
peak customer capacity, 213
peak minute, calculating throughput for, 208
peak period, 213
pending actions, 128, 129
people over processes, agile exhortation, F-23
percentages, as data type 87, 218

performance
    common issues with, 192–195
    defined, 191–192
    degrading of, 225, 244
    flexibility and, 240
    as a source of nonfunctional system aspects, F-70
    transactions and, 137
performance domain, 29–30, 191-238
performance requirement patterns, 191–238
performance targets, 192, 193–194
PERL scripts, 69
permissions. *See* privileges
personal contact details, data structure for, 96
personal name details, data structure for, 96
"Pervasive" requirement pattern classification, 35
pervasive requirements
    alerting readers to the presence of, 28
    defined, 20, 27
    grouping related, 27
    for inquiries, 159, 161
    for living entities, 131–132
    for reports, 166–167, 168
    writing, 47
post codes, unparochialness and, 259
postmortem, 42
power users, accessibility concerns and, 171, 174
preciseness of requirement patterns, 20
precision
    of calculations, 103
    of a glossary definition, 14, F-46
preemptive corrections, 225
preferences of users, 285
Prepare step in requirements process, 7, F-16–F-17
presentation unit, 176
preset thresholds, passing, 145
previous screen, returning to, 125
pricing changes, 129
primary programming language, 69
primary reviewers of requirements specification, F-19
principles, regarding requirements specification, 6–7, F-9
priorities, F-40–F-41
prioritizing requirements, 14
priority of a requirement, F-34, F-36, F-39–F-41, F-43
privacy requirements for reports, 166
privileges, 305
privilege types inquiry, 317
problems
    distinguishing from solutions, 9
    specifying, 6, F-9
procedures manual, documentation requirement, 83
processing abilities, accessibility concerns and, 171, 174, 182
processing load, 215
product mailing list, customers joining, 133
product restarts, need for, 229
production line, non-interference with, 139–140
programming language, 69, 188

progress bar, displaying, 204
project manager, F-3, F-15
proof of existence archiving, 111
prospective installations, scope of, 255
protection of data, 123
prototypes, developing, F-14
pseudo-localization, testing, 271
punctuation, unparochialness and, 259

Q
quality
    defining, 192
    shutdowns and, 231
    as a source of nonfunctional system aspects, F-70
    upgrade frequency and, 229
quality standards, 71, F-49
quantity limitations, removing, 241

R
range, expressing frequency as, 23
rationale of a requirement, F-42
readability of a requirement, F-34
rearchiving, 114
recent orders inquiry, 159
recorded event inquiry, 152
recovery of data, 123
refactoring, 239
reference numbering scheme, F-49
referenced requirements, 80–81
referenced specification, 79, 80
references
    for calculation formulas, 103
    details required, F-50–F-51
    to other glossaries, F-44
    withholding, F-49
References section of a requirements specification, 14–15, F-49–F-51
Refers to requirement pattern relationship, 32, 33
refer-to-requirements requirement pattern, 79–81
refinement requirements, 35–36
reflective monitoring of throughput, 210
refreshing user interface, 157, 159, 177, 188
regions, installing systems in varied geographic, 255
registering users, 284
registration, process of, 285
regulations
    accessibility, 169, 170, 184
    data longevity, 107, 109
rejection, during approval process, 320
"Related patterns" in section in requirement pattern, 22
relationships between requirements, F-43
relative volumes for throughput, 205, 206
releases, as independent of priority levels, F-40
relevance of glossary terms, 14, F-45
reliability
    of chronicles, 145
    system, 231

reloading of archived data, 116–117
remote access
    facilities, 234–235
    restricting access to, 311
removing requirements, F-38
renumbering requirements, F-38
reorganizing organizations, 329
repetition, avoiding, 7, F-48
repetitive strain injury, accessibility concerns
        and, 171, 174
replay attack on an inter-system interface, 305
replication of hardware, 231
reports
    access control, 190
    availability, 233
    content requirements, 164–165, 190
    defined, 189
    delivery mechanisms for, 190
    designing, 162, 190
    dynamic use, 214
    format considerations, 167, 190
    multiness requirements and, 263
    purging, 190
    recipients of, 163, 166, 190
    scalability requirements and, 245
    scheduling of, 190
    size limits on, 244
    static capacity, 217
report design changes, recording, 149
report design tool, 190
report fee requirement, 335
report instance, 189
report requirement pattern, 161–168
report run request, recording, 149
reporting infrastructure, 31, 155, 189–190
representative configuration values, 141
Request For Comment (RFC) standards, 74
requirements
    arguments against specifying, F-4
    audiences for, F-3
    case for specifying, F-4
    compared to requirement patterns, 21
    defined, 4, F-2, F-8
    grouping by functional area, 41
    identifying, 9, F-24
    impact of an agile outlook on, F-23
    indications of pattern use, 40
    introducing a variety into, 41
    items given for each, F-36–F-43
    lack of confidence in, F-4
    levels of detail for, 4, F-3
    nonfunctional, F-40
    not specifying for an infrastructure, F-66
    overall approaches to, 3, F-1
    presenting in a specification, F-34
    prioritizing, F-39

proportion covered by patterns, 41
putting customer in control, F-5
referencing an infrastructure, F-65
referencing applicable, 80
refinements of the main, 35–36
reflecting business rules, 38
relationships, F-43
removing, F-38
requirement patterns when defining, 39
responsibility for overall organization of, F-27
specifying, 4–5, F-3, F-28, F-64
treating constraints as, F-54
types of, 19
writing down during extreme programming, 10, F-26
requirement definitions, 13, F-33, F-35–F-36, F-42–F-43
Requirement format section, 13–14, F-33–F-43
requirement IDs, 13, F-33
    example of, F-35
    grouping, F-37
    qualities of, F-36–F-43
requirement pattern classifications, 34
requirement pattern domains. *See* domains
requirement pattern groups, 31–32, 33
requirement pattern use cases, 37–38
requirement priority. *See* priority of a requirement
requirement summary. *See* summary description
requirement template, 24, 46–47
requirement patterns. *See also specific names of
        requirement patterns*
    access control, 281
    applicability of, 24
    in association with extreme programming, 10, F-26
    benefits of using, 19, 40–41
    classifications of, 33–35
    commercial, 325
    contents of, 21–29
    data entity, 119–154
    defined, 19
    diversity of approaches to, 36–37
    drawbacks of, 41
    and extreme programming, F-25–F-26
    finding candidate, 43–44
    flexibility, 239–279
    fundamental, 51–84
    information, 85–117
    misapplying, 41
    naming, 21
    performance, 191–238
    refining, 42
    relationships between, 32–38
    relationships with domains and infrastructures, 30, 31
    during requirement definition, 39
    reviewing, 48
    sections of, 21
    sources of, 20
    specifying better in the future, 44
    tailoring, 41–42

requirement patterns, *continued*
use cases for, 37–38
user function, 155–190
using after the fact, 40
using and producing, 39–48
using to consider completeness, 40
writing, 21, 42–48
requirements approaches, diversity of, 36
Requirements Management Tools Survey, F-2
requirements process, 7–8, F-12–F-14, F-15
requirements specifications
contents of, 11–18, F-29–F-71
defined, 4, F-2
essential items of information in, F-33
example for infrastructures, F-66
example text for, F-35–F-36
formal and informal parts of, F-11–F-12
for an infrastructure, F-65, F-67
introduction of, F-33
language, 22
organizing, 11, F-29–F-30
reviewing, 8, 40, F-19
as a source of candidate infrastructures, F-64–F-65
suggested structure for, 11, F-29–F-30
requirements-take-too-long argument, F-4
resilience, 57, 58
resource checker utility, 269
resources, managing multiple sets of, 269
response time
evaluating, 203–204
scalability and, 242
response time requirement pattern, 195–204
responsiveness over plan, agile exhortation, F-23
restatement of a formal requirement, F-42
restoring data, 123
restructuring, corporate, 245
revenue model, 331–332
review cycles, F-20–F-21
reviewers, F-19, F-20
reviews, feedback from, 48
Revise after review step, 8, F-20–F-21
RFC (Request For Comment) standards, 74
roles, assigning to users, 285
rolling window, 188
rounding, 103
rule IDs, 100
run time, infrastructures used during, F-63

S

sales tax, 335
sales tax rate, 129
Sarbanes-Oxley Act (SOX), 75
scalability
dynamic capacity and, 212
of an interface, 57
specifying, 205

scalability requirement pattern, 241–246
scaling out, 242
scaling up, 242
scheduling of reports, 190
scope
defined, F-7
of the glossary, F-44
of a glossary definition, F-46
of a glossary term, F-49
of requirement ID uniqueness, F-36–F-37
writing, F-8
scope boundary, 15, F-55, F-56
scope document, F-31–F-32
Scope section of a requirements specification, 15–16, F-53, F-54–F-58
screen
refreshing, 177, 188
returning to previous, 125
screen focus, accessibility requirements, 179
screen size, accessibility requirements, 179
secondary reviewers, F-19
secret information, identifying users, 298
Section 508 of Rehabilitation Act, 170, 175, 186
sections in a requirement pattern, 21
security
against deliberate shutdowns, 231
archiving for, 110
extendability requirements and, 249, 252
of an interface, 57
outlawing bad practices, 293
requirements for good practices, 287, 292–293
requirements for interfaces, 60–61
requirements for reports, 166
as a source of nonfunctional system aspects, F-70
security breaches, helping users to spot, 298, 301–302
security procedures manual, 83
security risks during installation, 276
security violations, recording, 149
segregated data, 261–262, 269–270, 271
selection criteria
for inquiries, 157, 161
for recorded events, 152
semantic requirements, 178, 186
sender, verifying the identity of, 58, 59
sensitive data, recording access to, 148
sensitive information, 292
sensors, data recorded by, 123
separate requirements specification for a standard, 77–78
separator characters, 88
sequence numbers in templates, 25
sequential numbers, allocating, 99, 101
sequential requirement IDs, 13, F-37
sets of requirements, 20
severity level, 145, 150, 152–153
shutdowns, 225, 232. *See also* failures
"sign off" of requirements, F-21

signed numbers, data type, 87
simple data type, IDs as, 97
simplicity of identifiers, 98
simplification of transactions, 135
simultaneous customer capacity, 213
single requirement for standards compliance, 77
single site, installing system in, 255
sites, scaling number of, 245
sizing model, 195, 211, 216
skeleton pattern, 45
software
    for archiving, 116
    availability issues related to, 226
    changing at both ends of an interface, 59, 60
    data types represented in, 94
    for drivers, 251–252
    extending using, 246
    over documentation, agile exhortation, 8, F-23
    performance targets for, 192–193
    recording changes, 149
    scalability requirements and, 245
    for system integrity monitoring, 236
    writing to support documentation, 83
software download
    accessibility concerns, 177
    need for, 188
solutions
    distinguishing problems from, 9
    formulating based on requirements, F-8
    not specifying in requirements, 6, F-9
sort order for IDs, 99
sort sequence for inquiries, 157
sound, accessibility concerns and, 171, 174, 181–182
sound alerts, 182
sounds, 123
source code
    commenting, 84
    documentation, 83, 84
    for driver software, 252
SOX (Sarbanes-Oxley Act), 75
specific authorization, 281, 282
specific authorization requirement pattern, 47, 308–313
specific needs for accessibility, 168, 169, 172, 174–175, 178–182
specific privileges, 305
specifications, purpose of, F-2
spelling notes in a glossary, F-47
splitting a requirement pattern in two, 46–47
spreadsheets of mind-boggling complexity, 332
stale user sessions, 213, 215
standards
    categories of, 71–72
    complying with multiple versions, 72–73
    complying with parts of, 73
    contents of requirements mandating, 73–74
    defined, 71

defining an interface, 55
development considerations, 78–79
for documentation, 82
examples of, 74–77
location of, 74
making accessible, 78
multiple different for the same thing, 72–73
names of, 73
purposes of, 73
as a source of nonfunctional system aspects, F-70
specifying that a system comply with, 71
technology and, 66
testing considerations, 79
versions of, 73
standard patterns, agreement on, 36
standard-related requirements, prioritizing, 78
state transition diagram, 17, F-62–F-63
static capacity requirement pattern, 47, 215–217
statistical functions for viewing chronicles, 152
statistics on requirements for a system, 33–34
stopwatch, recording response times, 203
storage medium for archiving, 112
strategic stratosphere, report design and, 163
"strikethrough" text, F-38
style sheet, 177
subcalculations, in a calculation formula, 103, 106
subtotals on reports, 166
subtransactions, 134
suffix, adding to a previous requirement ID, F-38
suggestions, resolving conflicting, F-21
suitability conditions, 256
summary description, 14, F-34, F-36, F-41
support, accessible, 184
surreptitious unavailability, 221, 224–225, 238
switching time transaction, 200
systems
    accommodating old and new interface versions, 59, 60
    activities in building new, 5, F-6
    availability window of, 208, 219
    defined, 4, F-1
    describing purpose of, F-31
    difficulty of migrating from old, F-58
    driver type requirements for, 250–251
    at each end of an interface, 55
    human being as part of, 171
    load on, reducing, 214, 215, 245
    monitoring response times within, 202–203
    popular times for using, 208
    reliability of, 231
    replacing existing, F-58
    specifying, 6, F-10
system activity inquiry, 143
system building, specificity of, 254
system capacity. See dynamic capacity; static capacity
system clock, data longevity and, 109
system configuration. See configuration

system context diagram. *See* context diagrams
system defects, testing for, 238
system design, documentation requirement, 83
system designer, F-15
system events, recording significant, 148
system expansion, allowing for. *See* scalability
system failures, minimizing, 225
system flexibility. *See* flexibility
system glossary. *See* glossary
system gone live state, 143
system information, viewing of, 160
system monitor, requirements for, 234
system operation efforts, non-growth in, 244
system performance, 193
system processing state, 143
System Purpose section in requirements specification,
    12, F-31–F-32
system resources, freeing up, 214
system threshold, passing of defined, 148
system unavailable page, 224
systematic approach to capturing patterns, 43
system-generated passwords, no access via, 293
systemwide configuration values, 138, 139

T

table, distinguishing a list of requirements, F-34, F-35
taxes, 330–331
"TBD" paragraphs, removing, F-54
teams, splitting development between multiple, 54
technical data types, 86
technical standards, 71, 72, 76–77
technology
    constraints on the user interface, 188
    defined, 65
    description of, 66
    development considerations, 70
    examples of, 68–69
    for an interface, 55
    specifying to build or run a system, 65
    usage of, 67
    used in development, 66
    for user interface infrastructure, 187
    versions of, 67
    working with a range of, 67
    working with multiple, 70
technology requirement pattern, 65–70
telephone numbers, data type 92, 259
templates section of a requirement pattern, 21, 24–25
temporal parochialness, 256, 257
temporary dispensation from compliance to
        a standard, 73
terminology, variation in, 260
terms
    choosing new, F-45–F-46
    establishing the meaning of, F-44
    in a glossary, 14, F-45

listing alphabetically in a glossary, F-48
    of local scope, F-46
test system for external developers interface software, 61
testers, 47, 48, F-15
testing
    acceptance, 9, F-25
    accessibility, 186
    availability, 238
    calculation formula, 106–107
    chronicle, 153
    configuration, 144
    considerations for, 29
    considerations for interfaces, 65
    data archiving, 117
    data longevity, 109–110
    data structure, 96
    data types, 94
    of documentation, 84
    dynamic capacity, 215
    extendability, 253
    flexibility, 240
    ID, 101
    inquiries, 161
    of interfaces, 62
    living entities, 133, 144
    report, 167–168
    response time, 204
    scalability, 246
    static capacity, 217
    technology requirements demands on, 70
    throughput, 211
    transactions, 138
    unparochialness, 260–261
    using patterns during, 40
testing regime, F-27
tests
    exclusions and, F-60
    using requirements, F-3
text
    display, accessibility requirements, 179, 184
    equivalent of cosmetic script, 181
    not burying in code, 269
theme
    introduction explaining, 30
    for a new domain, 44
    of patterns in a domain, 29, 32
third-party interface development, 57, 61
third-party system, interfacing to, 54
threshold rates for fees, 333
throughput of an interface, 57
throughput requirement pattern, 204–211
throughput targets
    CPU cycle rate and, 207
    for inter-system interface, 206
    justification for, 209
    purpose of, 205
    selecting, 205, 206

timeframe for, 208, 209
transactions as, 206
tiered rates for fees, 333
time, 89–90
of system use, 208
systemwide aspects of, 93
time limits for data longevity, 108
time periods, measuring, 337
time, response. *See* response time
time to detect (availability), 232–234
time to fix (availability), 232, 235–237
time to react (availability), 232, 234–235
time zones, 90, 93, 133, 259
timed changes, 127–128, 129
timed responses, control of, 177
timeless requirements specification, 6, F-11, F-56
timestamps, 88, 90, 92, 153
title for each reference, F-50
"To Be Done" (TBD) paragraph format, F-18
top-level sections of requirements specification, F-29–F-30
totaling levels for reports, 165, 166
traceability, ID facilitating, F-35
traditional approach, 3, F-6
to specifying requirements, 7–8, F-1–F-2, F-12–F-22
traditional documentation, 84
traffic verification and recording, 57, 58–59, 60–61
training for installation, 277
transactions
determining origin of, 206
integrity of, 126
multiness of, 264
requirement pattern for, 133–138
restoring offline, 117
steps in, 125
switching time, 200
as throughput target, 206
transaction data scalability, 244
transaction fee requirement, 334
transaction monitor, 154
transaction number, 125
transaction requirement pattern, 133–138
transference of restrictions, 308, 312
transitions, state, 17, F-62
troubleshooting installation, 276

U

U.K. Data Protection Act (1998), 75, 292
U.K. Disability Discrimination Act, 170
UML (Unified Modeling Language) standard, 74
unaddable amounts, not sorting on, 270
unaddable data, 262, 270, 271
unapproved actions, storing, 323
unavailability, surreptitious, 221, 224–225, 238
unavailability window, 219
undecipherable form of passwords, 292
Unified Modeling Language (UML) standard, 74

uninstalling, 277, 279
unique identifiers, 98–99
for requirements, 13, F-33, F-36–F-37
scheme for assigning, 97
unique interface IDs, 52
unit IDs for organizations, 329
units, associated with values, 87
Universal Time Co-ordinated (UTC), 90, 92
unknown information, 160
unpaid fees, tracking, 336
unparochialness
content requirements, 256
examples of, 257
extra requirements for, 257–260
specifying, 254–255
templates for, 256
testing, 260–261
unparochialness requirement pattern, 254–261
unsigned numbers, data type, 87
upgrade from any previous version requirement, 277
upgrade instructions, documentation requirement, 83
upgrade requirements for an interface, 59–61
upgrades
as downtime, 225
duration of, 230
frequency of, 229–230
preparation for, 230
scalability requirements and, 245
testing, 278
uninstalling, 277
upgrading, 276
of an interface, 57
specifying requirements for, 277
by versions, 278
urgency of a requirement, F-39
U.S. Rehabilitation Act, Section 508, 170, 175, 186
usability, 168, 169, 175, 185, F-70. *See also* accessibility
use cases
compared to user stories, F-24
defined, F-13
for requirement patterns, 37–38
writing, F-13–F-14
use case diagram, F-13
users
allocating IDs to, 99
availability of system to. *See* availability
behavior of, 212–213
counting dynamic, 213
forcibly ejecting, 214
geographic distribution of, 209
limiting number of, 214
number of active, 149
with specific needs, 168, 169, 172, 174–175, 183–184.
See also accessibility
as system, 171
wait time warnings for, 203

user access state, specifying, 143
user access via Web browser, 68
user accountability, 282
user actions, 147, 148
user authentication, described, 281, 282
user authentication requirement pattern, 295–305
user authorization
    described, 281, 282
    inquiry requirement, 317
user authorization requirement pattern, 305–307
user classes, 285
user colors, accessibility requirements, 180
user de-registration, 287, 290
user experiences, distinct, 261, 267–269
user function domain, 29
user function requirement pattern, 155–190
user IDs, requirement for no special, 293
user interfaces
    allowing user to adjust to, 175
    capabilities, 187, 188
    inter-system interface requirement pattern not used
        for, 52
    multiness in, 267
    semantic requirements, 178, 186
    tailoring for specific needs, 183–184
user interface designer, F-15
user interface infrastructure, 155, 187–189
user preferences, 132–133
user registration, 281, 282
user registration requirement pattern, 284–295
user response time, 196, 201
user roles, 15, 316, F-55
user sessions
    allocating, 214
    created by authentication, 296
    ending, 298, 300–301
    viewing, 298, 303–304
user stories, 9, 10, F-24, F-26
user times per time zone, 93
user-accessible information, viewing of, 160
users
    blocking, 298, 302–303
    details about, 285
    performing their own registration, 284
    protection of, 298, 301
    registering, 284
    special processes for new, 287, 293–294
UTC (Universal Time Co-ordinated), 90, 92

V

valid interactions, testing for an interface, 65
values
    allowed, list of, 88
    of requirement patterns, 20, 45
variables, 103, 195

variants of a requirement pattern, 22
versions
    required for an upgrade, 277
    of a requirement pattern, 22
    of technology, 67
version history, F-51, F-53
version numbers
    in the document history, F-51
    of patterns, 22
    of references, F-50
    strategies for, F-52–F-53
viewing
    archived data, 114, 115–116
    of systemwide information, 160
vision, accessibility concerns and, 171, 173–174,
        178–181
visual cue for audio alert, 182
visually distinct requirements, F-34
voice use, accessibility concerns, 171, 174
Voluntary Product Accessibility Template (VPAT), 184

W

waiving a fee, 335
warnings about wait times, 203
waterfall approach to software development, F-6
Web browsers, 68, 188
Web content accessibility guidelines, 170
Web page display time, 200
Web pages, 123
Web site availability requirements, 223
"what changed" section of a document history, F-52
whole numbers, data type, 87
whole system, requirements for, 20
window, rolling, 188
window size, accessibility requirements, 179
Windows operating system, specifying, 69
Windows Vista password complexity requirements, 288
Word, specifying documentation in, 69
word processor table, presenting requirements with, F-34
World Wide Web Consortium, 74
Write draft requirements specification step, 8, F-18–F-19

X

X.509 standard, 76
XP. *See* extreme programming

Y

Y2K problem, 89, 256
year
    date storage by, 90
    financial, 259
    interest days in, 105
yes or no data type (Boolean), 88

About the Author

Stephen Withall has been working as a software professional since 1979, in a range of roles from programmer to chief technical officer. Along the way, he has accumulated many years experiencing both the satisfactions and the frustrations of business analysis, systems analysis, and specifying requirements. He has worked in diverse environments in companies big and small, in 17 countries across four continents. The first half of his career found him roaming the world of banking and finance, and the second  half (so far) in diverse kinds of e-commerce. He actively maintains his hands-on software development skills.

Stephen holds a BSc in Mathematical Sciences from Bristol University, U.K. He lives in Sydney, Australia, and he enjoys going to places where few others are. You can reach him at *http://www.withallyourequire.com.*

Manufactured by Amazon.ca
Bolton, ON

28402140R00212